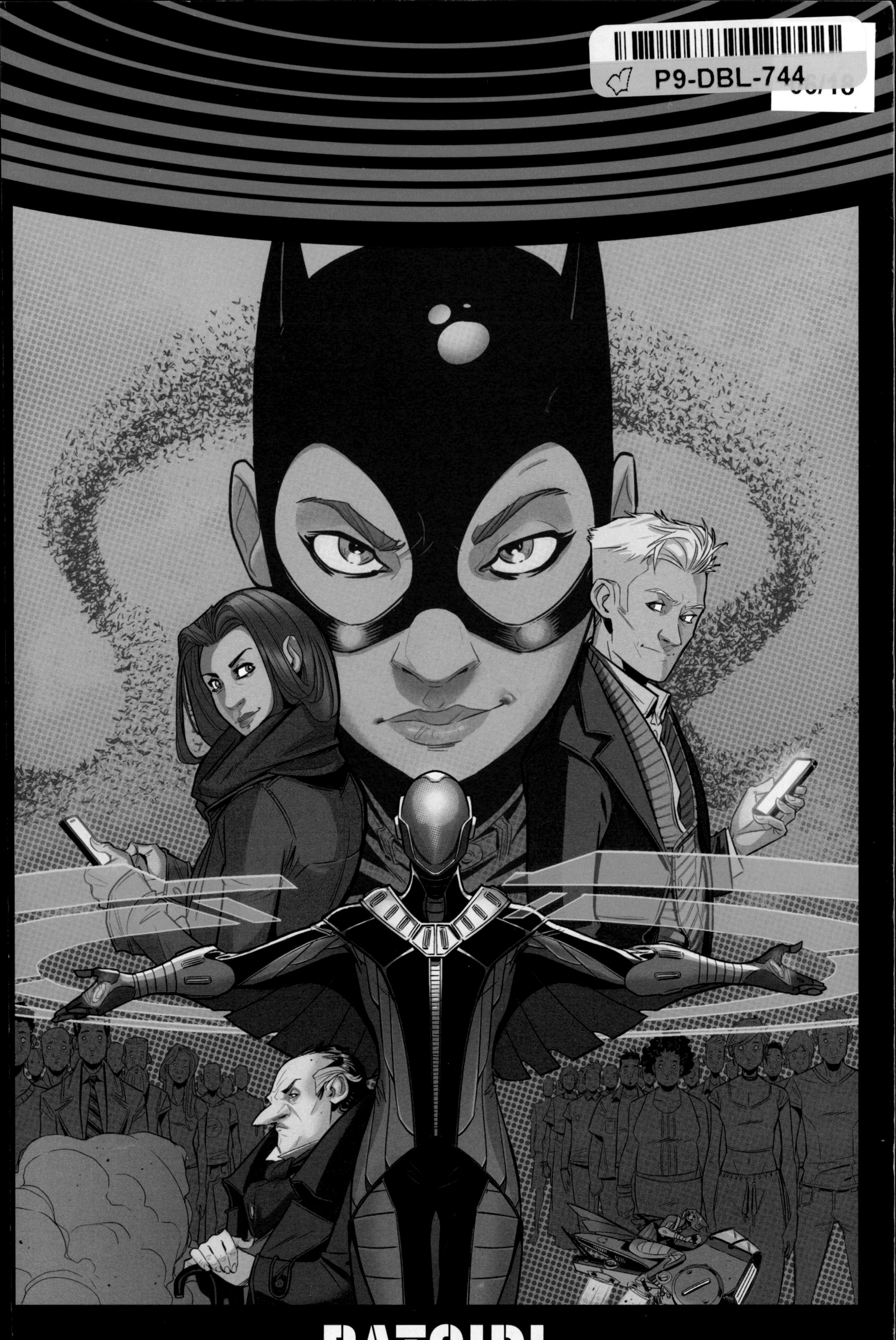

BATGIRL

VOL.2 SON OF PENGUIN

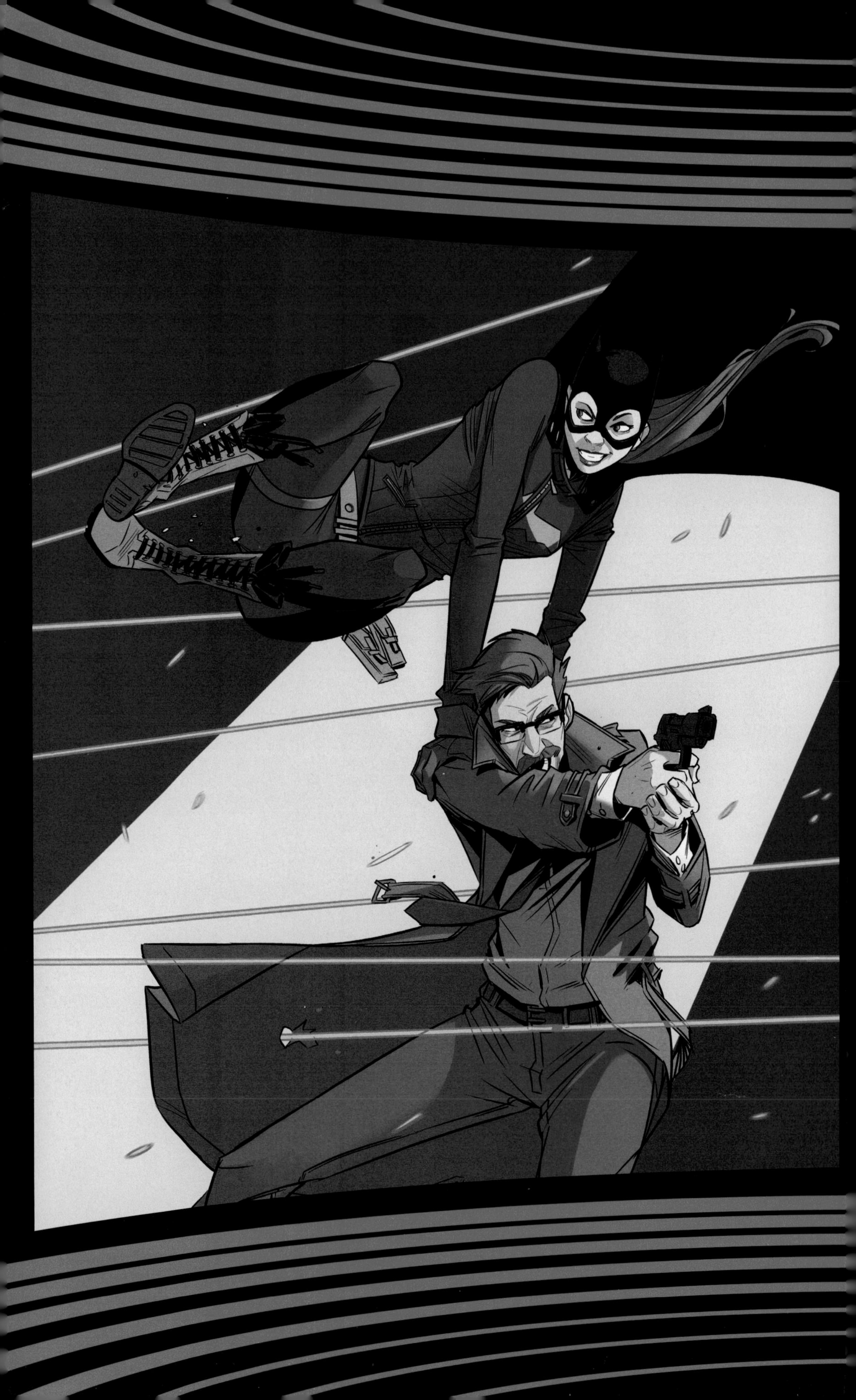

BATGIRL
VOL.2 SON OF PENGUIN

HOPE LARSON
VITA AYALA
writers

CHRIS WILDGOOSE
JON LAM
INAKI MIRANDA * ELEONORA CARLINI
artists

MAT LOPES
EVA DE LA CRUZ
colorists

DERON BENNETT
letterer

FRANCIS MANAPUL
collection cover artist

BATMAN created by BOB KANE with BILL FINGER
SUPERGIRL based on characters created by JERRY SIEGEL and JOE SHUSTER
By special arrangement with the Jerry Siegel family

MARK DOYLE Editor - Original Series ✴ **REBECCA TAYLOR** Associate Editor - Original Series ✴ **DAVE WIELGOSZ** Assistant Editor - Original Series
JEB WOODARD Group Editor - Collected Editions ✴ **ROBIN WILDMAN** Editor - Collected Edition
STEVE COOK Design Director - Books ✴ **MONIQUE GRUSPE** Publication Design

BOB HARRAS Senior VP - Editor-in-Chief, DC Comics
PAT McCALLUM Executive Editor, DC Comics

DIANE NELSON President ✴ **DAN DiDIO** Publisher ✴ **JIM LEE** Publisher ✴ **GEOFF JOHNS** President & Chief Creative Officer
AMIT DESAI Executive VP - Business & Marketing Strategy, Direct to Consumer & Global Franchise Management
SAM ADES Senior VP & General Manager, Digital Services ✴ **BOBBIE CHASE** VP & Executive Editor, Young Reader & Talent Development
MARK CHIARELLO Senior VP - Art, Design & Collected Editions ✴ **JOHN CUNNINGHAM** Senior VP - Sales & Trade Marketing
ANNE DePIES Senior VP - Business Strategy, Finance & Administration ✴ **DON FALLETTI** VP - Manufacturing Operations
LAWRENCE GANEM VP - Editorial Administration & Talent Relations ✴ **ALISON GILL** Senior VP - Manufacturing & Operations
HANK KANALZ Senior VP - Editorial Strategy & Administration ✴ **JAY KOGAN** VP - Legal Affairs ✴ **JACK MAHAN** VP - Business Affairs
NICK J. NAPOLITANO VP - Manufacturing Administration ✴ **EDDIE SCANNELL** VP - Consumer Marketing
COURTNEY SIMMONS Senior VP - Publicity & Communications ✴ **JIM (SKI) SOKOLOWSKI** VP - Comic Book Specialty Sales & Trade Marketing
NANCY SPEARS VP - Mass, Book, Digital Sales & Trade Marketing ✴ **MICHELE R. WELLS** VP - Content Strategy

BATGIRL VOL. 2: SON OF PENGUIN

DC Comics, 2900 West Alameda Ave., Burbank, CA 91505.
Printed by LSC Communications, Kendallville, IN, USA. 9/15/17. First Printing.
ISBN: 978-1-4012-7424-5

Library of Congress Cataloging-in-Publication Data is available.

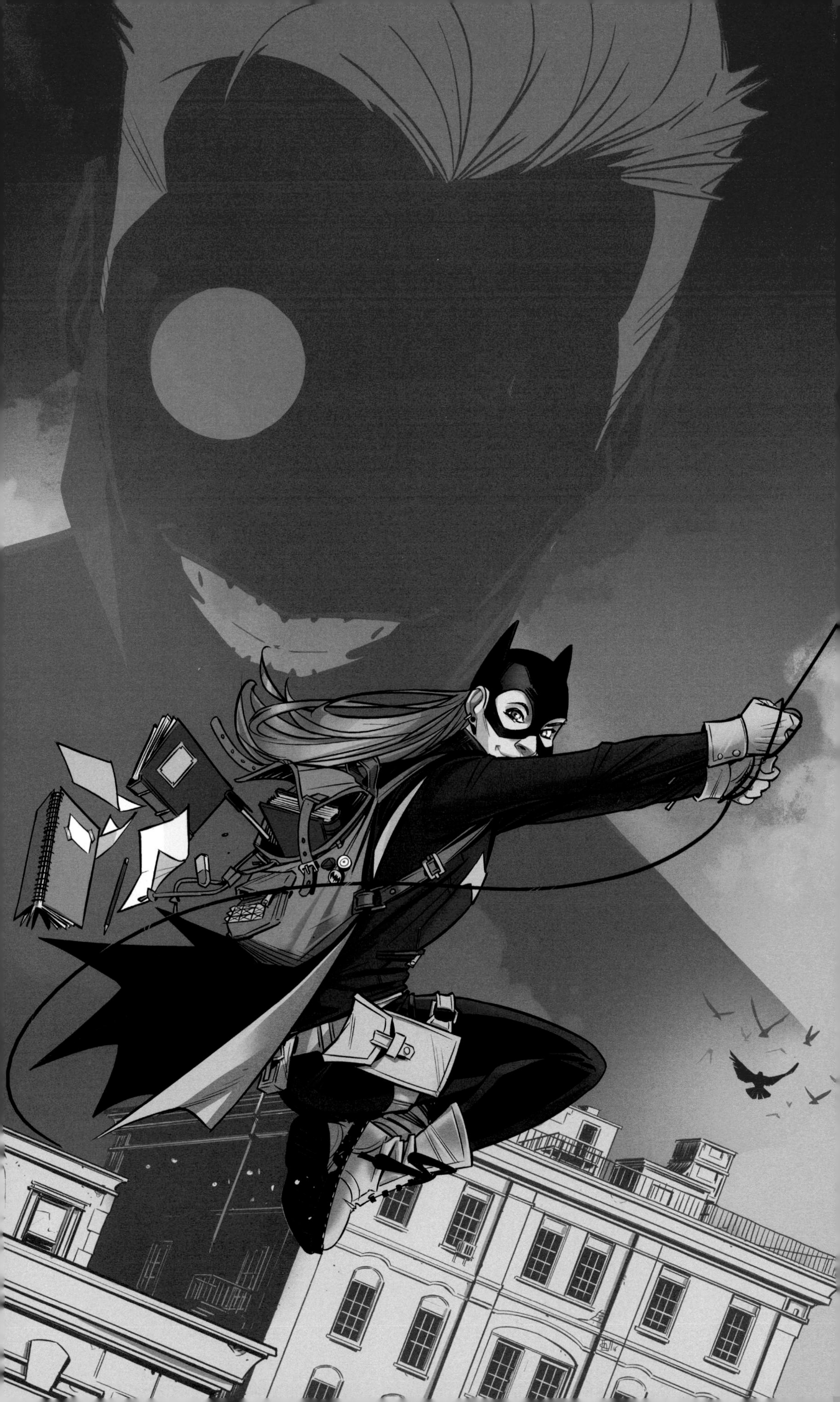

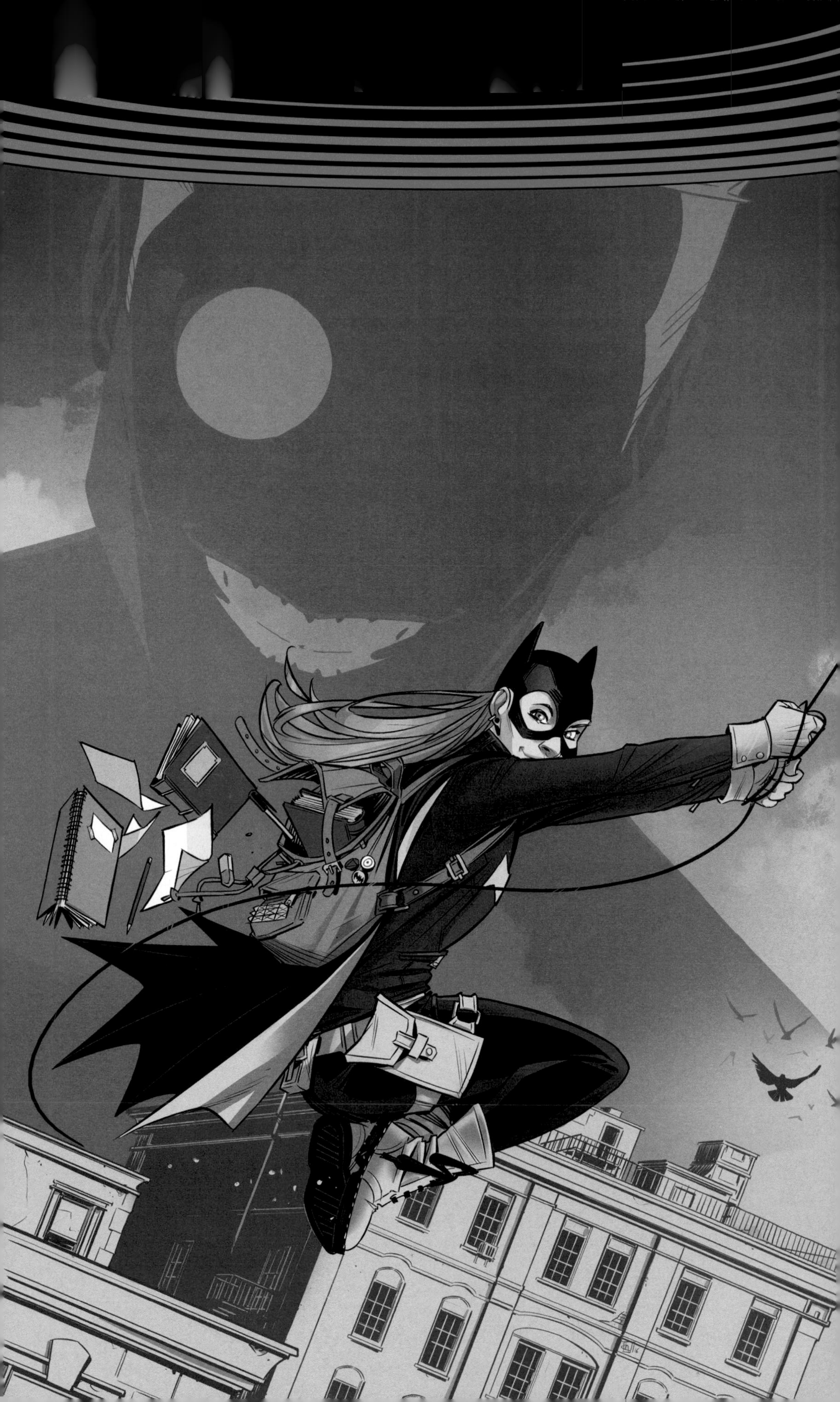

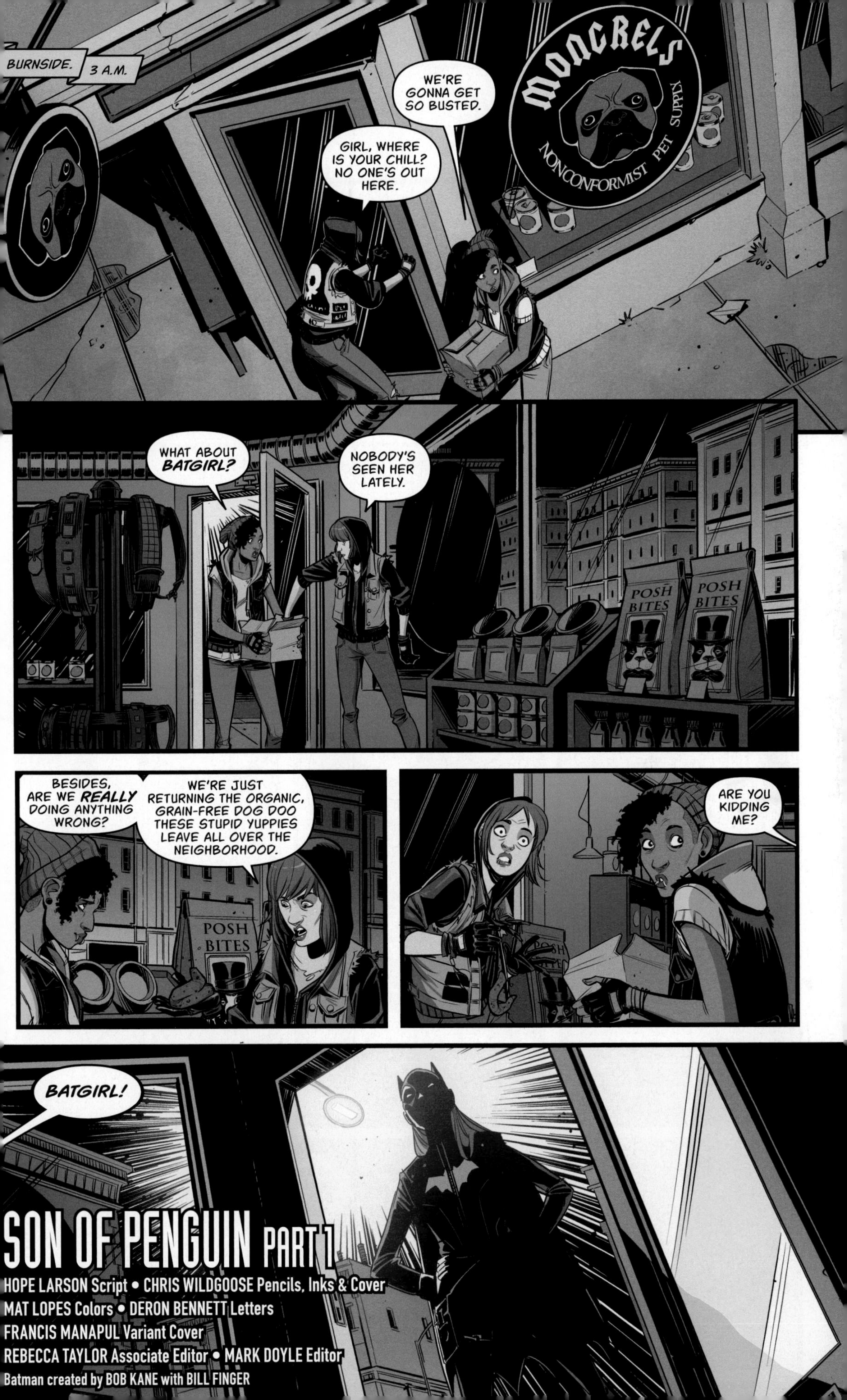
BURNSIDE.
3 A.M.
MONGRELS
NONCONFORMIST PET SUPPLY
WE'RE GONNA GET SO BUSTED.
GIRL, WHERE IS YOUR CHILL? NO ONE'S OUT HERE.
WHAT ABOUT BATGIRL?
NOBODY'S SEEN HER LATELY.
POSH BITES
POSH BITES
BESIDES, ARE WE REALLY DOING ANYTHING WRONG?
WE'RE JUST RETURNING THE ORGANIC, GRAIN-FREE DOG DOO THESE STUPID YUPPIES LEAVE ALL OVER THE NEIGHBORHOOD.
POSH BITES
ARE YOU KIDDING ME?
BATGIRL!

SON OF PENGUIN PART 1

HOPE LARSON Script • CHRIS WILDGOOSE Pencils, Inks & Cover
MAT LOPES Colors • DERON BENNETT Letters
FRANCIS MANAPUL Variant Cover
REBECCA TAYLOR Associate Editor • MARK DOYLE Editor
Batman created by BOB KANE with BILL FINGER

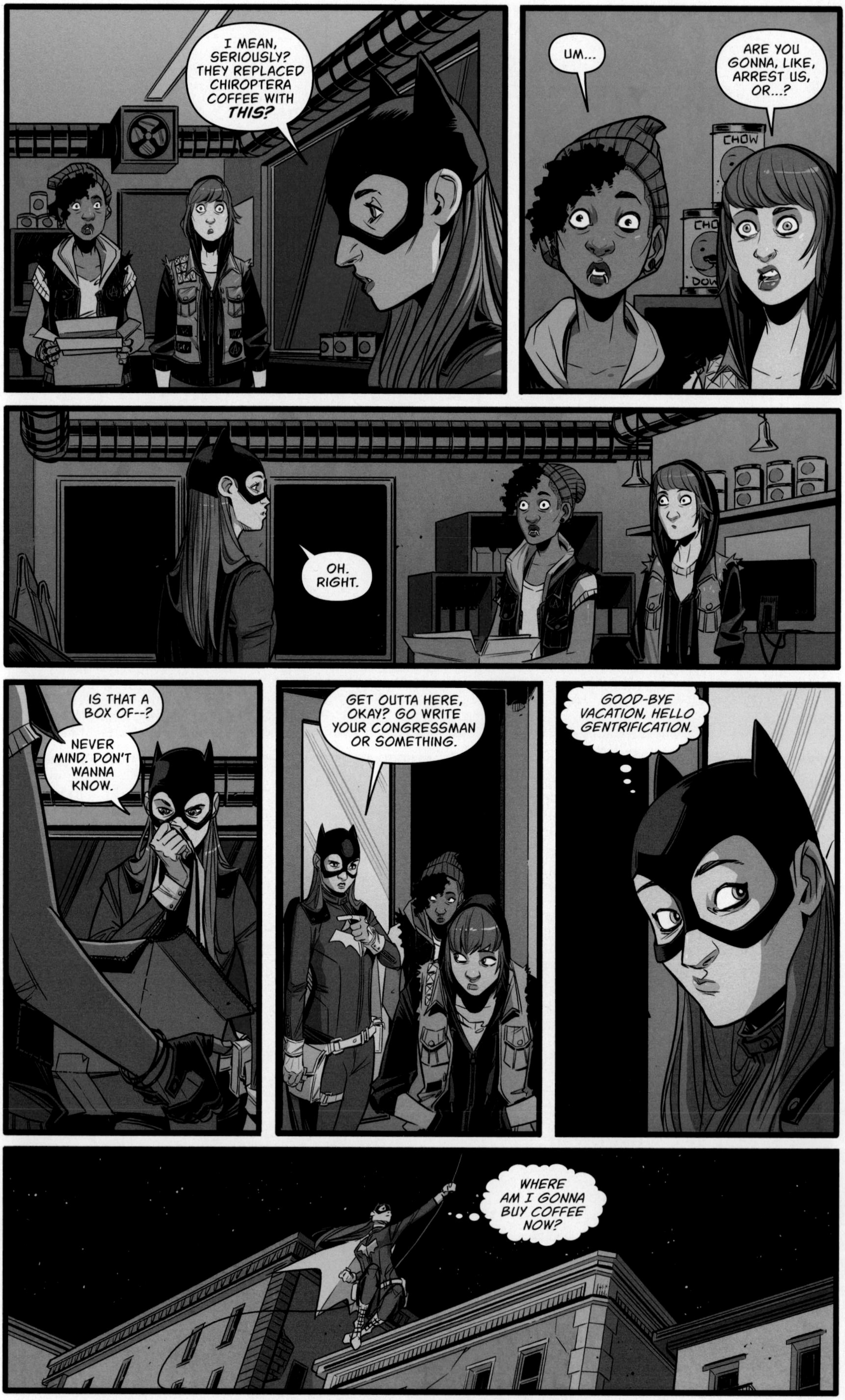

I MEAN, SERIOUSLY? THEY REPLACED CHIROPTERA COFFEE WITH *THIS?*
UM...
ARE YOU GONNA, LIKE, ARREST US, OR...?
CHOW
OH. RIGHT.
IS THAT A BOX OF--?
NEVER MIND. DON'T WANNA KNOW.
GET OUTTA HERE, OKAY? GO WRITE YOUR CONGRESSMAN OR SOMETHING.
GOOD-BYE VACATION, HELLO GENTRIFICATION.
WHERE AM I GONNA BUY COFFEE NOW?

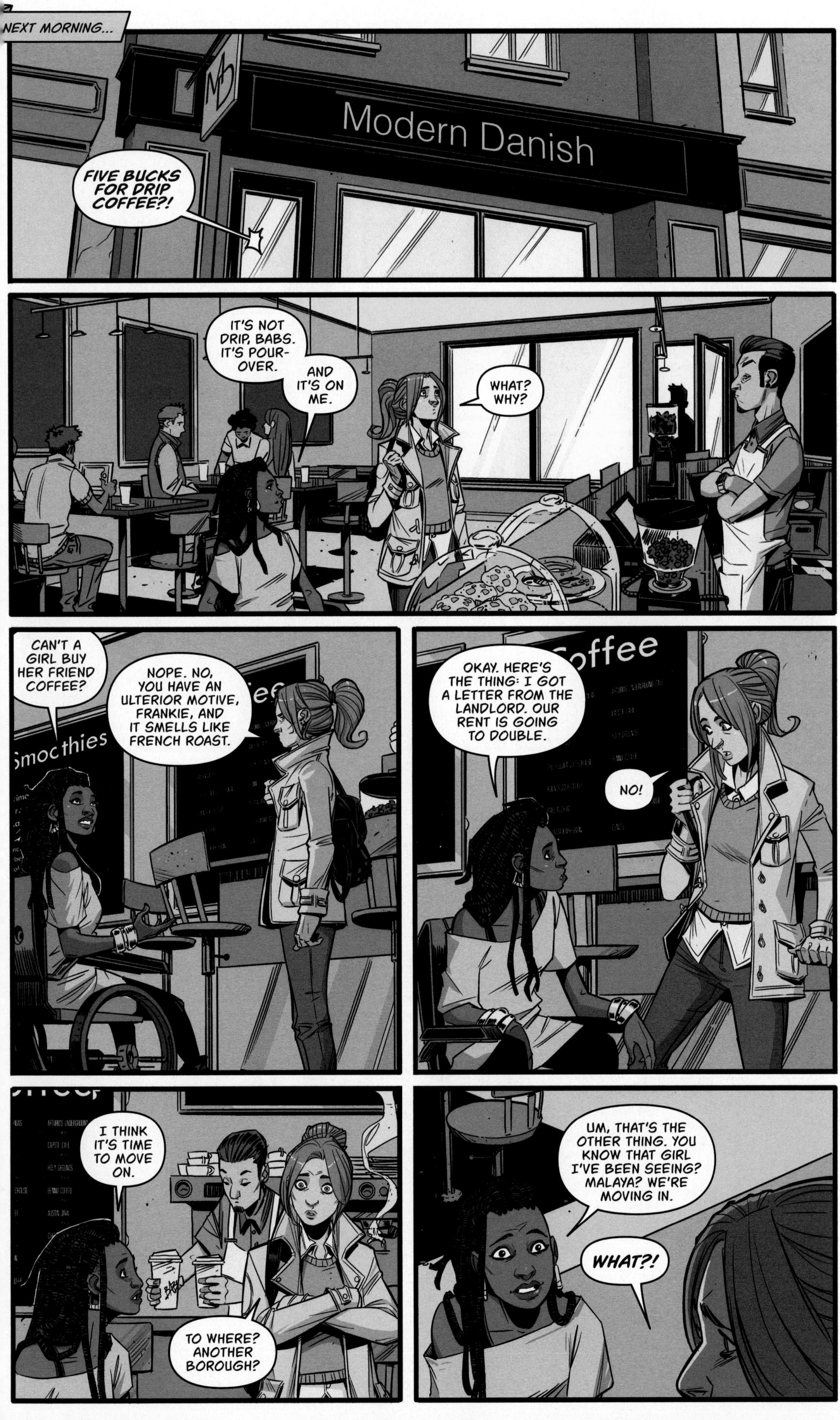
NEXT MORNING...
Modern Danish
FIVE BUCKS FOR DRIP COFFEE?!
IT'S NOT DRIP, BABS. IT'S POUR-OVER.
AND IT'S ON ME.
WHAT? WHY?
CAN'T A GIRL BUY HER FRIEND COFFEE?
NOPE. NO, YOU HAVE AN ULTERIOR MOTIVE, FRANKIE, AND IT SMELLS LIKE FRENCH ROAST.
Smoothies
Coffee
OKAY. HERE'S THE THING: I GOT A LETTER FROM THE LANDLORD. OUR RENT IS GOING TO DOUBLE.
NO!
I THINK IT'S TIME TO MOVE ON.
TO WHERE? ANOTHER BOROUGH?
UM, THAT'S THE OTHER THING. YOU KNOW THAT GIRL I'VE BEEN SEEING? MALAYA? WE'RE MOVING IN.
WHAT?!

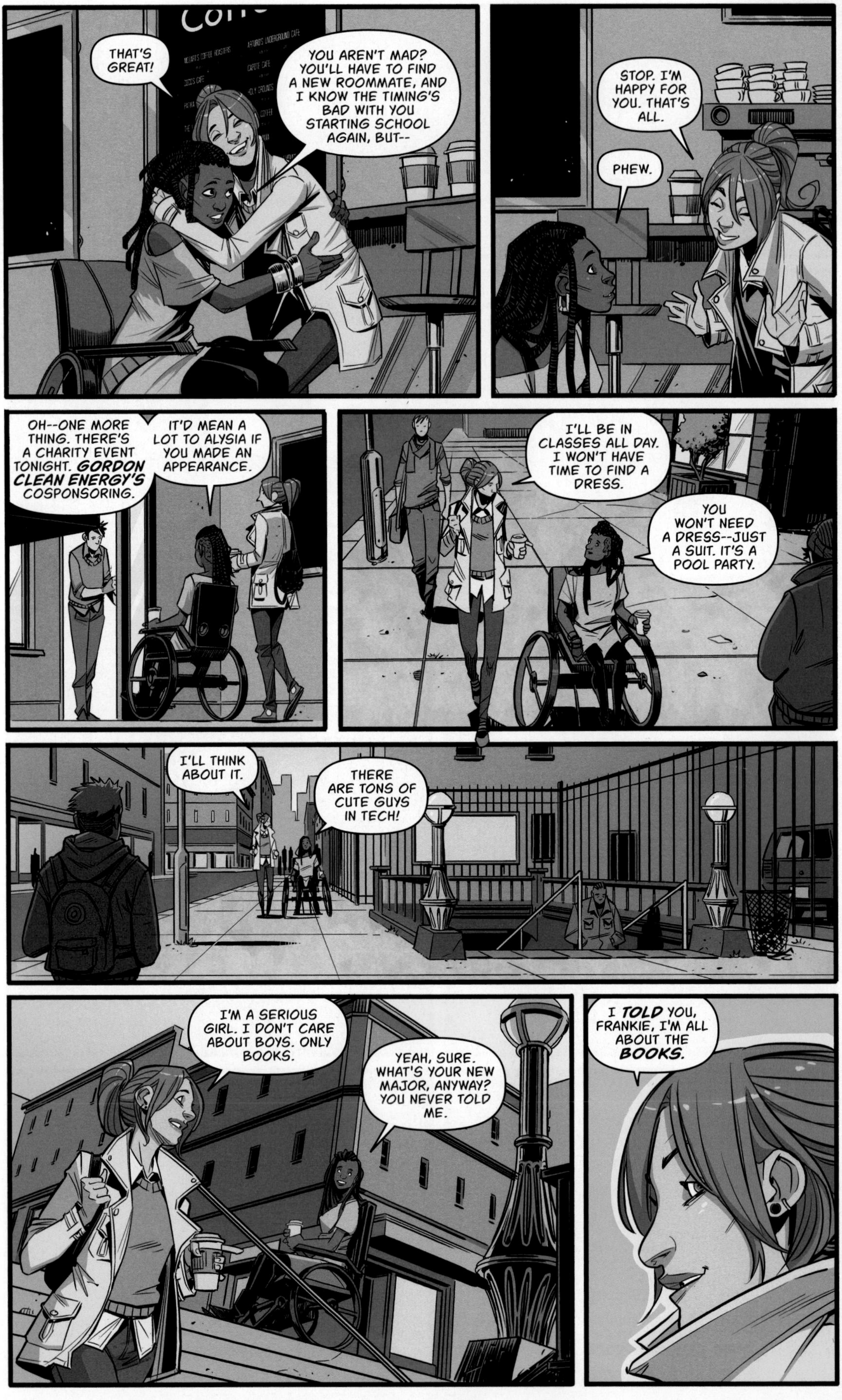
THAT'S GREAT!
YOU AREN'T MAD? YOU'LL HAVE TO FIND A NEW ROOMMATE, AND I KNOW THE TIMING'S BAD WITH YOU STARTING SCHOOL AGAIN, BUT--
STOP. I'M HAPPY FOR YOU. THAT'S ALL.
PHEW.
OH--ONE MORE THING. THERE'S A CHARITY EVENT TONIGHT. GORDON CLEAN ENERGY'S COSPONSORING.
IT'D MEAN A LOT TO ALYSIA IF YOU MADE AN APPEARANCE.
I'LL BE IN CLASSES ALL DAY. I WON'T HAVE TIME TO FIND A DRESS.
YOU WON'T NEED A DRESS--JUST A SUIT. IT'S A POOL PARTY.
I'LL THINK ABOUT IT.
THERE ARE TONS OF CUTE GUYS IN TECH!
I'M A SERIOUS GIRL. I DON'T CARE ABOUT BOYS. ONLY BOOKS.
YEAH, SURE. WHAT'S YOUR NEW MAJOR, ANYWAY? YOU NEVER TOLD ME.
I TOLD YOU, FRANKIE, I'M ALL ABOUT THE BOOKS.

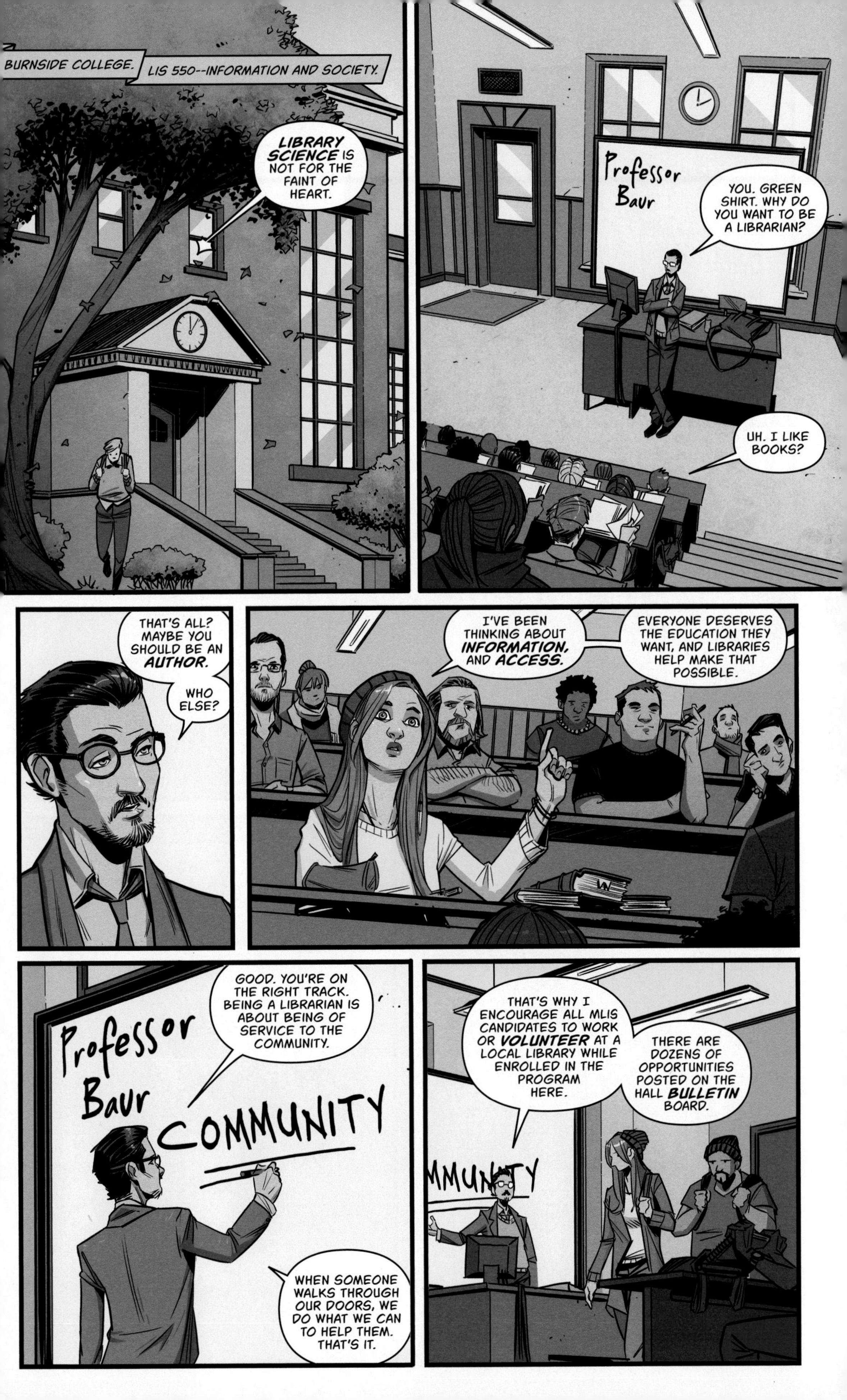
BURNSIDE COLLEGE.
LIS 550--INFORMATION AND SOCIETY.
LIBRARY SCIENCE IS NOT FOR THE FAINT OF HEART.
Professor Baur
YOU. GREEN SHIRT. WHY DO YOU WANT TO BE A LIBRARIAN?
UH. I LIKE BOOKS?
THAT'S ALL? MAYBE YOU SHOULD BE AN AUTHOR.
WHO ELSE?
I'VE BEEN THINKING ABOUT INFORMATION, AND ACCESS.
EVERYONE DESERVES THE EDUCATION THEY WANT, AND LIBRARIES HELP MAKE THAT POSSIBLE.
Professor Baur
COMMUNITY
GOOD. YOU'RE ON THE RIGHT TRACK. BEING A LIBRARIAN IS ABOUT BEING OF SERVICE TO THE COMMUNITY.
WHEN SOMEONE WALKS THROUGH OUR DOORS, WE DO WHAT WE CAN TO HELP THEM. THAT'S IT.
THAT'S WHY I ENCOURAGE ALL MLIS CANDIDATES TO WORK OR VOLUNTEER AT A LOCAL LIBRARY WHILE ENROLLED IN THE PROGRAM HERE.
THERE ARE DOZENS OF OPPORTUNITIES POSTED ON THE HALL BULLETIN BOARD.

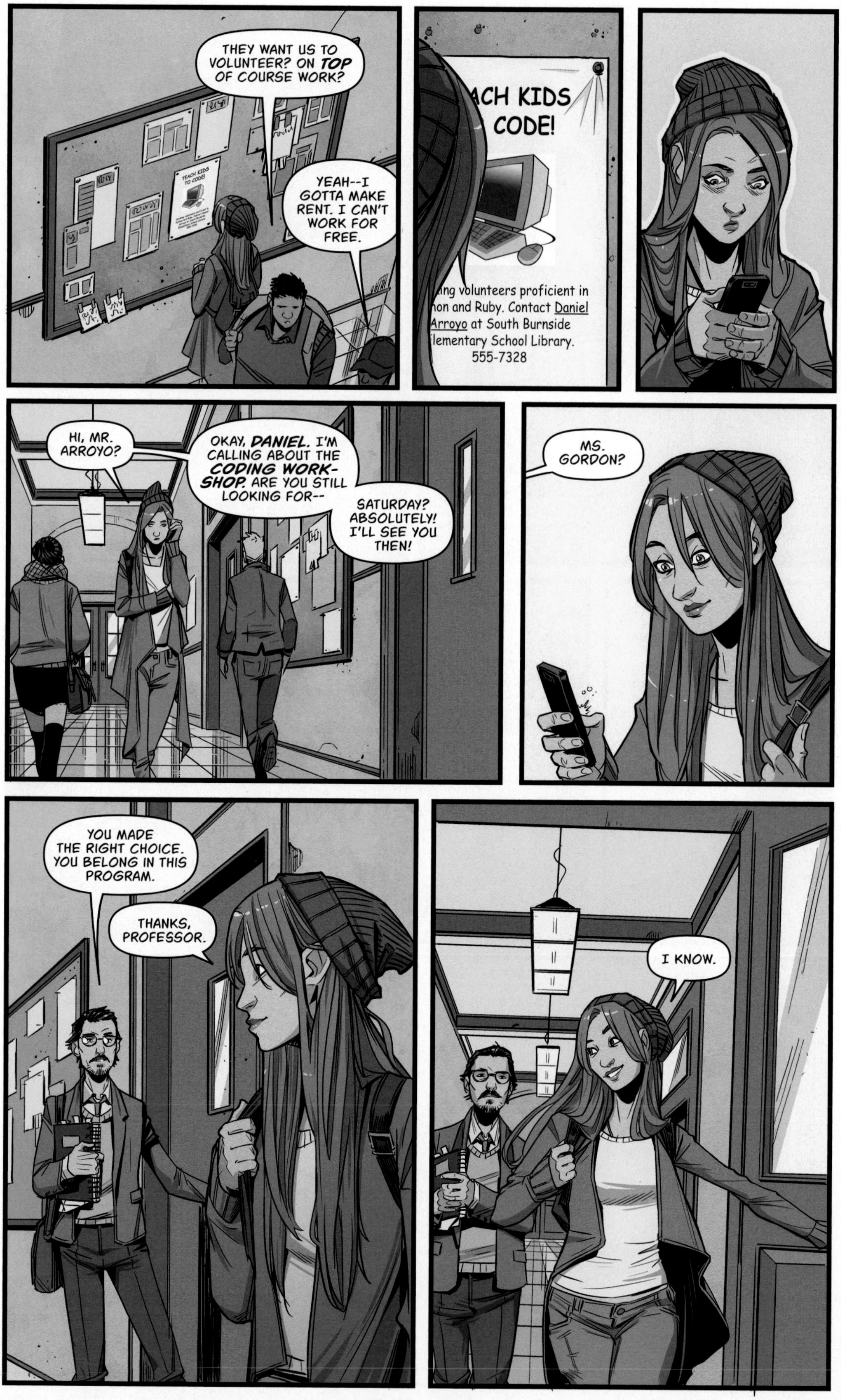
THEY WANT US TO VOLUNTEER? ON *TOP* OF COURSE WORK?
TEACH KIDS TO CODE!
YEAH--I GOTTA MAKE RENT. I CAN'T WORK FOR FREE.
ACH KIDS
CODE!
ing volunteers proficient in
hon and Ruby. Contact Daniel
Arroyo at South Burnside
lementary School Library.
555-7328
HI, MR. ARROYO?
OKAY, ***DANIEL.*** I'M CALLING ABOUT THE ***CODING WORK-SHOP.*** ARE YOU STILL LOOKING FOR--
SATURDAY? ABSOLUTELY! I'LL SEE YOU THEN!
MS. GORDON?
YOU MADE THE RIGHT CHOICE. YOU BELONG IN THIS PROGRAM.
THANKS, PROFESSOR.
I KNOW.

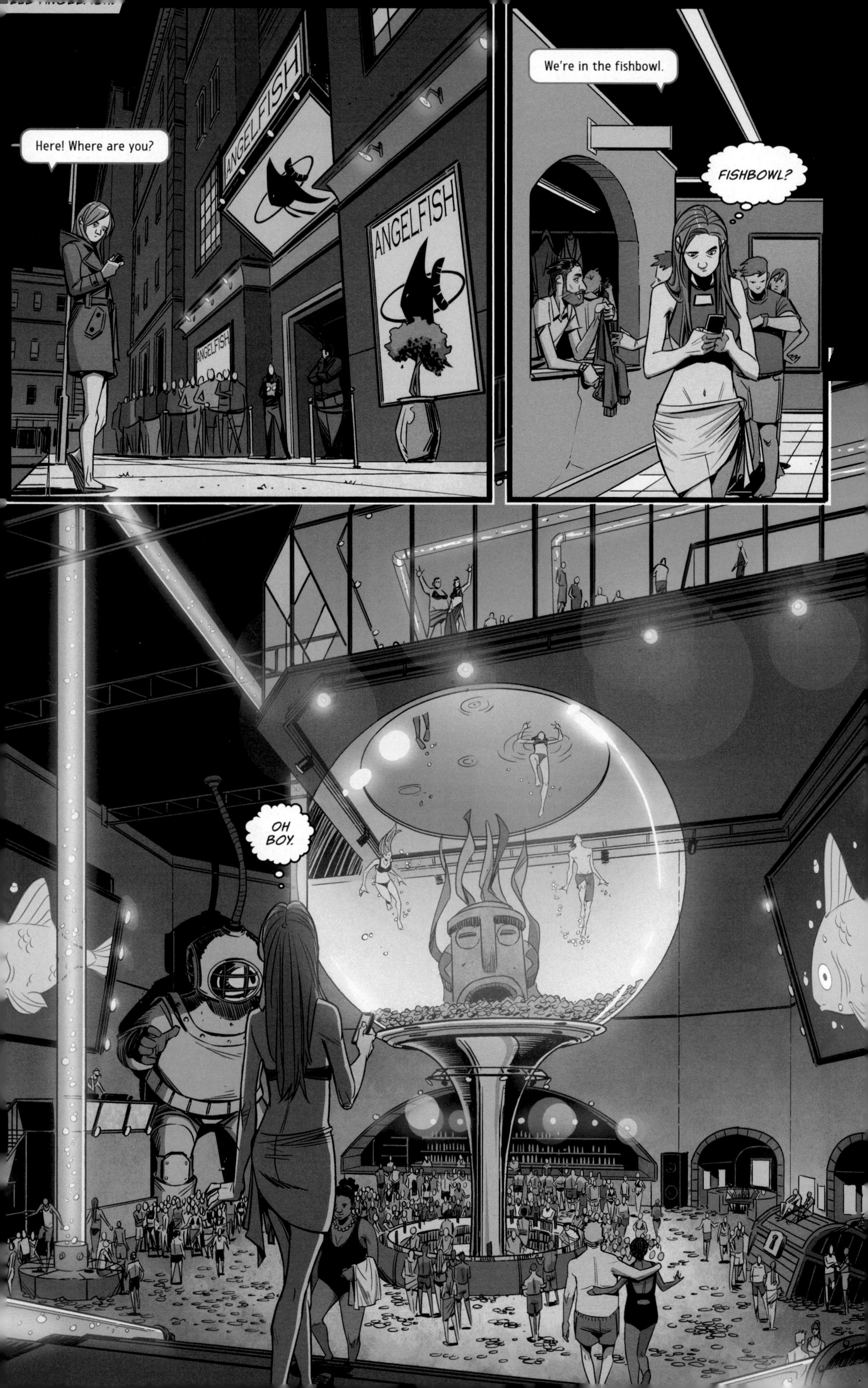
Here! Where are you?
ANGELFISH
ANGELFISH
ANGELFISH
We're in the fishbowl.
FISHBOWL?
OH BOY.

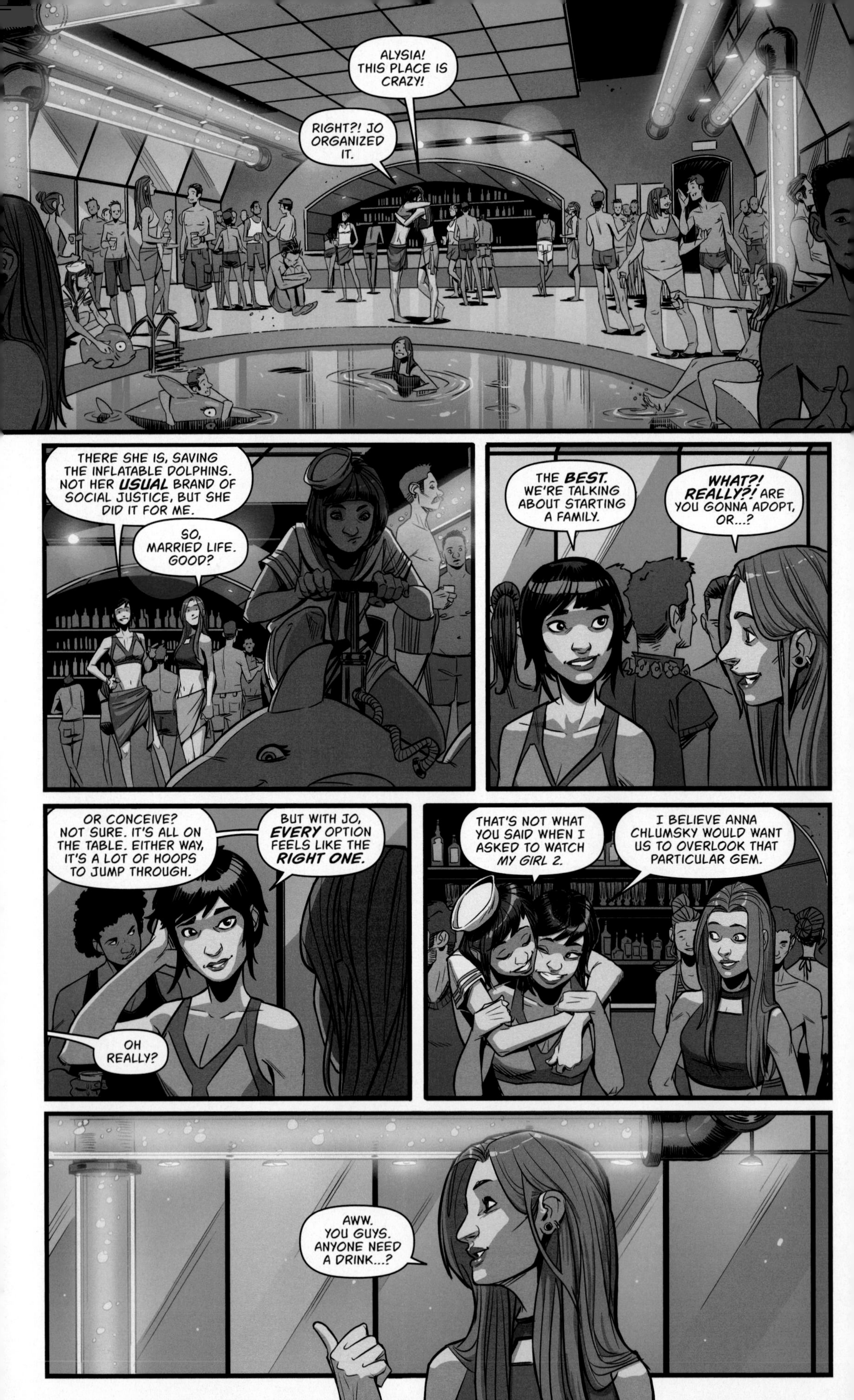
ALYSIA! THIS PLACE IS CRAZY!
RIGHT?! JO ORGANIZED IT.
THERE SHE IS, SAVING THE INFLATABLE DOLPHINS. NOT HER *USUAL* BRAND OF SOCIAL JUSTICE, BUT SHE DID IT FOR ME.
SO, MARRIED LIFE. GOOD?
THE **BEST.** WE'RE TALKING ABOUT STARTING A FAMILY.
WHAT?! REALLY?! ARE YOU GONNA ADOPT, OR...?
OR CONCEIVE? NOT SURE. IT'S ALL ON THE TABLE. EITHER WAY, IT'S A LOT OF HOOPS TO JUMP THROUGH.
BUT WITH JO, ***EVERY*** OPTION FEELS LIKE THE ***RIGHT ONE.***
OH REALLY?
THAT'S NOT WHAT YOU SAID WHEN I ASKED TO WATCH *MY GIRL 2.*
I BELIEVE ANNA CHLUMSKY WOULD WANT US TO OVERLOOK THAT PARTICULAR GEM.
AWW. YOU GUYS. ANYONE NEED A DRINK...?

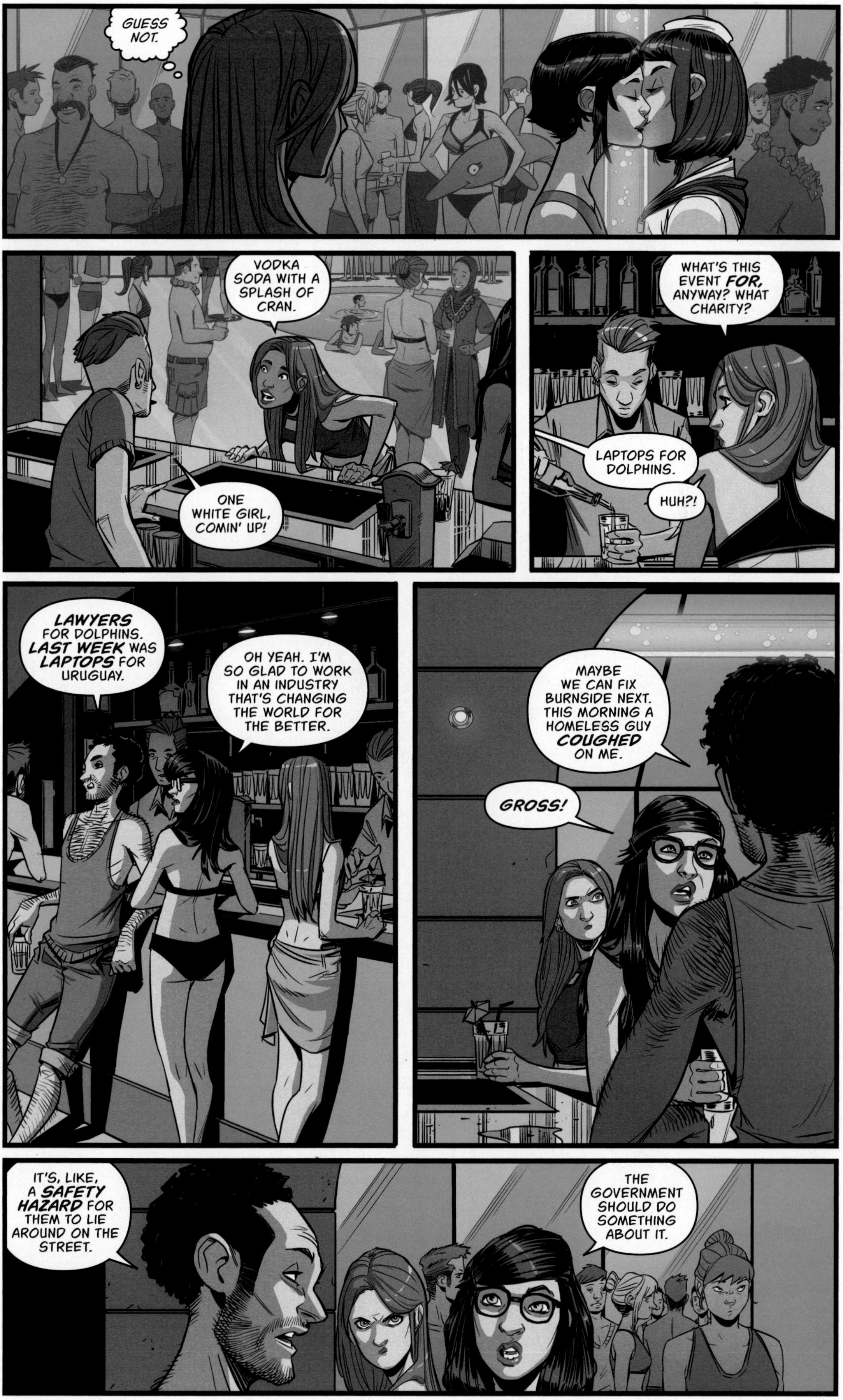
GUESS NOT.
VODKA SODA WITH A SPLASH OF CRAN.
ONE WHITE GIRL, COMIN' UP!
WHAT'S THIS EVENT FOR, ANYWAY? WHAT CHARITY?
LAPTOPS FOR DOLPHINS.
HUH?!
LAWYERS FOR DOLPHINS. LAST WEEK WAS LAPTOPS FOR URUGUAY.
OH YEAH. I'M SO GLAD TO WORK IN AN INDUSTRY THAT'S CHANGING THE WORLD FOR THE BETTER.
MAYBE WE CAN FIX BURNSIDE NEXT. THIS MORNING A HOMELESS GUY COUGHED ON ME.
GROSS!
IT'S, LIKE, A SAFETY HAZARD FOR THEM TO LIE AROUND ON THE STREET.
THE GOVERNMENT SHOULD DO SOMETHING ABOUT IT.

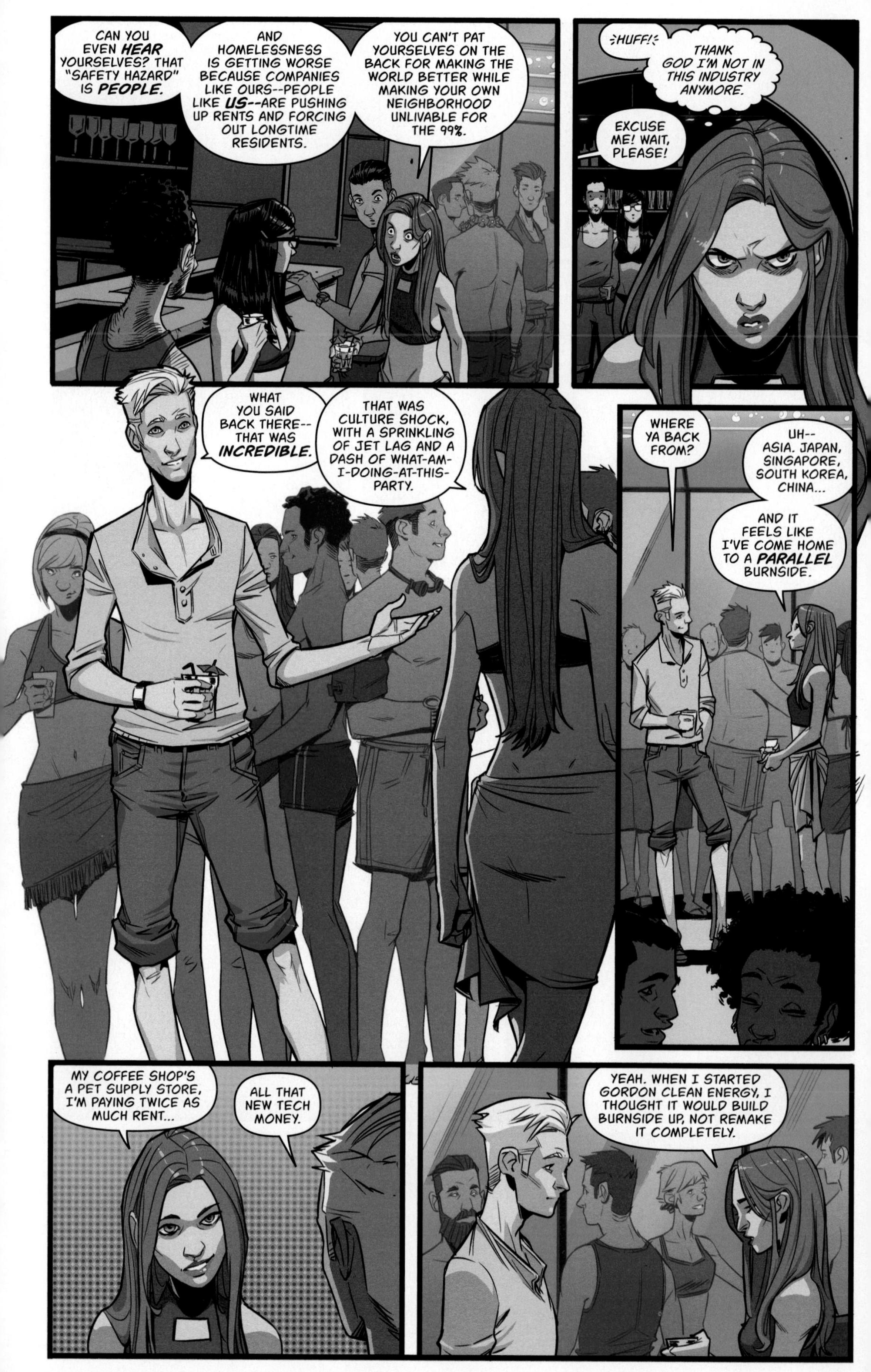

CAN YOU EVEN **HEAR** YOURSELVES? THAT "SAFETY HAZARD" IS **PEOPLE.**
AND HOMELESSNESS IS GETTING WORSE BECAUSE COMPANIES LIKE OURS--PEOPLE LIKE **US**--ARE PUSHING UP RENTS AND FORCING OUT LONGTIME RESIDENTS.
YOU CAN'T PAT YOURSELVES ON THE BACK FOR MAKING THE WORLD BETTER WHILE MAKING YOUR OWN NEIGHBORHOOD UNLIVABLE FOR THE 99%.
HUFF!
THANK GOD I'M NOT IN THIS INDUSTRY ANYMORE.
EXCUSE ME! WAIT, PLEASE!
WHAT YOU SAID BACK THERE--THAT WAS **INCREDIBLE.**
THAT WAS CULTURE SHOCK, WITH A SPRINKLING OF JET LAG AND A DASH OF WHAT-AM-I-DOING-AT-THIS-PARTY.
WHERE YA BACK FROM?
UH--ASIA. JAPAN, SINGAPORE, SOUTH KOREA, CHINA...
AND IT FEELS LIKE I'VE COME HOME TO A **PARALLEL** BURNSIDE.
MY COFFEE SHOP'S A PET SUPPLY STORE, I'M PAYING TWICE AS MUCH RENT...
ALL THAT NEW TECH MONEY.
YEAH. WHEN I STARTED GORDON CLEAN ENERGY, I THOUGHT IT WOULD BUILD BURNSIDE UP, NOT REMAKE IT COMPLETELY.

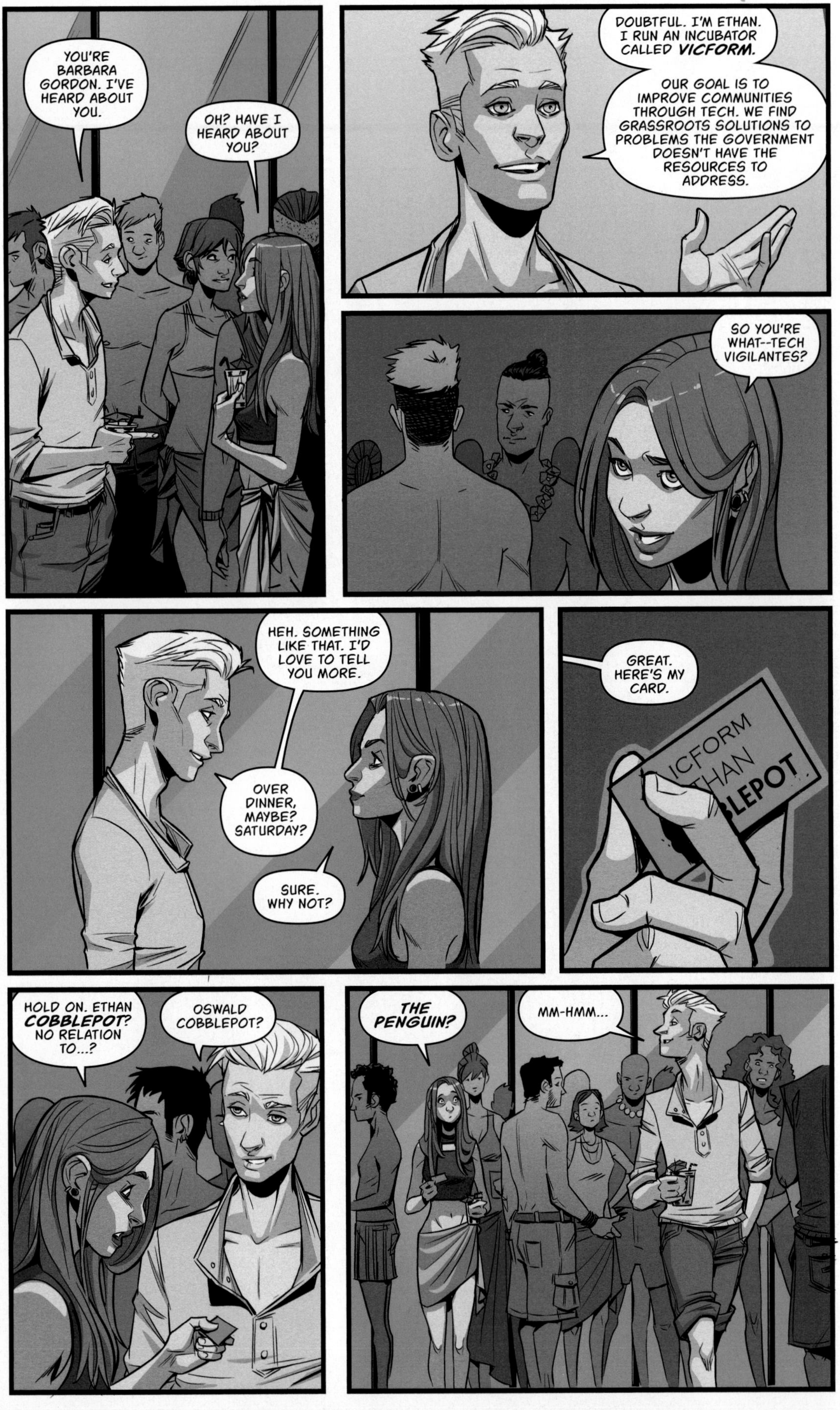
YOU'RE BARBARA GORDON. I'VE HEARD ABOUT YOU.
OH? HAVE I HEARD ABOUT YOU?
DOUBTFUL. I'M ETHAN. I RUN AN INCUBATOR CALLED **VICFORM.**
OUR GOAL IS TO IMPROVE COMMUNITIES THROUGH TECH. WE FIND GRASSROOTS SOLUTIONS TO PROBLEMS THE GOVERNMENT DOESN'T HAVE THE RESOURCES TO ADDRESS.
SO YOU'RE WHAT--TECH VIGILANTES?
HEH. SOMETHING LIKE THAT. I'D LOVE TO TELL YOU MORE.
OVER DINNER, MAYBE? SATURDAY?
SURE. WHY NOT?
GREAT. HERE'S MY CARD.
HOLD ON. ETHAN **COBBLEPOT?** NO RELATION TO...?
OSWALD COBBLEPOT?
THE PENGUIN?
MM-HMM...

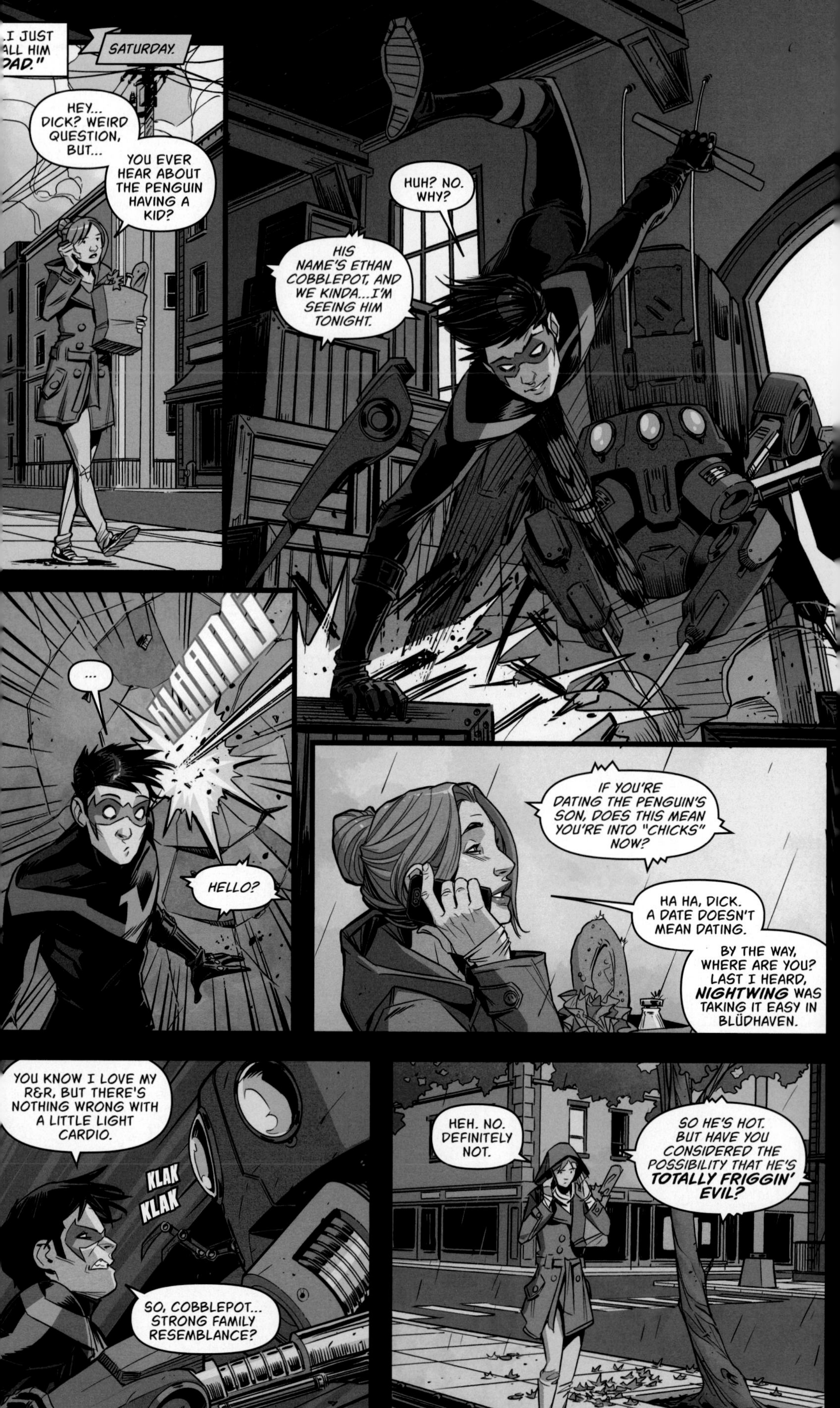

.I JUST ALL HIM DAD."
SATURDAY.
HEY... DICK? WEIRD QUESTION, BUT...
YOU EVER HEAR ABOUT THE PENGUIN HAVING A KID?
HUH? NO. WHY?
HIS NAME'S ETHAN COBBLEPOT, AND WE KINDA...I'M SEEING HIM TONIGHT.
KLANG
...
HELLO?
IF YOU'RE DATING THE PENGUIN'S SON, DOES THIS MEAN YOU'RE INTO "CHICKS" NOW?
HA HA, DICK. A DATE DOESN'T MEAN DATING.
BY THE WAY, WHERE ARE YOU? LAST I HEARD, NIGHTWING WAS TAKING IT EASY IN BLÜDHAVEN.
YOU KNOW I LOVE MY R&R, BUT THERE'S NOTHING WRONG WITH A LITTLE LIGHT CARDIO.
KLAK KLAK
SO, COBBLEPOT... STRONG FAMILY RESEMBLANCE?
HEH. NO. DEFINITELY NOT.
SO HE'S HOT. BUT HAVE YOU CONSIDERED THE POSSIBILITY THAT HE'S TOTALLY FRIGGIN' EVIL?

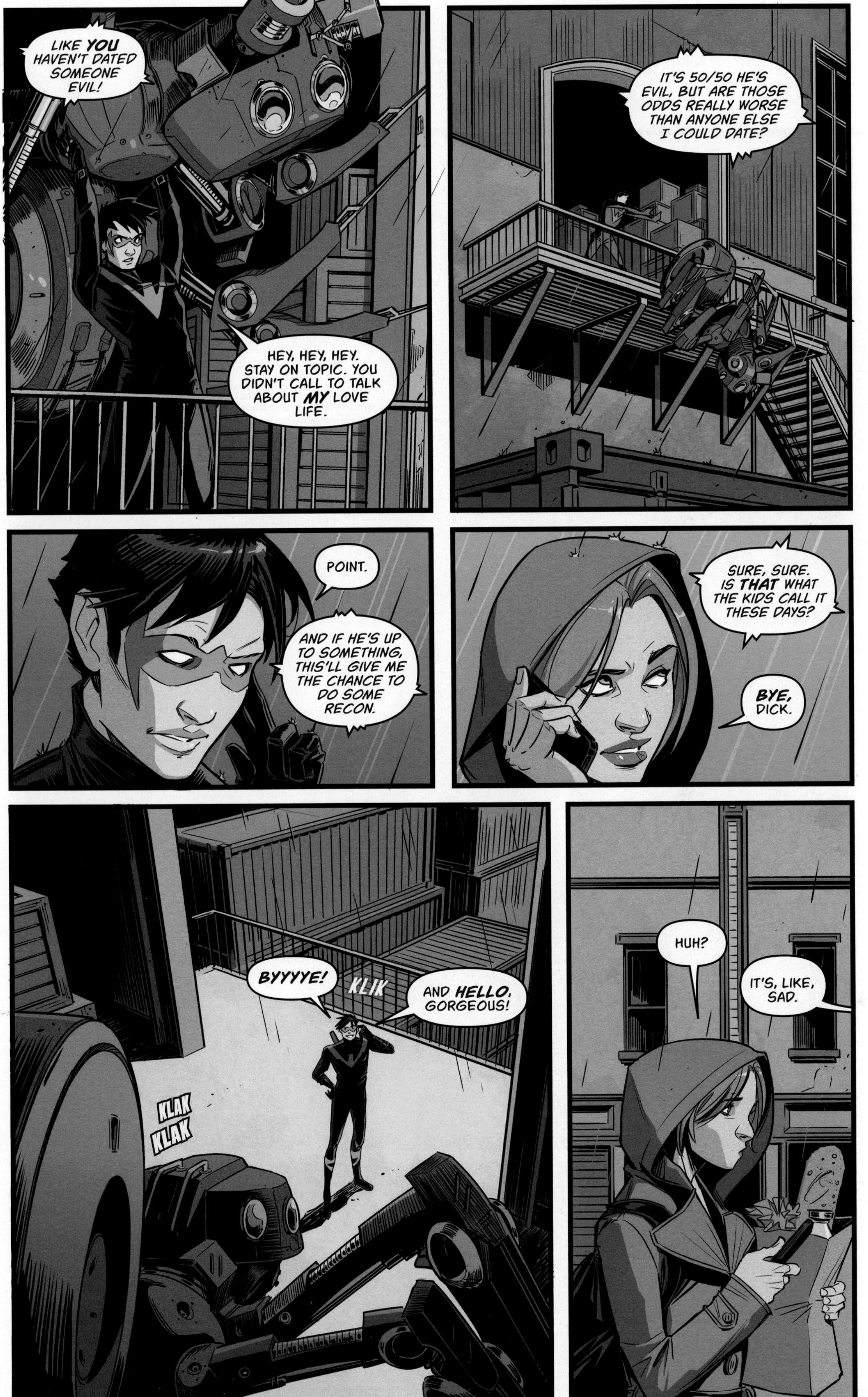
LIKE YOU HAVEN'T DATED SOMEONE EVIL!
HEY, HEY, HEY. STAY ON TOPIC. YOU DIDN'T CALL TO TALK ABOUT MY LOVE LIFE.
IT'S 50/50 HE'S EVIL, BUT ARE THOSE ODDS REALLY WORSE THAN ANYONE ELSE I COULD DATE?
POINT.
AND IF HE'S UP TO SOMETHING, THIS'LL GIVE ME THE CHANCE TO DO SOME RECON.
SURE, SURE. IS THAT WHAT THE KIDS CALL IT THESE DAYS?
BYE, DICK.
BYYYYE!
KLIK
AND HELLO, GORGEOUS!
KLAK KLAK
HUH?
IT'S, LIKE, SAD.

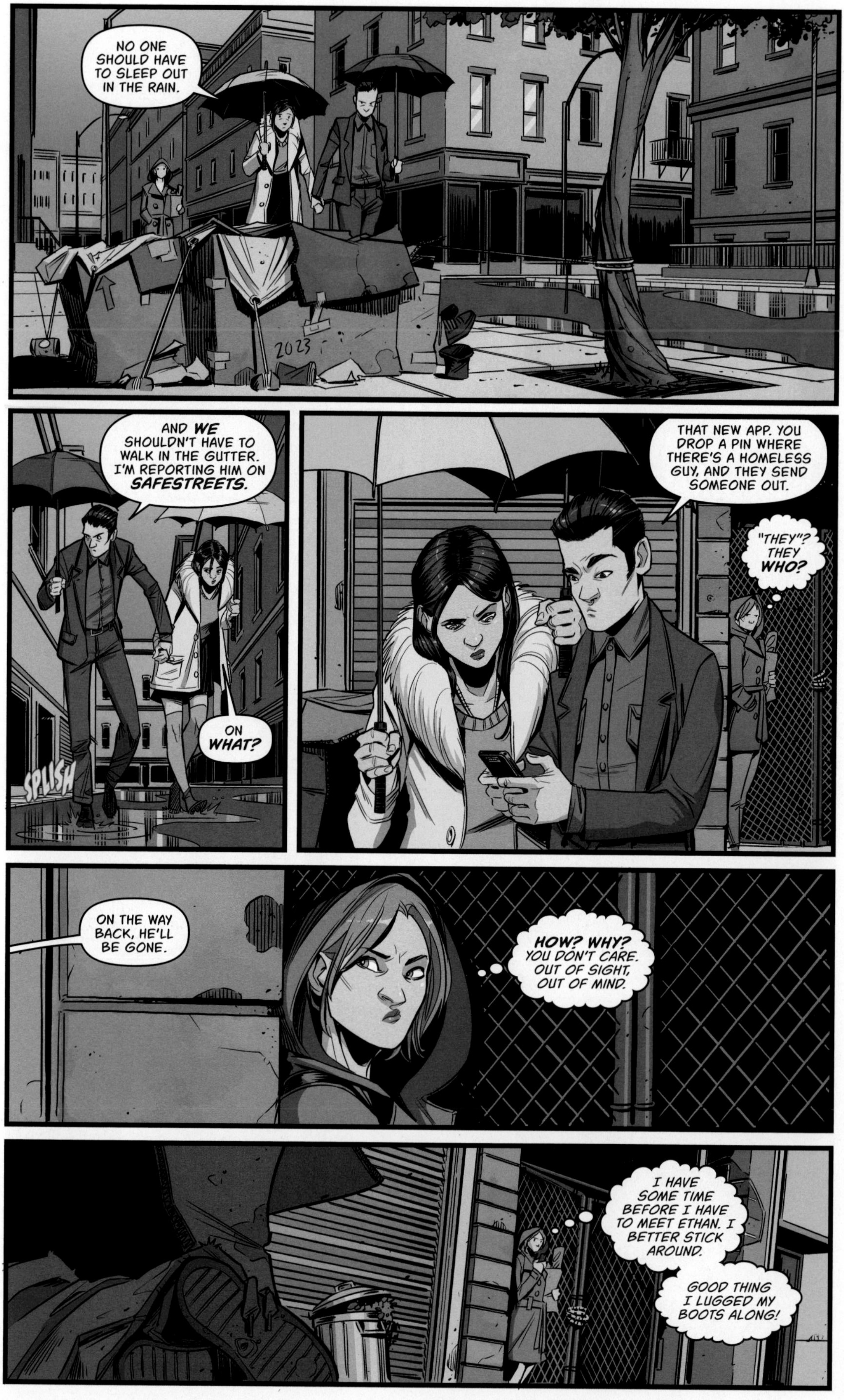
NO ONE SHOULD HAVE TO SLEEP OUT IN THE RAIN.
2023
AND WE SHOULDN'T HAVE TO WALK IN THE GUTTER. I'M REPORTING HIM ON SAFESTREETS.
ON WHAT?
SPLISH
THAT NEW APP. YOU DROP A PIN WHERE THERE'S A HOMELESS GUY, AND THEY SEND SOMEONE OUT.
"THEY"? THEY WHO?
ON THE WAY BACK, HE'LL BE GONE.
HOW? WHY? YOU DON'T CARE. OUT OF SIGHT, OUT OF MIND.
I HAVE SOME TIME BEFORE I HAVE TO MEET ETHAN. I BETTER STICK AROUND.
GOOD THING I LUGGED MY BOOTS ALONG!

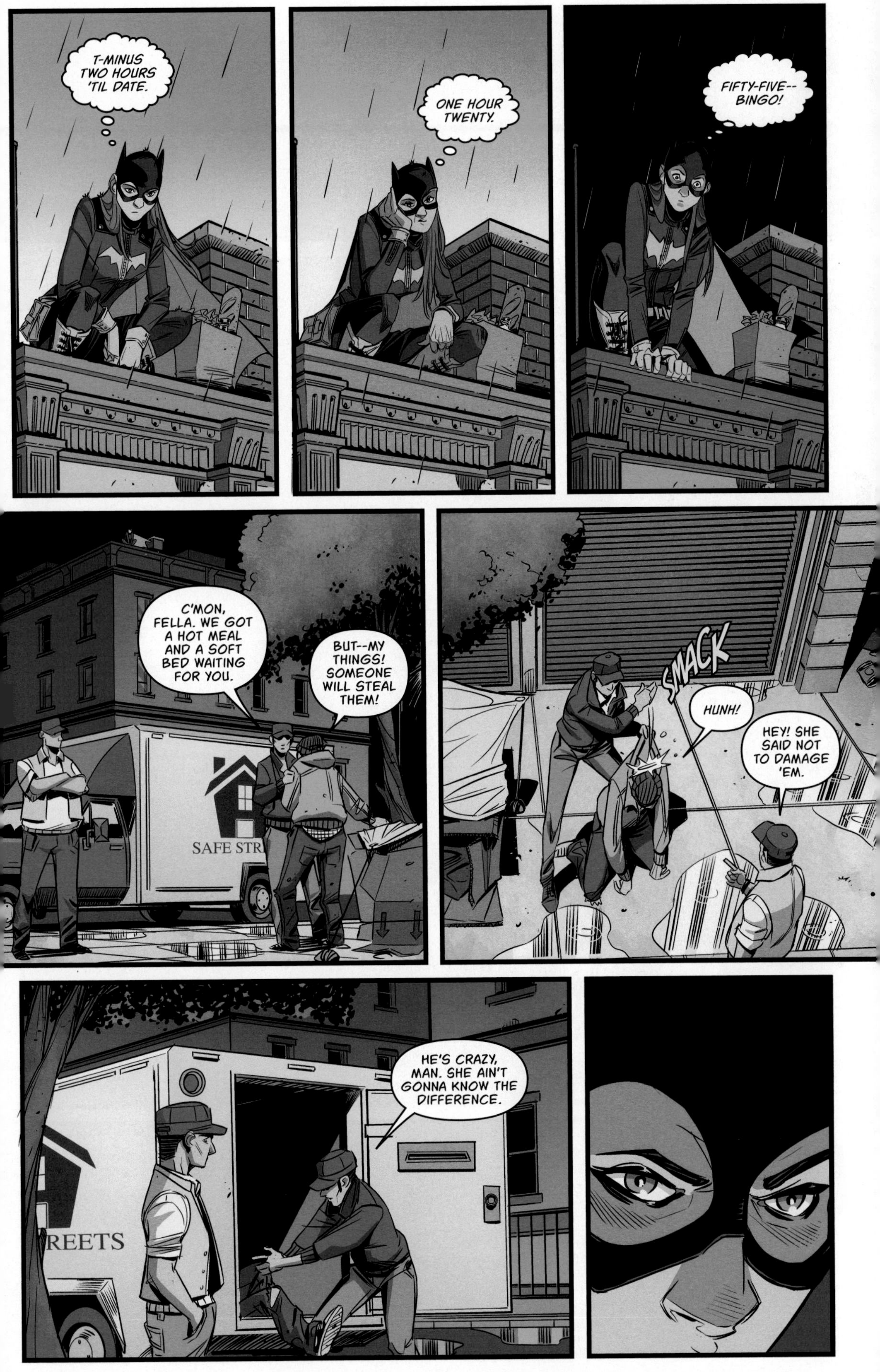
T-MINUS TWO HOURS 'TIL DATE.
ONE HOUR TWENTY.
FIFTY-FIVE-- BINGO!
C'MON, FELLA. WE GOT A HOT MEAL AND A SOFT BED WAITING FOR YOU.
BUT--MY THINGS! SOMEONE WILL STEAL THEM!
SAFE STR
SMACK
HUNH!
HEY! SHE SAID NOT TO DAMAGE 'EM.
HE'S CRAZY, MAN. SHE AIN'T GONNA KNOW THE DIFFERENCE.
REETS

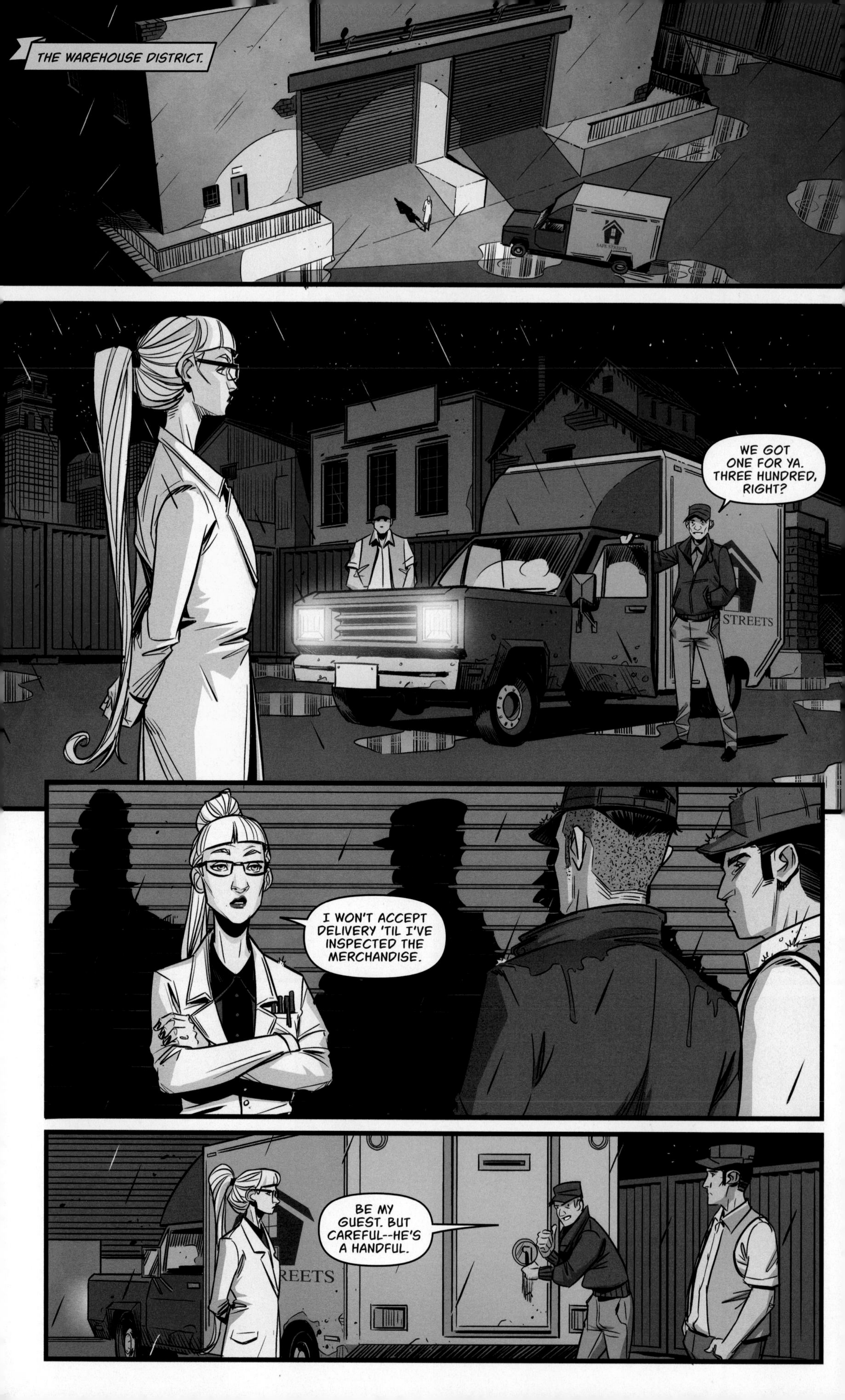
THE WAREHOUSE DISTRICT.
SAFE STREETS
WE GOT ONE FOR YA. THREE HUNDRED, RIGHT?
STREETS
I WON'T ACCEPT DELIVERY 'TIL I'VE INSPECTED THE MERCHANDISE.
BE MY GUEST. BUT CAREFUL--HE'S A HANDFUL.
REETS

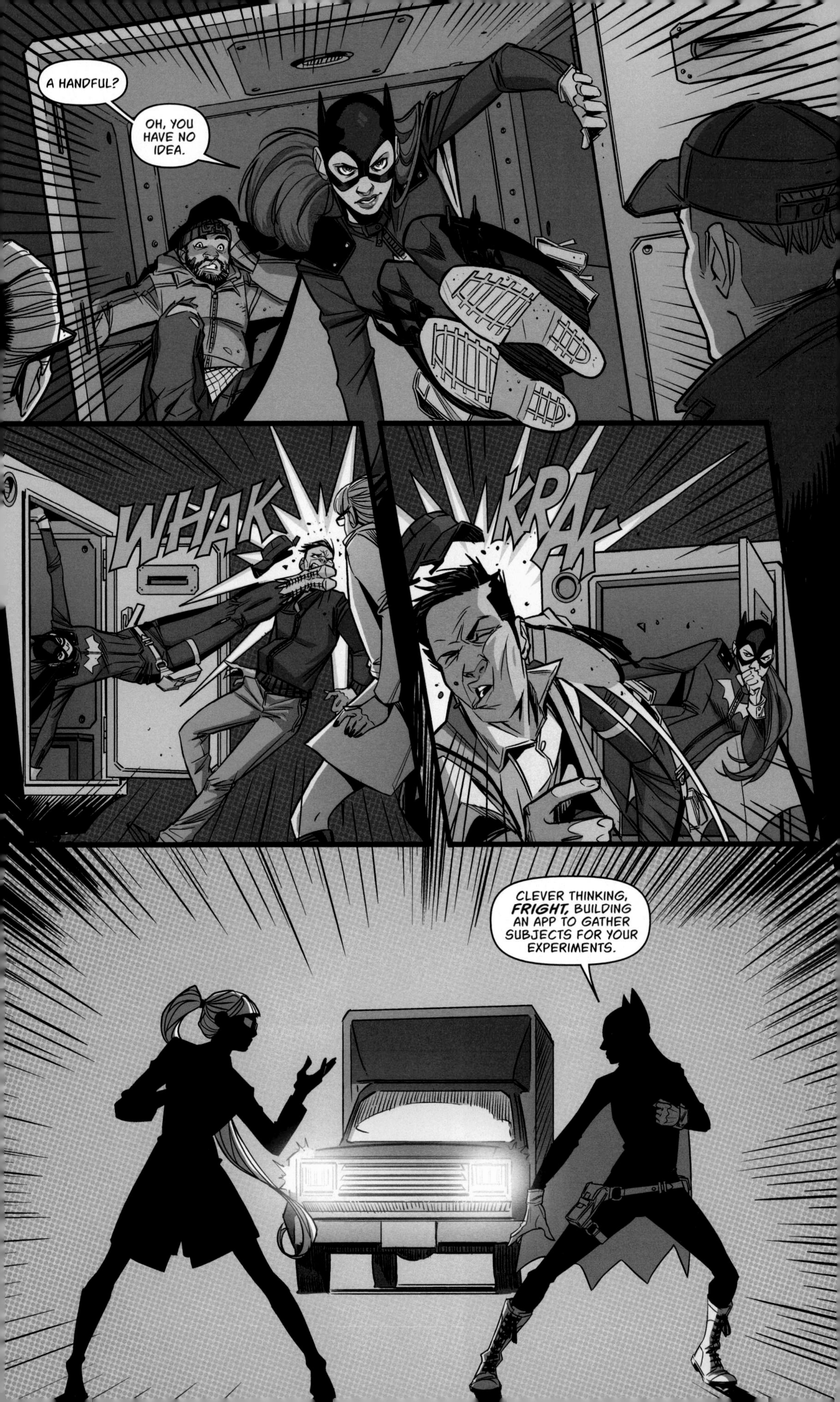
A HANDFUL?
OH, YOU HAVE NO IDEA.
WHAK
KRAK
CLEVER THINKING, FRIGHT, BUILDING AN APP TO GATHER SUBJECTS FOR YOUR EXPERIMENTS.

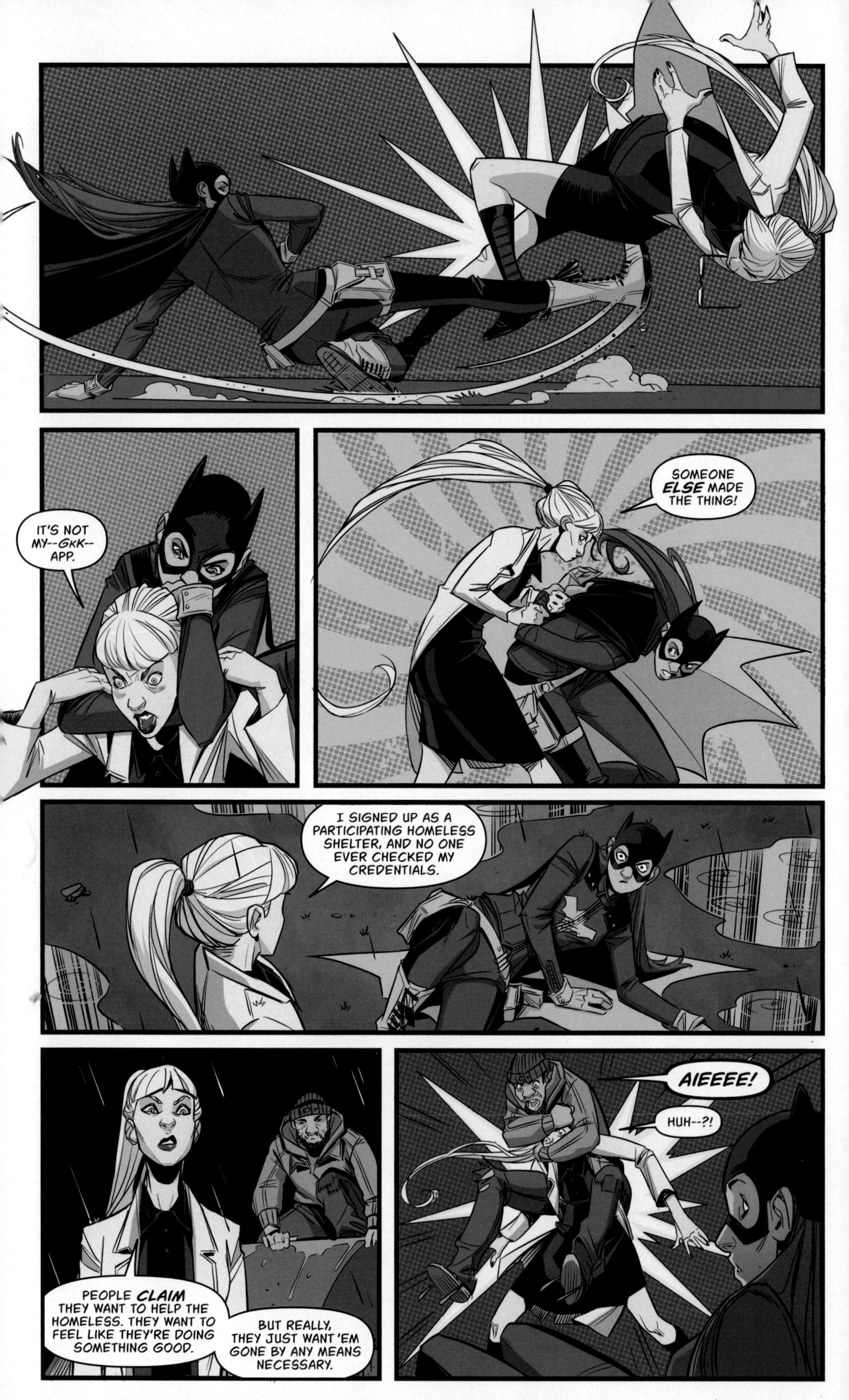
IT'S NOT MY--GKK--APP.
SOMEONE ELSE MADE THE THING!
I SIGNED UP AS A PARTICIPATING HOMELESS SHELTER, AND NO ONE EVER CHECKED MY CREDENTIALS.
PEOPLE CLAIM THEY WANT TO HELP THE HOMELESS. THEY WANT TO FEEL LIKE THEY'RE DOING SOMETHING GOOD.
BUT REALLY, THEY JUST WANT 'EM GONE BY ANY MEANS NECESSARY.
AIEEEE!
HUH--?!

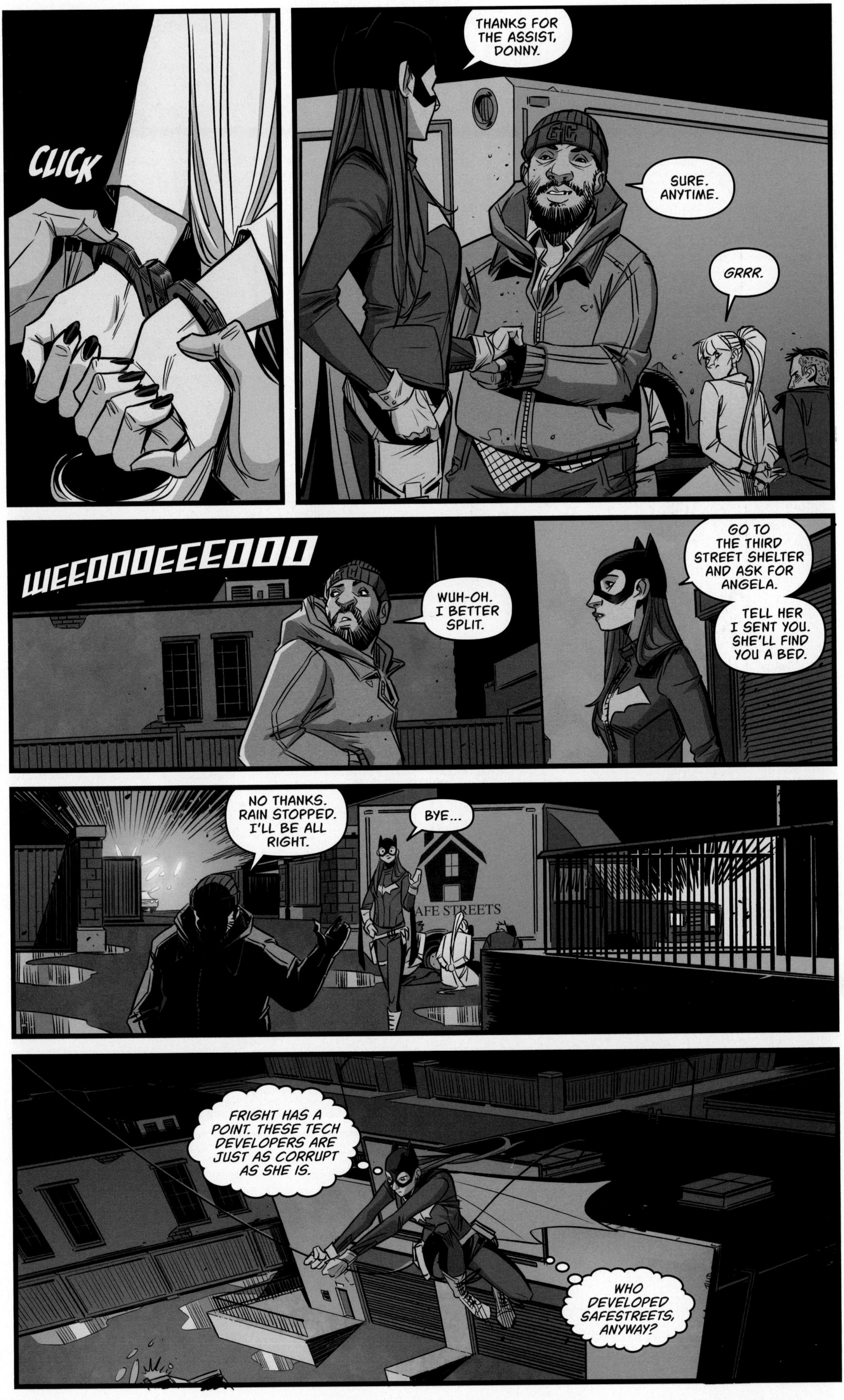
CLICK
THANKS FOR THE ASSIST, DONNY.
SURE. ANYTIME.
GRRR.
WEEOOOEEEOOO
WUH-OH. I BETTER SPLIT.
GO TO THE THIRD STREET SHELTER AND ASK FOR ANGELA.
TELL HER I SENT YOU. SHE'LL FIND YOU A BED.
NO THANKS. RAIN STOPPED. I'LL BE ALL RIGHT.
BYE...
AFE STREETS
FRIGHT HAS A POINT. THESE TECH DEVELOPERS ARE JUST AS CORRUPT AS SHE IS.
WHO DEVELOPED SAFESTREETS, ANYWAY?

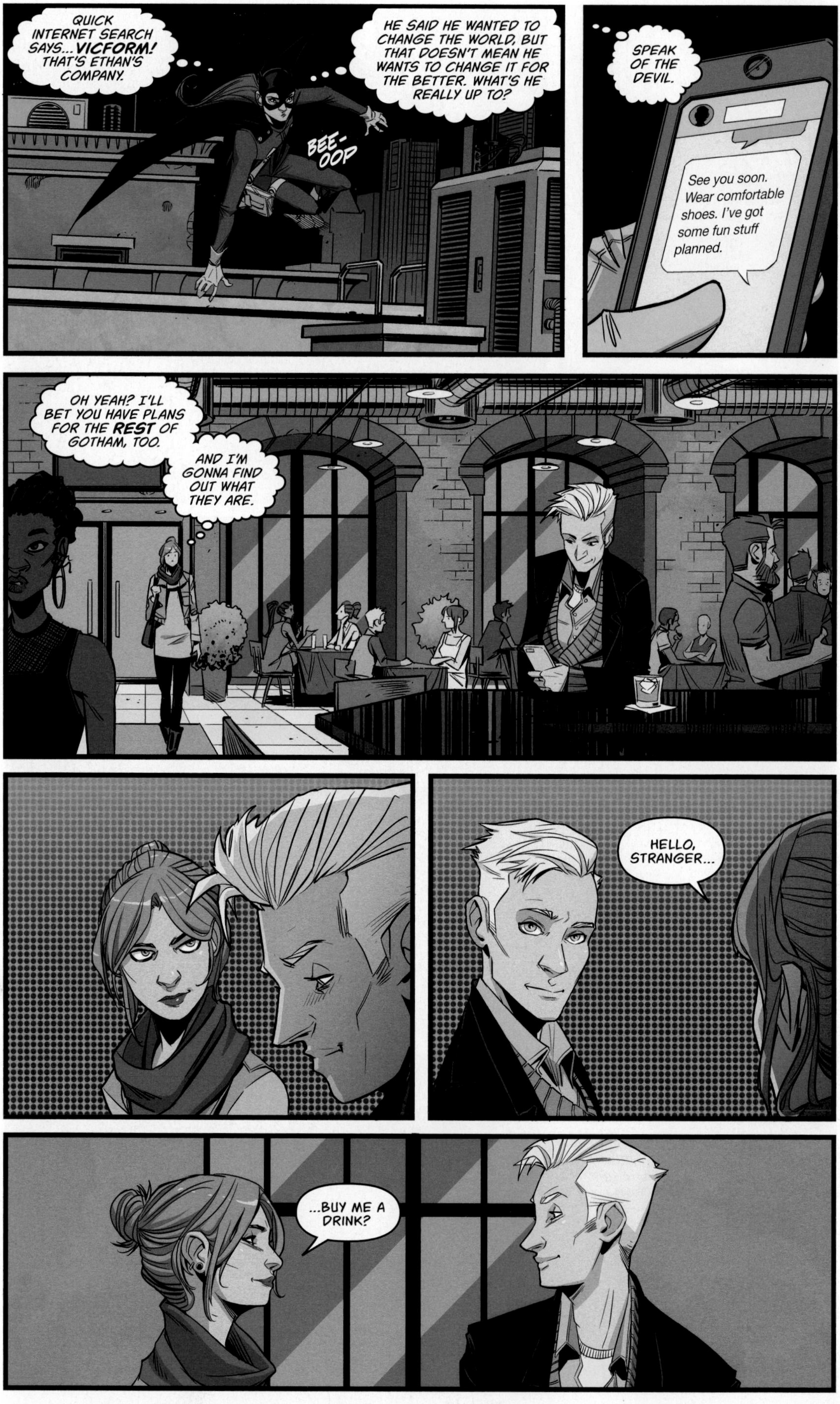
QUICK INTERNET SEARCH SAYS... VICFORM! THAT'S ETHAN'S COMPANY.
HE SAID HE WANTED TO CHANGE THE WORLD, BUT THAT DOESN'T MEAN HE WANTS TO CHANGE IT FOR THE BETTER. WHAT'S HE REALLY UP TO?
BEE-OOP
SPEAK OF THE DEVIL.
See you soon. Wear comfortable shoes. I've got some fun stuff planned.
OH YEAH? I'LL BET YOU HAVE PLANS FOR THE REST OF GOTHAM, TOO.
AND I'M GONNA FIND OUT WHAT THEY ARE.
HELLO, STRANGER...
...BUY ME A DRINK?

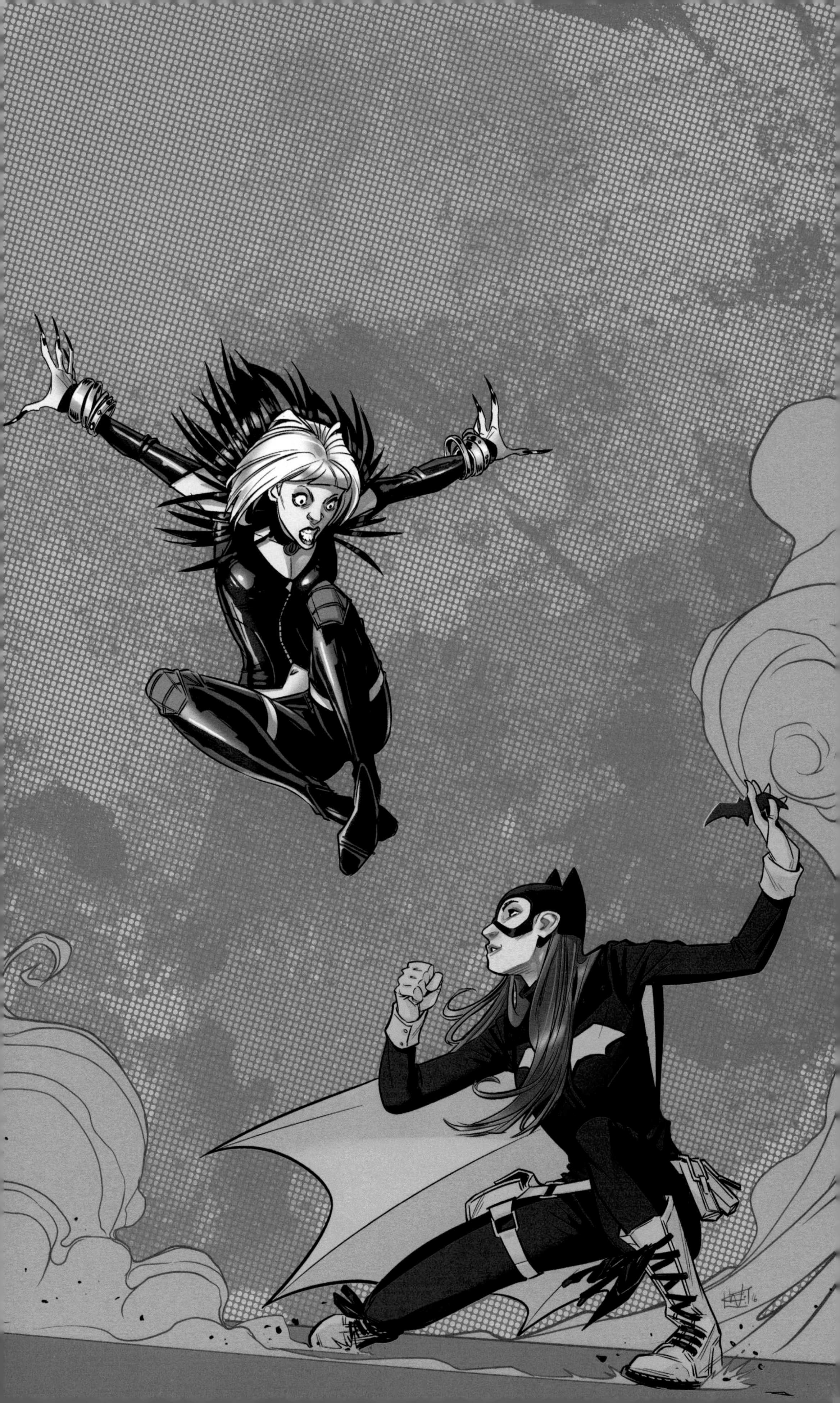

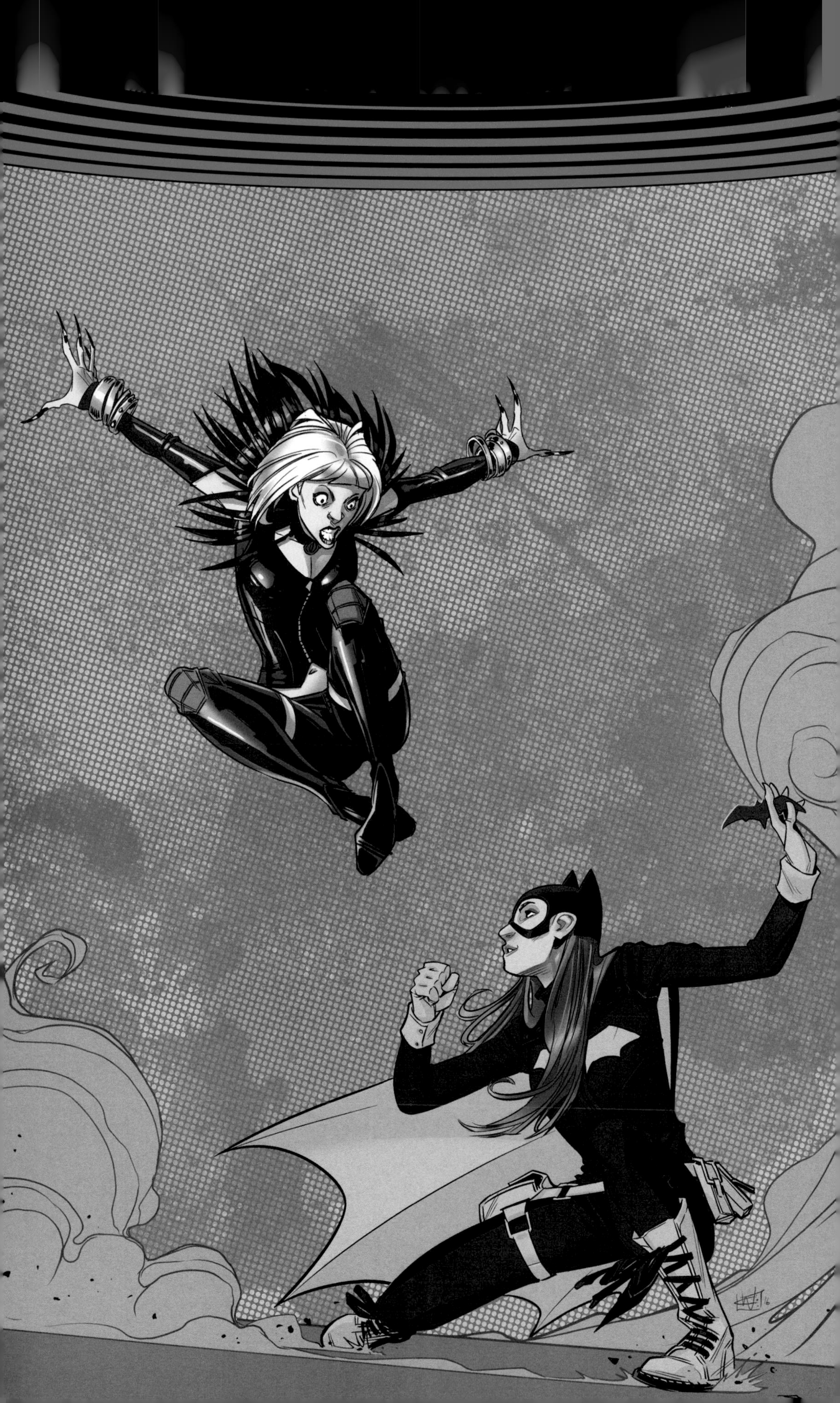

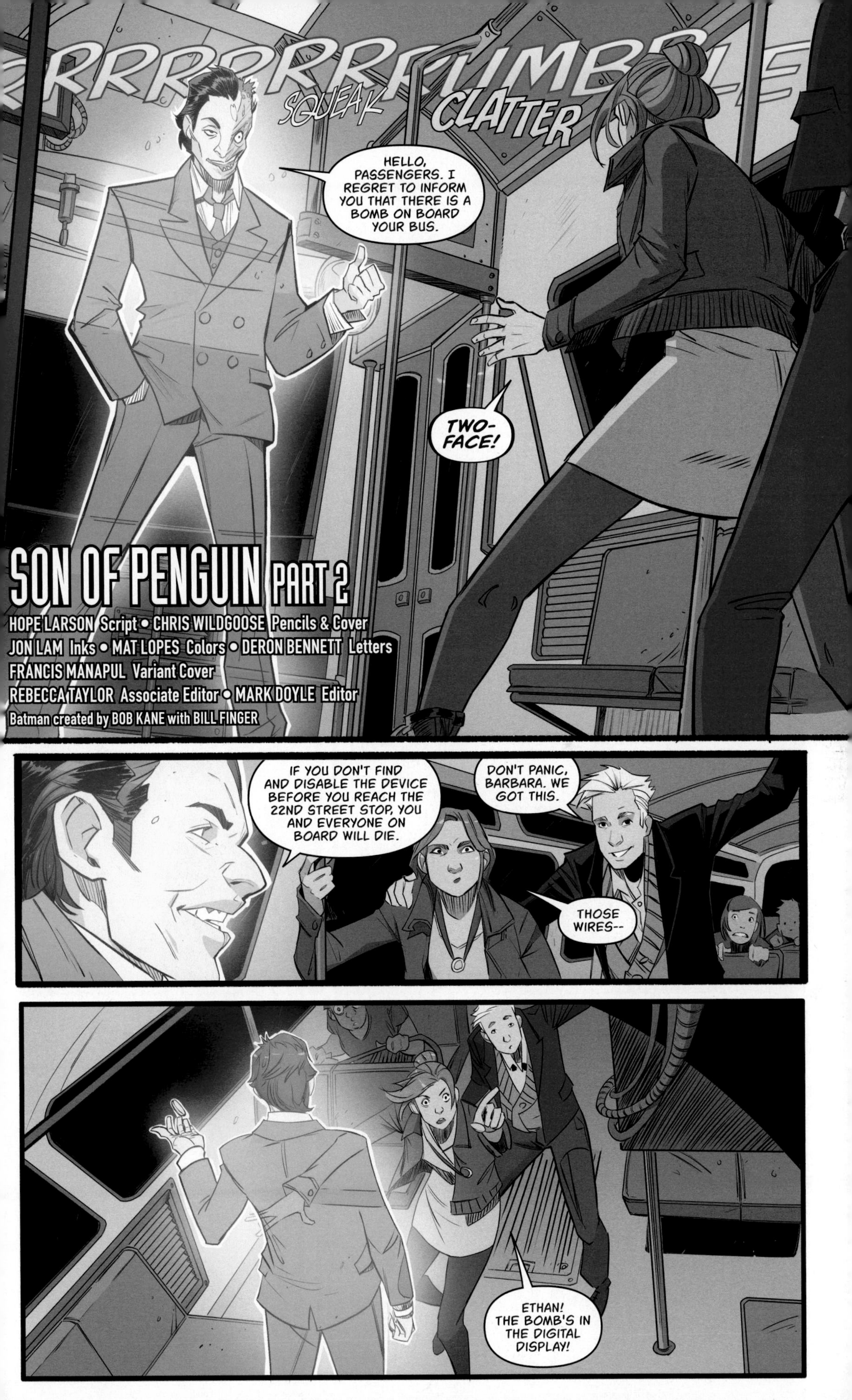
RRRRRRRRRUMBBLE
SQUEAK
CLATTER
HELLO, PASSENGERS. I REGRET TO INFORM YOU THAT THERE IS A BOMB ON BOARD YOUR BUS.
TWO-FACE!
SON OF PENGUIN PART 2
HOPE LARSON Script • CHRIS WILDGOOSE Pencils & Cover
JON LAM Inks • MAT LOPES Colors • DERON BENNETT Letters
FRANCIS MANAPUL Variant Cover
REBECCA TAYLOR Associate Editor • MARK DOYLE Editor
Batman created by BOB KANE with BILL FINGER
IF YOU DON'T FIND AND DISABLE THE DEVICE BEFORE YOU REACH THE 22ND STREET STOP, YOU AND EVERYONE ON BOARD WILL DIE.
DON'T PANIC, BARBARA. WE GOT THIS.
THOSE WIRES--
ETHAN! THE BOMB'S IN THE DIGITAL DISPLAY!

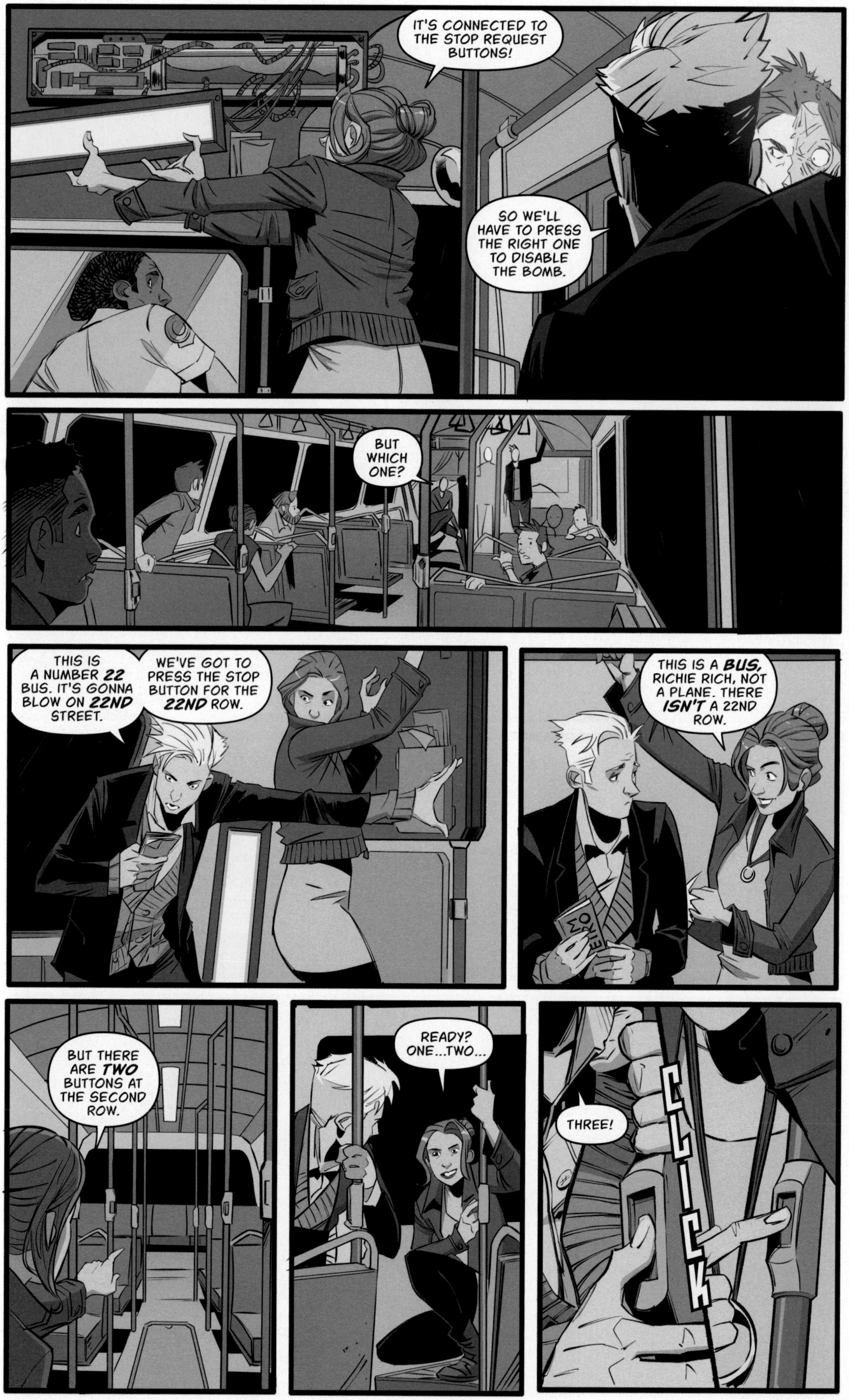
IT'S CONNECTED TO THE STOP REQUEST BUTTONS!
SO WE'LL HAVE TO PRESS THE RIGHT ONE TO DISABLE THE BOMB.
BUT WHICH ONE?
THIS IS A NUMBER 22 BUS. IT'S GONNA BLOW ON 22ND STREET.
WE'VE GOT TO PRESS THE STOP BUTTON FOR THE 22ND ROW.
THIS IS A BUS, RICHIE RICH, NOT A PLANE. THERE ISN'T A 22ND ROW.
BUT THERE ARE TWO BUTTONS AT THE SECOND ROW.
READY? ONE...TWO...
THREE!
CLICK

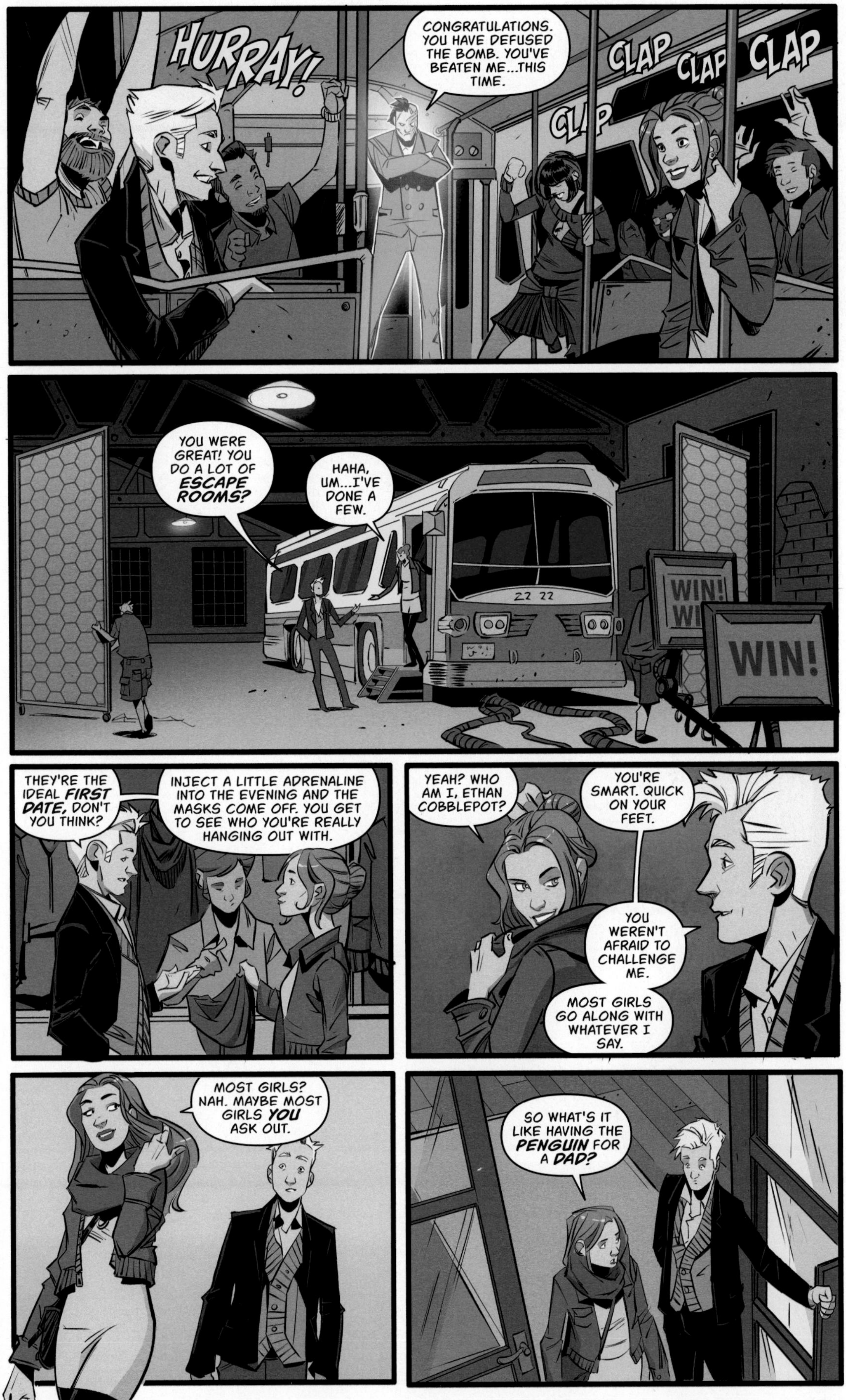
HURRAY!
CONGRATULATIONS. YOU HAVE DEFUSED THE BOMB. YOU'VE BEATEN ME...THIS TIME.
CLAP CLAP CLAP
CLAP
YOU WERE GREAT! YOU DO A LOT OF ESCAPE ROOMS?
HAHA, UM...I'VE DONE A FEW.
22 22
WIN! WI
WIN!
THEY'RE THE IDEAL FIRST DATE, DON'T YOU THINK?
INJECT A LITTLE ADRENALINE INTO THE EVENING AND THE MASKS COME OFF. YOU GET TO SEE WHO YOU'RE REALLY HANGING OUT WITH.
YEAH? WHO AM I, ETHAN COBBLEPOT?
YOU'RE SMART. QUICK ON YOUR FEET.
YOU WEREN'T AFRAID TO CHALLENGE ME.
MOST GIRLS GO ALONG WITH WHATEVER I SAY.
MOST GIRLS? NAH. MAYBE MOST GIRLS YOU ASK OUT.
SO WHAT'S IT LIKE HAVING THE PENGUIN FOR A DAD?

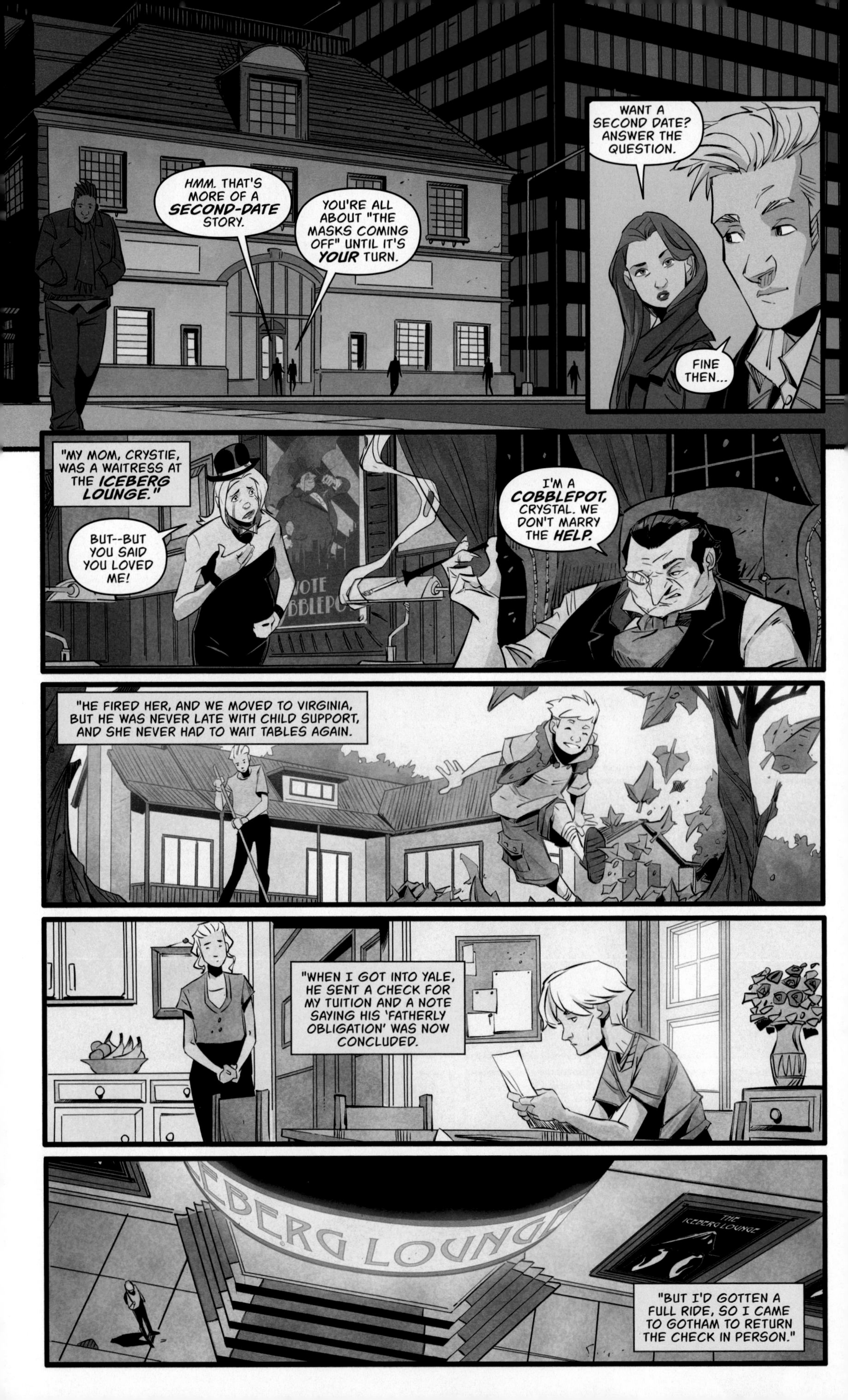
HMM. THAT'S MORE OF A SECOND-DATE STORY.
YOU'RE ALL ABOUT "THE MASKS COMING OFF" UNTIL IT'S YOUR TURN.
WANT A SECOND DATE? ANSWER THE QUESTION.
FINE THEN...
"MY MOM, CRYSTIE, WAS A WAITRESS AT THE ICEBERG LOUNGE."
BUT--BUT YOU SAID YOU LOVED ME!
I'M A COBBLEPOT, CRYSTAL. WE DON'T MARRY THE HELP.
"HE FIRED HER, AND WE MOVED TO VIRGINIA, BUT HE WAS NEVER LATE WITH CHILD SUPPORT, AND SHE NEVER HAD TO WAIT TABLES AGAIN.
"WHEN I GOT INTO YALE, HE SENT A CHECK FOR MY TUITION AND A NOTE SAYING HIS 'FATHERLY OBLIGATION' WAS NOW CONCLUDED.
ICEBERG LOUNGE
THE ICEBERG LOUNGE
"BUT I'D GOTTEN A FULL RIDE, SO I CAME TO GOTHAM TO RETURN THE CHECK IN PERSON."

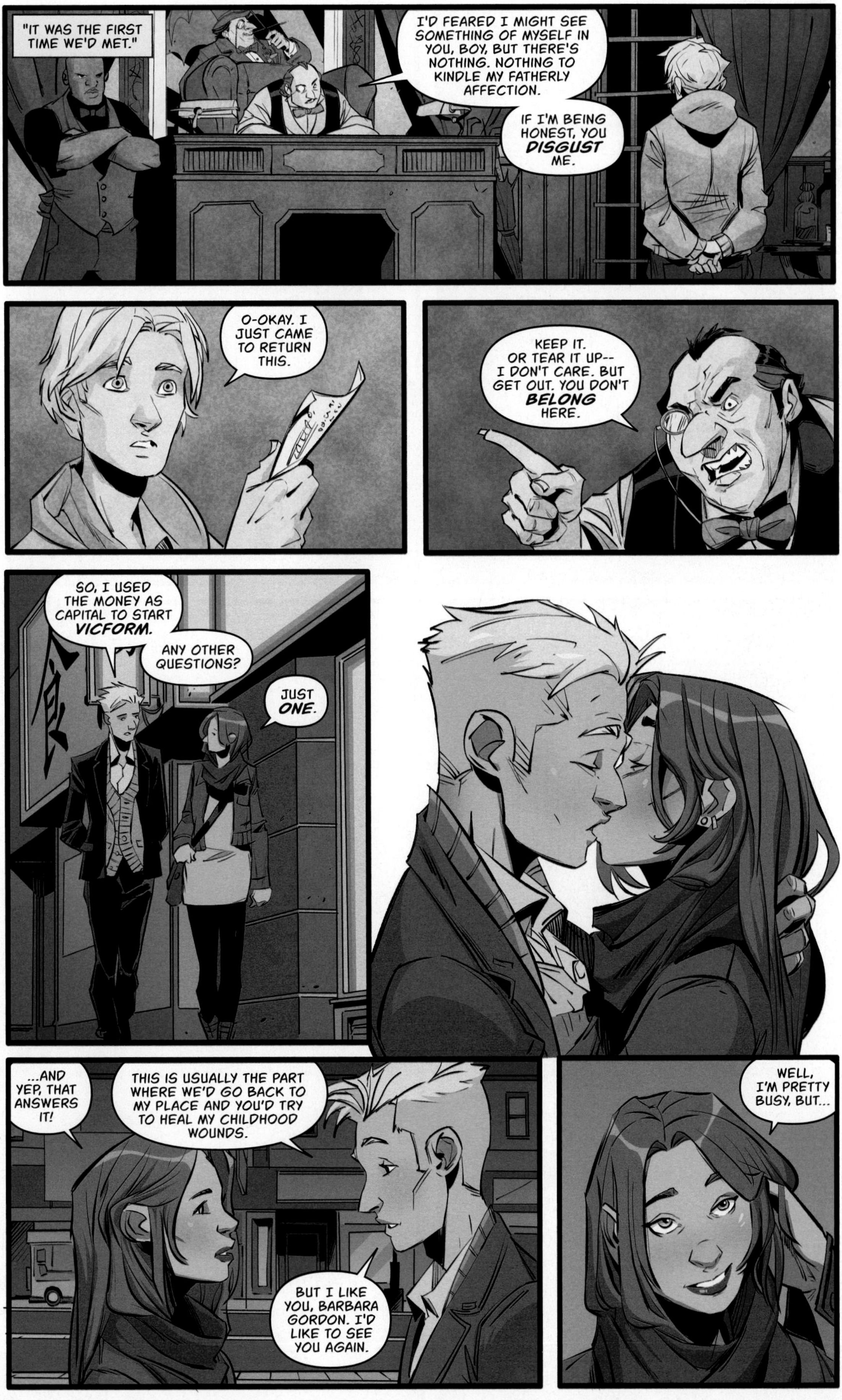
"IT WAS THE FIRST TIME WE'D MET."
I'D FEARED I MIGHT SEE SOMETHING OF MYSELF IN YOU, BOY, BUT THERE'S NOTHING. NOTHING TO KINDLE MY FATHERLY AFFECTION.
IF I'M BEING HONEST, YOU DISGUST ME.
O-OKAY. I JUST CAME TO RETURN THIS.
KEEP IT. OR TEAR IT UP-- I DON'T CARE. BUT GET OUT. YOU DON'T BELONG HERE.
SO, I USED THE MONEY AS CAPITAL TO START VICFORM.
ANY OTHER QUESTIONS?
JUST ONE.
...AND YEP, THAT ANSWERS IT!
THIS IS USUALLY THE PART WHERE WE'D GO BACK TO MY PLACE AND YOU'D TRY TO HEAL MY CHILDHOOD WOUNDS.
BUT I LIKE YOU, BARBARA GORDON. I'D LIKE TO SEE YOU AGAIN.
WELL, I'M PRETTY BUSY, BUT...

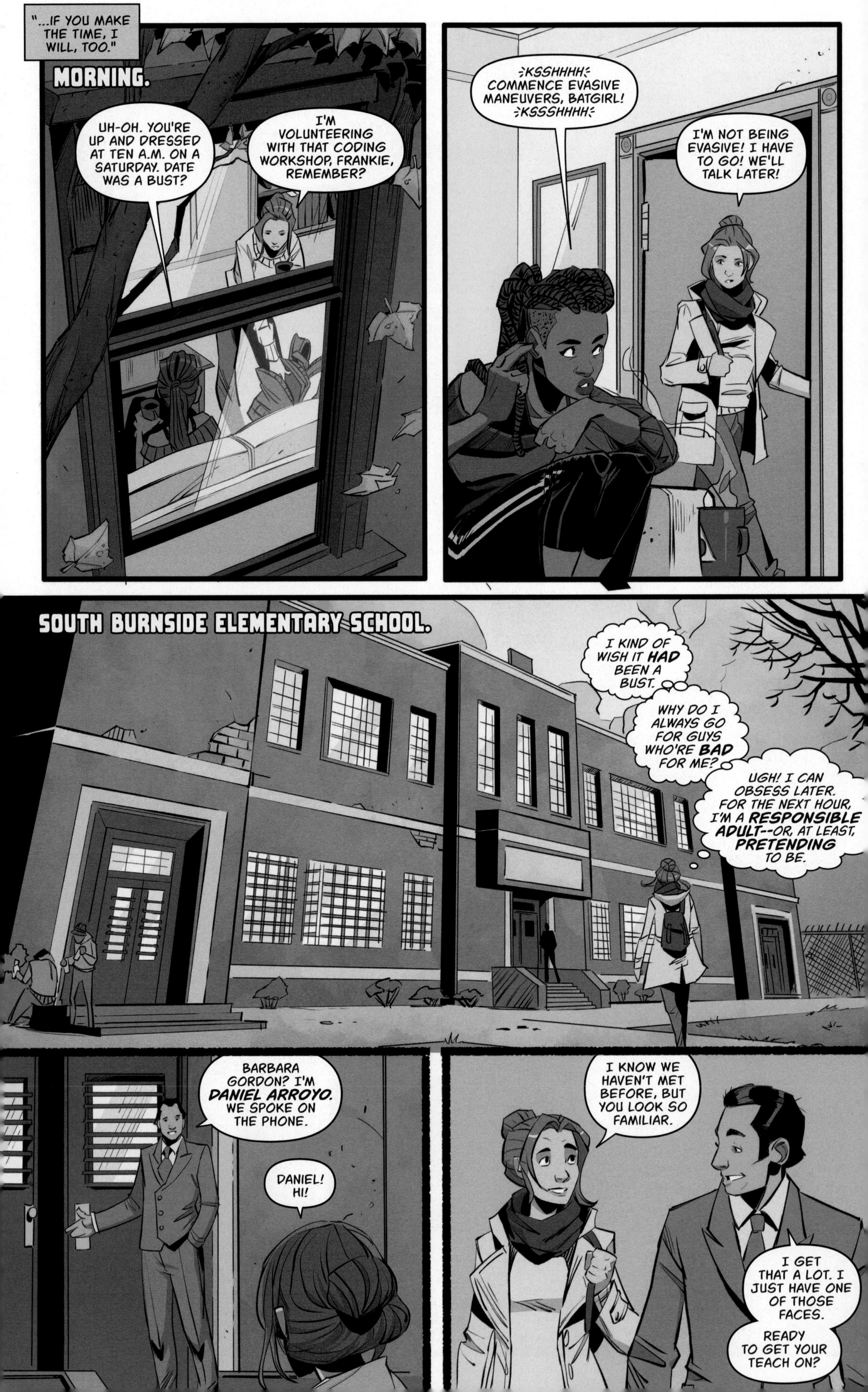
"...IF YOU MAKE THE TIME, I WILL, TOO."
MORNING.
UH-OH. YOU'RE UP AND DRESSED AT TEN A.M. ON A SATURDAY. DATE WAS A BUST?
I'M VOLUNTEERING WITH THAT CODING WORKSHOP, FRANKIE, REMEMBER?
KSSHHHH COMMENCE EVASIVE MANEUVERS, BATGIRL! KSSSHHHH
I'M NOT BEING EVASIVE! I HAVE TO GO! WE'LL TALK LATER!
SOUTH BURNSIDE ELEMENTARY SCHOOL.
I KIND OF WISH IT HAD BEEN A BUST.
WHY DO I ALWAYS GO FOR GUYS WHO'RE BAD FOR ME?
UGH! I CAN OBSESS LATER. FOR THE NEXT HOUR, I'M A RESPONSIBLE ADULT--OR, AT LEAST, PRETENDING TO BE.
BARBARA GORDON? I'M DANIEL ARROYO. WE SPOKE ON THE PHONE.
DANIEL! HI!
I KNOW WE HAVEN'T MET BEFORE, BUT YOU LOOK SO FAMILIAR.
I GET THAT A LOT. I JUST HAVE ONE OF THOSE FACES.
READY TO GET YOUR TEACH ON?

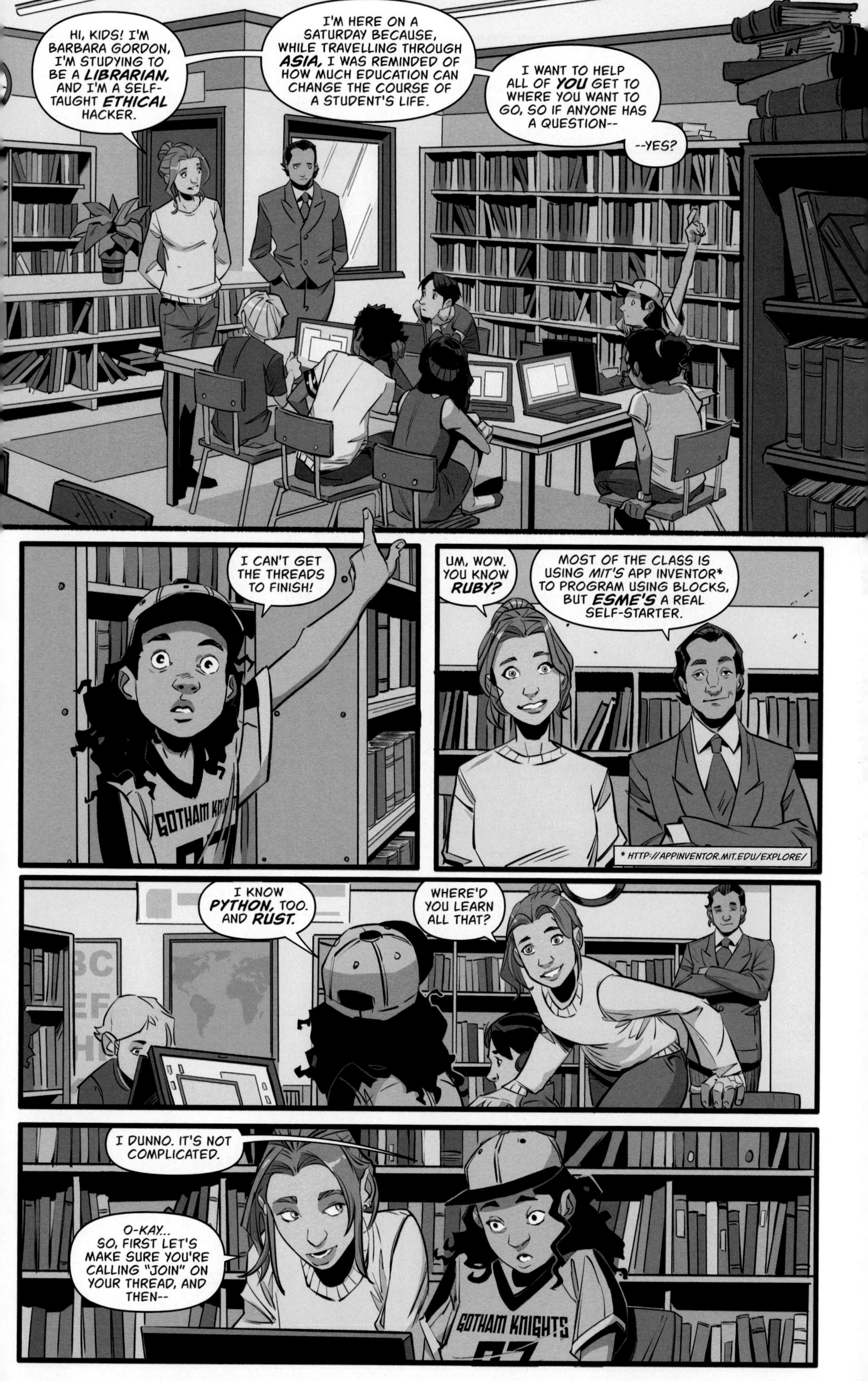
HI, KIDS! I'M BARBARA GORDON, I'M STUDYING TO BE A LIBRARIAN, AND I'M A SELF-TAUGHT ETHICAL HACKER.
I'M HERE ON A SATURDAY BECAUSE, WHILE TRAVELLING THROUGH ASIA, I WAS REMINDED OF HOW MUCH EDUCATION CAN CHANGE THE COURSE OF A STUDENT'S LIFE.
I WANT TO HELP ALL OF YOU GET TO WHERE YOU WANT TO GO, SO IF ANYONE HAS A QUESTION--
--YES?
I CAN'T GET THE THREADS TO FINISH!
GOTHAM KNIGHTS
UM, WOW. YOU KNOW RUBY?
MOST OF THE CLASS IS USING MIT'S APP INVENTOR* TO PROGRAM USING BLOCKS, BUT ESME'S A REAL SELF-STARTER.
* HTTP://APPINVENTOR.MIT.EDU/EXPLORE/
I KNOW PYTHON, TOO. AND RUST.
WHERE'D YOU LEARN ALL THAT?
I DUNNO. IT'S NOT COMPLICATED.
O-KAY... SO, FIRST LET'S MAKE SURE YOU'RE CALLING "JOIN" ON YOUR THREAD, AND THEN--
GOTHAM KNIGHTS

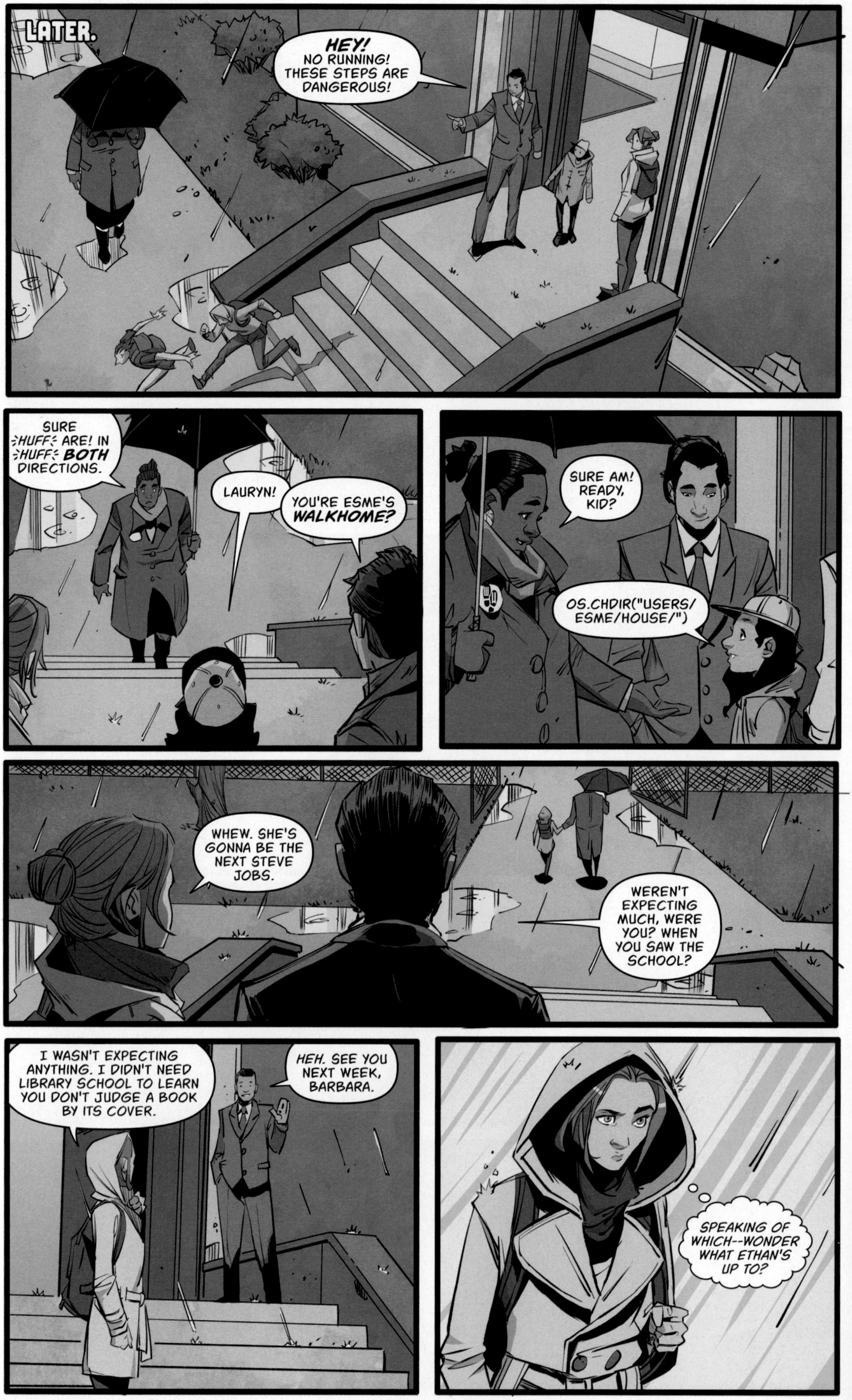
LATER.
HEY! NO RUNNING! THESE STEPS ARE DANGEROUS!
SURE ~HUFF~ ARE! IN ~HUFF~ BOTH DIRECTIONS.
LAURYN!
YOU'RE ESME'S WALKHOME?
SURE AM! READY, KID?
OS.CHDIR("USERS/ ESME/HOUSE/")
WHEW. SHE'S GONNA BE THE NEXT STEVE JOBS.
WEREN'T EXPECTING MUCH, WERE YOU? WHEN YOU SAW THE SCHOOL?
I WASN'T EXPECTING ANYTHING. I DIDN'T NEED LIBRARY SCHOOL TO LEARN YOU DON'T JUDGE A BOOK BY ITS COVER.
HEH. SEE YOU NEXT WEEK, BARBARA.
SPEAKING OF WHICH--WONDER WHAT ETHAN'S UP TO?

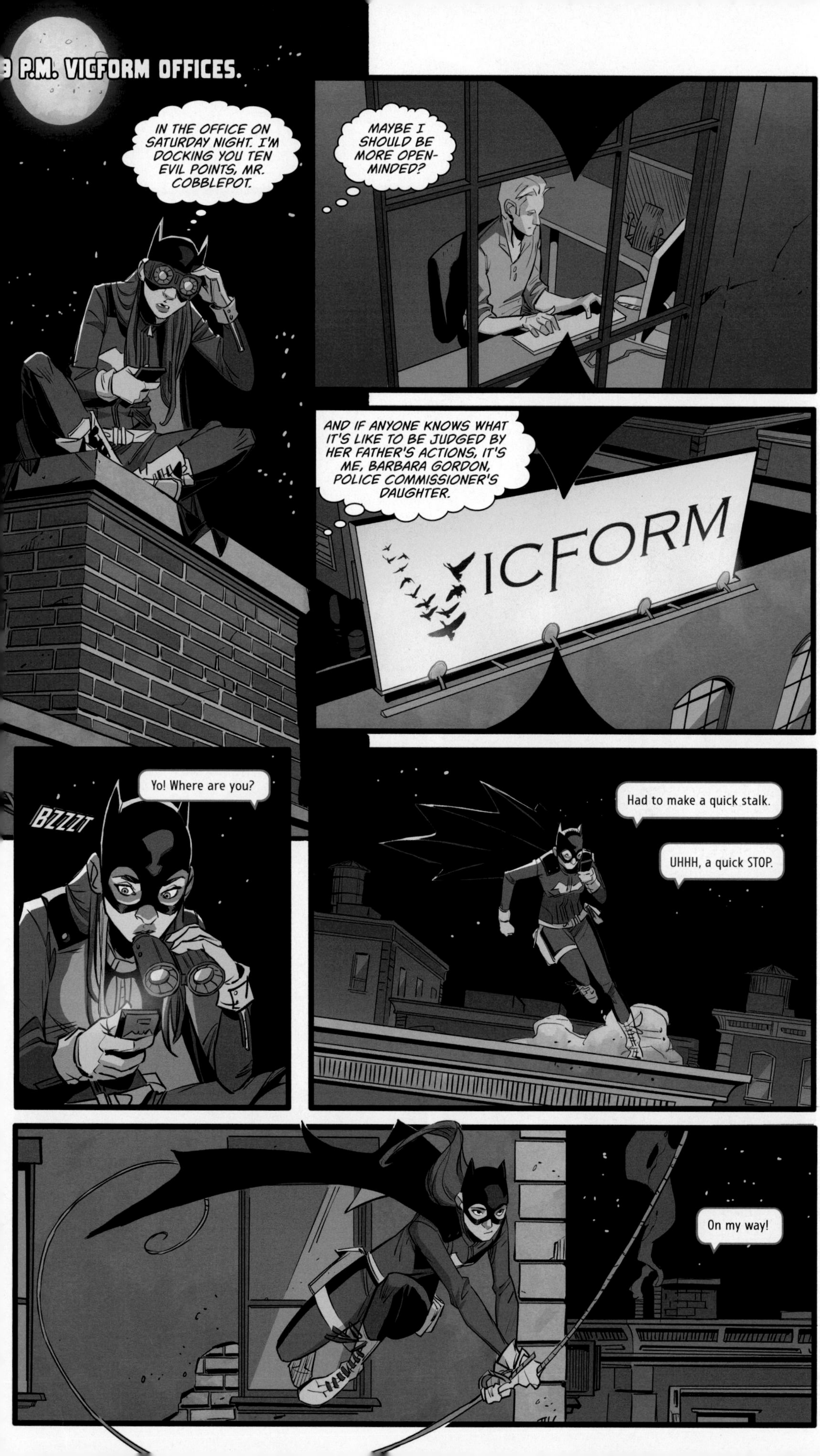
9 P.M. VICFORM OFFICES.
IN THE OFFICE ON SATURDAY NIGHT. I'M DOCKING YOU TEN EVIL POINTS, MR. COBBLEPOT.
MAYBE I SHOULD BE MORE OPEN-MINDED?
AND IF ANYONE KNOWS WHAT IT'S LIKE TO BE JUDGED BY HER FATHER'S ACTIONS, IT'S ME, BARBARA GORDON, POLICE COMMISSIONER'S DAUGHTER.
VICFORM
BZZZT
Yo! Where are you?
Had to make a quick stalk.
UHHH, a quick STOP.
On my way!

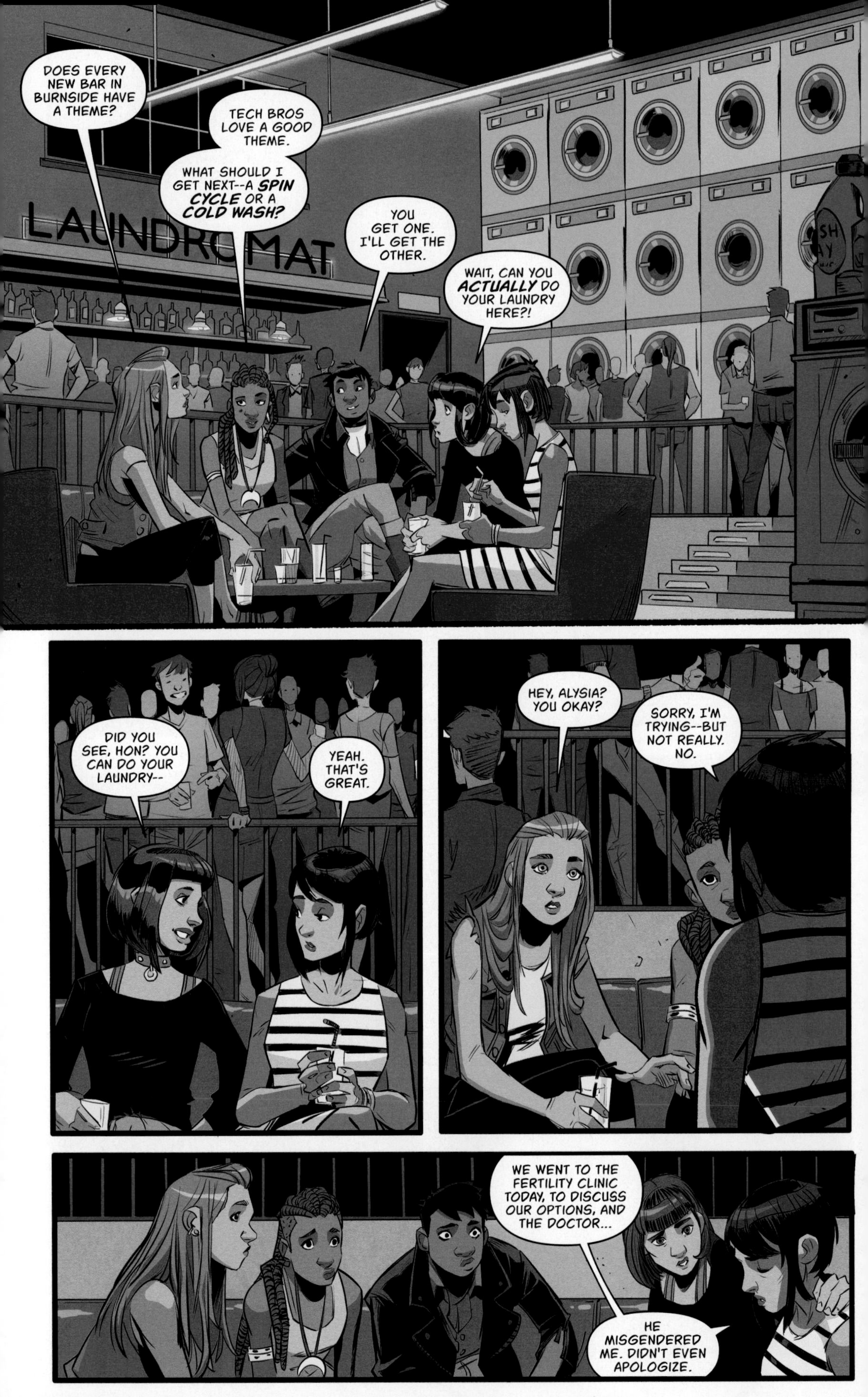
DOES EVERY NEW BAR IN BURNSIDE HAVE A THEME?
TECH BROS LOVE A GOOD THEME.
WHAT SHOULD I GET NEXT--A SPIN CYCLE OR A COLD WASH?
LAUNDROMAT
YOU GET ONE. I'LL GET THE OTHER.
WAIT, CAN YOU ACTUALLY DO YOUR LAUNDRY HERE?!
DID YOU SEE, HON? YOU CAN DO YOUR LAUNDRY--
YEAH. THAT'S GREAT.
HEY, ALYSIA? YOU OKAY?
SORRY, I'M TRYING--BUT NOT REALLY. NO.
WE WENT TO THE FERTILITY CLINIC TODAY, TO DISCUSS OUR OPTIONS, AND THE DOCTOR...
HE MISGENDERED ME. DIDN'T EVEN APOLOGIZE.

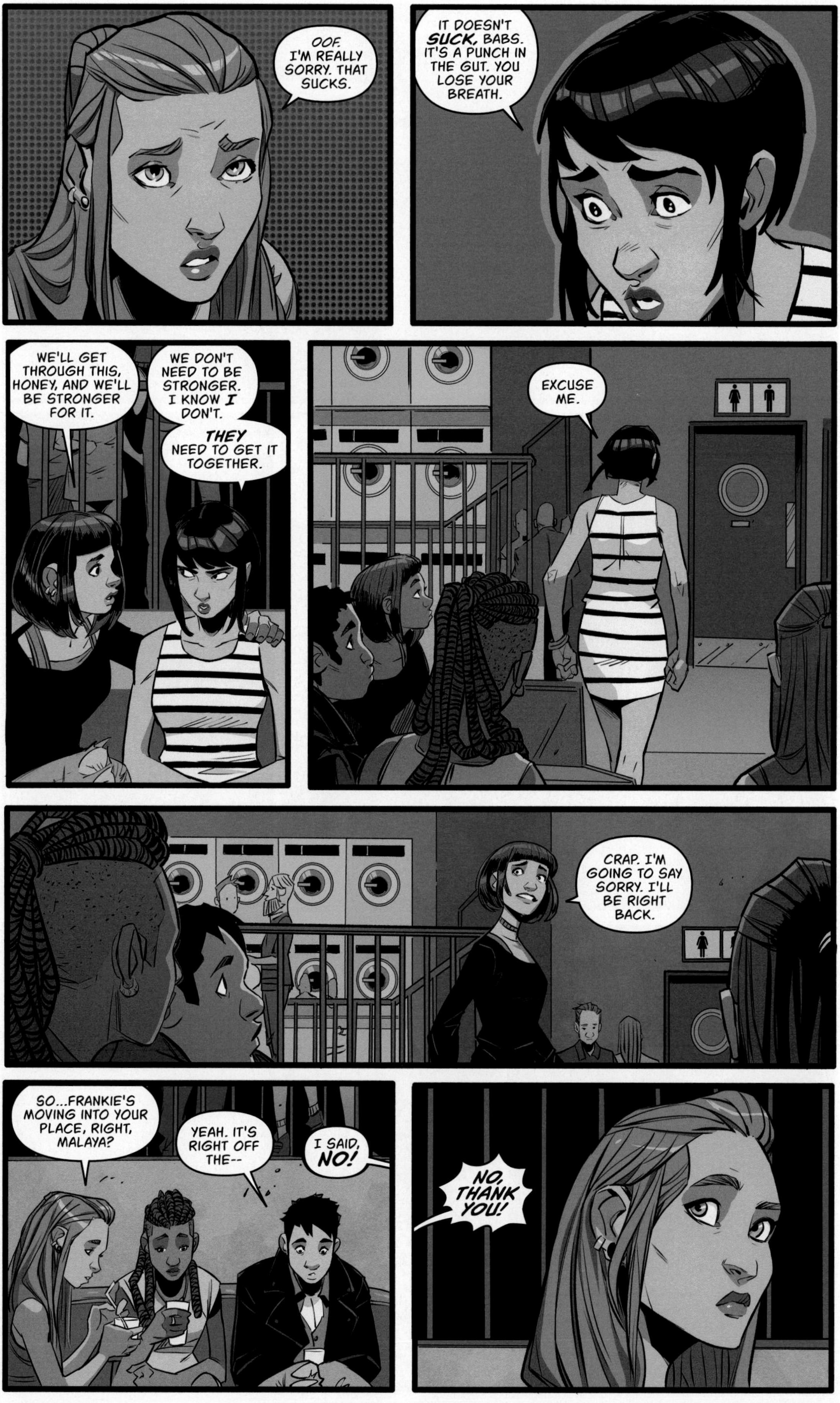

OOF. I'M REALLY SORRY. THAT SUCKS.
IT DOESN'T SUCK, BABS. IT'S A PUNCH IN THE GUT. YOU LOSE YOUR BREATH.
WE'LL GET THROUGH THIS, HONEY, AND WE'LL BE STRONGER FOR IT.
WE DON'T NEED TO BE STRONGER. I KNOW I DON'T.
THEY NEED TO GET IT TOGETHER.
EXCUSE ME.
CRAP. I'M GOING TO SAY SORRY. I'LL BE RIGHT BACK.
SO...FRANKIE'S MOVING INTO YOUR PLACE, RIGHT, MALAYA?
YEAH. IT'S RIGHT OFF THE--
I SAID, NO!
NO, THANK YOU!

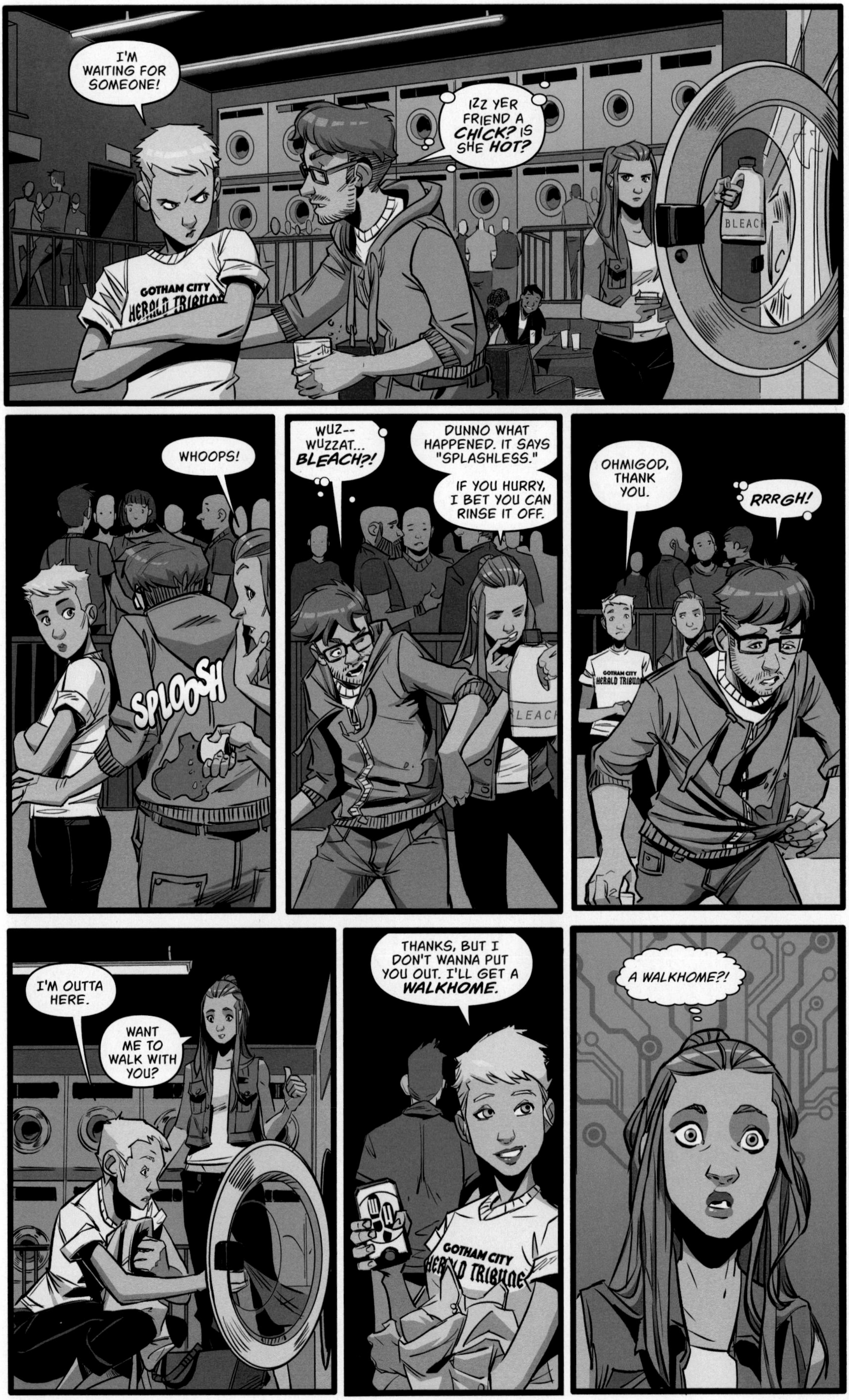
I'M WAITING FOR SOMEONE!
IZZ YER FRIEND A CHICK? IS SHE HOT?
BLEACH
GOTHAM CITY HERALD TRIBUNE
WHOOPS!
SPLOOSH
WUZ-- WUZZAT... BLEACH?!
DUNNO WHAT HAPPENED. IT SAYS "SPLASHLESS."
IF YOU HURRY, I BET YOU CAN RINSE IT OFF.
BLEACH
OHMIGOD, THANK YOU.
RRRGH!
GOTHAM CITY HERALD TRIBUNE
I'M OUTTA HERE.
WANT ME TO WALK WITH YOU?
THANKS, BUT I DON'T WANNA PUT YOU OUT. I'LL GET A WALKHOME.
GOTHAM CITY HERALD TRIBUNE
A WALKHOME?!

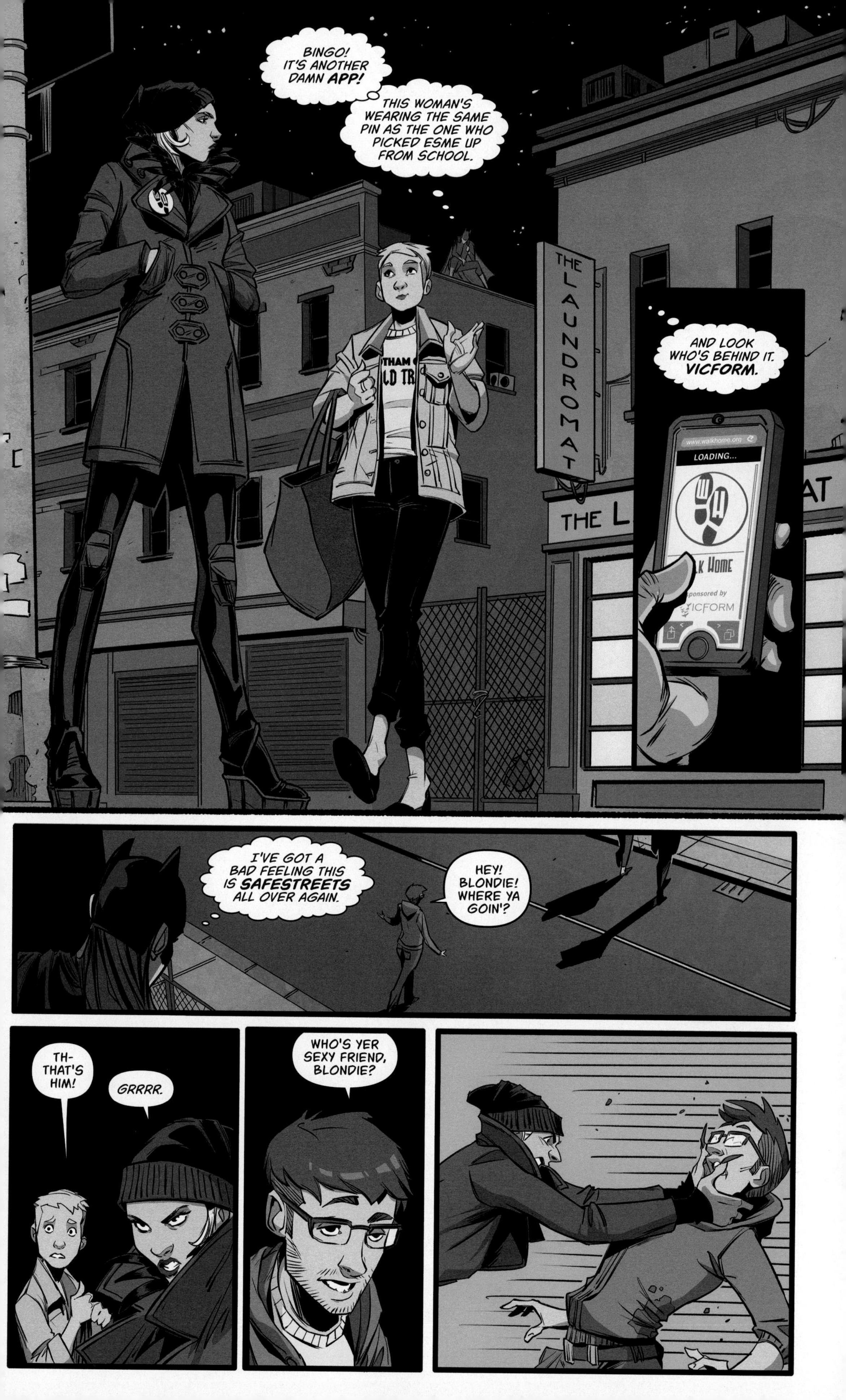
BINGO! IT'S ANOTHER DAMN APP!
THIS WOMAN'S WEARING THE SAME PIN AS THE ONE WHO PICKED ESME UP FROM SCHOOL.
THE LAUNDROMAT
AND LOOK WHO'S BEHIND IT. VICFORM.
www.walkhome.org
LOADING...
sponsored by
I'VE GOT A BAD FEELING THIS IS SAFESTREETS ALL OVER AGAIN.
HEY! BLONDIE! WHERE YA GOIN'?
TH- THAT'S HIM!
GRRRR.
WHO'S YER SEXY FRIEND, BLONDIE?

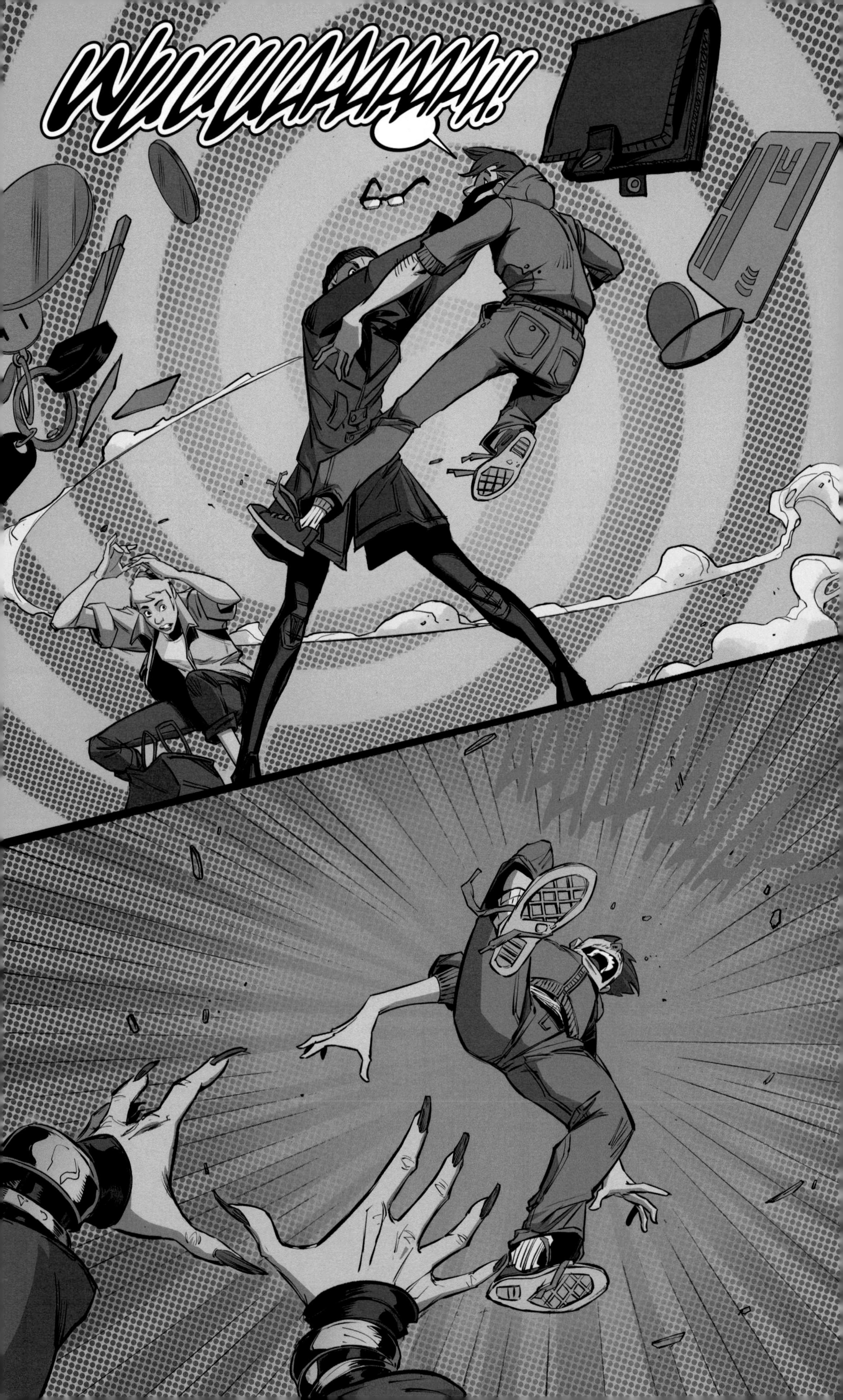
WHUUUAAAA!!
AAAAAAAA

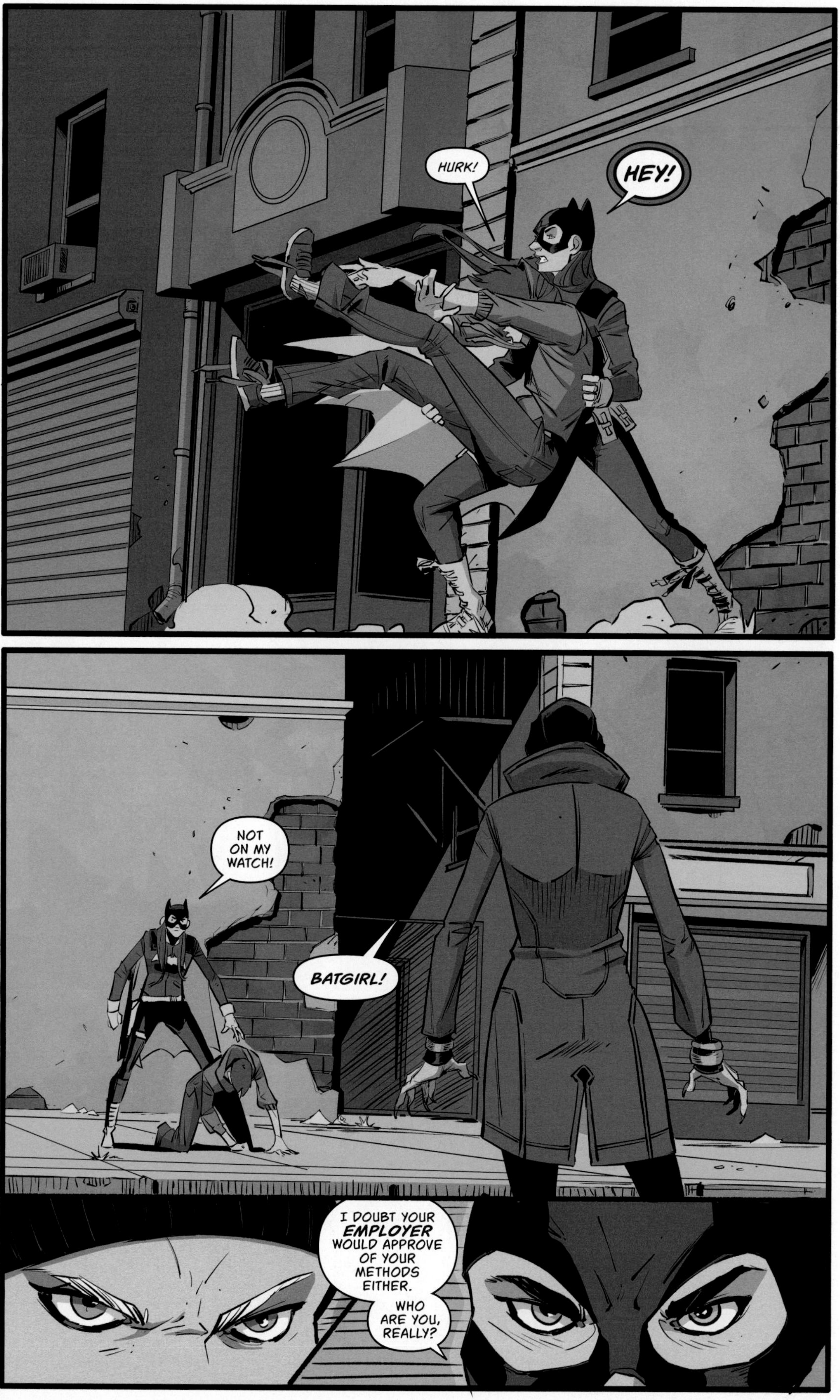
HURK!
HEY!
NOT ON MY WATCH!
BATGIRL!
I DOUBT YOUR EMPLOYER WOULD APPROVE OF YOUR METHODS EITHER.
WHO ARE YOU, REALLY?

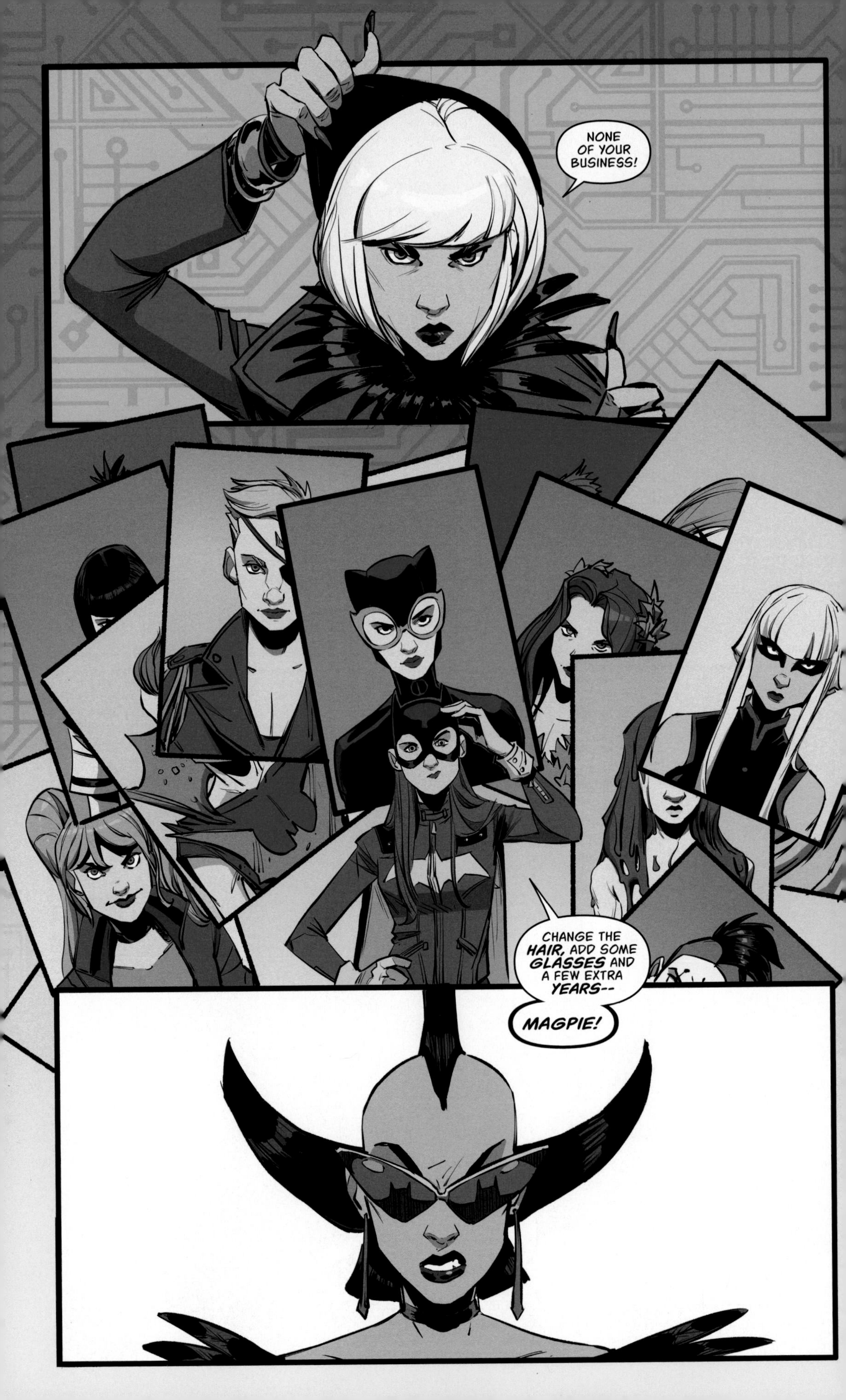
NONE OF YOUR BUSINESS!
CHANGE THE HAIR, ADD SOME GLASSES AND A FEW EXTRA YEARS--
MAGPIE!

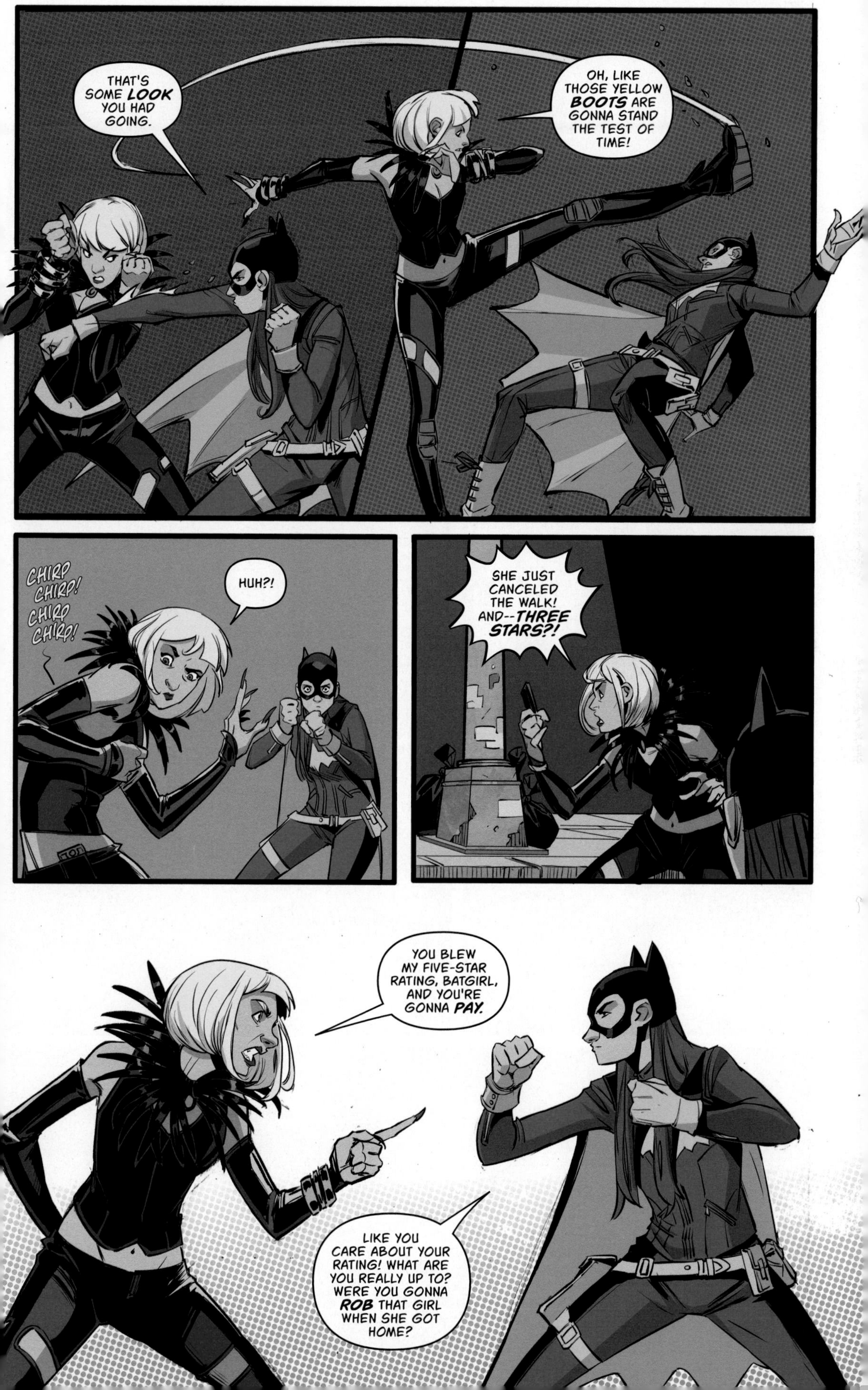
THAT'S SOME LOOK YOU HAD GOING.
OH, LIKE THOSE YELLOW BOOTS ARE GONNA STAND THE TEST OF TIME!
CHIRP CHIRP! CHIRP CHIRP!
HUH?!
SHE JUST CANCELED THE WALK! AND--THREE STARS?!
YOU BLEW MY FIVE-STAR RATING, BATGIRL, AND YOU'RE GONNA PAY.
LIKE YOU CARE ABOUT YOUR RATING! WHAT ARE YOU REALLY UP TO? WERE YOU GONNA ROB THAT GIRL WHEN SHE GOT HOME?

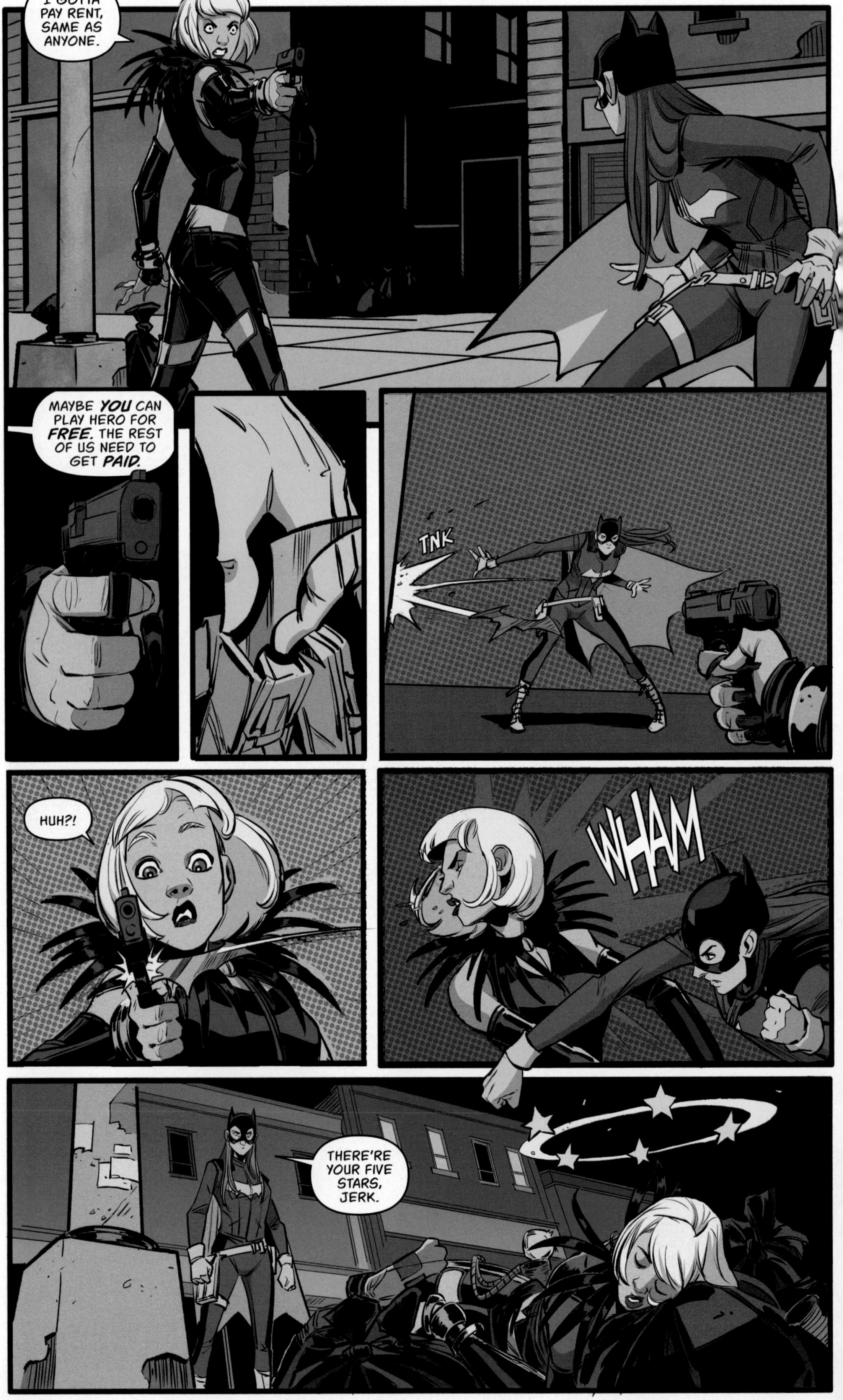
I GOTTA PAY RENT, SAME AS ANYONE.
MAYBE *YOU* CAN PLAY HERO FOR *FREE.* THE REST OF US NEED TO GET *PAID.*
TNK
HUH?!
WHAM
THERE'RE YOUR FIVE STARS, JERK.

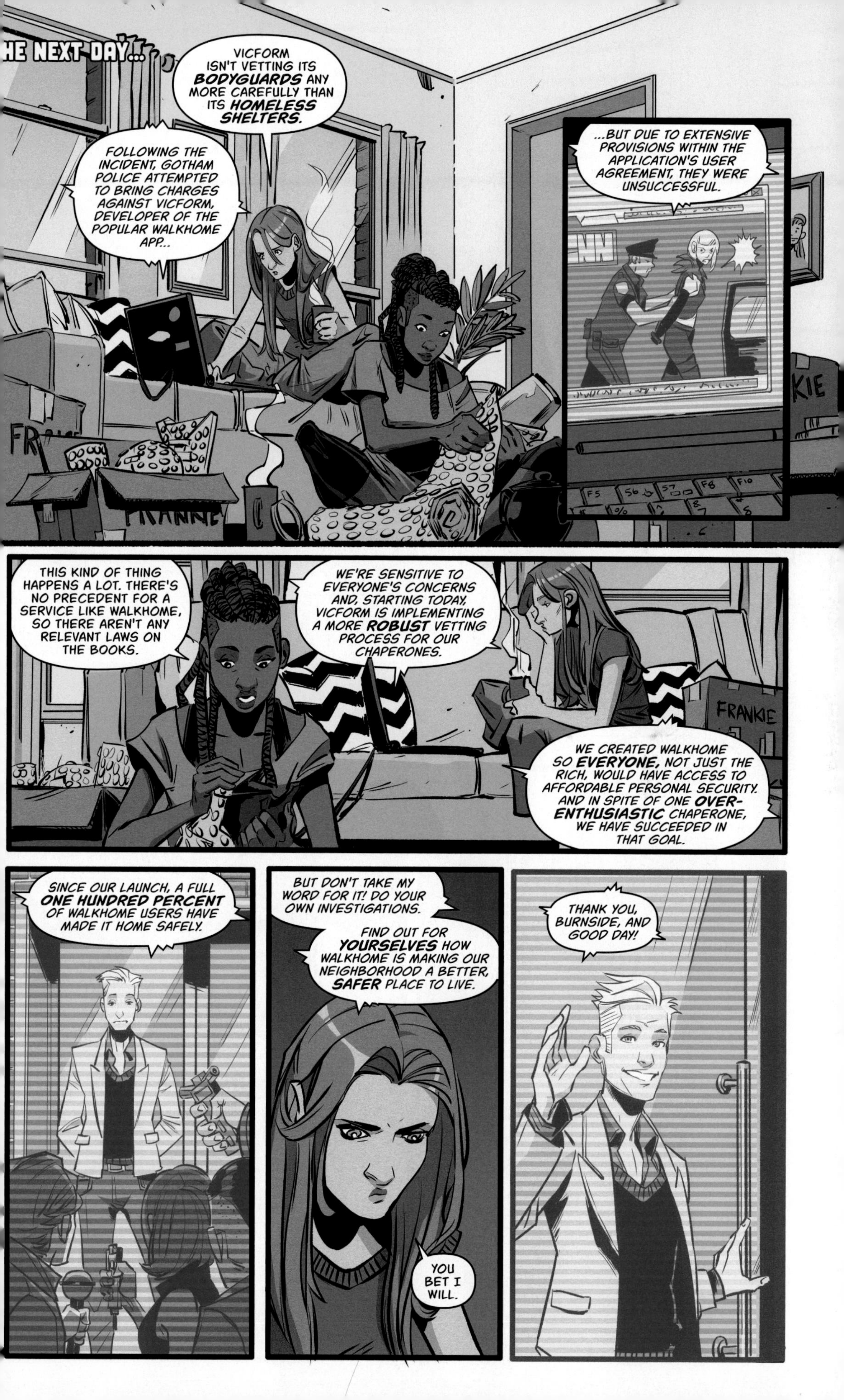

THE NEXT DAY...
FOLLOWING THE INCIDENT, GOTHAM POLICE ATTEMPTED TO BRING CHARGES AGAINST VICFORM, DEVELOPER OF THE POPULAR WALKHOME APP...
VICFORM ISN'T VETTING ITS BODYGUARDS ANY MORE CAREFULLY THAN ITS HOMELESS SHELTERS.
...BUT DUE TO EXTENSIVE PROVISIONS WITHIN THE APPLICATION'S USER AGREEMENT, THEY WERE UNSUCCESSFUL.
FRANKIE
THIS KIND OF THING HAPPENS A LOT. THERE'S NO PRECEDENT FOR A SERVICE LIKE WALKHOME, SO THERE AREN'T ANY RELEVANT LAWS ON THE BOOKS.
WE'RE SENSITIVE TO EVERYONE'S CONCERNS AND, STARTING TODAY, VICFORM IS IMPLEMENTING A MORE ROBUST VETTING PROCESS FOR OUR CHAPERONES.
FRANKIE
WE CREATED WALKHOME SO EVERYONE, NOT JUST THE RICH, WOULD HAVE ACCESS TO AFFORDABLE PERSONAL SECURITY. AND IN SPITE OF ONE OVER-ENTHUSIASTIC CHAPERONE, WE HAVE SUCCEEDED IN THAT GOAL.
SINCE OUR LAUNCH, A FULL ONE HUNDRED PERCENT OF WALKHOME USERS HAVE MADE IT HOME SAFELY.
BUT DON'T TAKE MY WORD FOR IT! DO YOUR OWN INVESTIGATIONS.
FIND OUT FOR YOURSELVES HOW WALKHOME IS MAKING OUR NEIGHBORHOOD A BETTER, SAFER PLACE TO LIVE.
YOU BET I WILL.
THANK YOU, BURNSIDE, AND GOOD DAY!

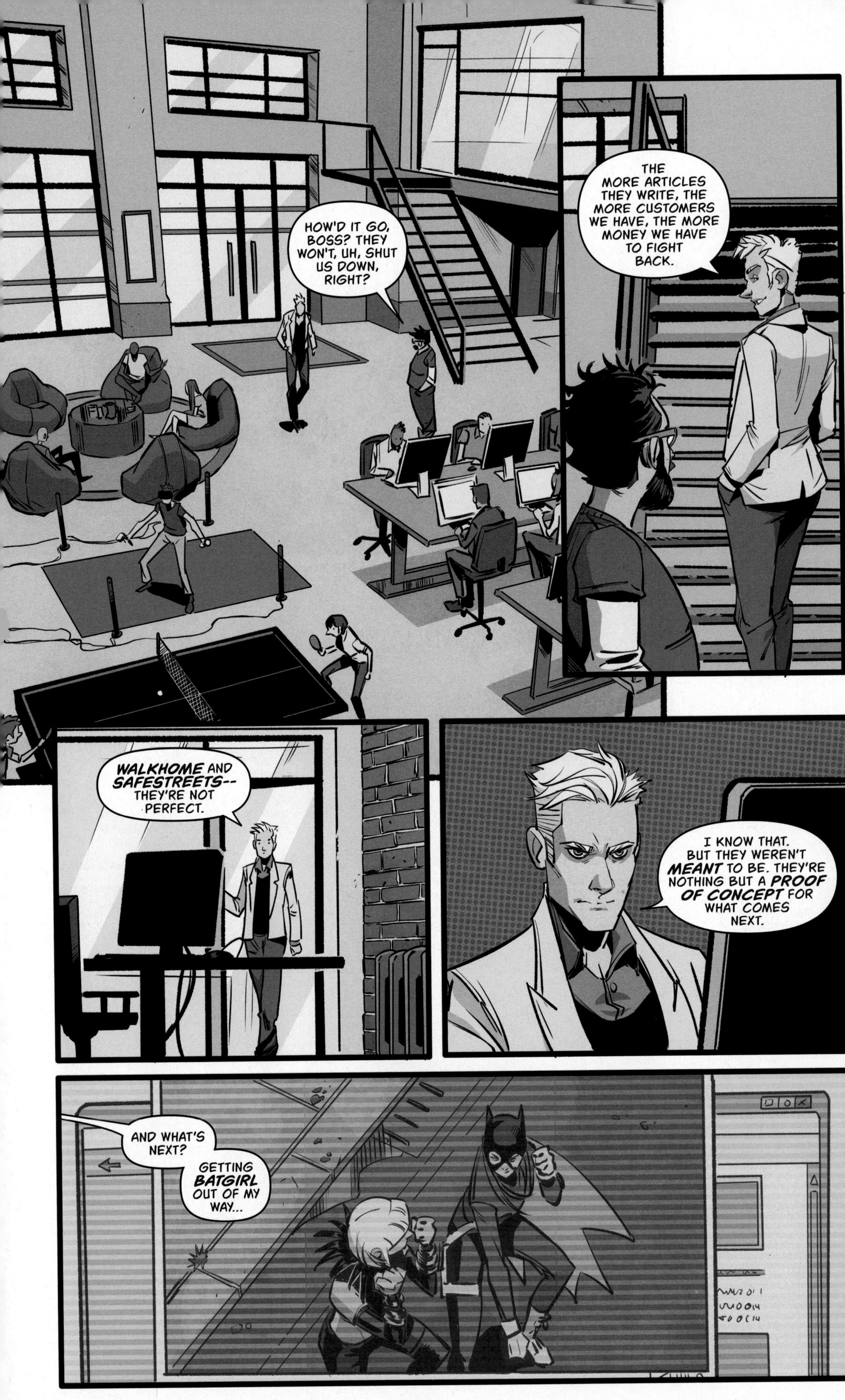
HOW'D IT GO, BOSS? THEY WON'T, UH, SHUT US DOWN, RIGHT?
THE MORE ARTICLES THEY WRITE, THE MORE CUSTOMERS WE HAVE, THE MORE MONEY WE HAVE TO FIGHT BACK.
WALKHOME AND SAFESTREETS-- THEY'RE NOT PERFECT.
I KNOW THAT. BUT THEY WEREN'T MEANT TO BE. THEY'RE NOTHING BUT A PROOF OF CONCEPT FOR WHAT COMES NEXT.
AND WHAT'S NEXT?
GETTING BATGIRL OUT OF MY WAY...

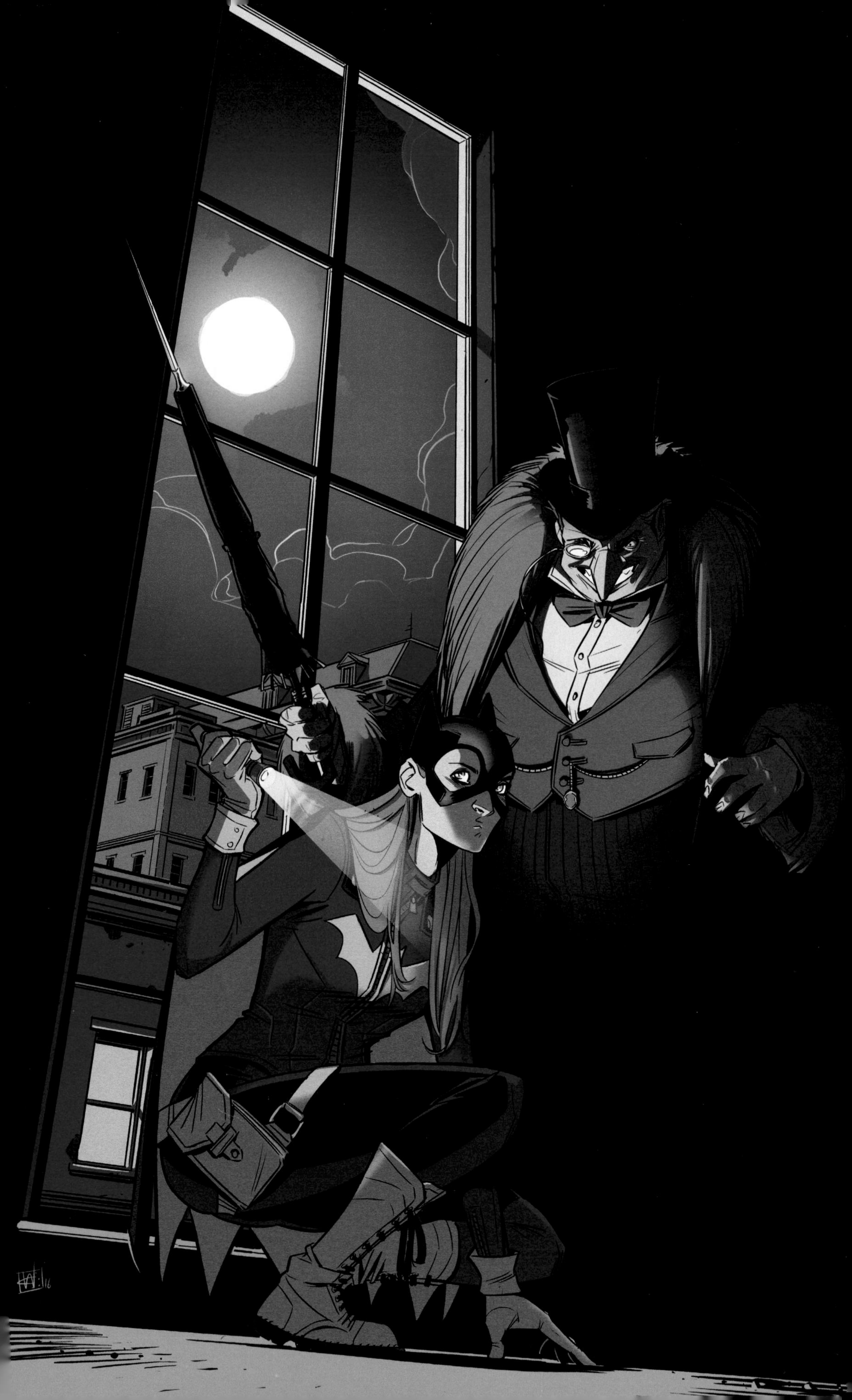

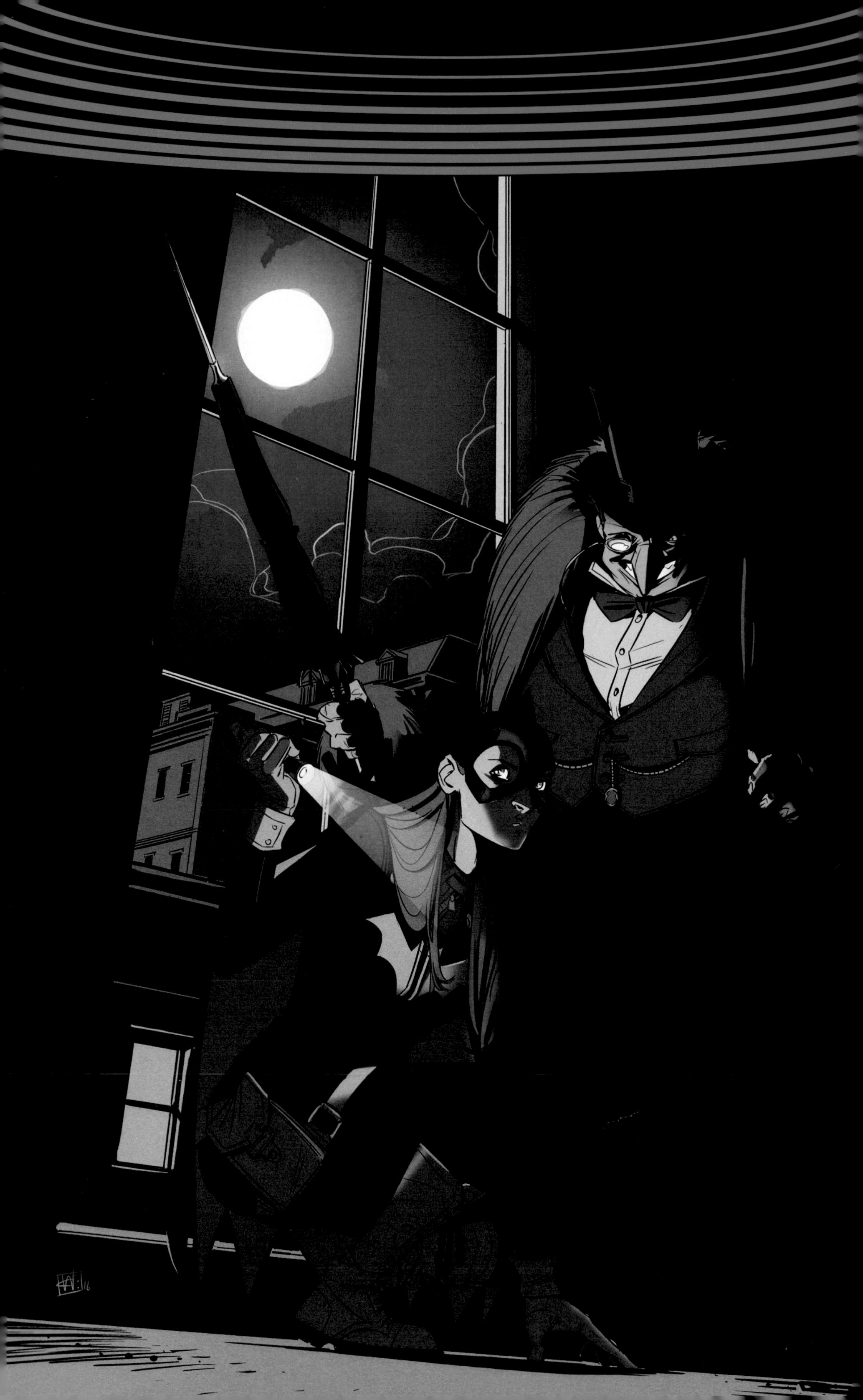

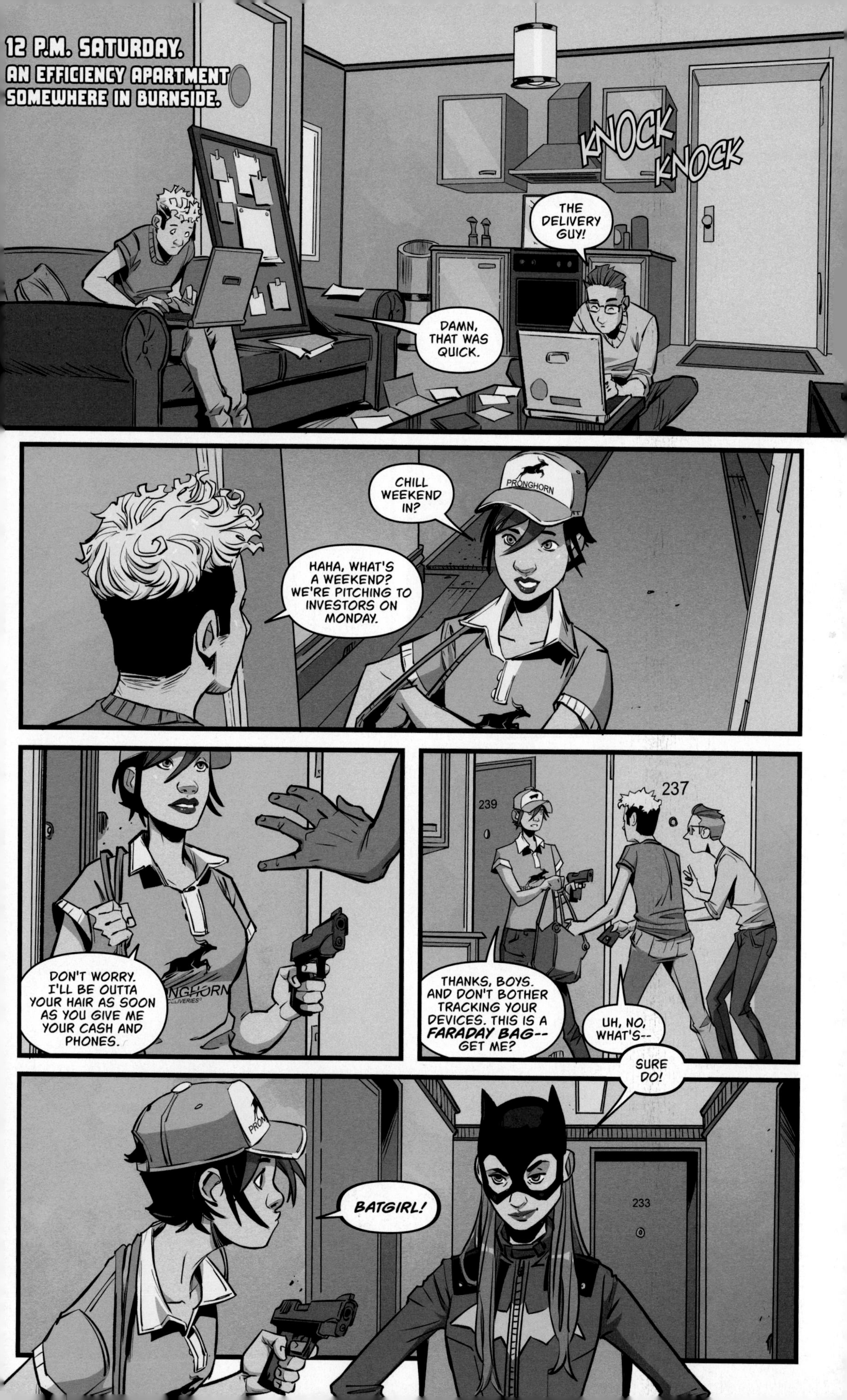
12 P.M. SATURDAY.
AN EFFICIENCY APARTMENT SOMEWHERE IN BURNSIDE.
KNOCK KNOCK
THE DELIVERY GUY!
DAMN, THAT WAS QUICK.
CHILL WEEKEND IN?
HAHA, WHAT'S A WEEKEND? WE'RE PITCHING TO INVESTORS ON MONDAY.
PRONGHORN
DON'T WORRY. I'LL BE OUTTA YOUR HAIR AS SOON AS YOU GIVE ME YOUR CASH AND PHONES.
239
237
THANKS, BOYS. AND DON'T BOTHER TRACKING YOUR DEVICES. THIS IS A FARADAY BAG-- GET ME?
UH, NO, WHAT'S--
SURE DO!
233
BATGIRL!

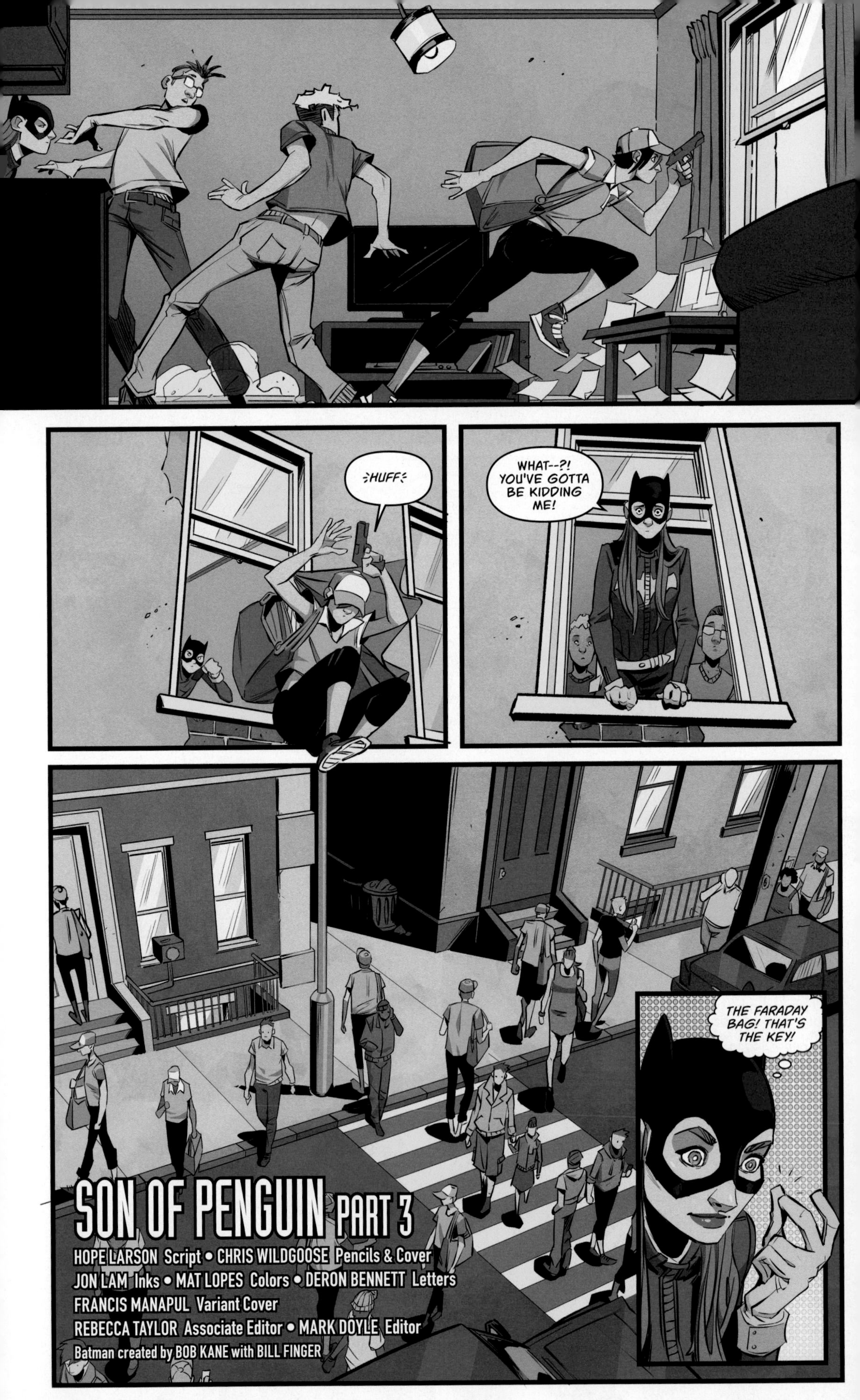

HUFF
WHAT--?! YOU'VE GOTTA BE KIDDING ME!
THE FARADAY BAG! THAT'S THE KEY!
SON OF PENGUIN PART 3
HOPE LARSON Script • CHRIS WILDGOOSE Pencils & Cover
JON LAM Inks • MAT LOPES Colors • DERON BENNETT Letters
FRANCIS MANAPUL Variant Cover
REBECCA TAYLOR Associate Editor • MARK DOYLE Editor
Batman created by BOB KANE with BILL FINGER

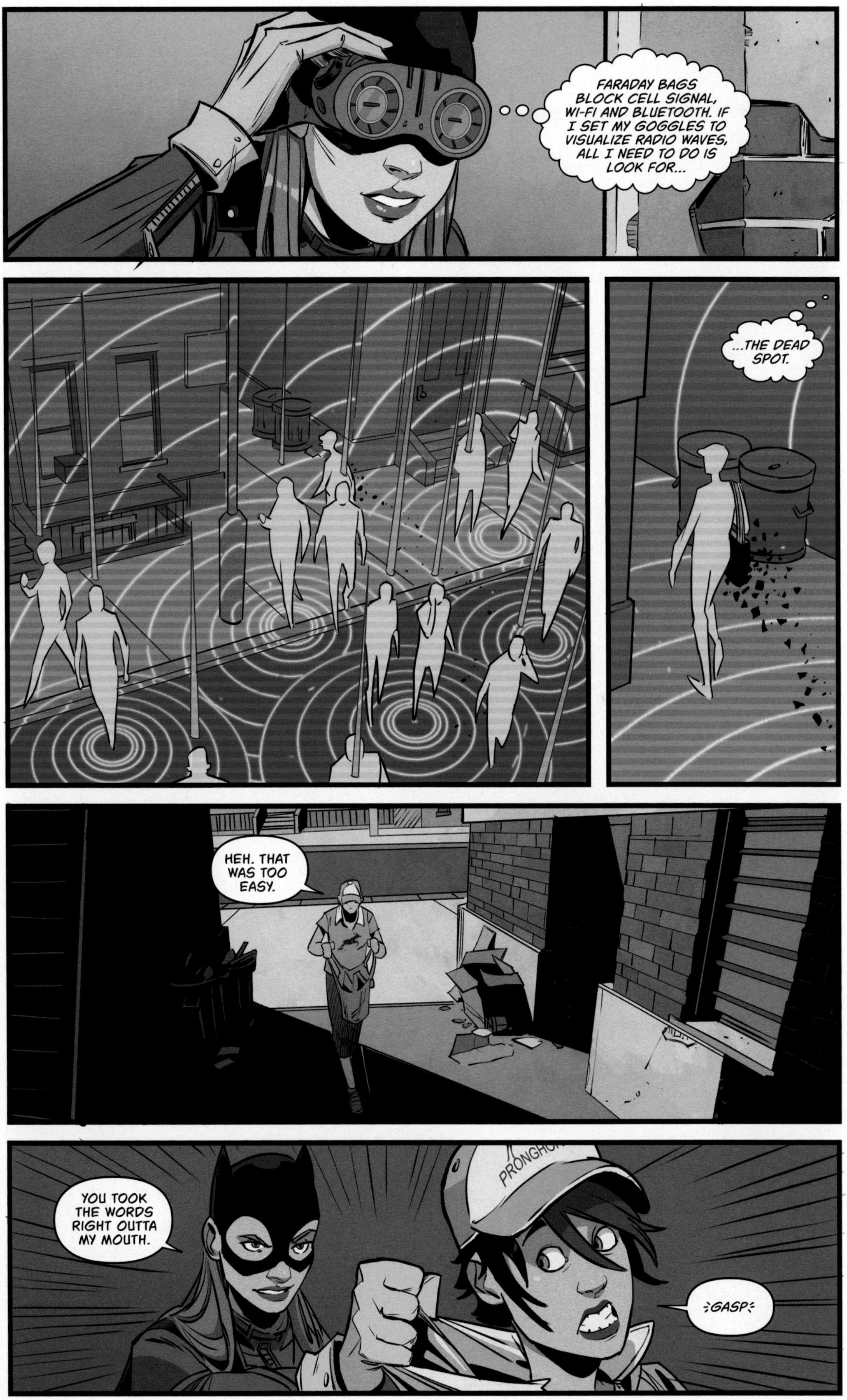
FARADAY BAGS BLOCK CELL SIGNAL, WI-FI AND BLUETOOTH. IF I SET MY GOGGLES TO VISUALIZE RADIO WAVES, ALL I NEED TO DO IS LOOK FOR...
...THE DEAD SPOT.
HEH. THAT WAS TOO EASY.
YOU TOOK THE WORDS RIGHT OUTTA MY MOUTH.
PRONGHORN
GASP

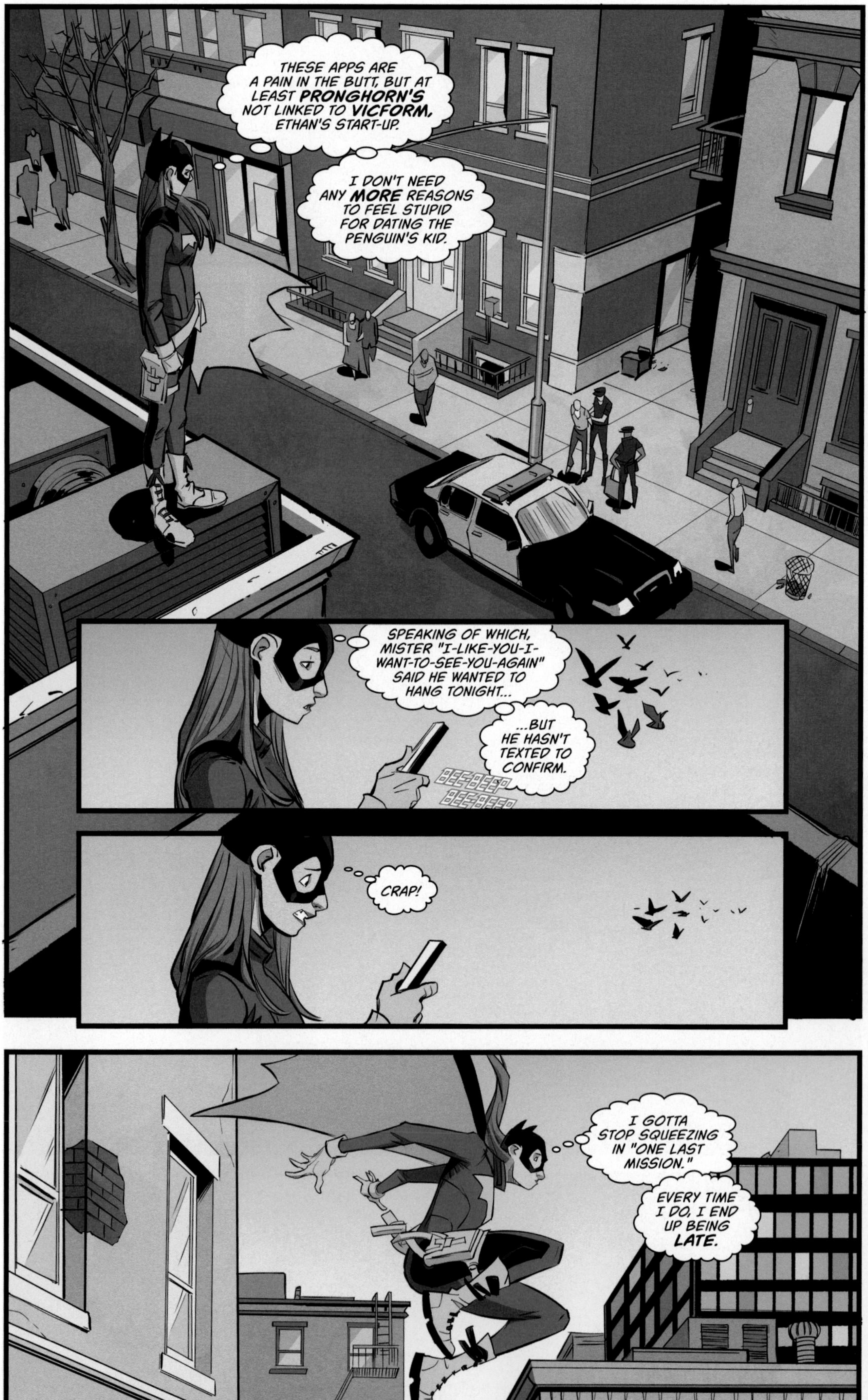
THESE APPS ARE A PAIN IN THE BUTT, BUT AT LEAST PRONGHORN'S NOT LINKED TO VICFORM, ETHAN'S START-UP.
I DON'T NEED ANY MORE REASONS TO FEEL STUPID FOR DATING THE PENGUIN'S KID.
SPEAKING OF WHICH, MISTER "I-LIKE-YOU-I-WANT-TO-SEE-YOU-AGAIN" SAID HE WANTED TO HANG TONIGHT...
...BUT HE HASN'T TEXTED TO CONFIRM.
BEEBEEP BEEBEEP
CRAP!
I GOTTA STOP SQUEEZING IN "ONE LAST MISSION."
EVERY TIME I DO, I END UP BEING LATE.

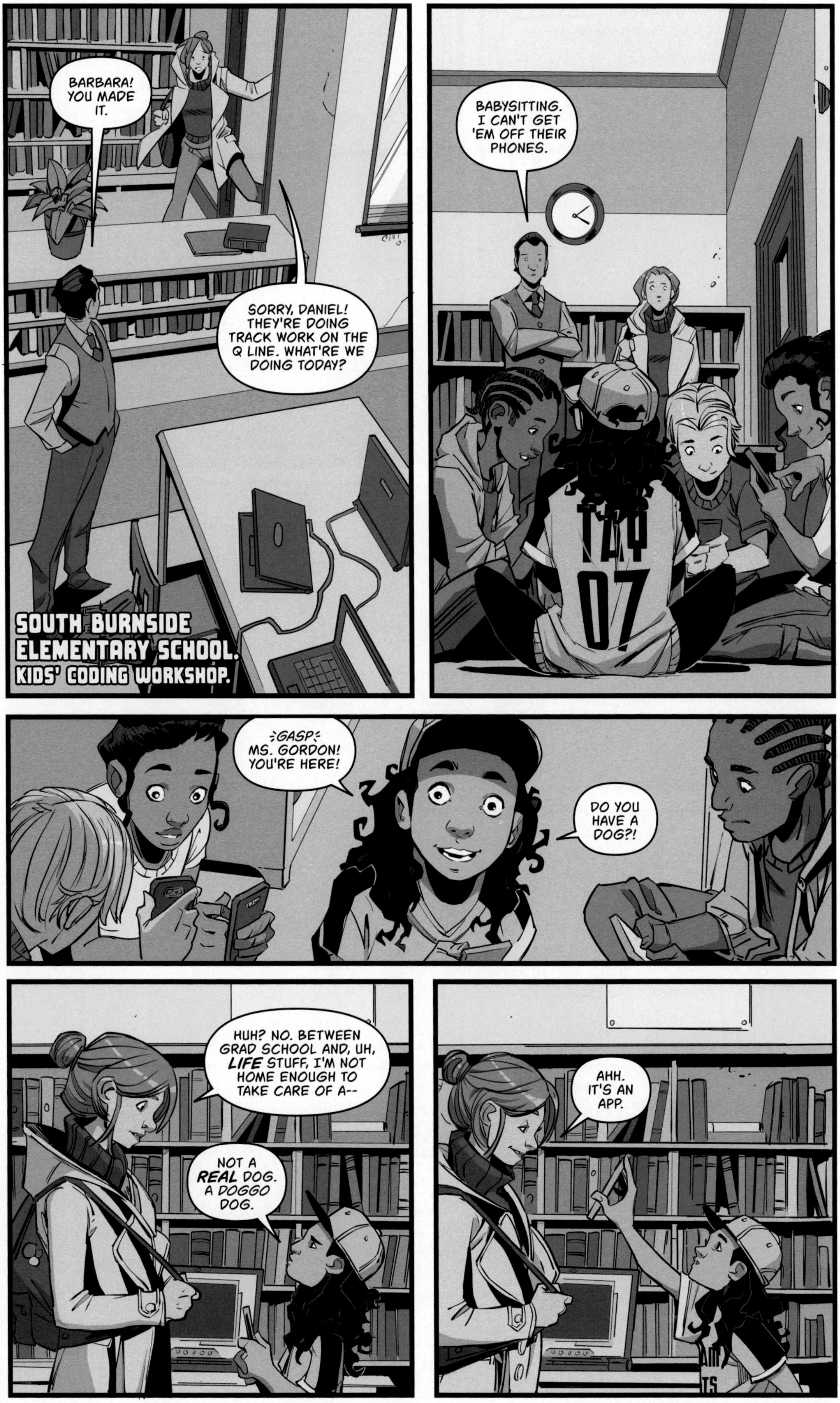
BARBARA! YOU MADE IT.
SORRY, DANIEL! THEY'RE DOING TRACK WORK ON THE Q LINE. WHAT'RE WE DOING TODAY?
SOUTH BURNSIDE ELEMENTARY SCHOOL. KIDS' CODING WORKSHOP.
BABYSITTING. I CAN'T GET 'EM OFF THEIR PHONES.
TAY 07
GASP MS. GORDON! YOU'RE HERE!
DO YOU HAVE A DOG?!
HUH? NO. BETWEEN GRAD SCHOOL AND, UH, LIFE STUFF, I'M NOT HOME ENOUGH TO TAKE CARE OF A--
NOT A REAL DOG. A DOGGO DOG.
AHH. IT'S AN APP.

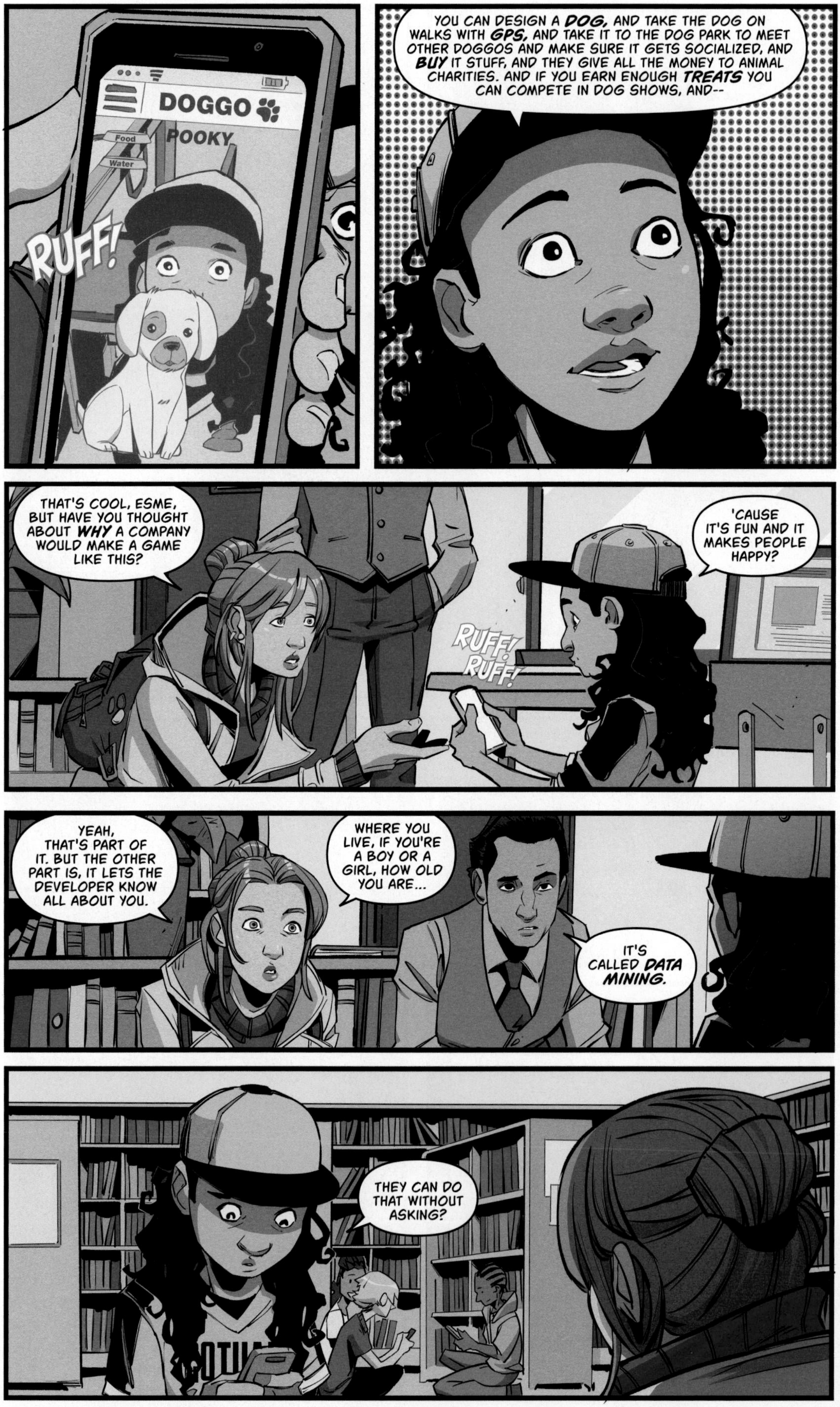

DOGGO
POOKY
Food
Water
RUFF!
YOU CAN DESIGN A DOG, AND TAKE THE DOG ON WALKS WITH GPS, AND TAKE IT TO THE DOG PARK TO MEET OTHER DOGGOS AND MAKE SURE IT GETS SOCIALIZED, AND BUY IT STUFF, AND THEY GIVE ALL THE MONEY TO ANIMAL CHARITIES. AND IF YOU EARN ENOUGH TREATS YOU CAN COMPETE IN DOG SHOWS, AND--
THAT'S COOL, ESME, BUT HAVE YOU THOUGHT ABOUT WHY A COMPANY WOULD MAKE A GAME LIKE THIS?
'CAUSE IT'S FUN AND IT MAKES PEOPLE HAPPY?
RUFF! RUFF!
YEAH, THAT'S PART OF IT. BUT THE OTHER PART IS, IT LETS THE DEVELOPER KNOW ALL ABOUT YOU.
WHERE YOU LIVE, IF YOU'RE A BOY OR A GIRL, HOW OLD YOU ARE...
IT'S CALLED DATA MINING.
THEY CAN DO THAT WITHOUT ASKING?

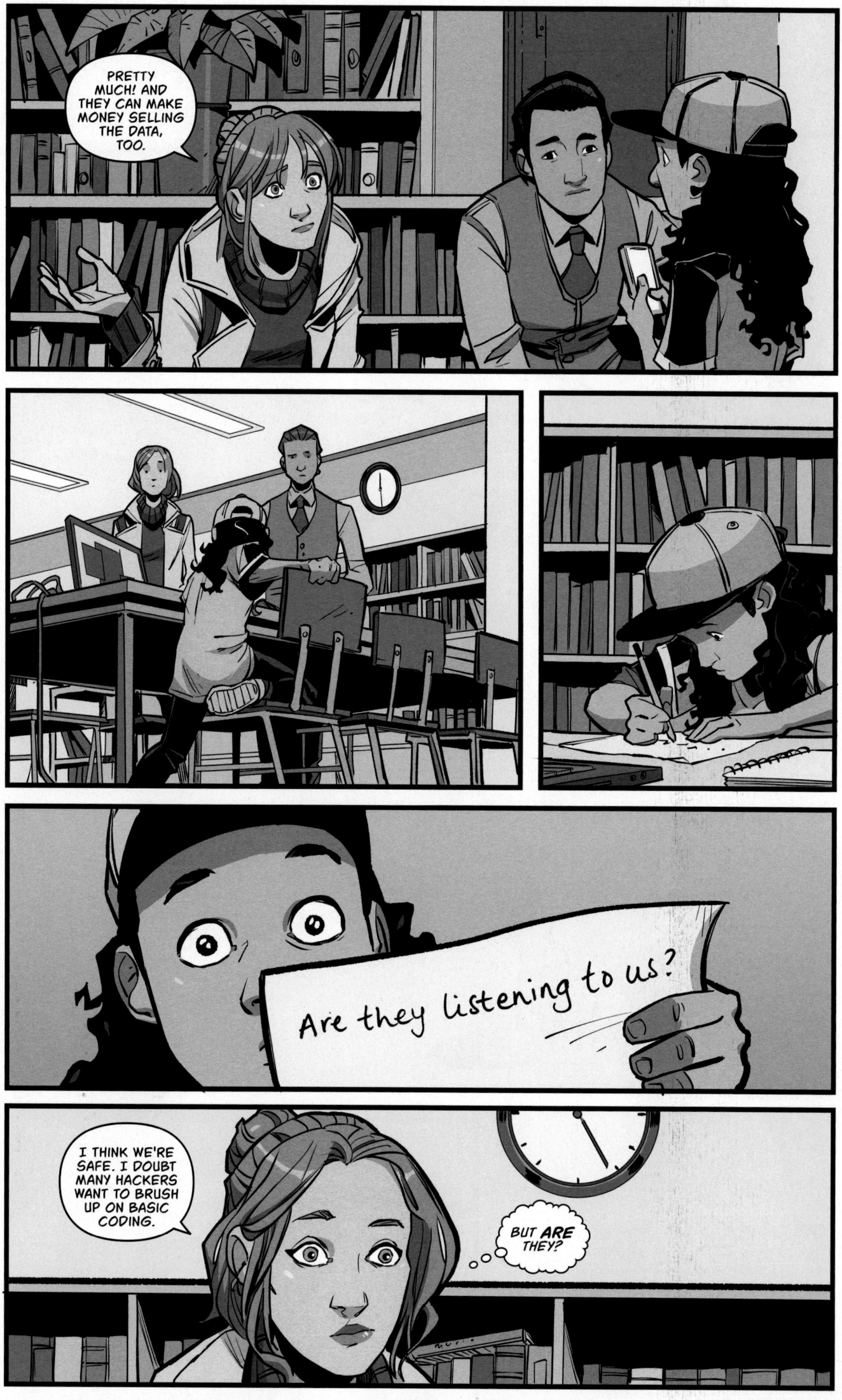
PRETTY MUCH! AND THEY CAN MAKE MONEY SELLING THE DATA, TOO.
Are they listening to us?
I THINK WE'RE SAFE. I DOUBT MANY HACKERS WANT TO BRUSH UP ON BASIC CODING.
BUT ARE THEY?

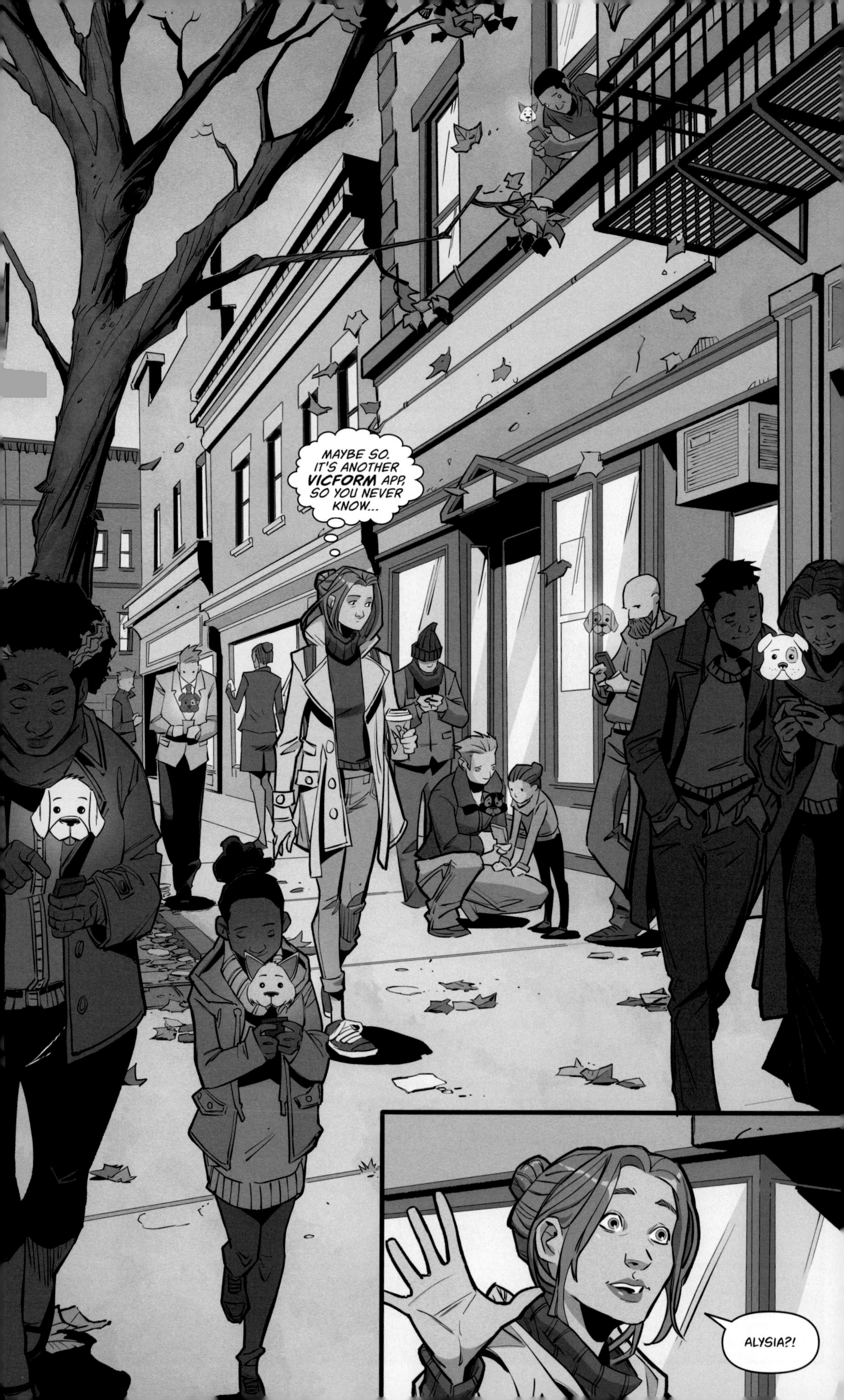
MAYBE SO. IT'S ANOTHER VICFORM APP, SO YOU NEVER KNOW...
ALYSIA?!

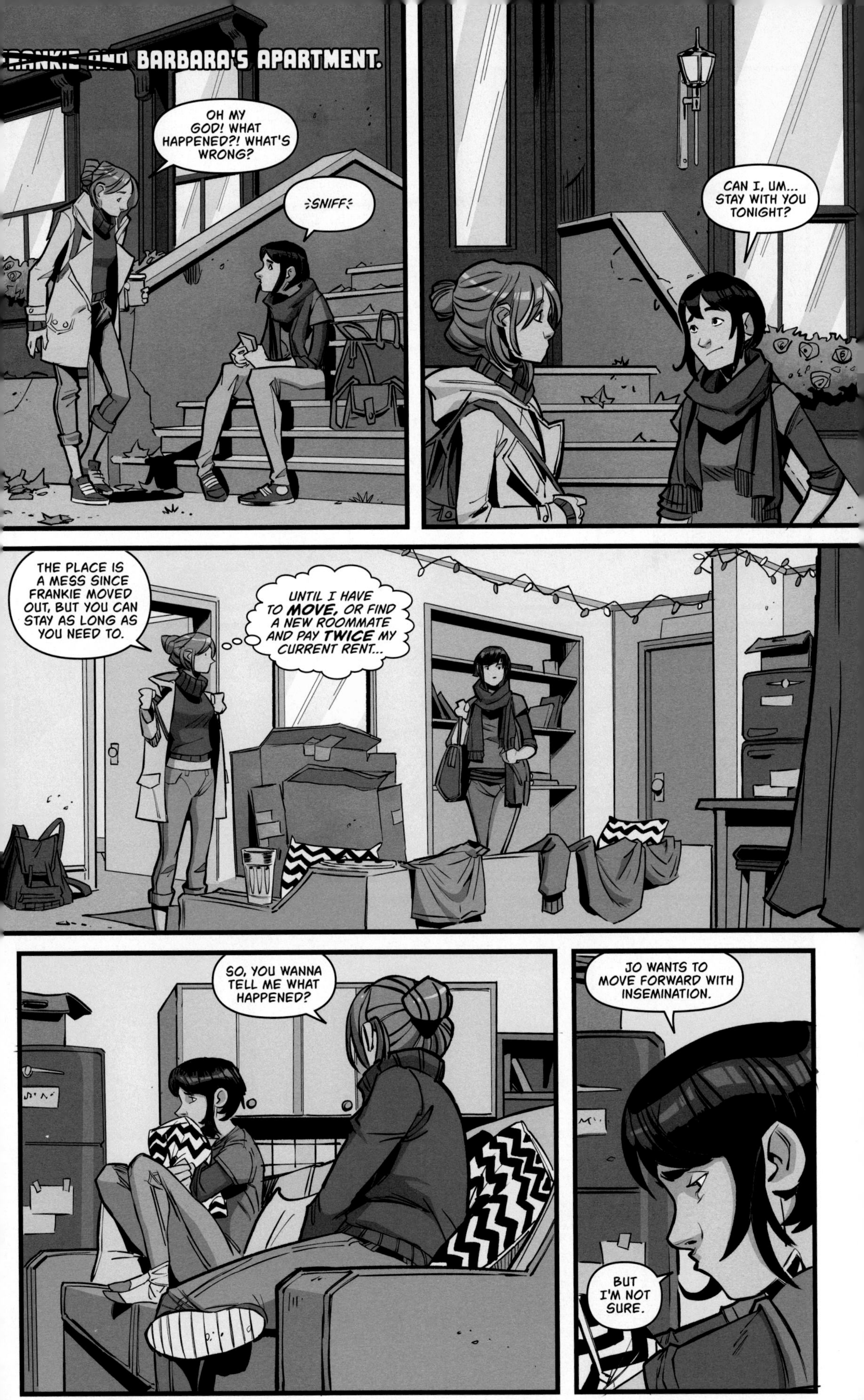
~~FRANKIE AND~~ BARBARA'S APARTMENT.
OH MY GOD! WHAT HAPPENED?! WHAT'S WRONG?
SNIFF
CAN I, UM... STAY WITH YOU TONIGHT?
THE PLACE IS A MESS SINCE FRANKIE MOVED OUT, BUT YOU CAN STAY AS LONG AS YOU NEED TO.
UNTIL I HAVE TO MOVE, OR FIND A NEW ROOMMATE AND PAY TWICE MY CURRENT RENT...
SO, YOU WANNA TELL ME WHAT HAPPENED?
JO WANTS TO MOVE FORWARD WITH INSEMINATION.
BUT I'M NOT SURE.

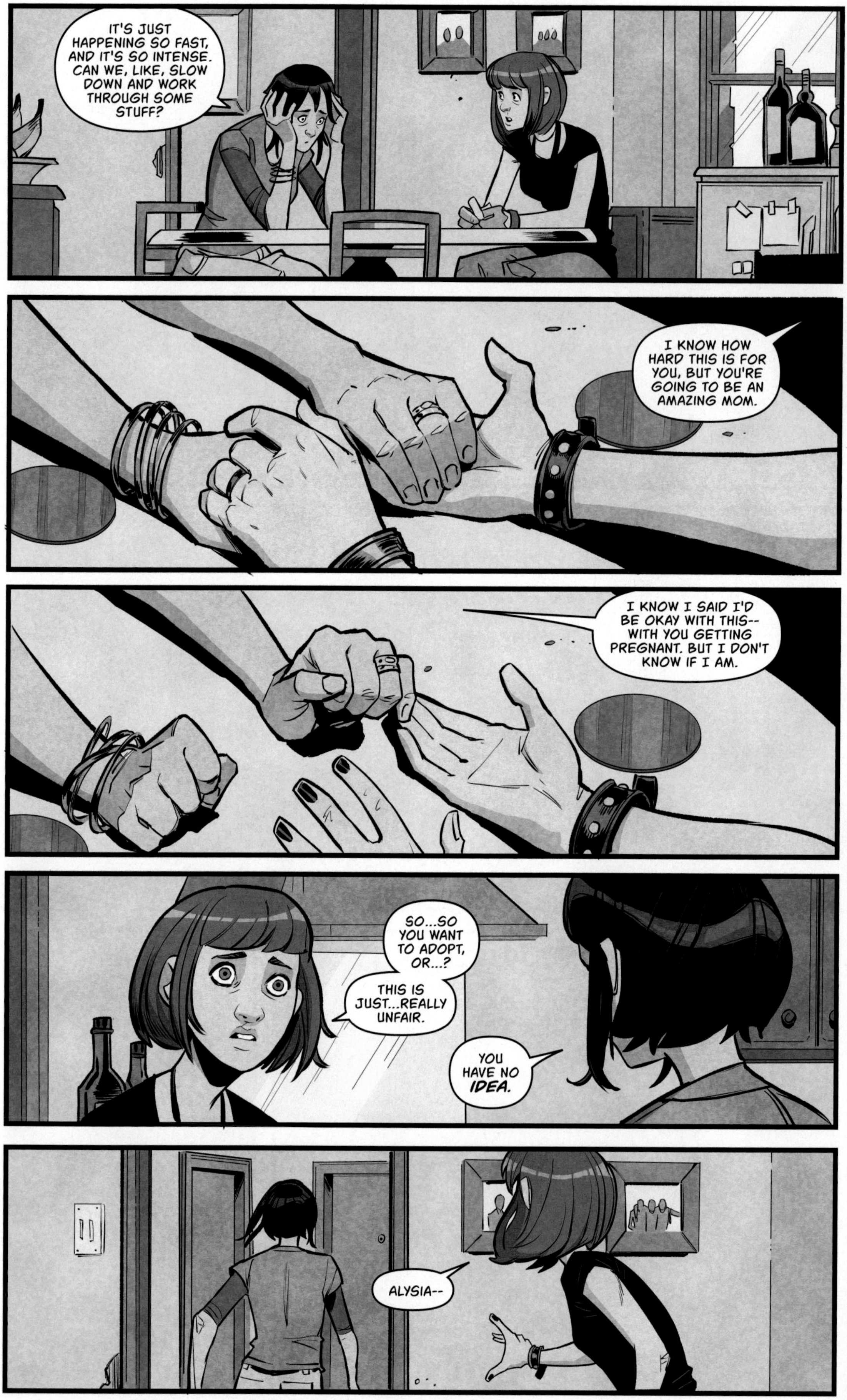
IT'S JUST HAPPENING SO FAST, AND IT'S SO INTENSE. CAN WE, LIKE, SLOW DOWN AND WORK THROUGH SOME STUFF?
I KNOW HOW HARD THIS IS FOR YOU, BUT YOU'RE GOING TO BE AN AMAZING MOM.
I KNOW I SAID I'D BE OKAY WITH THIS-- WITH YOU GETTING PREGNANT. BUT I DON'T KNOW IF I AM.
SO...SO YOU WANT TO ADOPT, OR...?
THIS IS JUST...REALLY UNFAIR.
YOU HAVE NO IDEA.
ALYSIA--

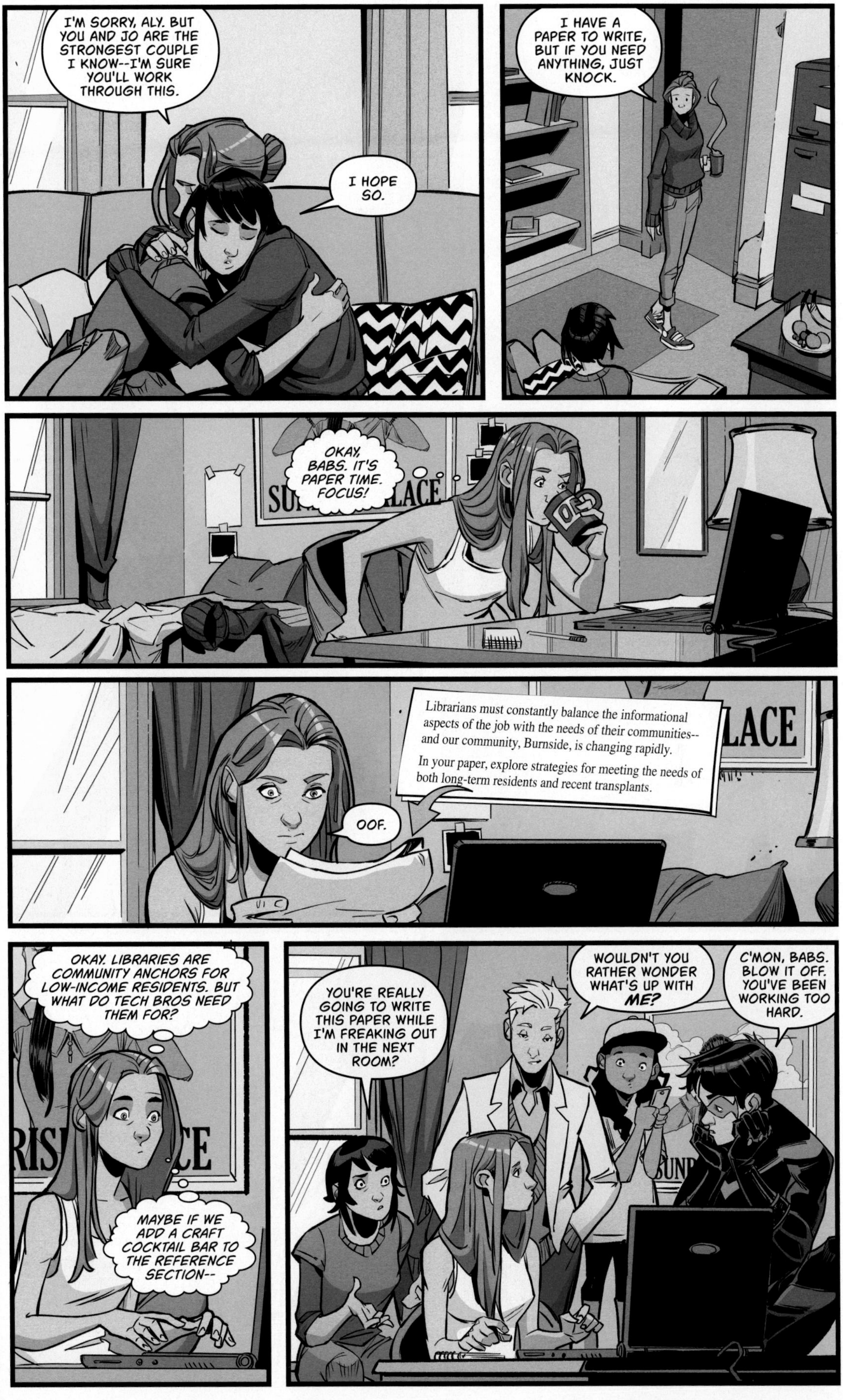
I'M SORRY, ALY. BUT YOU AND JO ARE THE STRONGEST COUPLE I KNOW--I'M SURE YOU'LL WORK THROUGH THIS.
I HOPE SO.
I HAVE A PAPER TO WRITE, BUT IF YOU NEED ANYTHING, JUST KNOCK.
OKAY, BABS. IT'S PAPER TIME. FOCUS!
Librarians must constantly balance the informational aspects of the job with the needs of their communities--and our community, Burnside, is changing rapidly.
In your paper, explore strategies for meeting the needs of both long-term residents and recent transplants.
OOF.
OKAY. LIBRARIES ARE COMMUNITY ANCHORS FOR LOW-INCOME RESIDENTS. BUT WHAT DO TECH BROS NEED THEM FOR?
MAYBE IF WE ADD A CRAFT COCKTAIL BAR TO THE REFERENCE SECTION--
YOU'RE REALLY GOING TO WRITE THIS PAPER WHILE I'M FREAKING OUT IN THE NEXT ROOM?
WOULDN'T YOU RATHER WONDER WHAT'S UP WITH ME?
C'MON, BABS. BLOW IT OFF. YOU'VE BEEN WORKING TOO HARD.

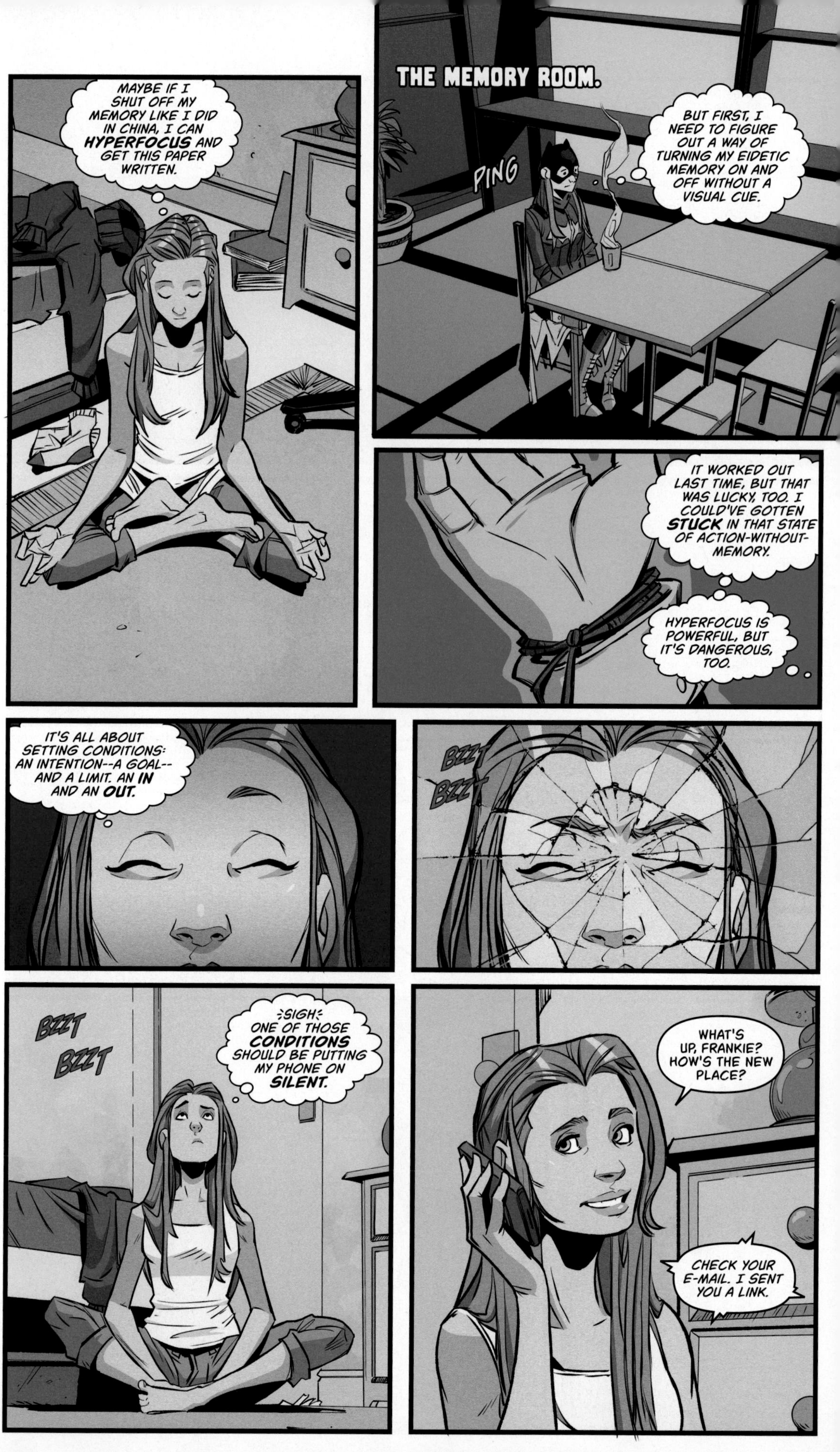
MAYBE IF I SHUT OFF MY MEMORY LIKE I DID IN CHINA, I CAN HYPERFOCUS AND GET THIS PAPER WRITTEN.
THE MEMORY ROOM.
PING
BUT FIRST, I NEED TO FIGURE OUT A WAY OF TURNING MY EIDETIC MEMORY ON AND OFF WITHOUT A VISUAL CUE.
IT WORKED OUT LAST TIME, BUT THAT WAS LUCKY, TOO. I COULD'VE GOTTEN STUCK IN THAT STATE OF ACTION-WITHOUT-MEMORY.
HYPERFOCUS IS POWERFUL, BUT IT'S DANGEROUS, TOO.
IT'S ALL ABOUT SETTING CONDITIONS: AN INTENTION--A GOAL--AND A LIMIT. AN IN AND AN OUT.
BZZT BZZT
BZZT BZZT
SIGH ONE OF THOSE CONDITIONS SHOULD BE PUTTING MY PHONE ON SILENT.
WHAT'S UP, FRANKIE? HOW'S THE NEW PLACE?
CHECK YOUR E-MAIL. I SENT YOU A LINK.

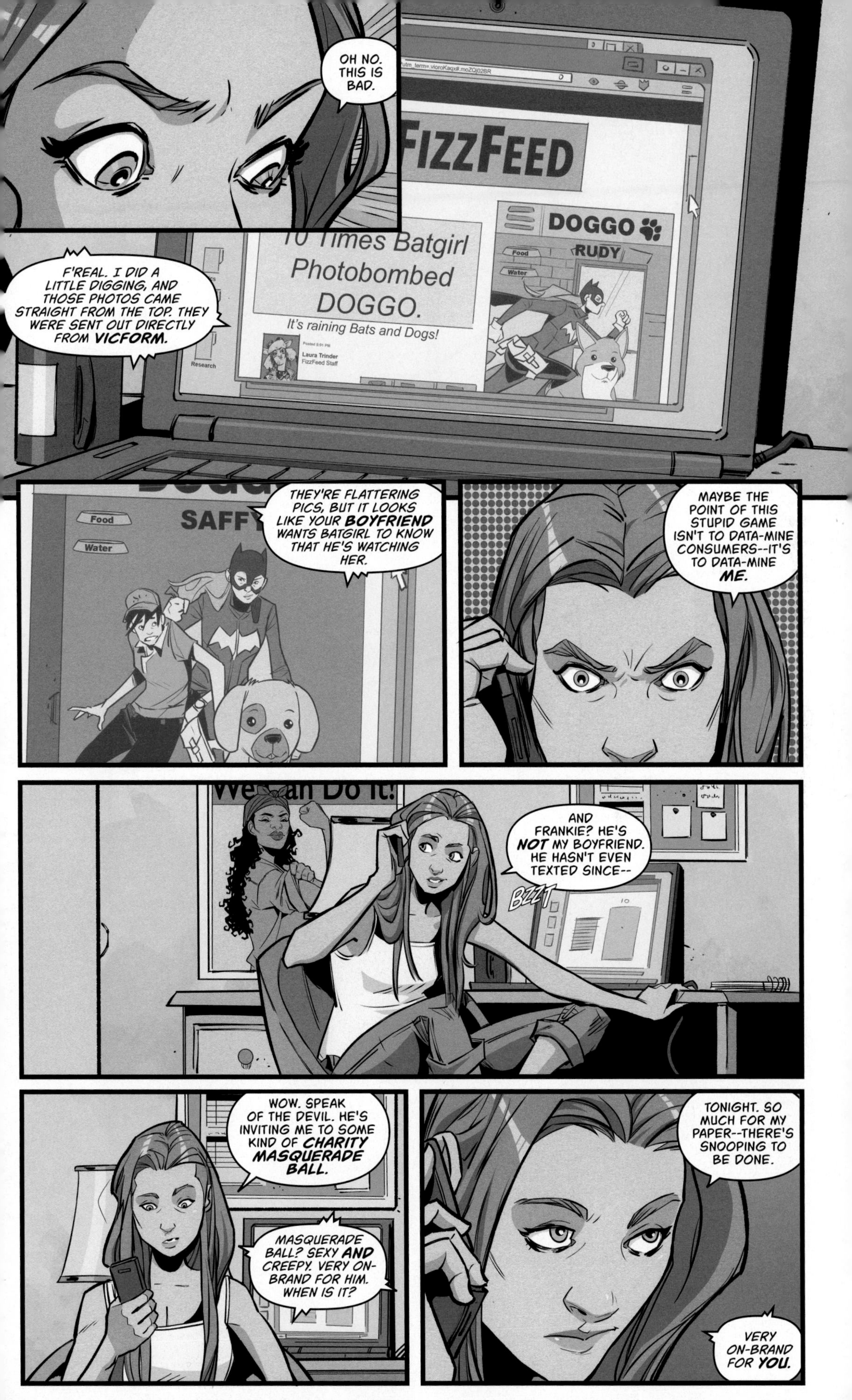

OH NO. THIS IS BAD.
FIZZFEED
DOGGO
RUDY
Food
Water
10 Times Batgirl Photobombed DOGGO.
It's raining Bats and Dogs!
Laura Trinder
FizzFeed Staff
Research
F'REAL. I DID A LITTLE DIGGING, AND THOSE PHOTOS CAME STRAIGHT FROM THE TOP. THEY WERE SENT OUT DIRECTLY FROM VICFORM.
Food
Water
SAFFY
THEY'RE FLATTERING PICS, BUT IT LOOKS LIKE YOUR BOYFRIEND WANTS BATGIRL TO KNOW THAT HE'S WATCHING HER.
MAYBE THE POINT OF THIS STUPID GAME ISN'T TO DATA-MINE CONSUMERS--IT'S TO DATA-MINE ME.
AND FRANKIE? HE'S NOT MY BOYFRIEND. HE HASN'T EVEN TEXTED SINCE--
BZZZT
WOW. SPEAK OF THE DEVIL. HE'S INVITING ME TO SOME KIND OF CHARITY MASQUERADE BALL.
MASQUERADE BALL? SEXY AND CREEPY. VERY ON-BRAND FOR HIM. WHEN IS IT?
TONIGHT. SO MUCH FOR MY PAPER--THERE'S SNOOPING TO BE DONE.
VERY ON-BRAND FOR YOU.

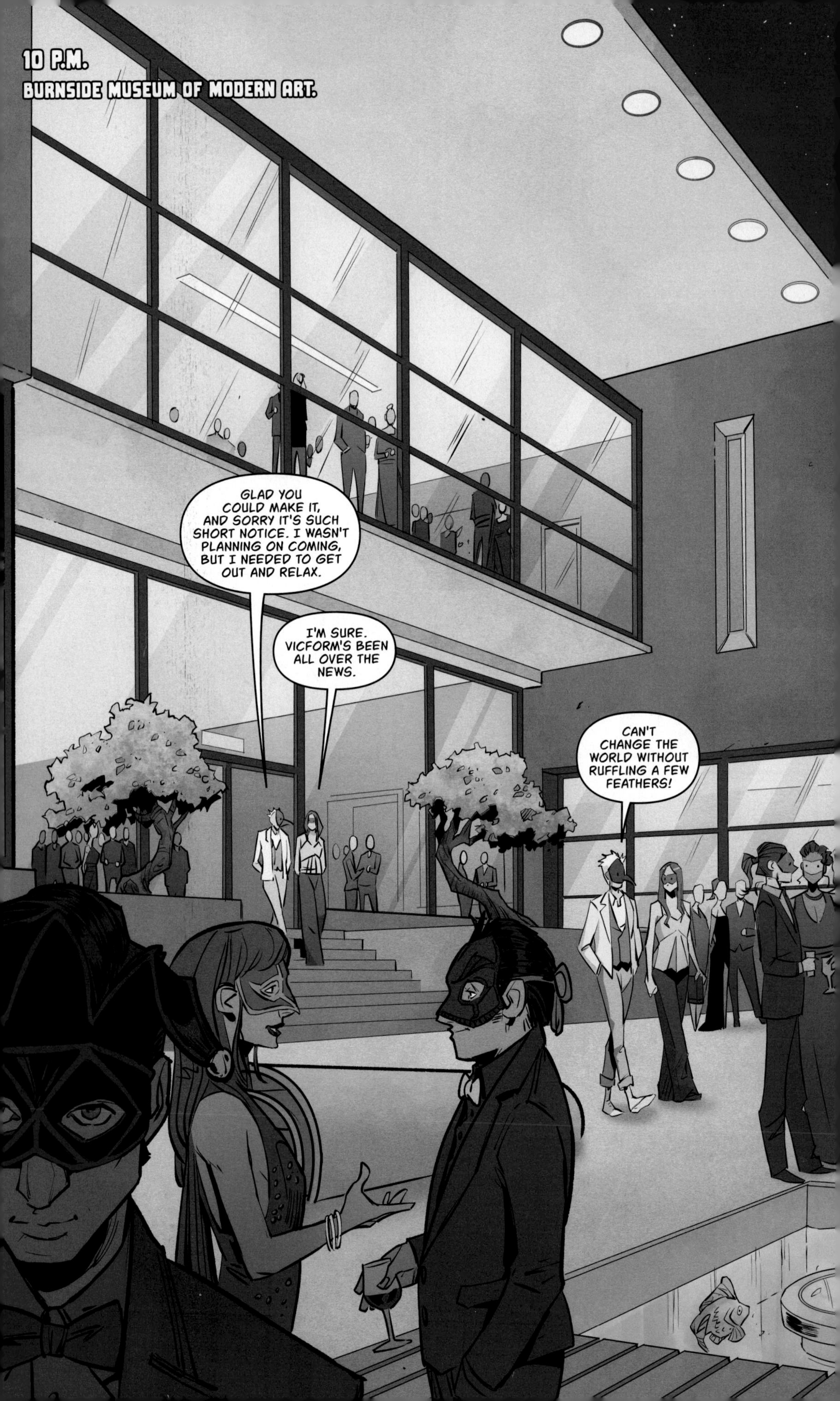
10 P.M.
BURNSIDE MUSEUM OF MODERN ART.
GLAD YOU COULD MAKE IT, AND SORRY IT'S SUCH SHORT NOTICE. I WASN'T PLANNING ON COMING, BUT I NEEDED TO GET OUT AND RELAX.
I'M SURE. VICFORM'S BEEN ALL OVER THE NEWS.
CAN'T CHANGE THE WORLD WITHOUT RUFFLING A FEW FEATHERS!

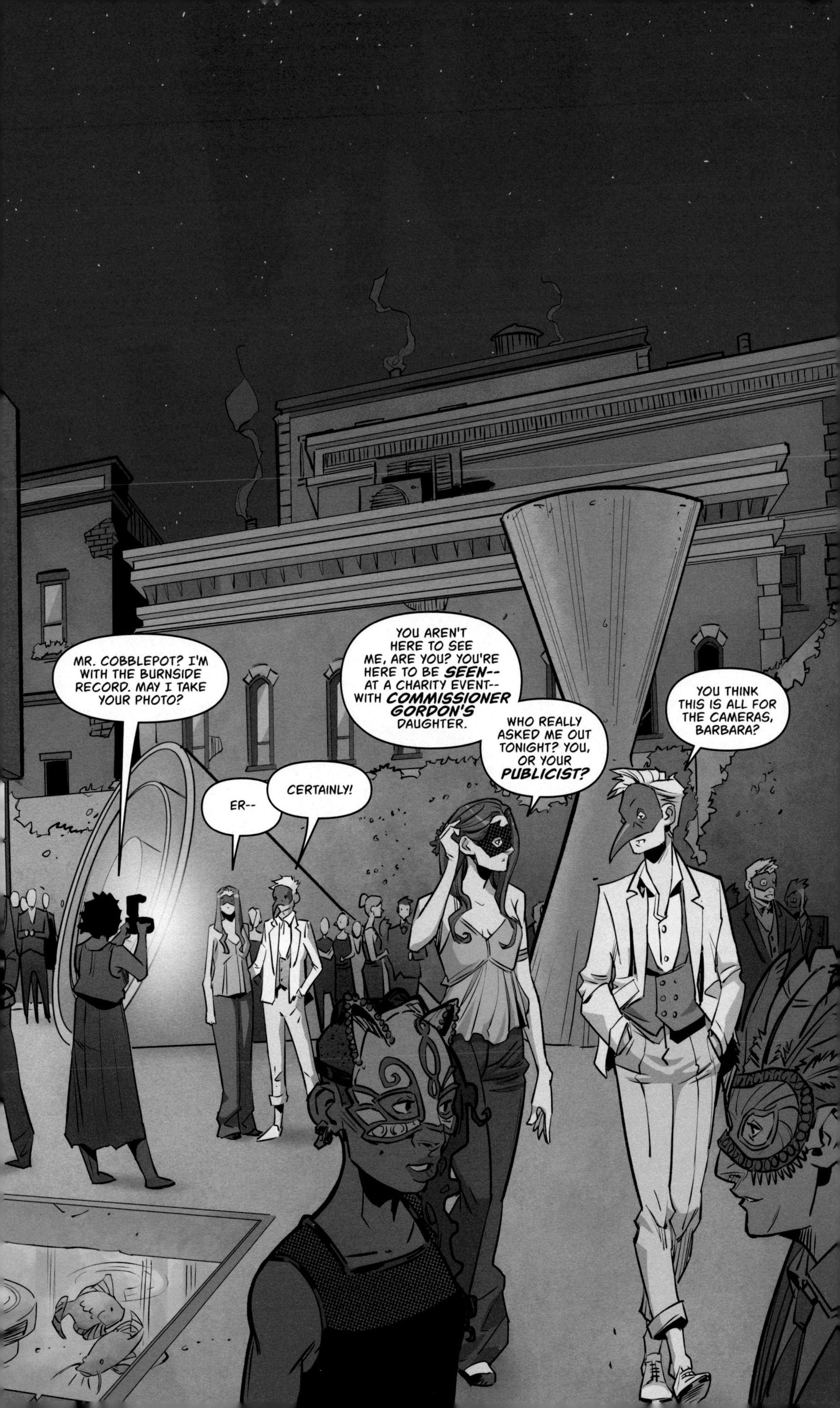

MR. COBBLEPOT? I'M WITH THE BURNSIDE RECORD. MAY I TAKE YOUR PHOTO?
ER--
CERTAINLY!
YOU AREN'T HERE TO SEE ME, ARE YOU? YOU'RE HERE TO BE SEEN--AT A CHARITY EVENT--WITH COMMISSIONER GORDON'S DAUGHTER.
WHO REALLY ASKED ME OUT TONIGHT? YOU, OR YOUR PUBLICIST?
YOU THINK THIS IS ALL FOR THE CAMERAS, BARBARA?

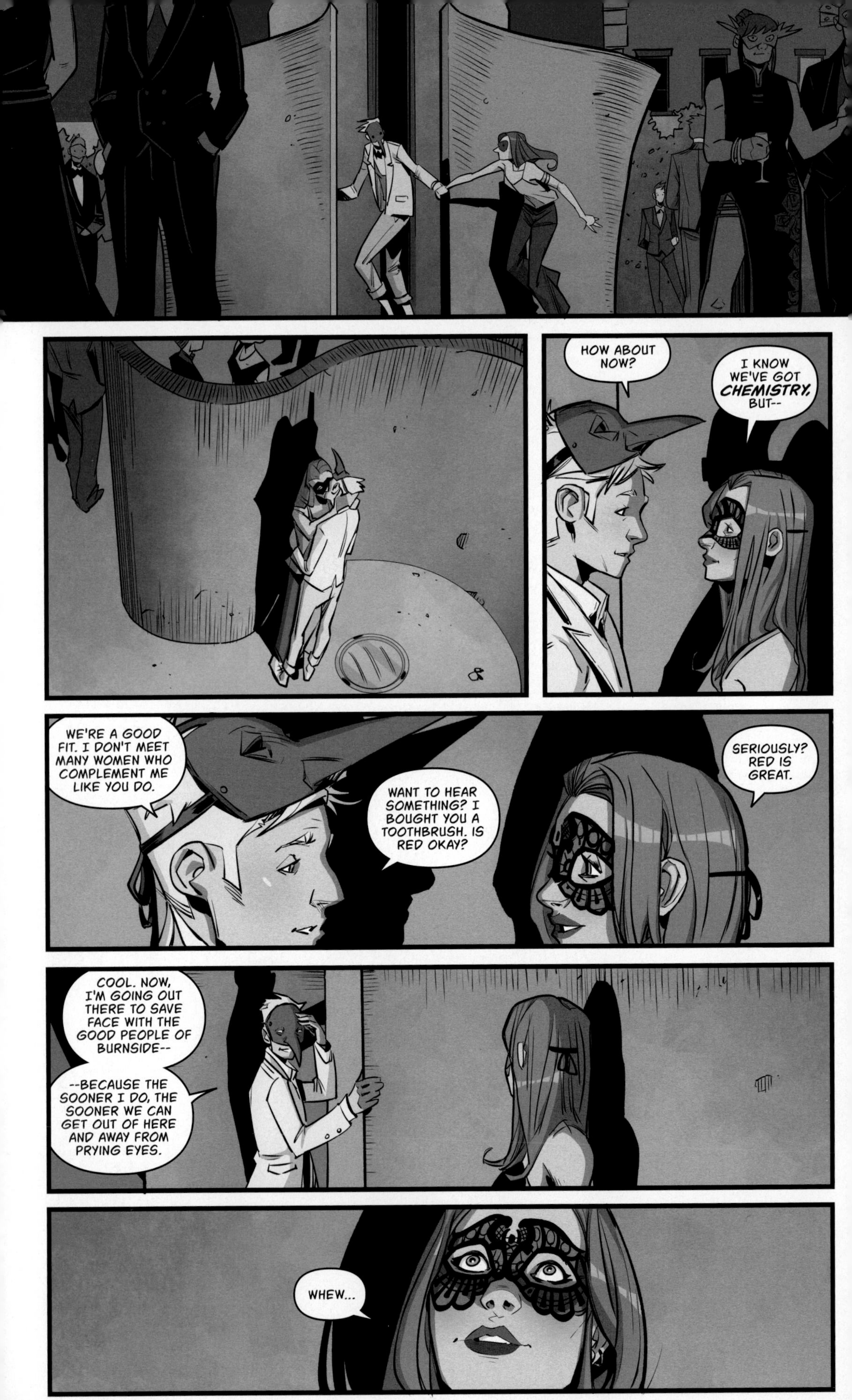
HOW ABOUT NOW?
I KNOW WE'VE GOT CHEMISTRY, BUT--
WE'RE A GOOD FIT. I DON'T MEET MANY WOMEN WHO COMPLEMENT ME LIKE YOU DO.
WANT TO HEAR SOMETHING? I BOUGHT YOU A TOOTHBRUSH. IS RED OKAY?
SERIOUSLY? RED IS GREAT.
COOL. NOW, I'M GOING OUT THERE TO SAVE FACE WITH THE GOOD PEOPLE OF BURNSIDE--
--BECAUSE THE SOONER I DO, THE SOONER WE CAN GET OUT OF HERE AND AWAY FROM PRYING EYES.
WHEW...

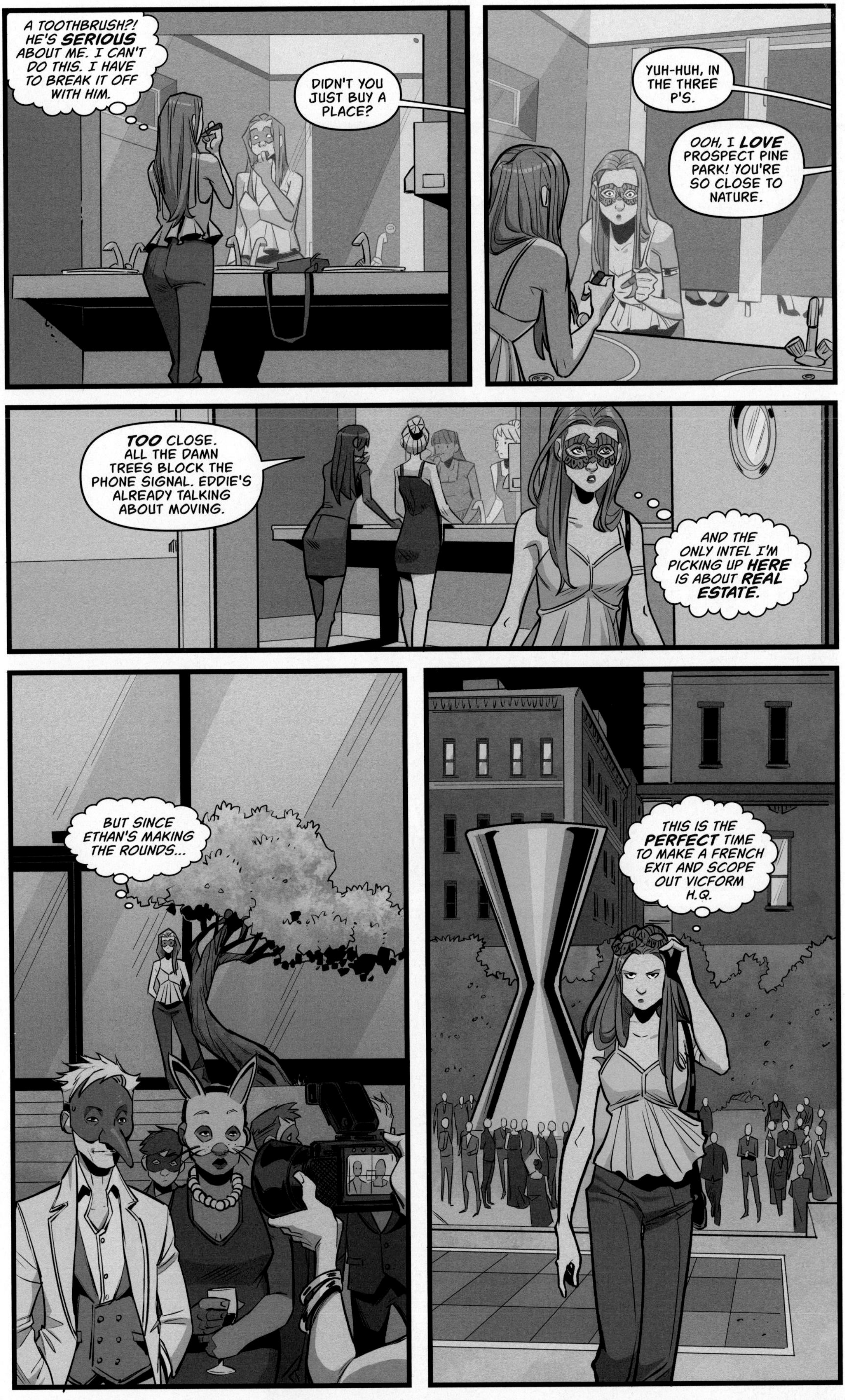
A TOOTHBRUSH?! HE'S SERIOUS ABOUT ME. I CAN'T DO THIS. I HAVE TO BREAK IT OFF WITH HIM.
DIDN'T YOU JUST BUY A PLACE?
YUH-HUH, IN THE THREE P'S.
OOH, I LOVE PROSPECT PINE PARK! YOU'RE SO CLOSE TO NATURE.
TOO CLOSE. ALL THE DAMN TREES BLOCK THE PHONE SIGNAL. EDDIE'S ALREADY TALKING ABOUT MOVING.
AND THE ONLY INTEL I'M PICKING UP HERE IS ABOUT REAL ESTATE.
BUT SINCE ETHAN'S MAKING THE ROUNDS...
THIS IS THE PERFECT TIME TO MAKE A FRENCH EXIT AND SCOPE OUT VICFORM H.Q.

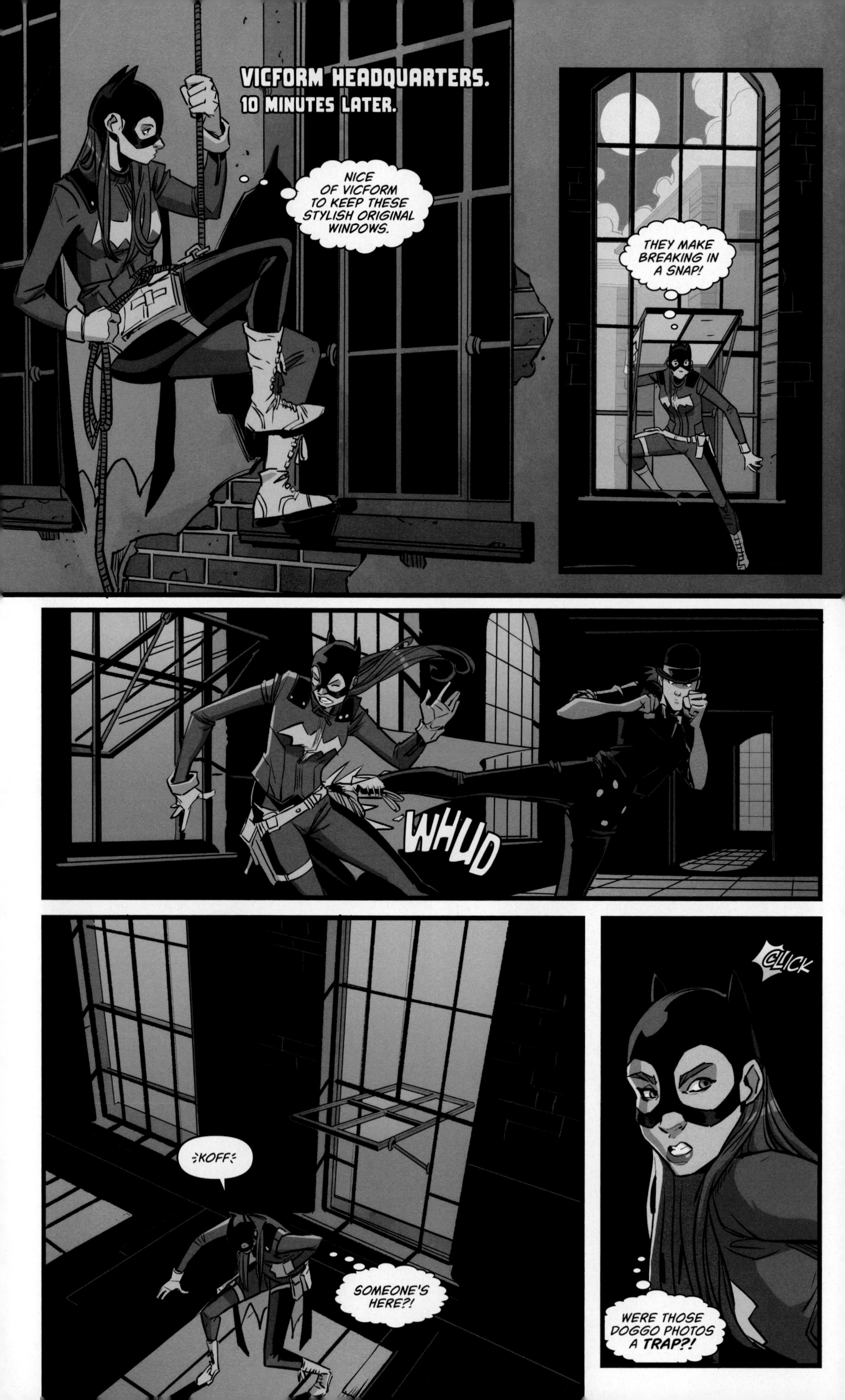

VICFORM HEADQUARTERS.
10 MINUTES LATER.
NICE OF VICFORM TO KEEP THESE STYLISH ORIGINAL WINDOWS.
THEY MAKE BREAKING IN A SNAP!
WHUD
KOFF
SOMEONE'S HERE?!
CLICK
WERE THOSE DOGGO PHOTOS A TRAP?!

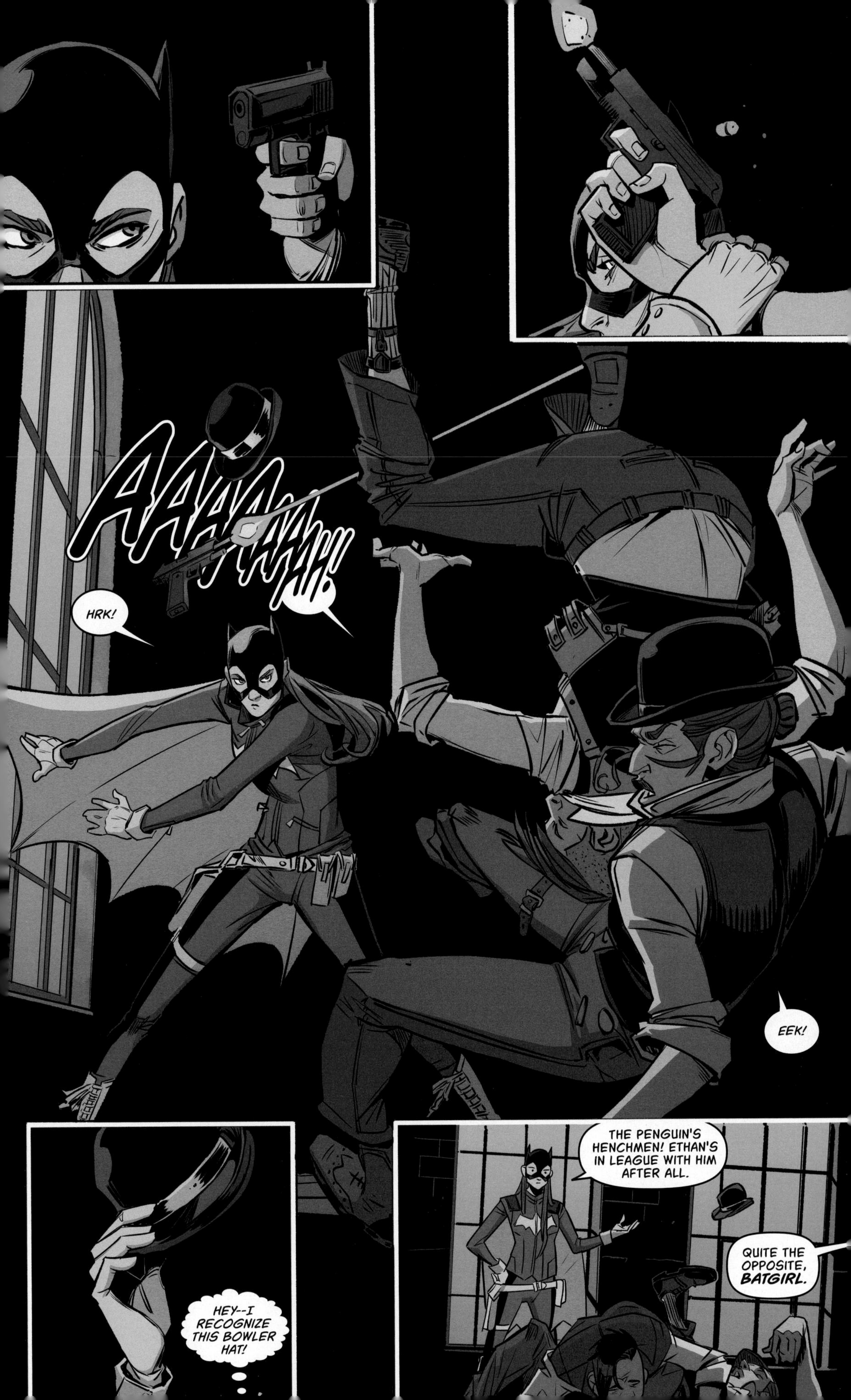
AAAAAAAH!
HRK!
EEK!
HEY--I RECOGNIZE THIS BOWLER HAT!
THE PENGUIN'S HENCHMEN! ETHAN'S IN LEAGUE WITH HIM AFTER ALL.
QUITE THE OPPOSITE, **BATGIRL.**

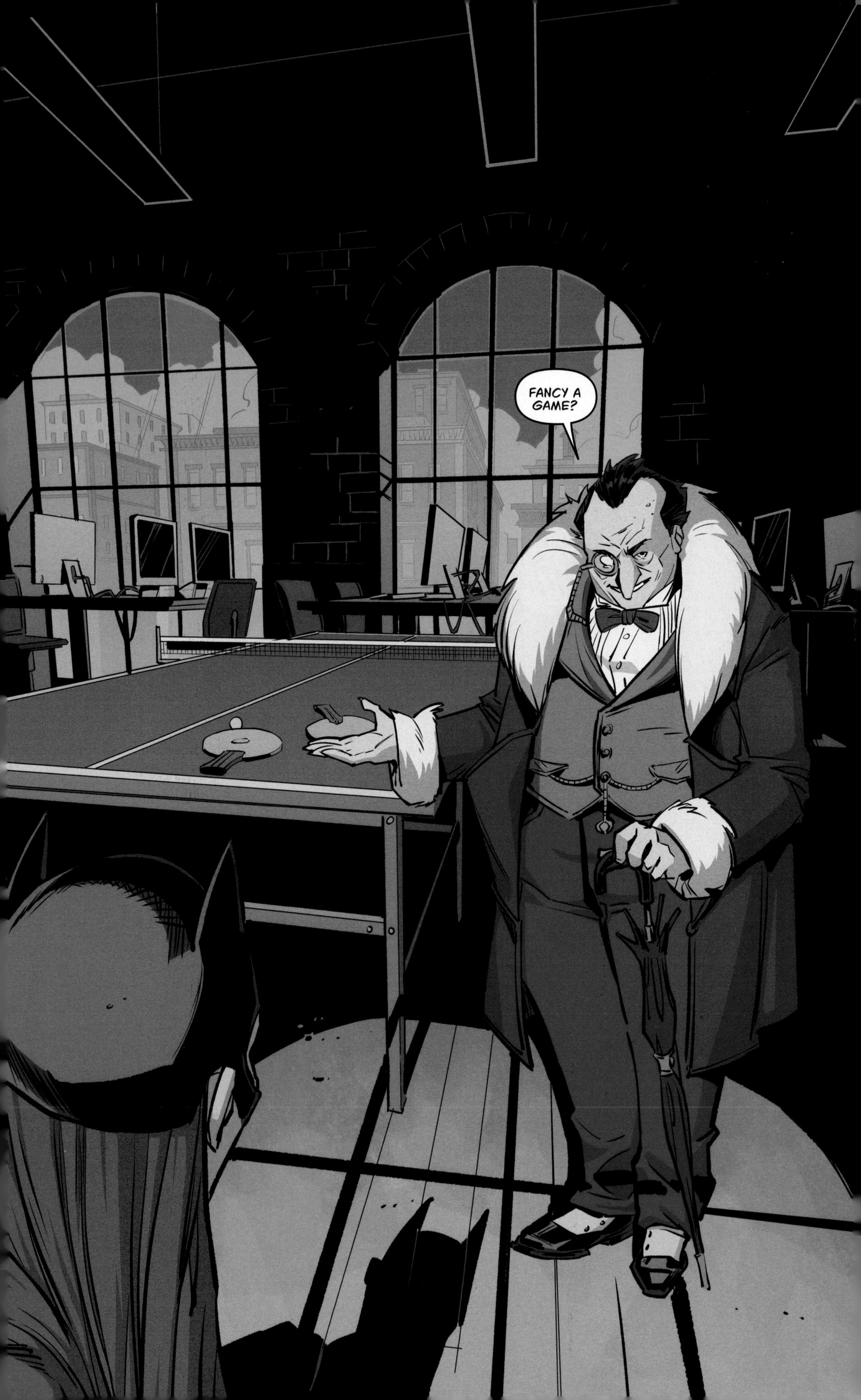
FANCY A GAME?

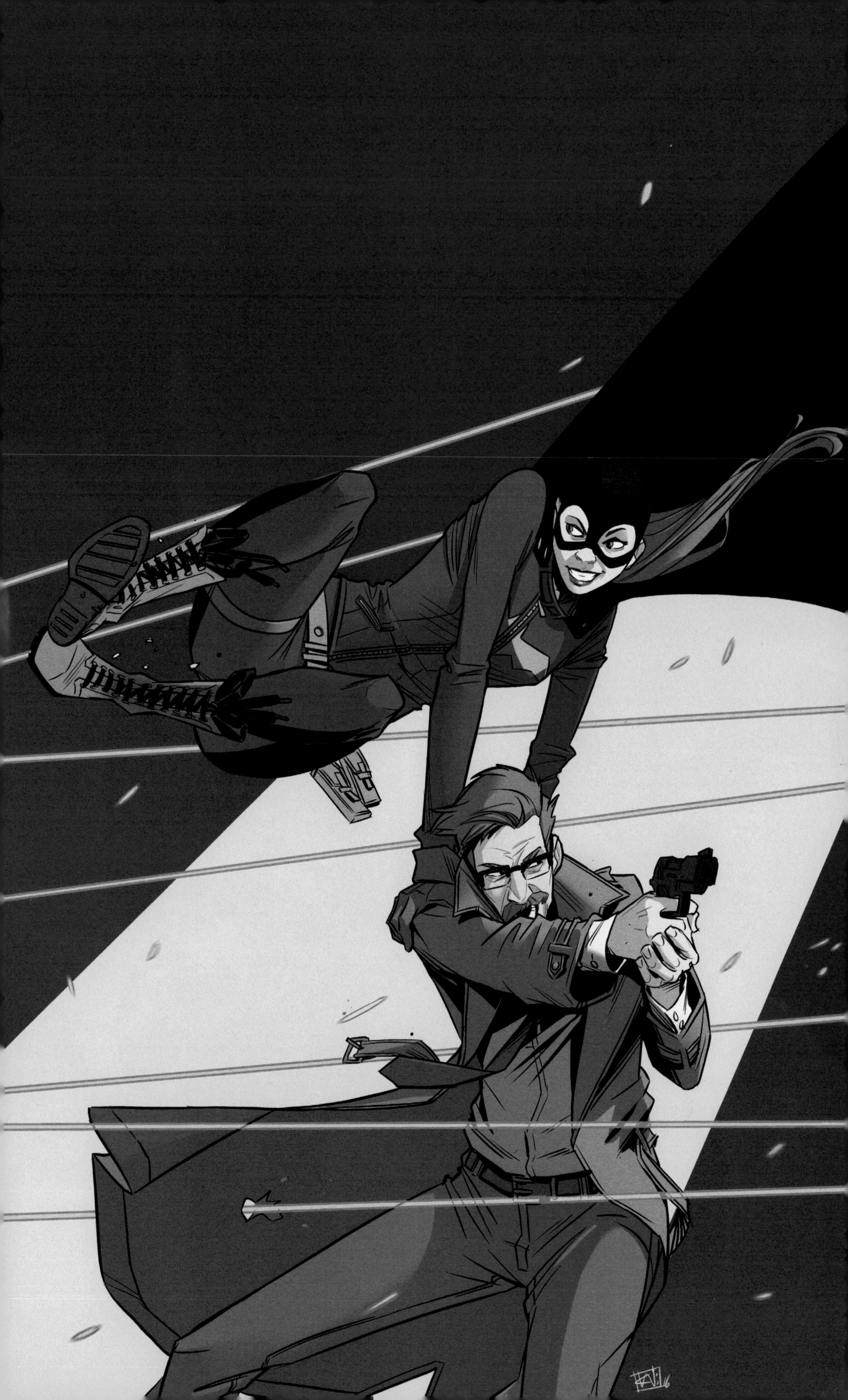

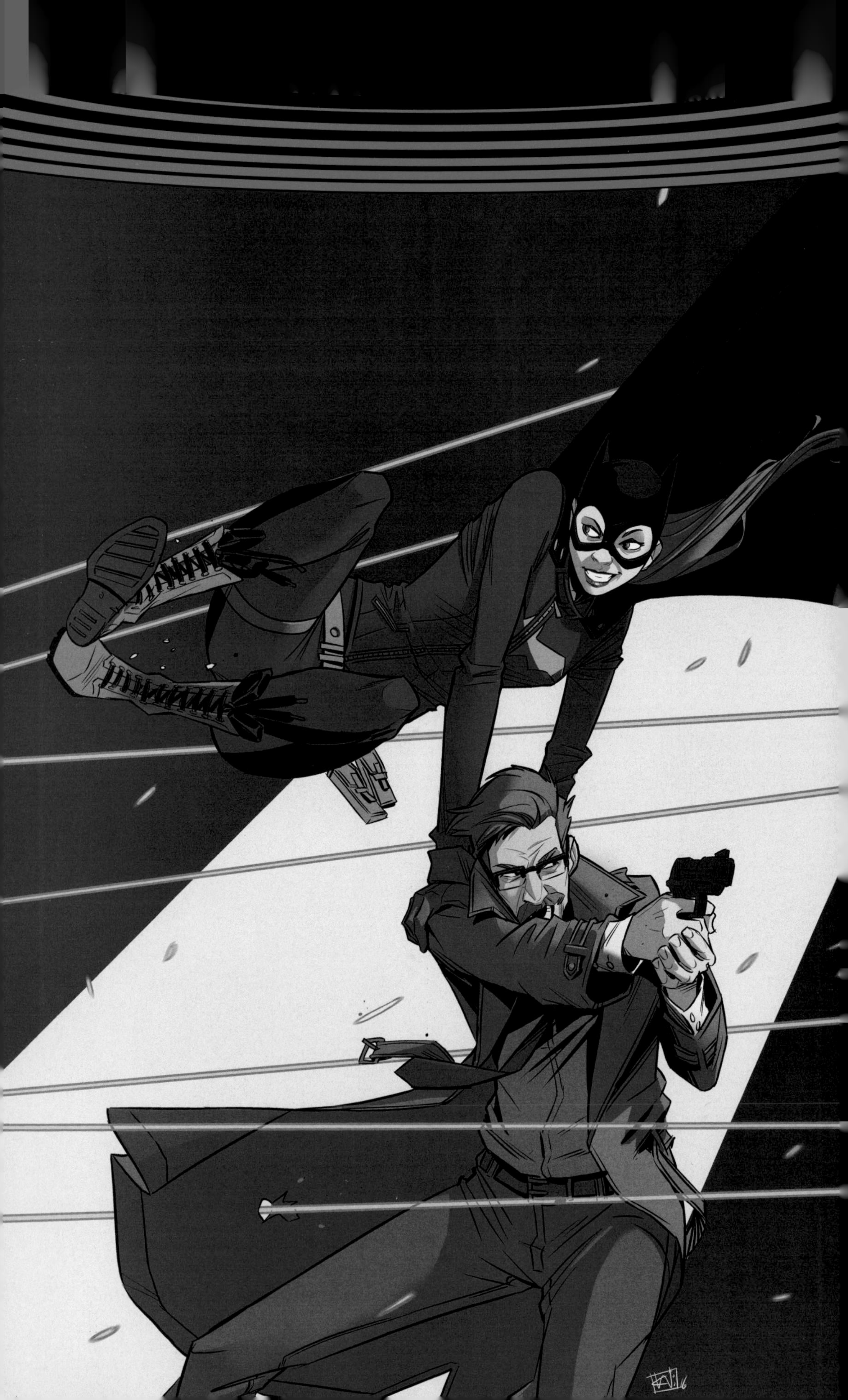

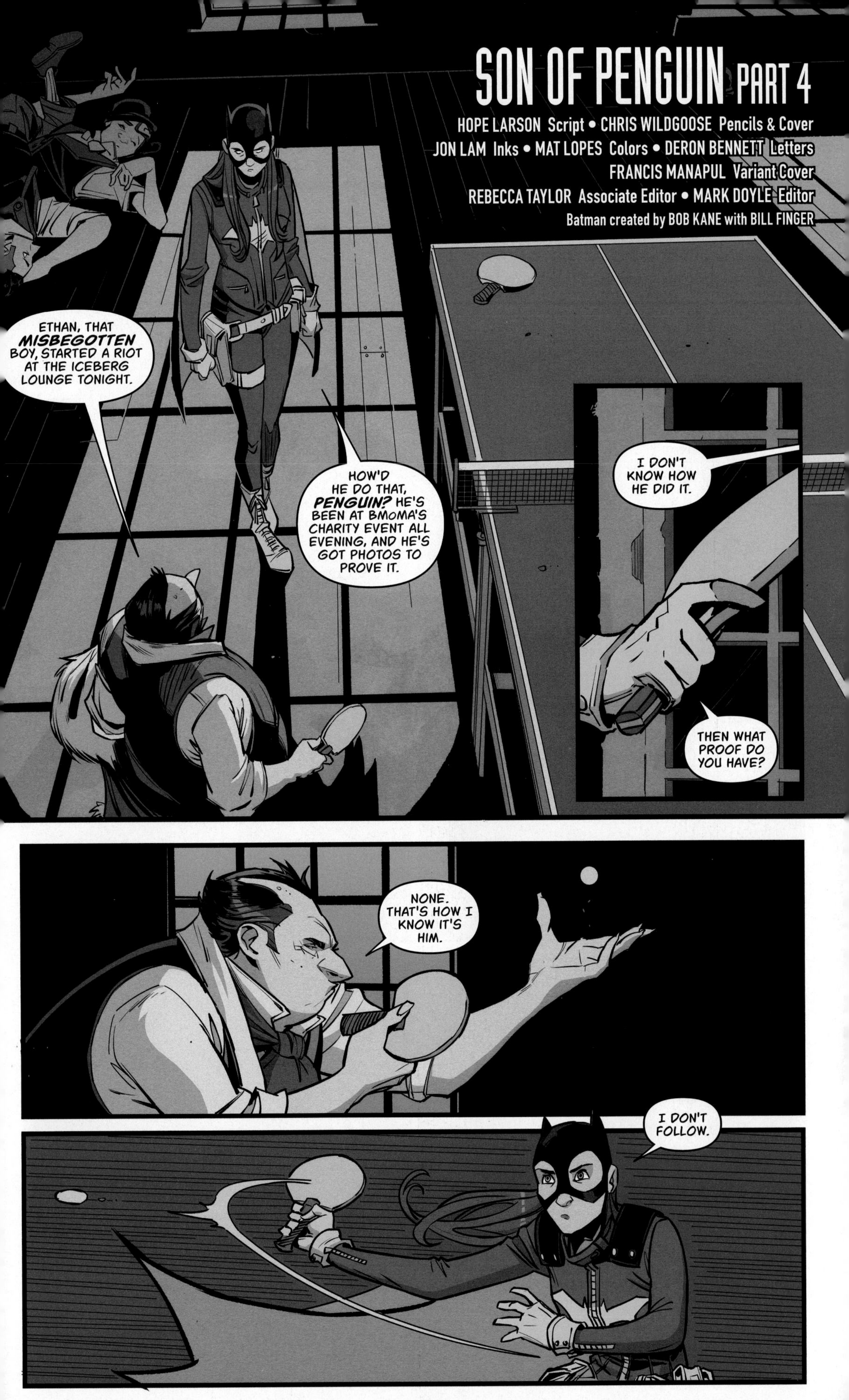
SON OF PENGUIN PART 4
HOPE LARSON Script • CHRIS WILDGOOSE Pencils & Cover
JON LAM Inks • MAT LOPES Colors • DERON BENNETT Letters
FRANCIS MANAPUL Variant Cover
REBECCA TAYLOR Associate Editor • MARK DOYLE Editor
Batman created by BOB KANE with BILL FINGER
ETHAN, THAT MISBEGOTTEN BOY, STARTED A RIOT AT THE ICEBERG LOUNGE TONIGHT.
HOW'D HE DO THAT, PENGUIN? HE'S BEEN AT BMOMA'S CHARITY EVENT ALL EVENING, AND HE'S GOT PHOTOS TO PROVE IT.
I DON'T KNOW HOW HE DID IT.
THEN WHAT PROOF DO YOU HAVE?
NONE. THAT'S HOW I KNOW IT'S HIM.
I DON'T FOLLOW.

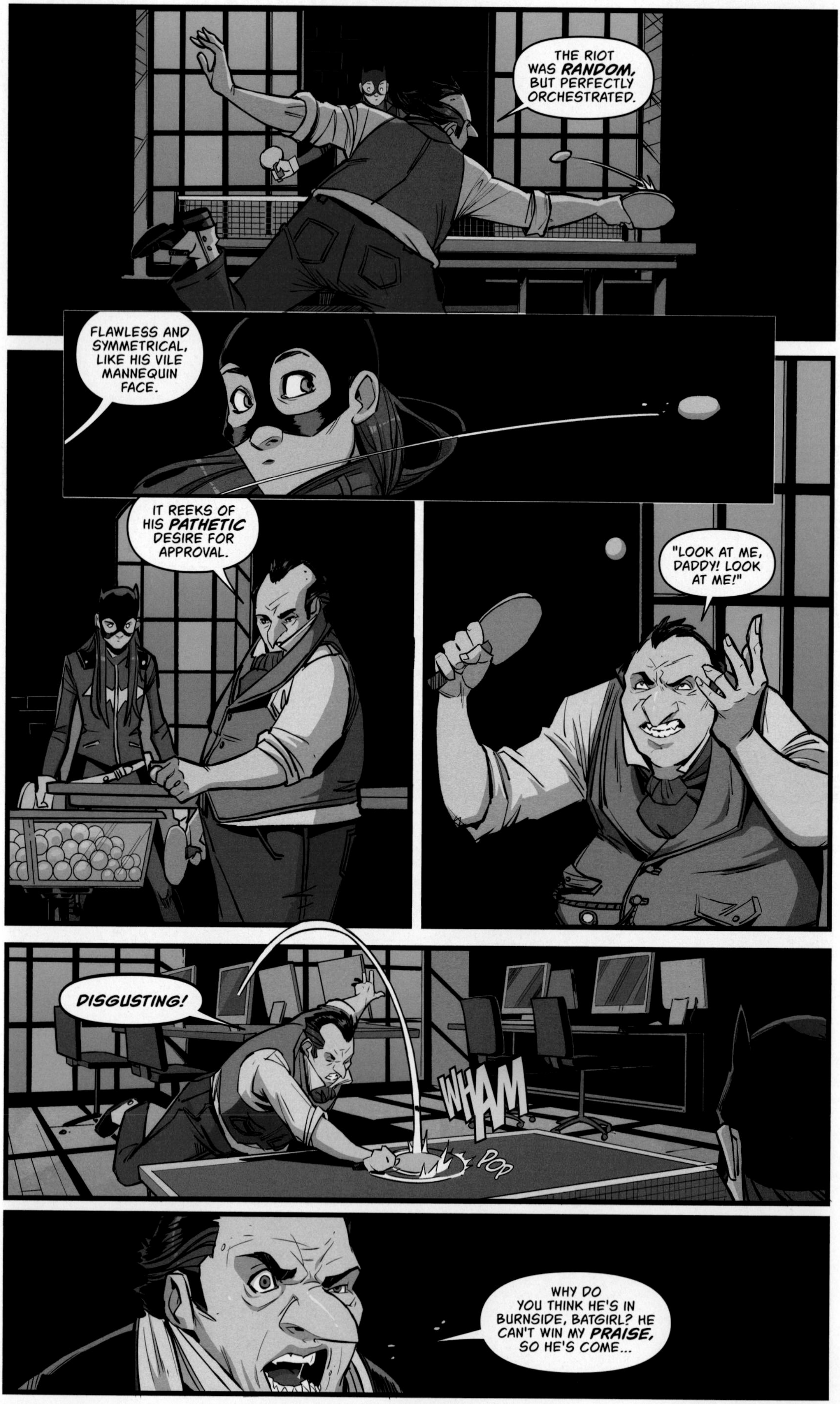

THE RIOT WAS RANDOM, BUT PERFECTLY ORCHESTRATED.
FLAWLESS AND SYMMETRICAL, LIKE HIS VILE MANNEQUIN FACE.
IT REEKS OF HIS PATHETIC DESIRE FOR APPROVAL.
"LOOK AT ME, DADDY! LOOK AT ME!"
DISGUSTING!
WHAM
POP
WHY DO YOU THINK HE'S IN BURNSIDE, BATGIRL? HE CAN'T WIN MY PRAISE, SO HE'S COME...

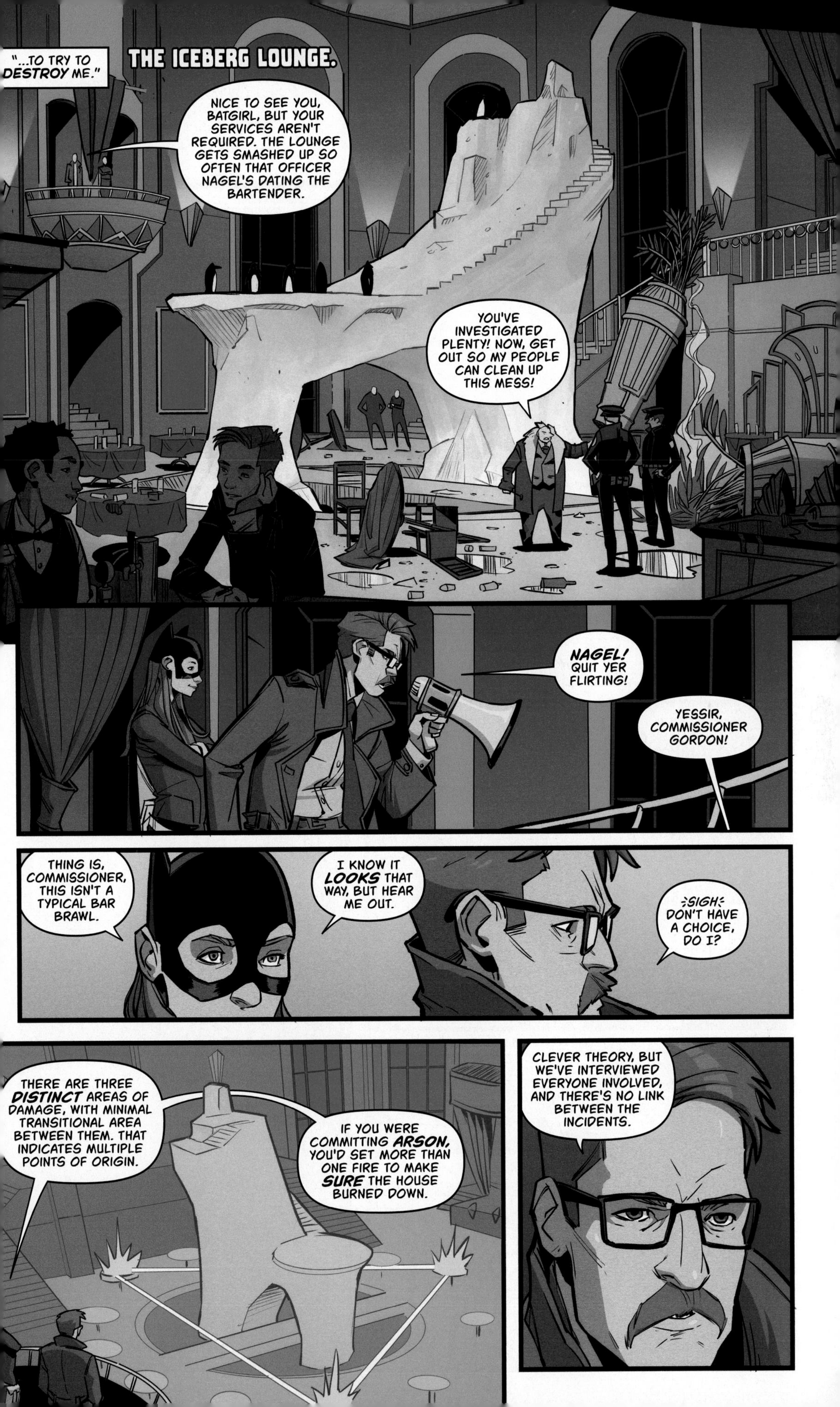
"...TO TRY TO DESTROY ME."
THE ICEBERG LOUNGE.
NICE TO SEE YOU, BATGIRL, BUT YOUR SERVICES AREN'T REQUIRED. THE LOUNGE GETS SMASHED UP SO OFTEN THAT OFFICER NAGEL'S DATING THE BARTENDER.
YOU'VE INVESTIGATED PLENTY! NOW, GET OUT SO MY PEOPLE CAN CLEAN UP THIS MESS!
NAGEL! QUIT YER FLIRTING!
YESSIR, COMMISSIONER GORDON!
THING IS, COMMISSIONER, THIS ISN'T A TYPICAL BAR BRAWL.
I KNOW IT LOOKS THAT WAY, BUT HEAR ME OUT.
SIGH DON'T HAVE A CHOICE, DO I?
THERE ARE THREE DISTINCT AREAS OF DAMAGE, WITH MINIMAL TRANSITIONAL AREA BETWEEN THEM. THAT INDICATES MULTIPLE POINTS OF ORIGIN.
IF YOU WERE COMMITTING ARSON, YOU'D SET MORE THAN ONE FIRE TO MAKE SURE THE HOUSE BURNED DOWN.
CLEVER THEORY, BUT WE'VE INTERVIEWED EVERYONE INVOLVED, AND THERE'S NO LINK BETWEEN THE INCIDENTS.

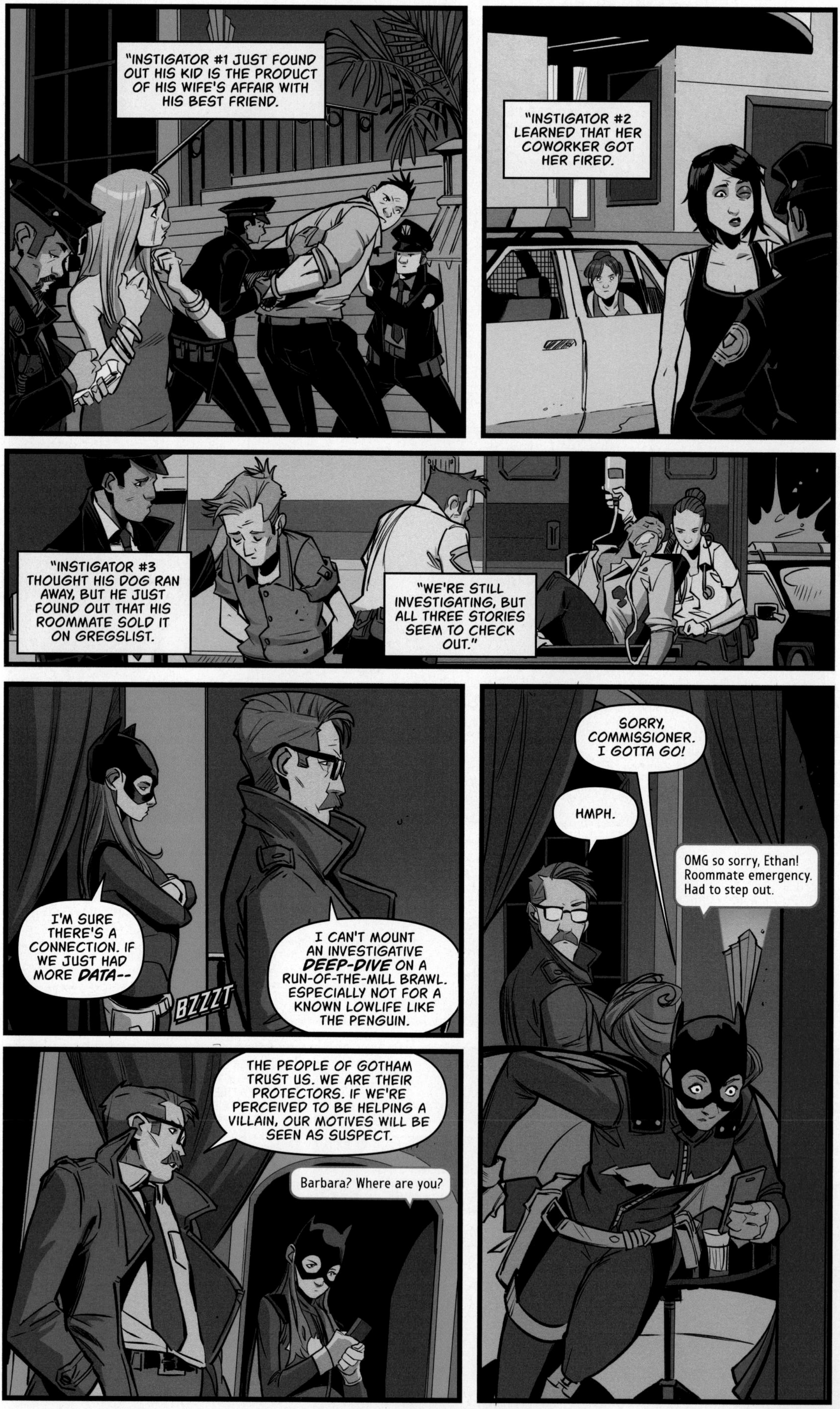
"INSTIGATOR #1 JUST FOUND OUT HIS KID IS THE PRODUCT OF HIS WIFE'S AFFAIR WITH HIS BEST FRIEND.
"INSTIGATOR #2 LEARNED THAT HER COWORKER GOT HER FIRED.
"INSTIGATOR #3 THOUGHT HIS DOG RAN AWAY, BUT HE JUST FOUND OUT THAT HIS ROOMMATE SOLD IT ON GREGSLIST.
"WE'RE STILL INVESTIGATING, BUT ALL THREE STORIES SEEM TO CHECK OUT."
I'M SURE THERE'S A CONNECTION. IF WE JUST HAD MORE DATA--
BZZZT
I CAN'T MOUNT AN INVESTIGATIVE DEEP-DIVE ON A RUN-OF-THE-MILL BRAWL. ESPECIALLY NOT FOR A KNOWN LOWLIFE LIKE THE PENGUIN.
THE PEOPLE OF GOTHAM TRUST US. WE ARE THEIR PROTECTORS. IF WE'RE PERCEIVED TO BE HELPING A VILLAIN, OUR MOTIVES WILL BE SEEN AS SUSPECT.
Barbara? Where are you?
SORRY, COMMISSIONER. I GOTTA GO!
HMPH.
OMG so sorry, Ethan! Roommate emergency. Had to step out.

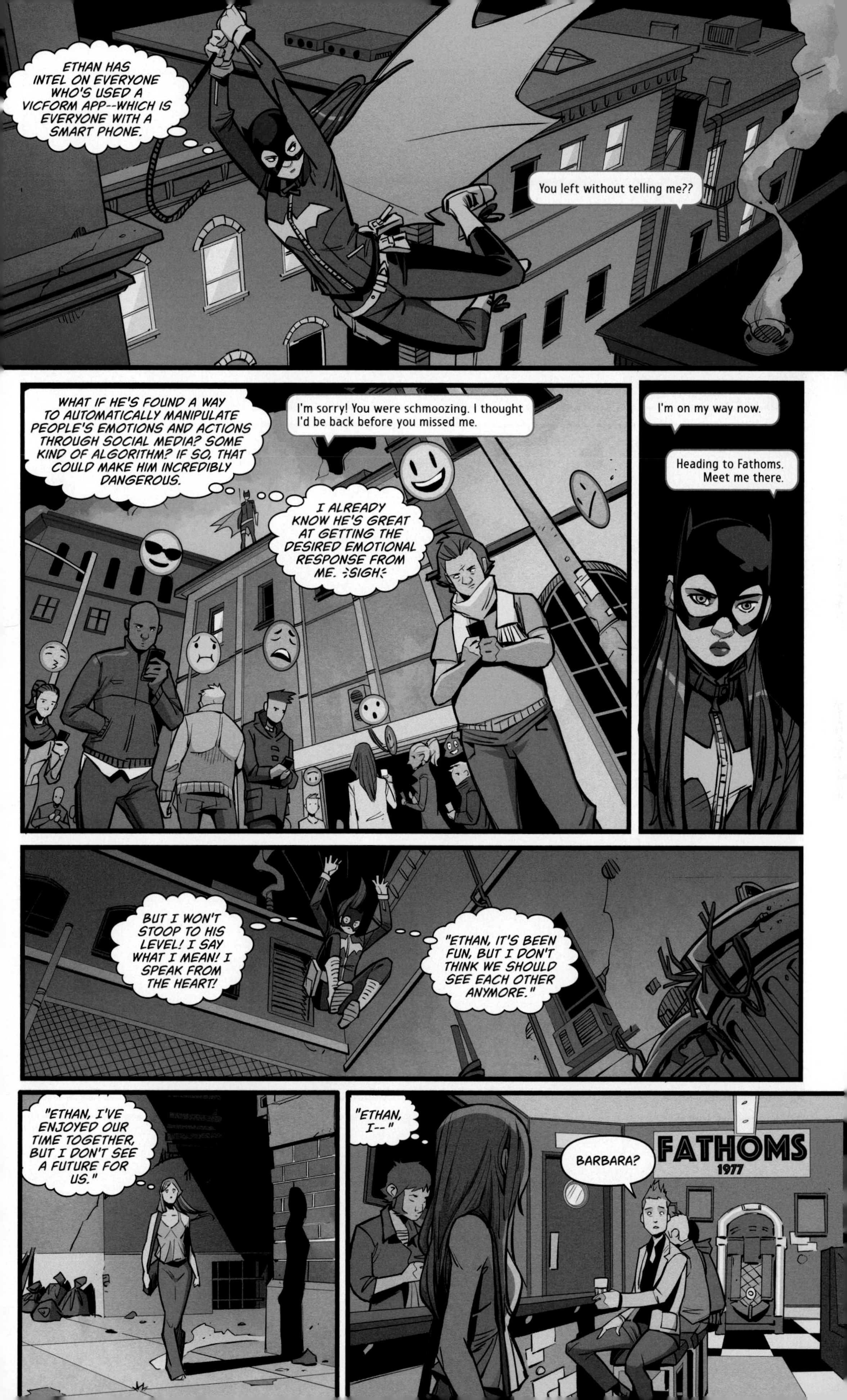
ETHAN HAS INTEL ON EVERYONE WHO'S USED A VICFORM APP--WHICH IS EVERYONE WITH A SMART PHONE.
You left without telling me??
WHAT IF HE'S FOUND A WAY TO AUTOMATICALLY MANIPULATE PEOPLE'S EMOTIONS AND ACTIONS THROUGH SOCIAL MEDIA? SOME KIND OF ALGORITHM? IF SO, THAT COULD MAKE HIM INCREDIBLY DANGEROUS.
I'm sorry! You were schmoozing. I thought I'd be back before you missed me.
I ALREADY KNOW HE'S GREAT AT GETTING THE DESIRED EMOTIONAL RESPONSE FROM ME. SIGH
I'm on my way now.
Heading to Fathoms. Meet me there.
BUT I WON'T STOOP TO HIS LEVEL! I SAY WHAT I MEAN! I SPEAK FROM THE HEART!
"ETHAN, IT'S BEEN FUN, BUT I DON'T THINK WE SHOULD SEE EACH OTHER ANYMORE."
"ETHAN, I'VE ENJOYED OUR TIME TOGETHER, BUT I DON'T SEE A FUTURE FOR US."
"ETHAN, I--"
BARBARA?
FATHOMS
1977

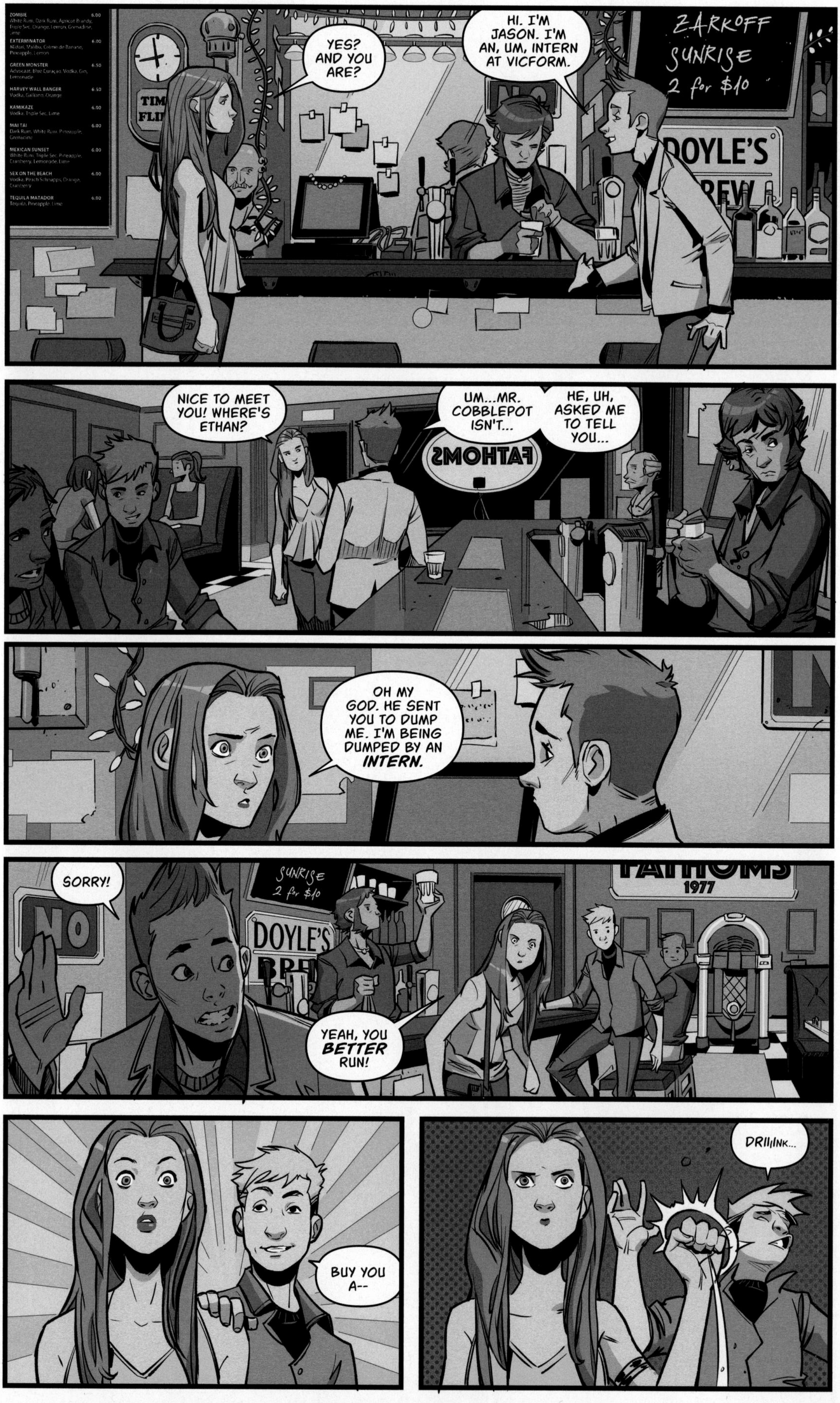
ZOMBIE 6.00
White Rum, Dark Rum, Apricot Brandy, Triple Sec, Orange, Lemon, Grenadine, Lime
EXTERMINATOR 6.00
Midori, Malibu, Crème de Banane, Pineapple, Lemon
GREEN MONSTER 6.50
Advocaat, Blue Curaçao, Vodka, Gin, Lemonade
HARVEY WALL BANGER 6.50
Vodka, Galliano, Orange
KAMIKAZE 6.00
Vodka, Triple Sec, Lime
MAI TAI 6.00
Dark Rum, White Rum, Pineapple, Grenadine
MEXICAN SUNSET 6.00
White Rum, Triple Sec, Pineapple, Cranberry, Lemonade, Lime
SEX ON THE BEACH 6.00
Vodka, Peach Schnapps, Orange, Cranberry
TEQUILA MATADOR 6.00
Tequila, Pineapple, Lime
ZARKOFF SUNRISE 2 for $10
YES? AND YOU ARE?
HI. I'M JASON. I'M AN, UM, INTERN AT VICFORM.
DOYLE'S
NICE TO MEET YOU! WHERE'S ETHAN?
UM...MR. COBBLEPOT ISN'T...
HE, UH, ASKED ME TO TELL YOU...
FATHOMS
OH MY GOD. HE SENT YOU TO DUMP ME. I'M BEING DUMPED BY AN INTERN.
SORRY!
SUNRISE 2 for $10
NO
DOYLE'S
FATHOMS 1977
YEAH, YOU BETTER RUN!
BUY YOU A--
DRIIIINK...

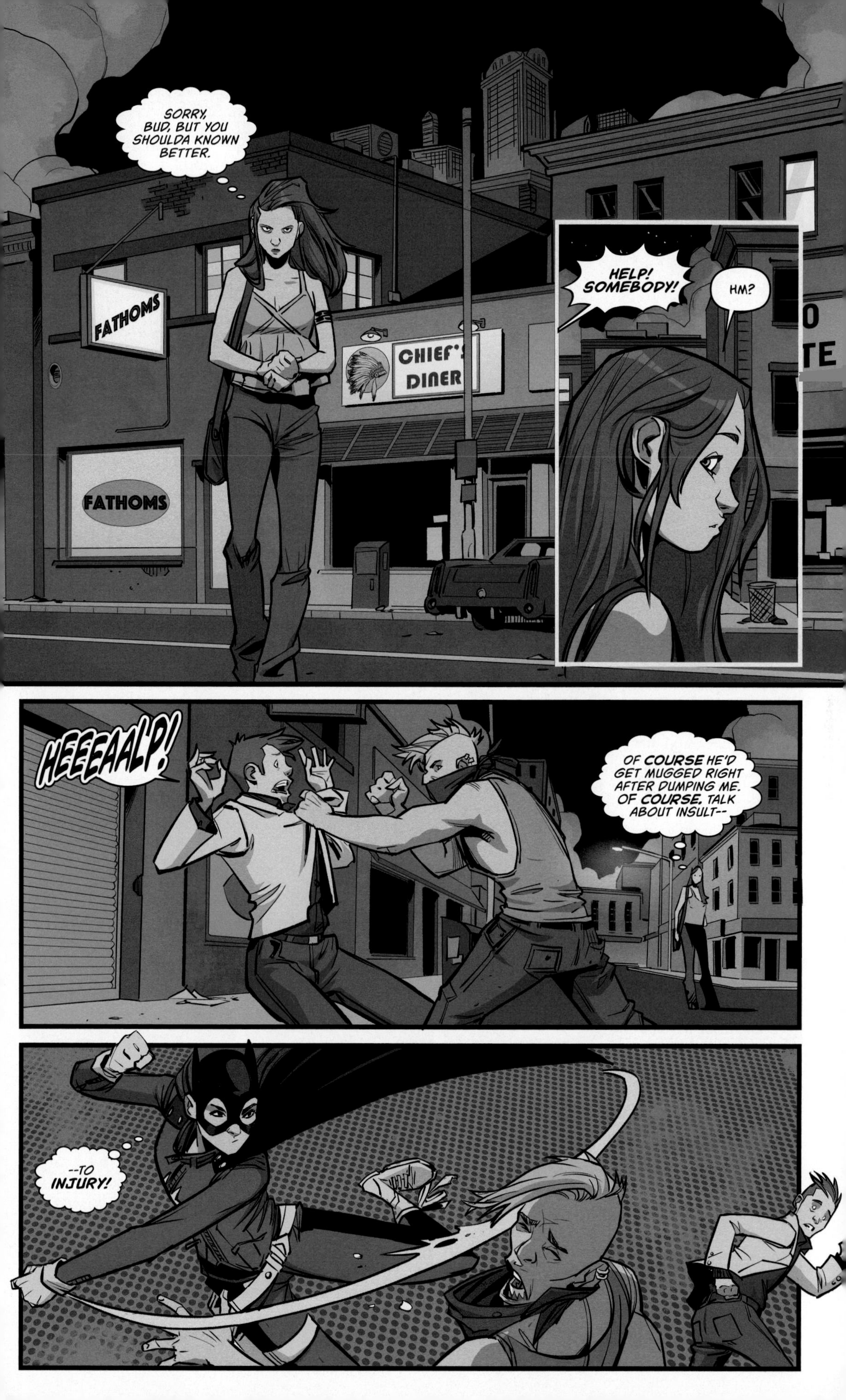
SORRY, BUD, BUT YOU SHOULDA KNOWN BETTER.
FATHOMS
CHIEF'S DINER
FATHOMS
HELP! SOMEBODY!
HM?
HEEEAALP!
OF COURSE HE'D GET MUGGED RIGHT AFTER DUMPING ME. OF COURSE. TALK ABOUT INSULT--
--TO INJURY!

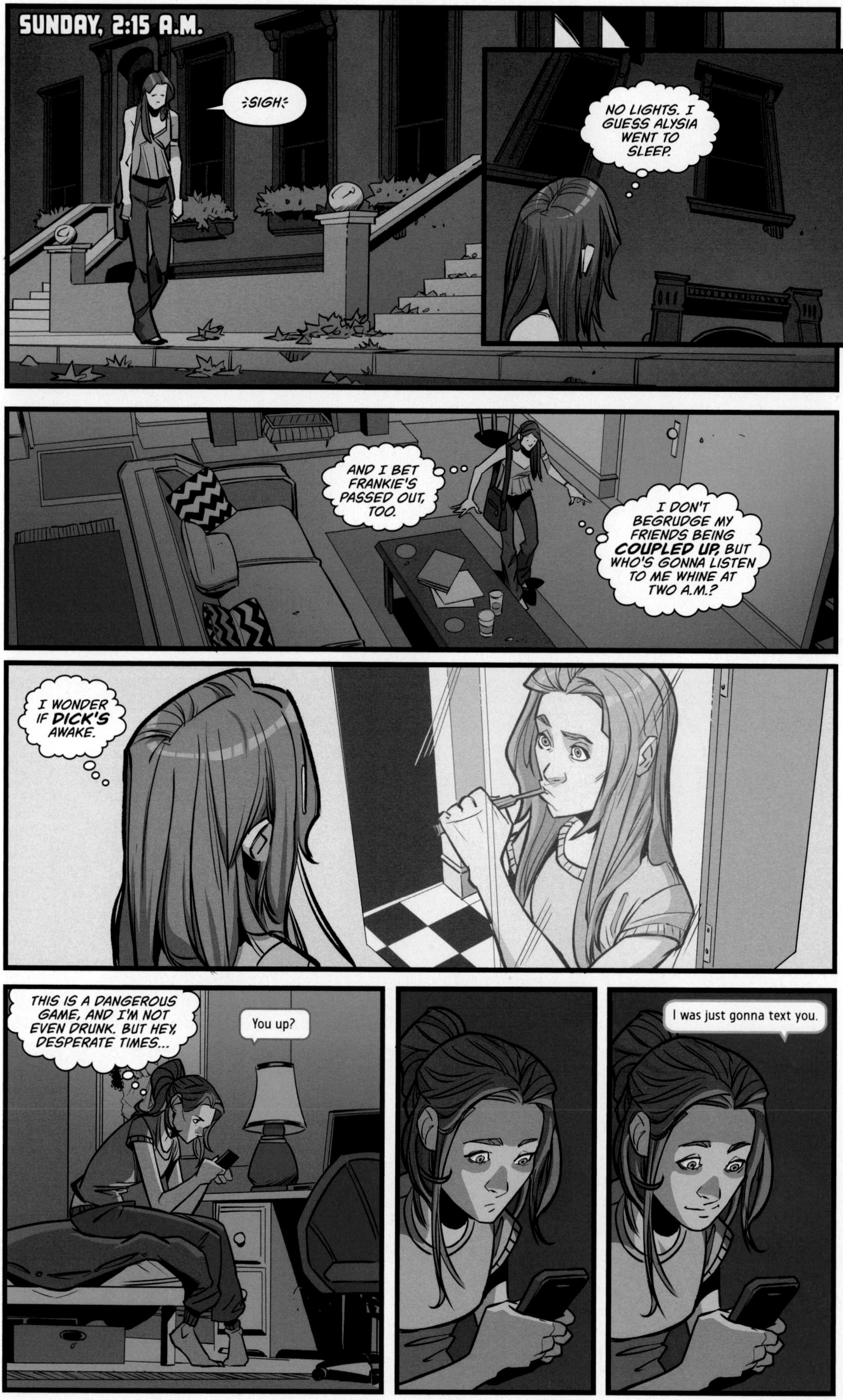
SUNDAY, 2:15 A.M.
SIGH
NO LIGHTS. I GUESS ALYSIA WENT TO SLEEP.
AND I BET FRANKIE'S PASSED OUT, TOO.
I DON'T BEGRUDGE MY FRIENDS BEING COUPLED UP, BUT WHO'S GONNA LISTEN TO ME WHINE AT TWO A.M.?
I WONDER IF DICK'S AWAKE.
THIS IS A DANGEROUS GAME, AND I'M NOT EVEN DRUNK. BUT HEY, DESPERATE TIMES...
You up?
I was just gonna text you.

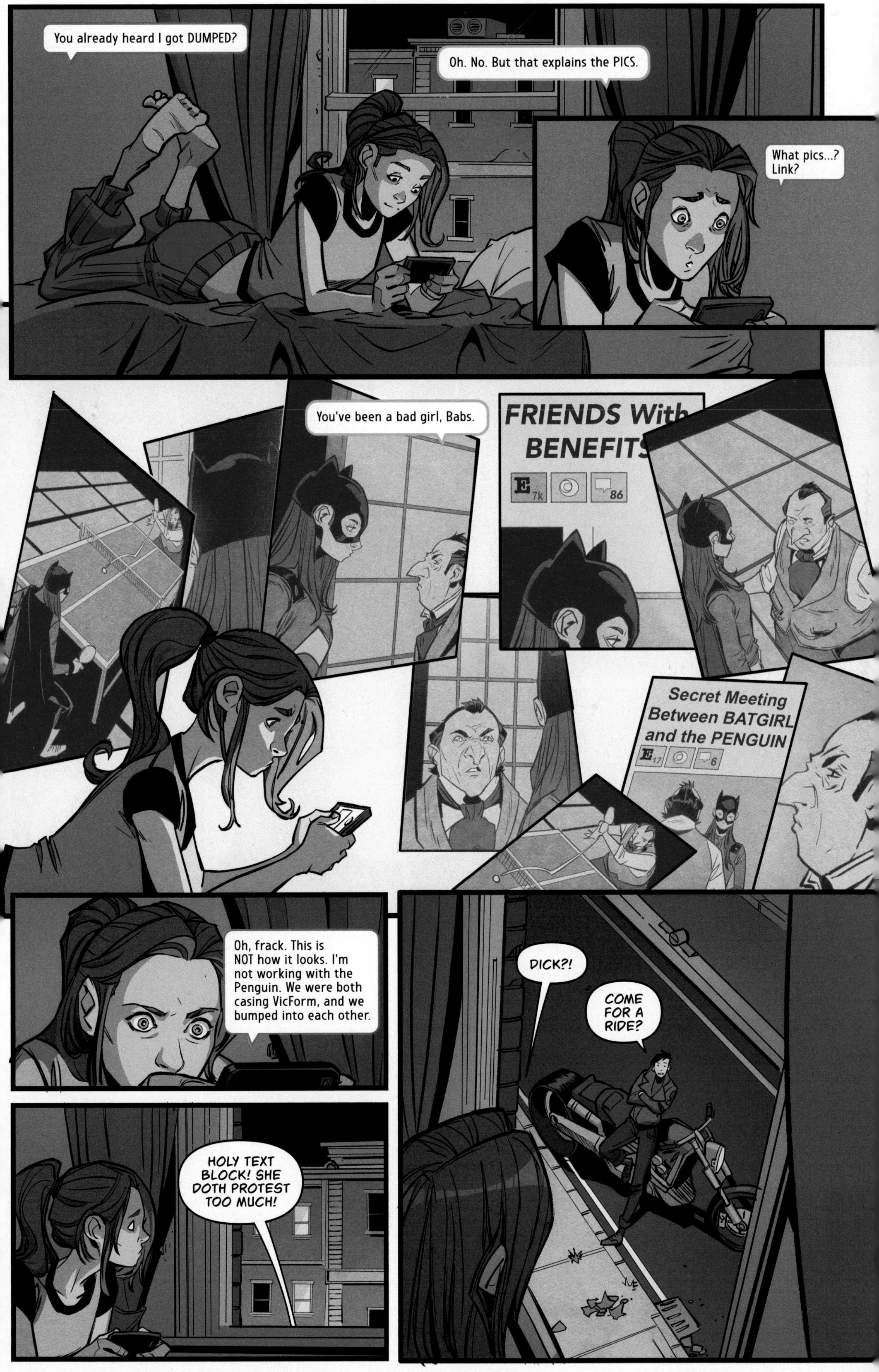

You already heard I got DUMPED?
Oh. No. But that explains the PICS.
What pics...? Link?
You've been a bad girl, Babs.
FRIENDS With BENEFITS
7k
86
Secret Meeting Between BATGIRL and the PENGUIN
17
6
Oh, frack. This is NOT how it looks. I'm not working with the Penguin. We were both casing VicForm, and we bumped into each other.
HOLY TEXT BLOCK! SHE DOTH PROTEST TOO MUCH!
DICK?!
COME FOR A RIDE?

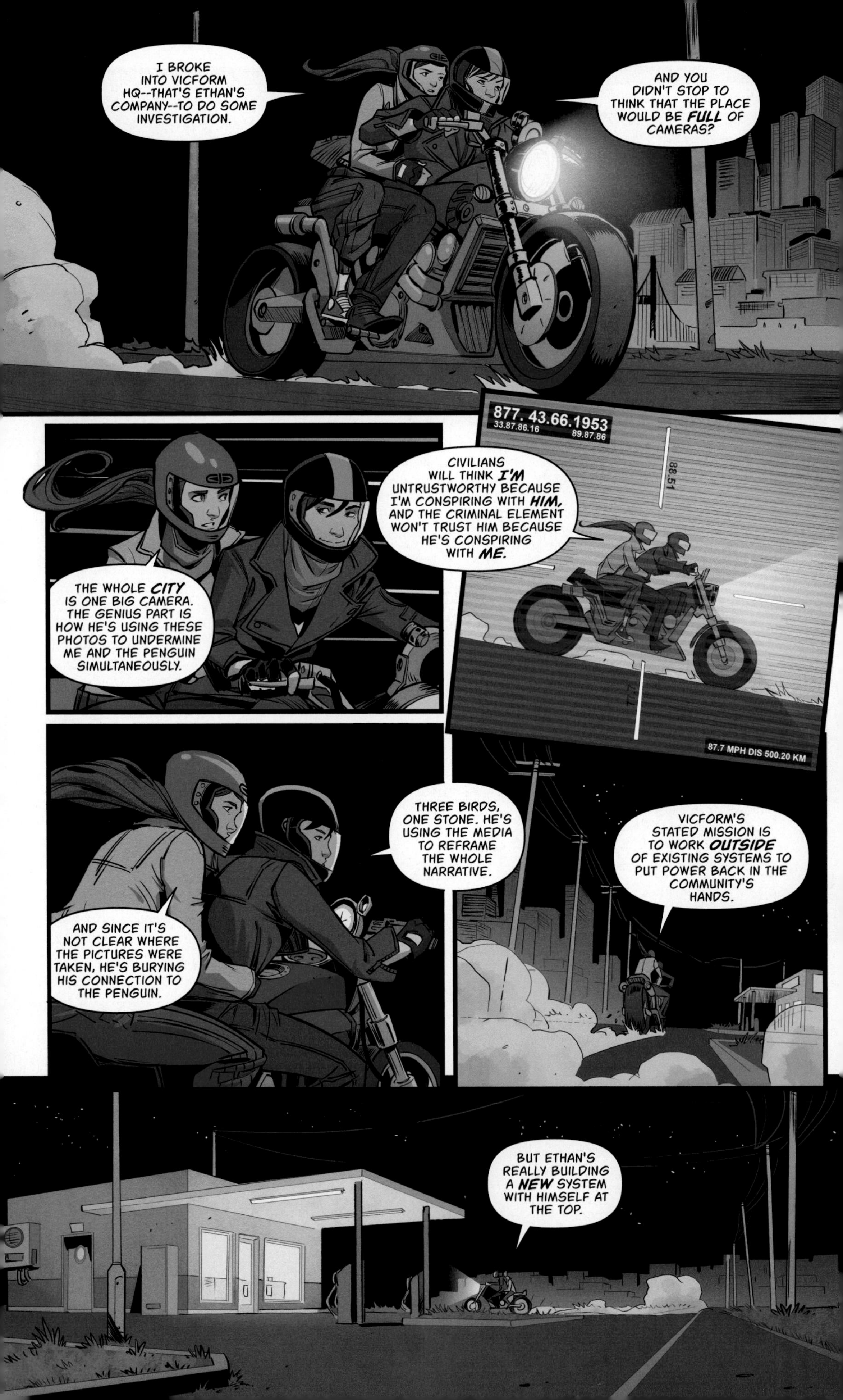
I BROKE INTO VICFORM HQ--THAT'S ETHAN'S COMPANY--TO DO SOME INVESTIGATION.
AND YOU DIDN'T STOP TO THINK THAT THE PLACE WOULD BE FULL OF CAMERAS?
THE WHOLE CITY IS ONE BIG CAMERA. THE GENIUS PART IS HOW HE'S USING THESE PHOTOS TO UNDERMINE ME AND THE PENGUIN SIMULTANEOUSLY.
877. 43.66.1953
33.87.86.16
89.87.86
88.51
CIVILIANS WILL THINK I'M UNTRUSTWORTHY BECAUSE I'M CONSPIRING WITH HIM, AND THE CRIMINAL ELEMENT WON'T TRUST HIM BECAUSE HE'S CONSPIRING WITH ME.
87.7 MPH DIS 500.20 KM
AND SINCE IT'S NOT CLEAR WHERE THE PICTURES WERE TAKEN, HE'S BURYING HIS CONNECTION TO THE PENGUIN.
THREE BIRDS, ONE STONE. HE'S USING THE MEDIA TO REFRAME THE WHOLE NARRATIVE.
VICFORM'S STATED MISSION IS TO WORK OUTSIDE OF EXISTING SYSTEMS TO PUT POWER BACK IN THE COMMUNITY'S HANDS.
BUT ETHAN'S REALLY BUILDING A NEW SYSTEM WITH HIMSELF AT THE TOP.

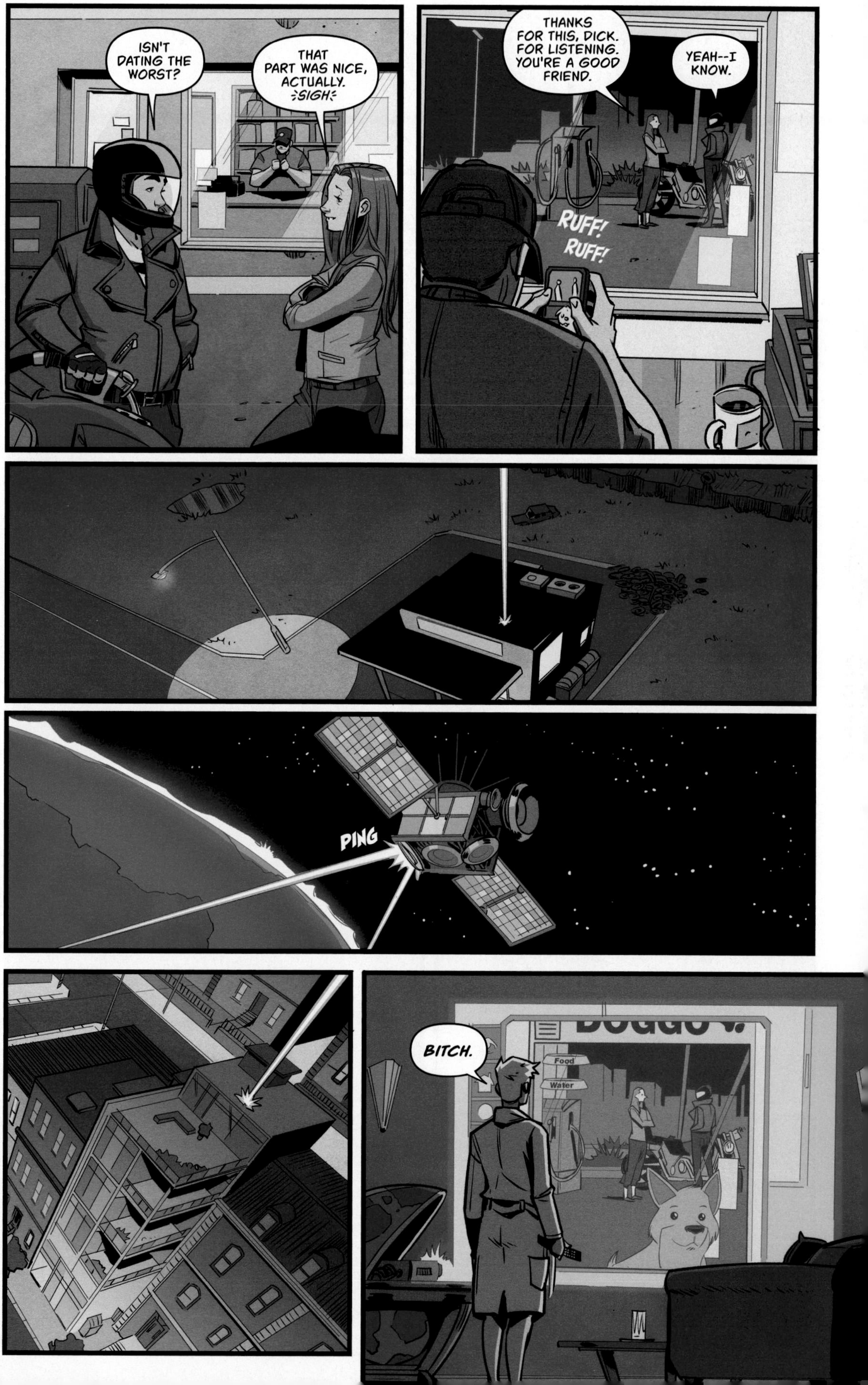
ISN'T DATING THE WORST?
THAT PART WAS NICE, ACTUALLY. *SIGH*
THANKS FOR THIS, DICK. FOR LISTENING. YOU'RE A GOOD FRIEND.
YEAH--I KNOW.
RUFF! RUFF!
PING
BITCH.
Food
Water

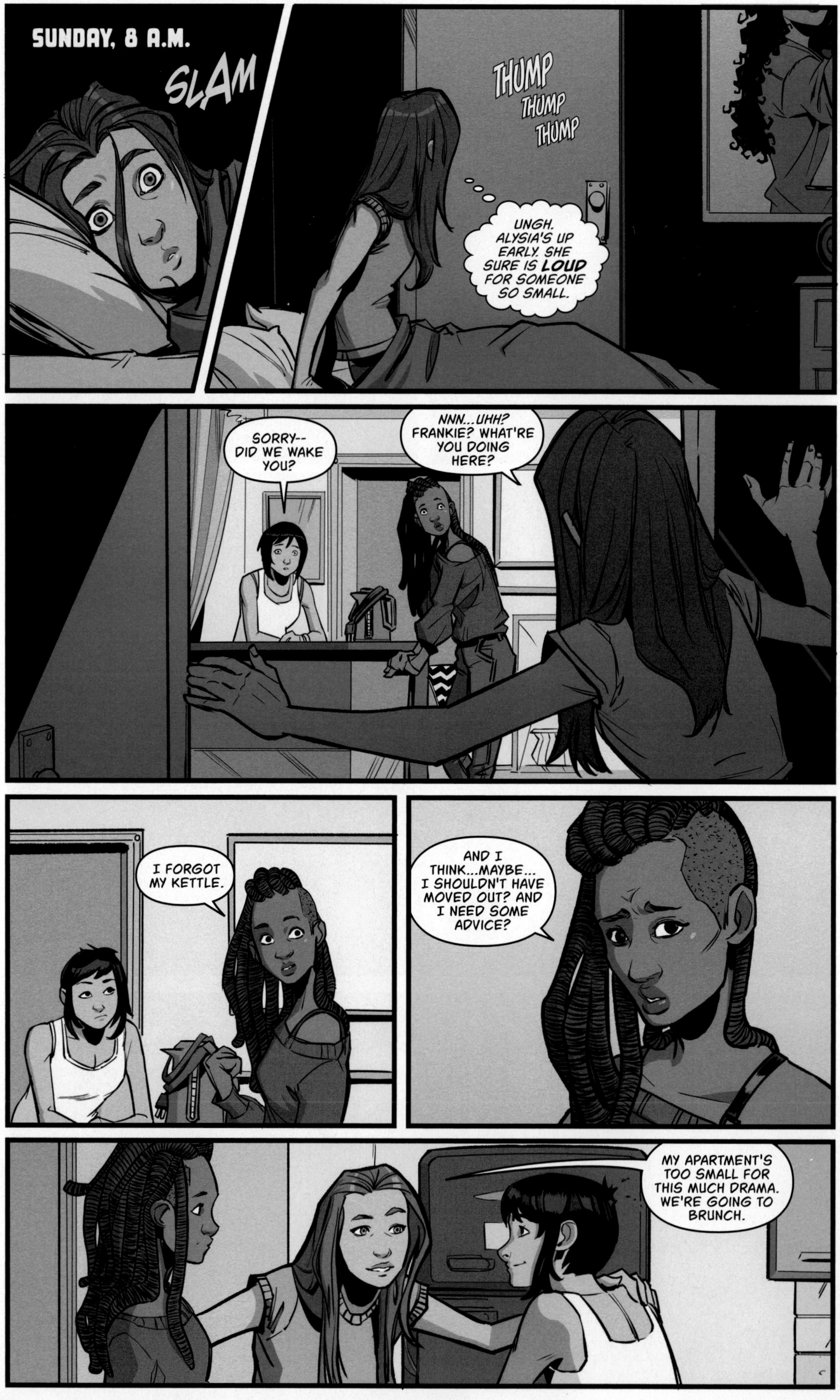
SUNDAY, 8 A.M.
SLAM
THUMP THUMP THUMP
UNGH. ALYSIA'S UP EARLY. SHE SURE IS **LOUD** FOR SOMEONE SO SMALL.
SORRY-- DID WE WAKE YOU?
NNN...UHH? FRANKIE? WHAT'RE YOU DOING HERE?
I FORGOT MY KETTLE.
AND I THINK...MAYBE... I SHOULDN'T HAVE MOVED OUT? AND I NEED SOME ADVICE?
MY APARTMENT'S TOO SMALL FOR THIS MUCH DRAMA. WE'RE GOING TO BRUNCH.

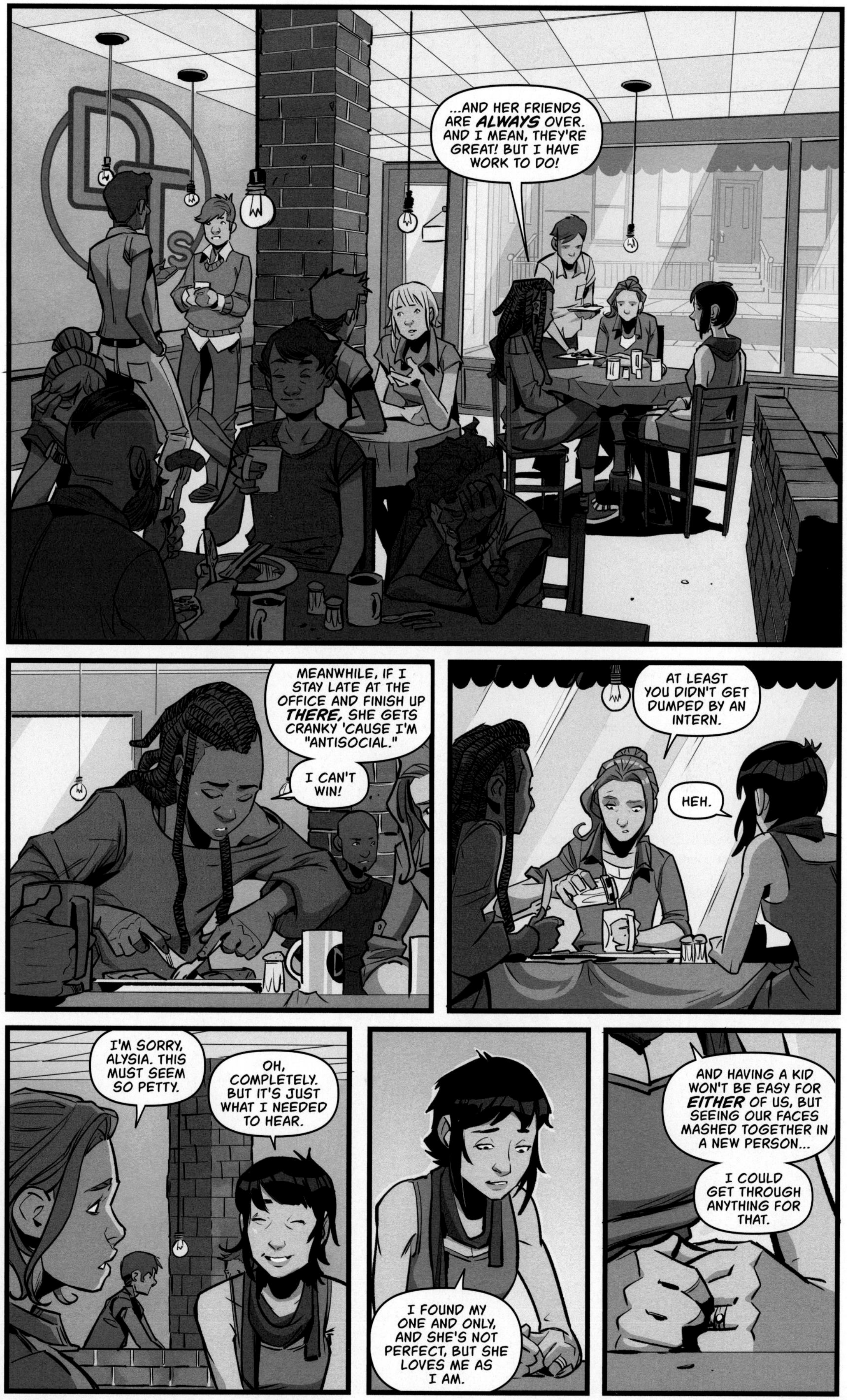
...AND HER FRIENDS ARE **ALWAYS** OVER. AND I MEAN, THEY'RE GREAT! BUT I HAVE WORK TO DO!
MEANWHILE, IF I STAY LATE AT THE OFFICE AND FINISH UP **THERE,** SHE GETS CRANKY 'CAUSE I'M "ANTISOCIAL."
I CAN'T WIN!
AT LEAST YOU DIDN'T GET DUMPED BY AN INTERN.
HEH.
I'M SORRY, ALYSIA. THIS MUST SEEM SO PETTY.
OH, COMPLETELY. BUT IT'S JUST WHAT I NEEDED TO HEAR.
I FOUND MY ONE AND ONLY, AND SHE'S NOT PERFECT, BUT SHE LOVES ME AS I AM.
AND HAVING A KID WON'T BE EASY FOR **EITHER** OF US, BUT SEEING OUR FACES MASHED TOGETHER IN A NEW PERSON...
I COULD GET THROUGH ANYTHING FOR THAT.

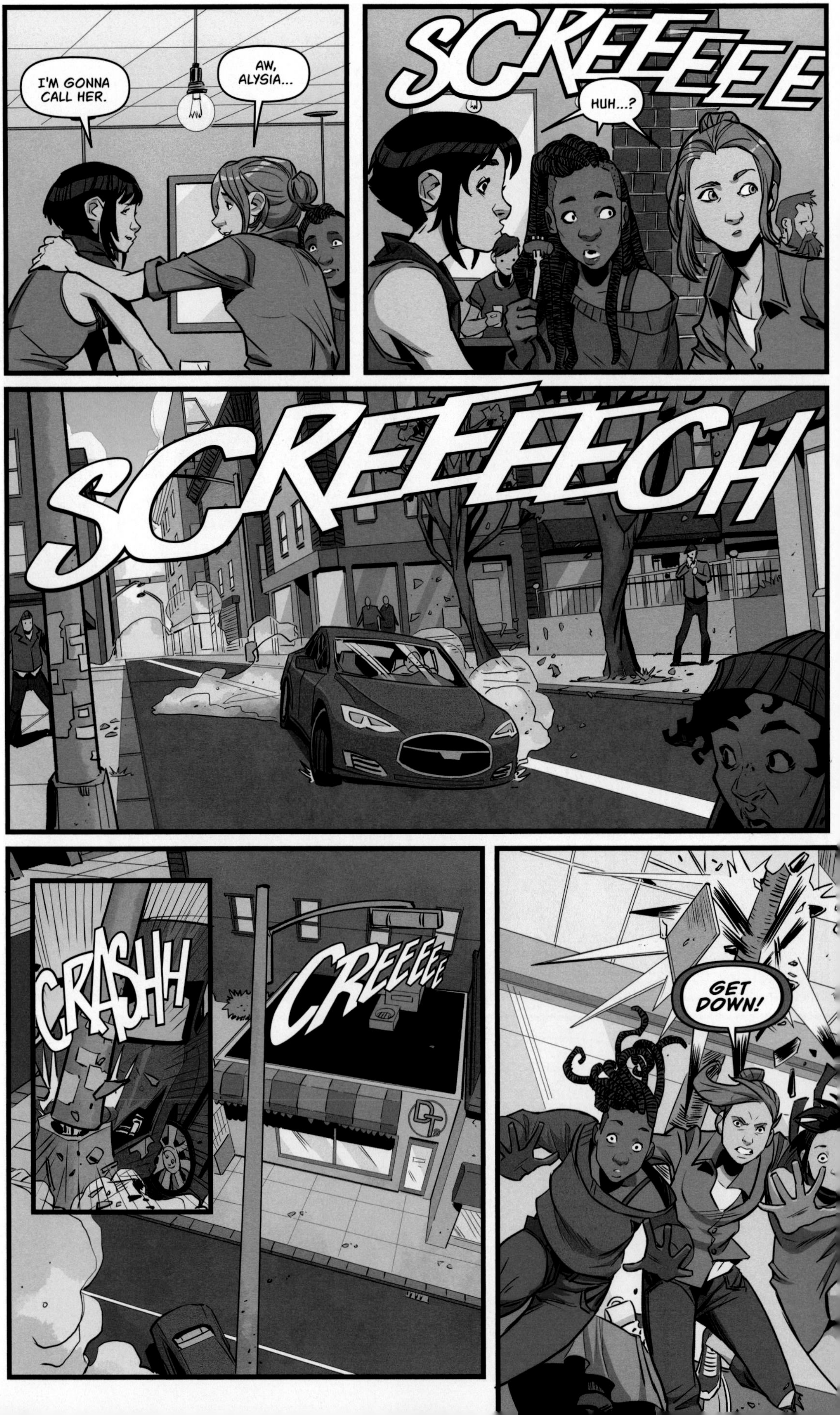
I'M GONNA CALL HER.
AW, ALYSIA...
SCREEEEEE
HUH...?
SCREEEECH
CRASHH
CREEEEEE
GET DOWN!

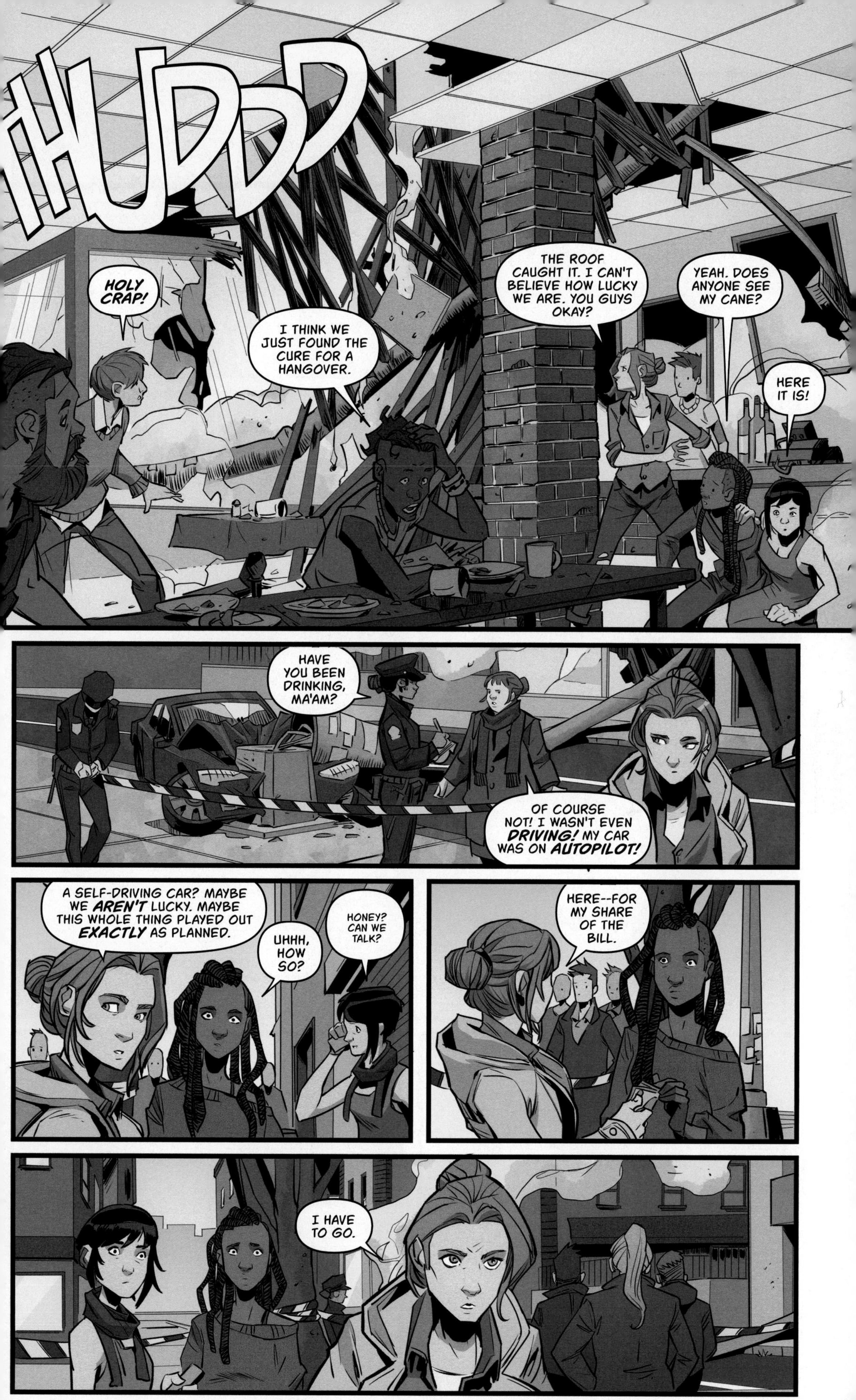
THUDDD
HOLY CRAP!
I THINK WE JUST FOUND THE CURE FOR A HANGOVER.
THE ROOF CAUGHT IT. I CAN'T BELIEVE HOW LUCKY WE ARE. YOU GUYS OKAY?
YEAH. DOES ANYONE SEE MY CANE?
HERE IT IS!
HAVE YOU BEEN DRINKING, MA'AM?
OF COURSE NOT! I WASN'T EVEN DRIVING! MY CAR WAS ON AUTOPILOT!
A SELF-DRIVING CAR? MAYBE WE AREN'T LUCKY. MAYBE THIS WHOLE THING PLAYED OUT EXACTLY AS PLANNED.
UHHH, HOW SO?
HONEY? CAN WE TALK?
HERE--FOR MY SHARE OF THE BILL.
I HAVE TO GO.

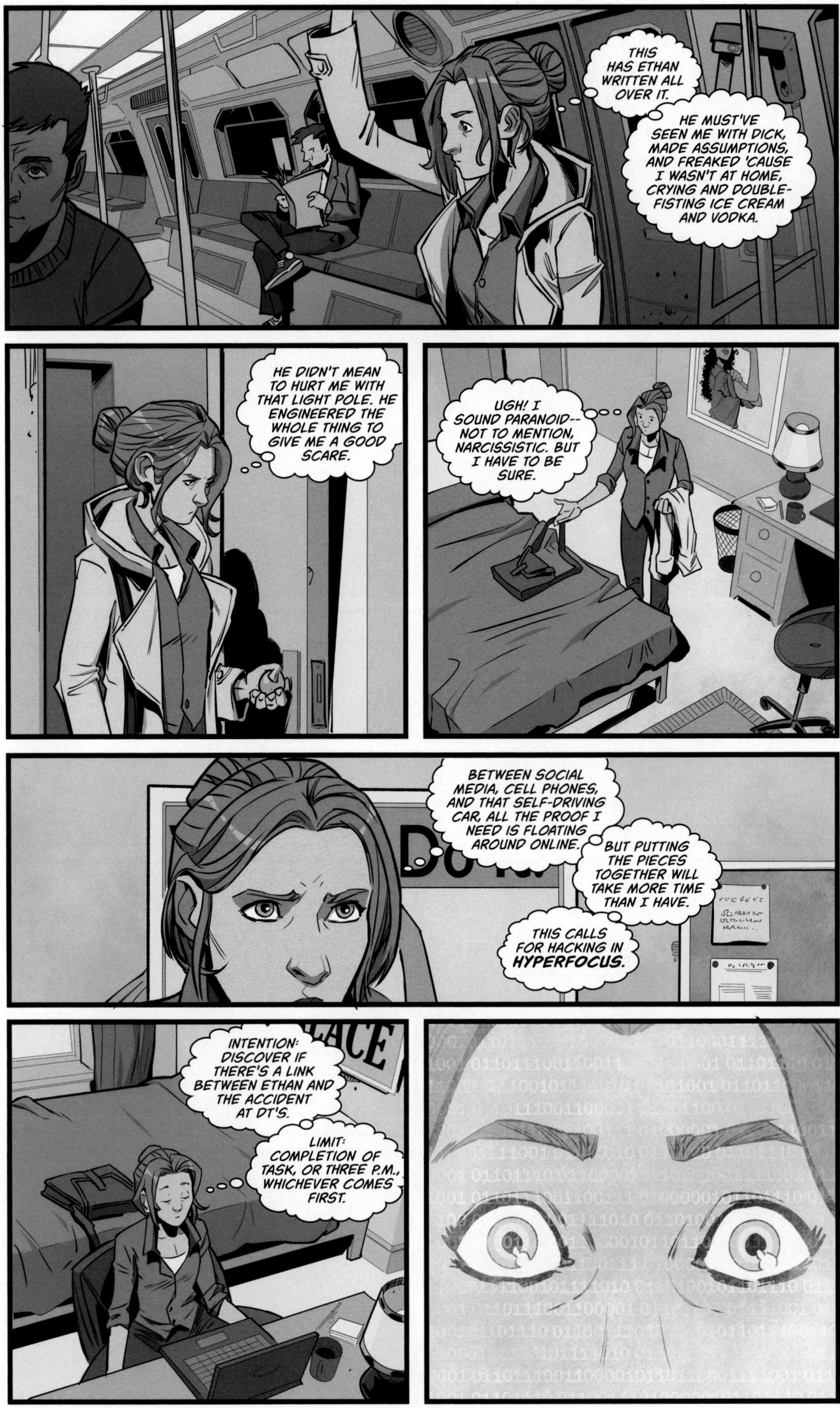
THIS HAS ETHAN WRITTEN ALL OVER IT.
HE MUST'VE SEEN ME WITH DICK, MADE ASSUMPTIONS, AND FREAKED 'CAUSE I WASN'T AT HOME, CRYING AND DOUBLE-FISTING ICE CREAM AND VODKA.
HE DIDN'T MEAN TO HURT ME WITH THAT LIGHT POLE. HE ENGINEERED THE WHOLE THING TO GIVE ME A GOOD SCARE.
UGH! I SOUND PARANOID-- NOT TO MENTION, NARCISSISTIC. BUT I HAVE TO BE SURE.
BETWEEN SOCIAL MEDIA, CELL PHONES, AND THAT SELF-DRIVING CAR, ALL THE PROOF I NEED IS FLOATING AROUND ONLINE.
BUT PUTTING THE PIECES TOGETHER WILL TAKE MORE TIME THAN I HAVE.
THIS CALLS FOR HACKING IN HYPERFOCUS.
INTENTION: DISCOVER IF THERE'S A LINK BETWEEN ETHAN AND THE ACCIDENT AT DT'S.
LIMIT: COMPLETION OF TASK, OR THREE P.M., WHICHEVER COMES FIRST.

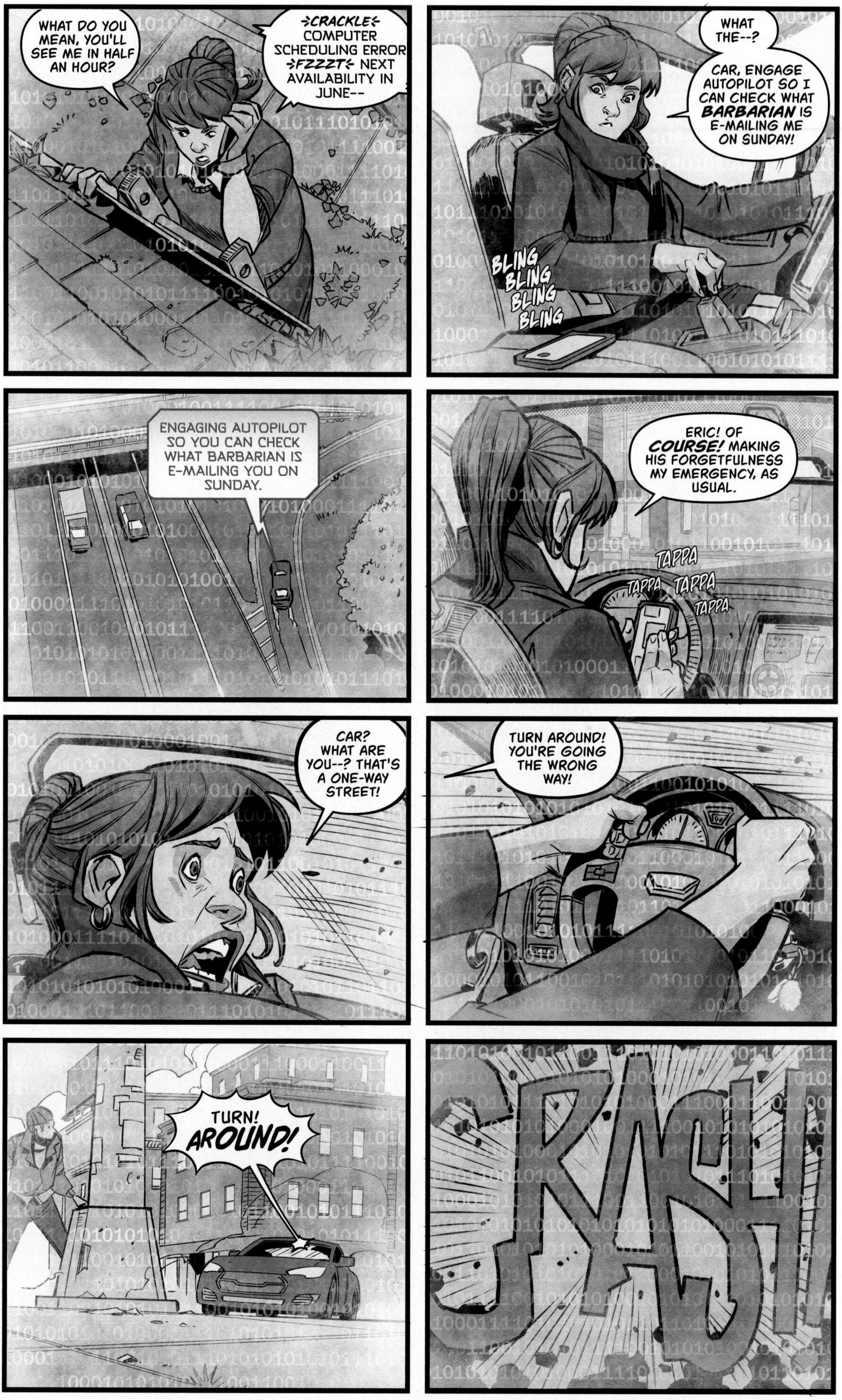
WHAT DO YOU MEAN, YOU'LL SEE ME IN HALF AN HOUR?
-CRACKLE- COMPUTER SCHEDULING ERROR -FZZZT- NEXT AVAILABILITY IN JUNE--
WHAT THE--?
CAR, ENGAGE AUTOPILOT SO I CAN CHECK WHAT BARBARIAN IS E-MAILING ME ON SUNDAY!
BLING BLING BLING BLING
ENGAGING AUTOPILOT SO YOU CAN CHECK WHAT BARBARIAN IS E-MAILING YOU ON SUNDAY.
ERIC! OF COURSE! MAKING HIS FORGETFULNESS MY EMERGENCY, AS USUAL.
TAPPA TAPPA TAPPA TAPPA
CAR? WHAT ARE YOU--? THAT'S A ONE-WAY STREET!
TURN AROUND! YOU'RE GOING THE WRONG WAY!
TURN! AROUND!
CRASH!

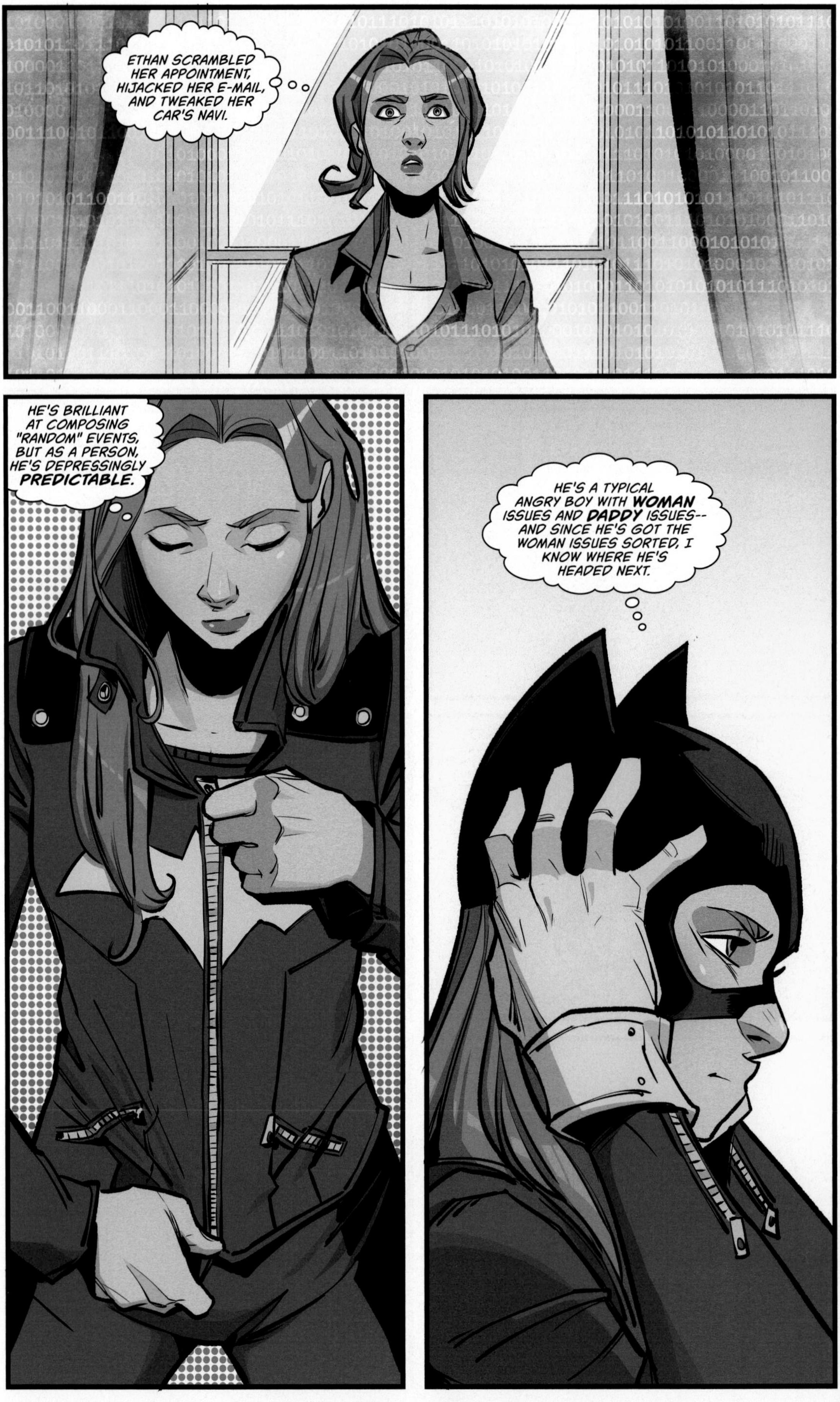
ETHAN SCRAMBLED HER APPOINTMENT, HIJACKED HER E-MAIL, AND TWEAKED HER CAR'S NAVI.
HE'S BRILLIANT AT COMPOSING "RANDOM" EVENTS, BUT AS A PERSON, HE'S DEPRESSINGLY PREDICTABLE.
HE'S A TYPICAL ANGRY BOY WITH WOMAN ISSUES AND DADDY ISSUES-- AND SINCE HE'S GOT THE WOMAN ISSUES SORTED, I KNOW WHERE HE'S HEADED NEXT.

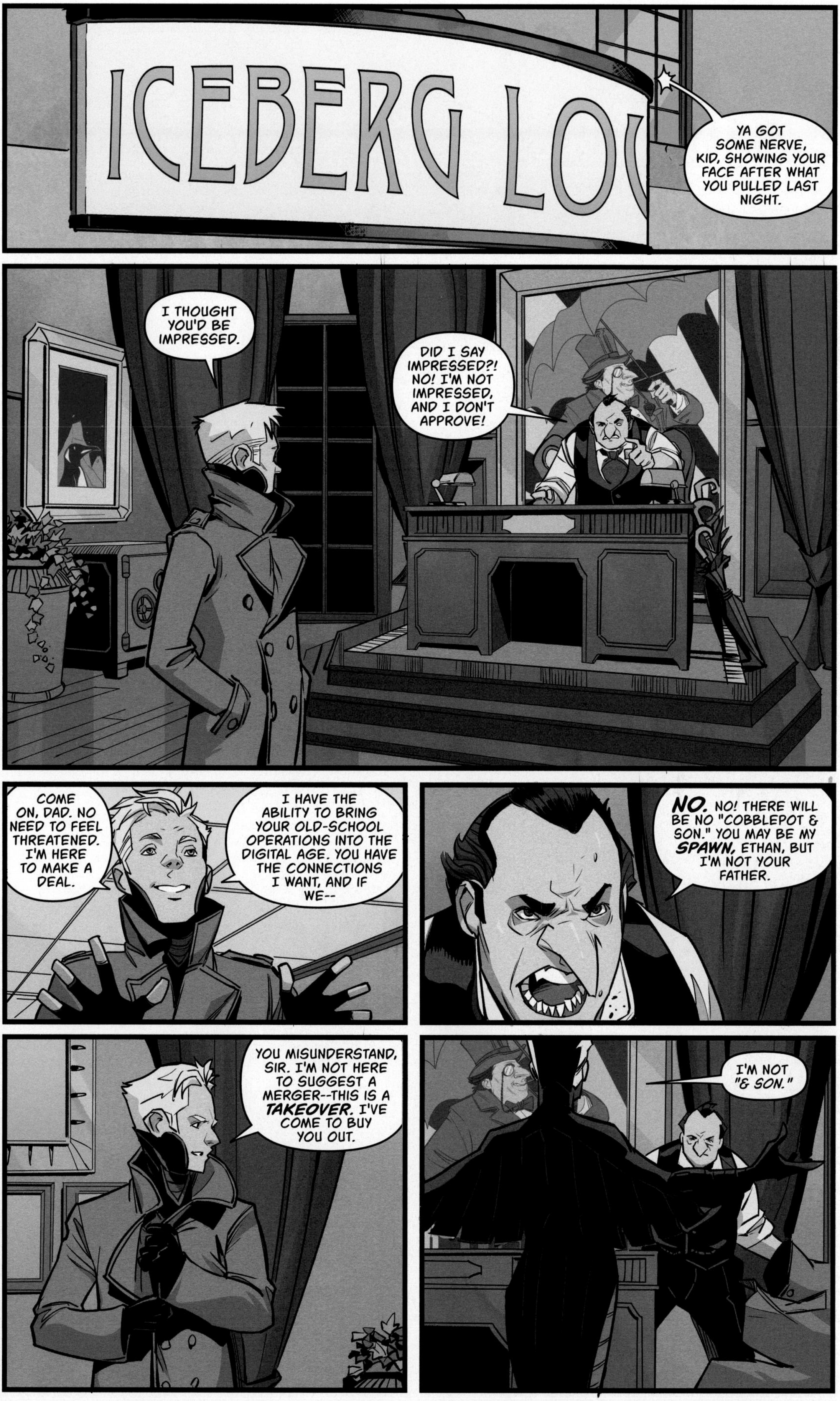
ICEBERG LOU
YA GOT SOME NERVE, KID, SHOWING YOUR FACE AFTER WHAT YOU PULLED LAST NIGHT.
I THOUGHT YOU'D BE IMPRESSED.
DID I SAY IMPRESSED?! NO! I'M NOT IMPRESSED, AND I DON'T APPROVE!
COME ON, DAD. NO NEED TO FEEL THREATENED. I'M HERE TO MAKE A DEAL.
I HAVE THE ABILITY TO BRING YOUR OLD-SCHOOL OPERATIONS INTO THE DIGITAL AGE. YOU HAVE THE CONNECTIONS I WANT, AND IF WE--
NO. NO! THERE WILL BE NO "COBBLEPOT & SON." YOU MAY BE MY SPAWN, ETHAN, BUT I'M NOT YOUR FATHER.
YOU MISUNDERSTAND, SIR. I'M NOT HERE TO SUGGEST A MERGER--THIS IS A TAKEOVER. I'VE COME TO BUY YOU OUT.
I'M NOT "& SON."

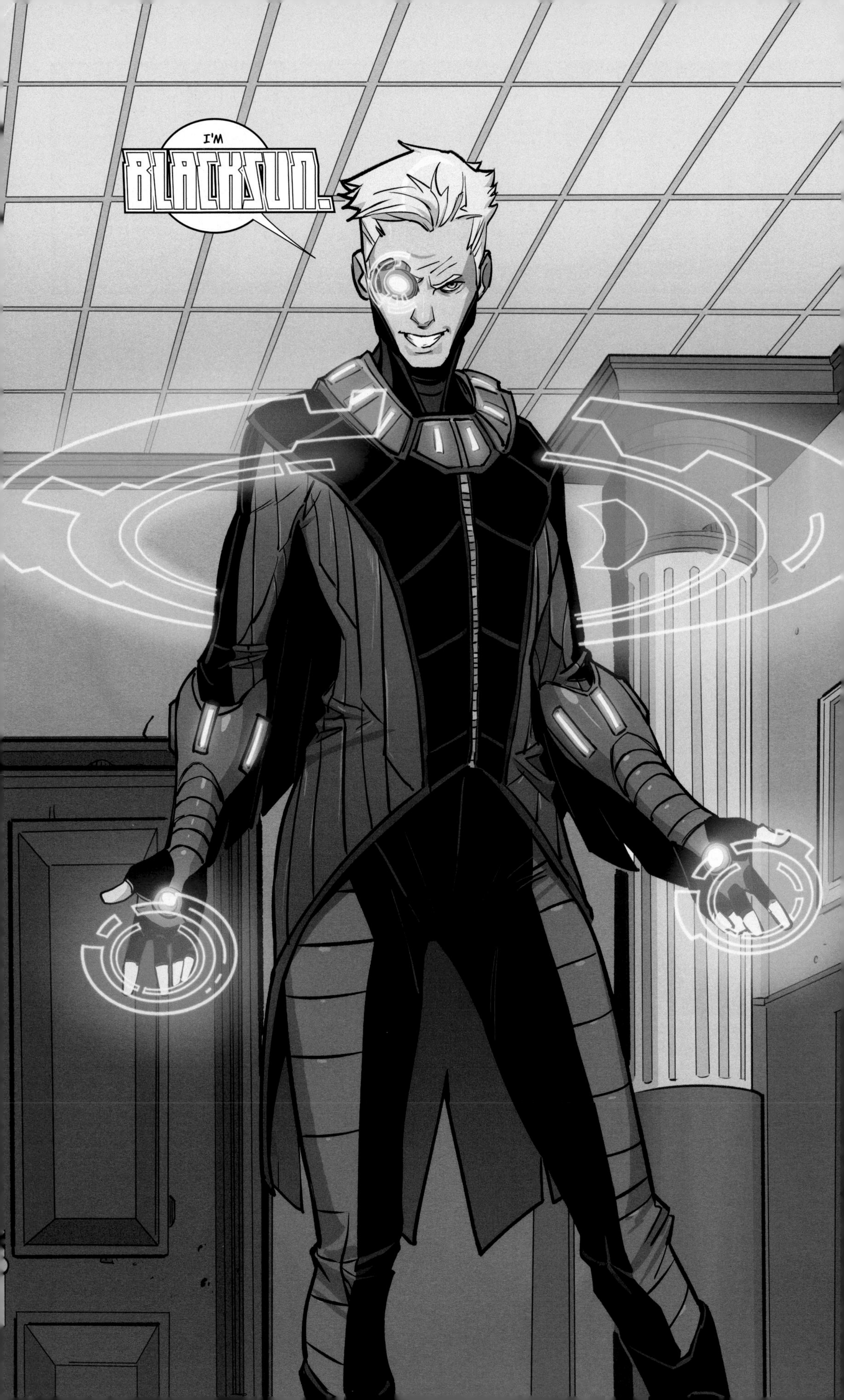
I'M BLACKSUN.

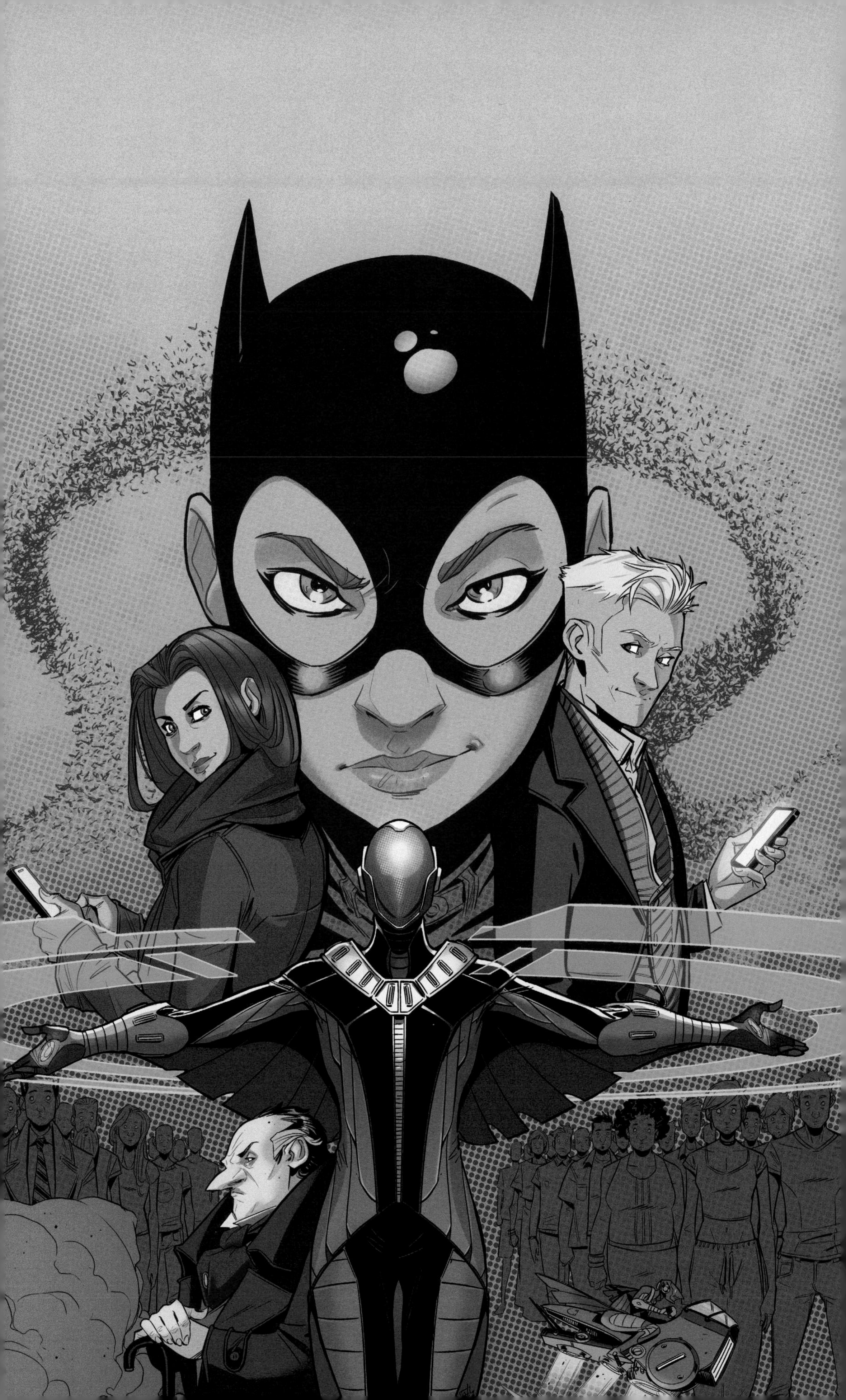

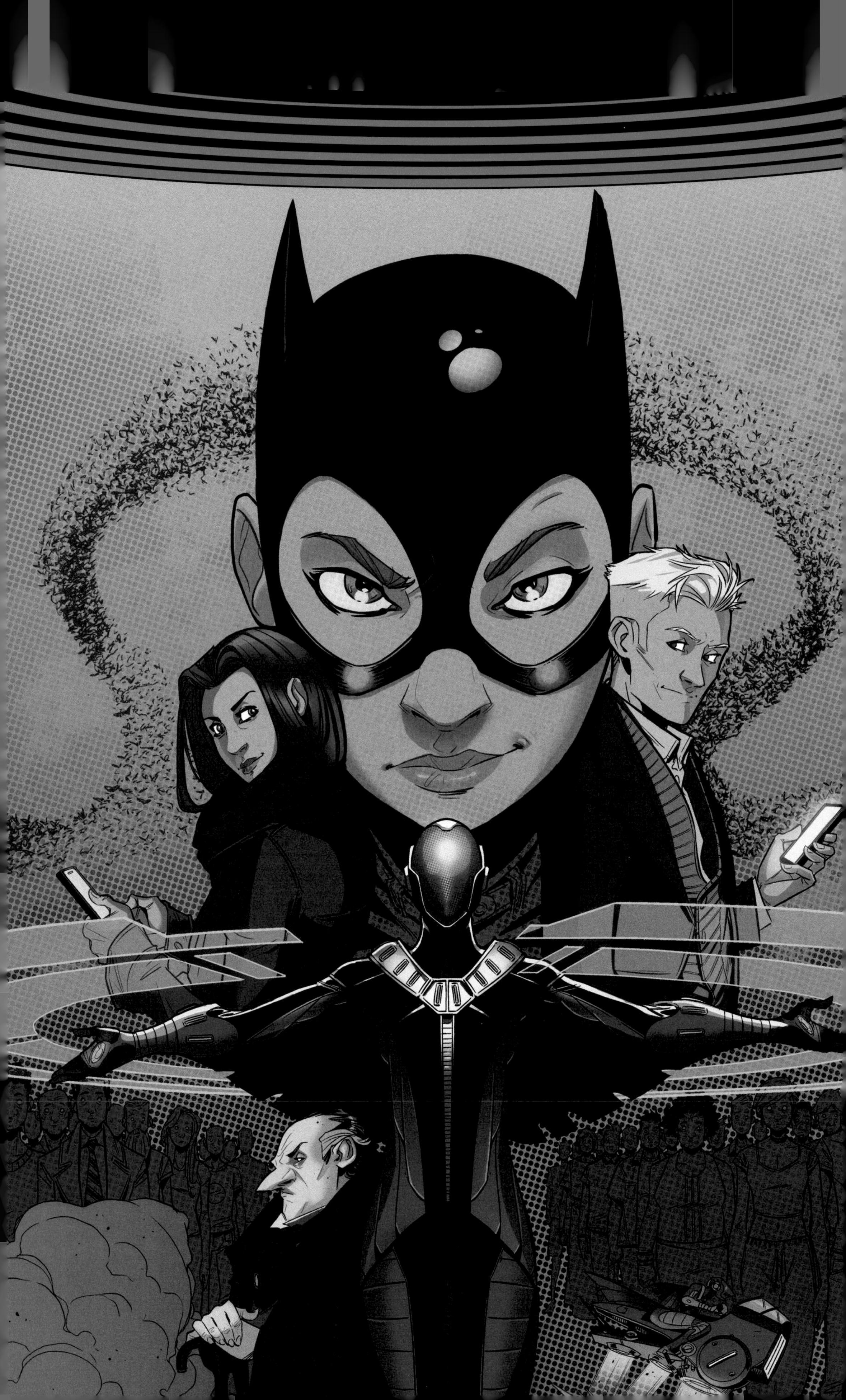

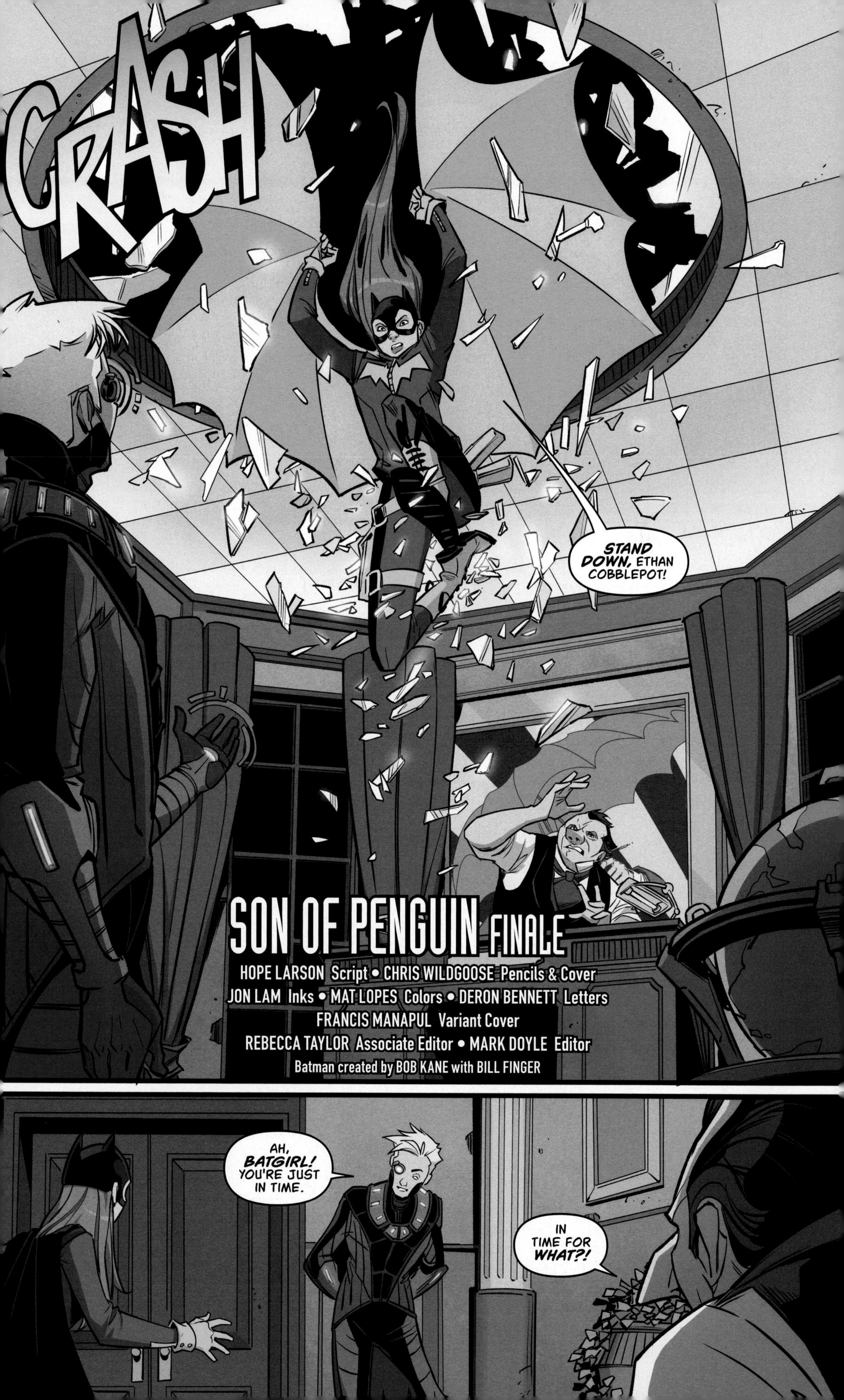
CRASH
STAND DOWN, ETHAN COBBLEPOT!
SON OF PENGUIN FINALE
HOPE LARSON Script • CHRIS WILDGOOSE Pencils & Cover
JON LAM Inks • MAT LOPES Colors • DERON BENNETT Letters
FRANCIS MANAPUL Variant Cover
REBECCA TAYLOR Associate Editor • MARK DOYLE Editor
Batman created by BOB KANE with BILL FINGER
AH, BATGIRL! YOU'RE JUST IN TIME.
IN TIME FOR WHAT?!

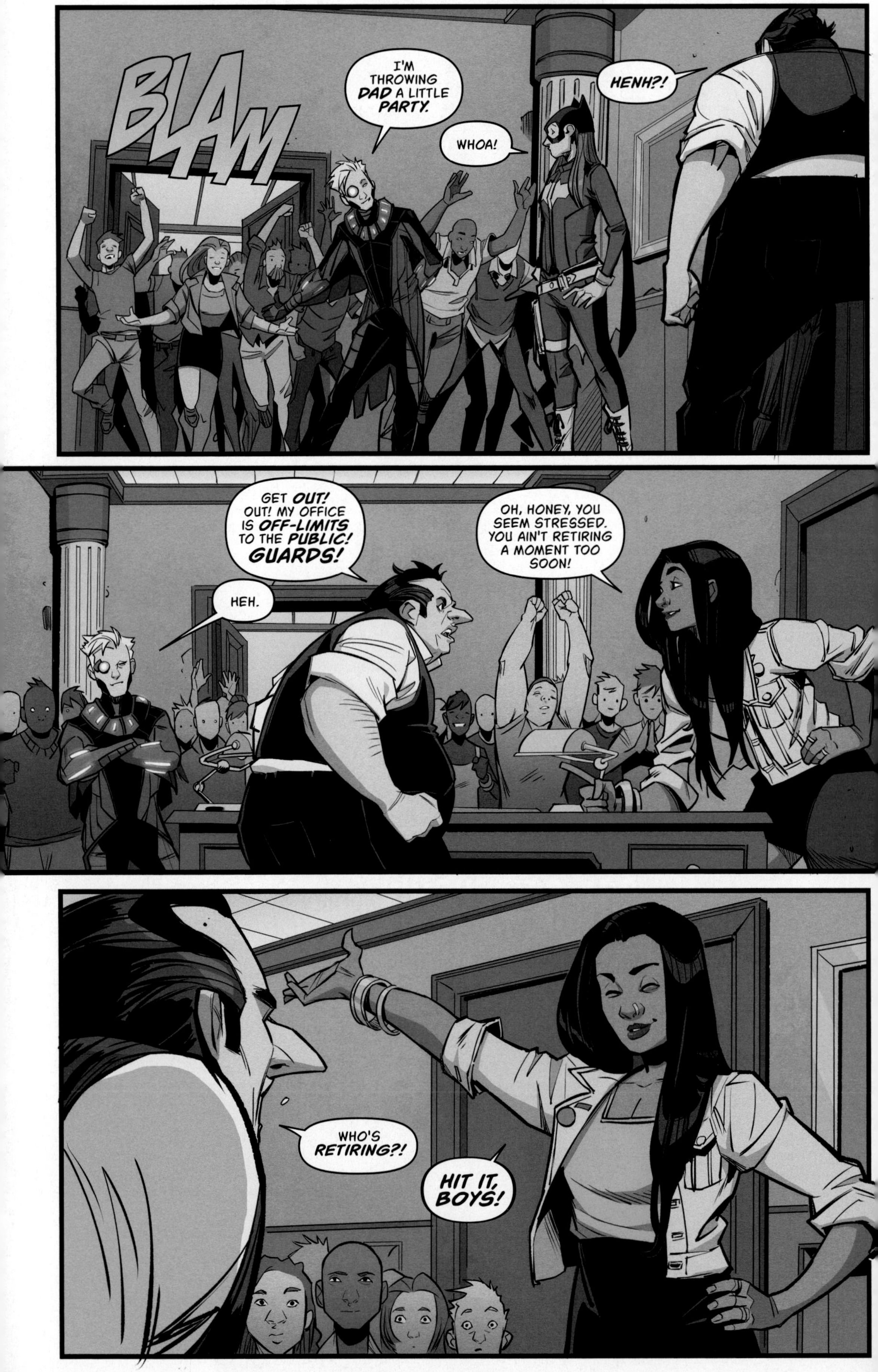
BLAM
I'M THROWING DAD A LITTLE PARTY.
WHOA!
HENH?!
GET OUT! OUT! MY OFFICE IS OFF-LIMITS TO THE PUBLIC! GUARDS!
HEH.
OH, HONEY, YOU SEEM STRESSED. YOU AIN'T RETIRING A MOMENT TOO SOON!
WHO'S RETIRING?!
HIT IT, BOYS!

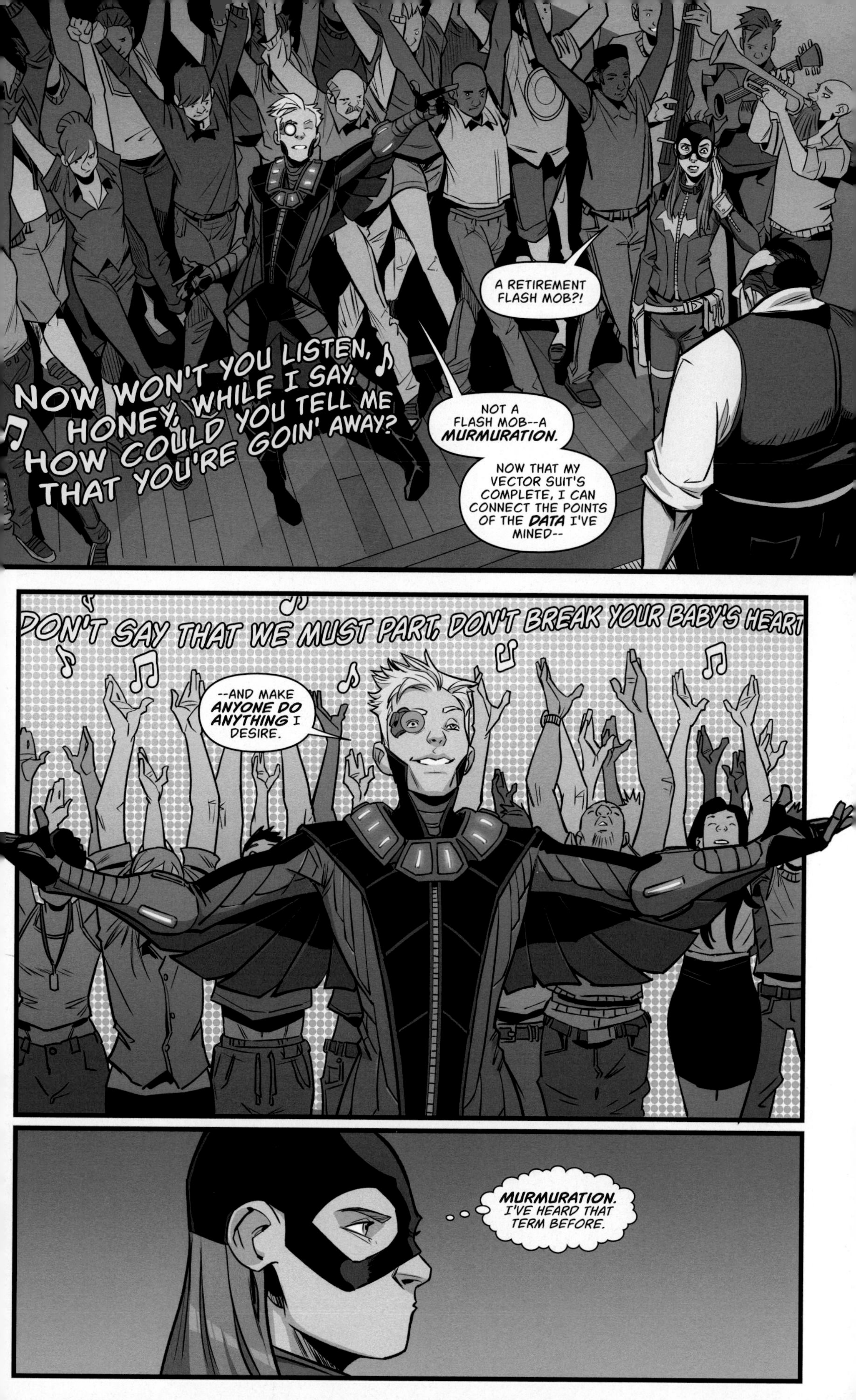

NOW WON'T YOU LISTEN, HONEY, WHILE I SAY, HOW COULD YOU TELL ME THAT YOU'RE GOIN' AWAY?
A RETIREMENT FLASH MOB?!
NOT A FLASH MOB--A MURMURATION.
NOW THAT MY VECTOR SUIT'S COMPLETE, I CAN CONNECT THE POINTS OF THE DATA I'VE MINED--
DON'T SAY THAT WE MUST PART, DON'T BREAK YOUR BABY'S HEART
--AND MAKE ANYONE DO ANYTHING I DESIRE.
MURMURATION. I'VE HEARD THAT TERM BEFORE.

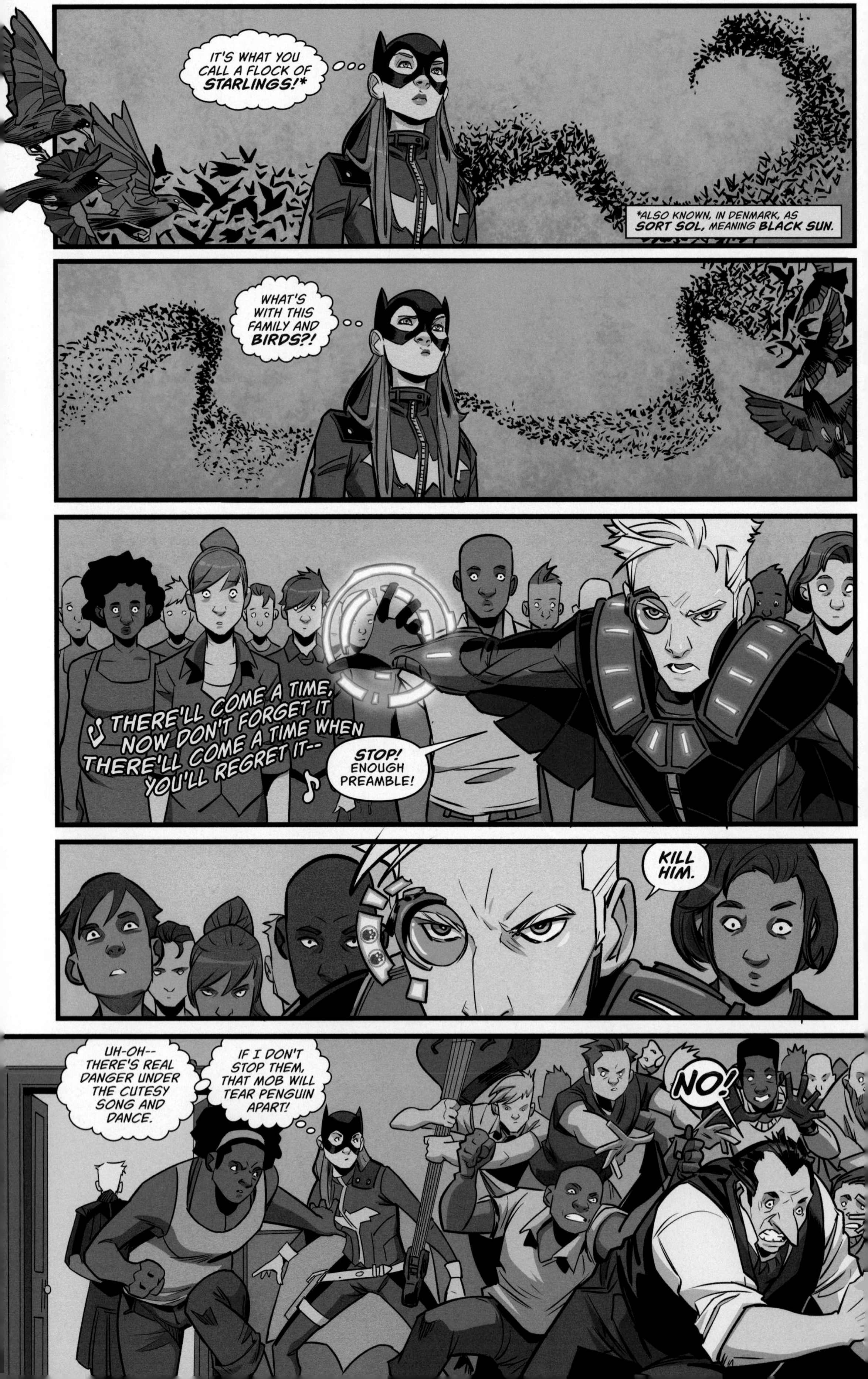
IT'S WHAT YOU CALL A FLOCK OF STARLINGS!*
*ALSO KNOWN, IN DENMARK, AS SORT SOL, MEANING BLACK SUN.
WHAT'S WITH THIS FAMILY AND BIRDS?!
THERE'LL COME A TIME, NOW DON'T FORGET IT NOW THERE'LL COME A TIME WHEN YOU'LL REGRET IT--
STOP! ENOUGH PREAMBLE!
KILL HIM.
UH-OH-- THERE'S REAL DANGER UNDER THE CUTESY SONG AND DANCE.
IF I DON'T STOP THEM, THAT MOB WILL TEAR PENGUIN APART!
NO!

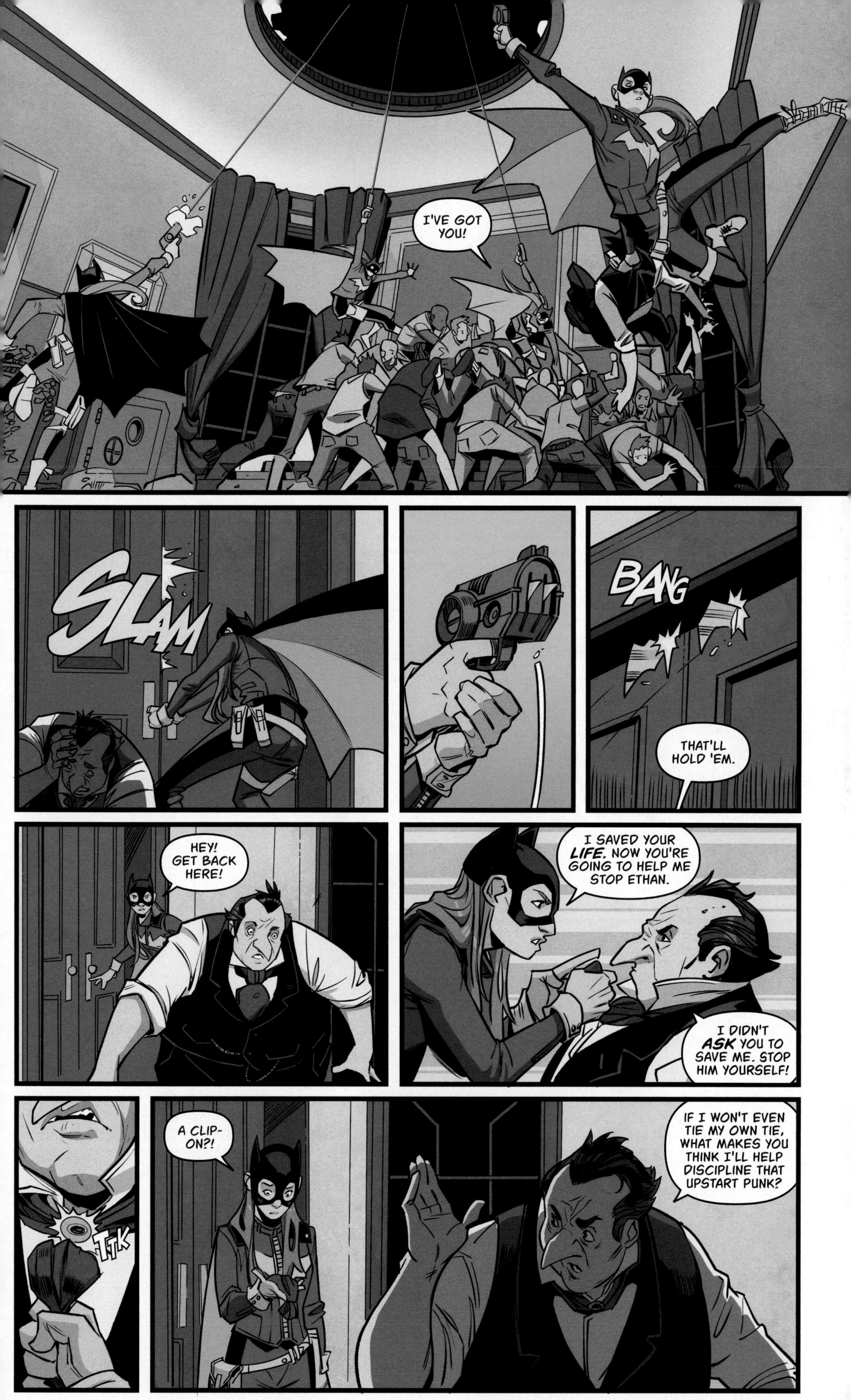
I'VE GOT YOU!
SLAM
BANG
THAT'LL HOLD 'EM.
HEY! GET BACK HERE!
I SAVED YOUR LIFE. NOW YOU'RE GOING TO HELP ME STOP ETHAN.
I DIDN'T ASK YOU TO SAVE ME. STOP HIM YOURSELF!
TTK
A CLIP-ON?!
IF I WON'T EVEN TIE MY OWN TIE, WHAT MAKES YOU THINK I'LL HELP DISCIPLINE THAT UPSTART PUNK?

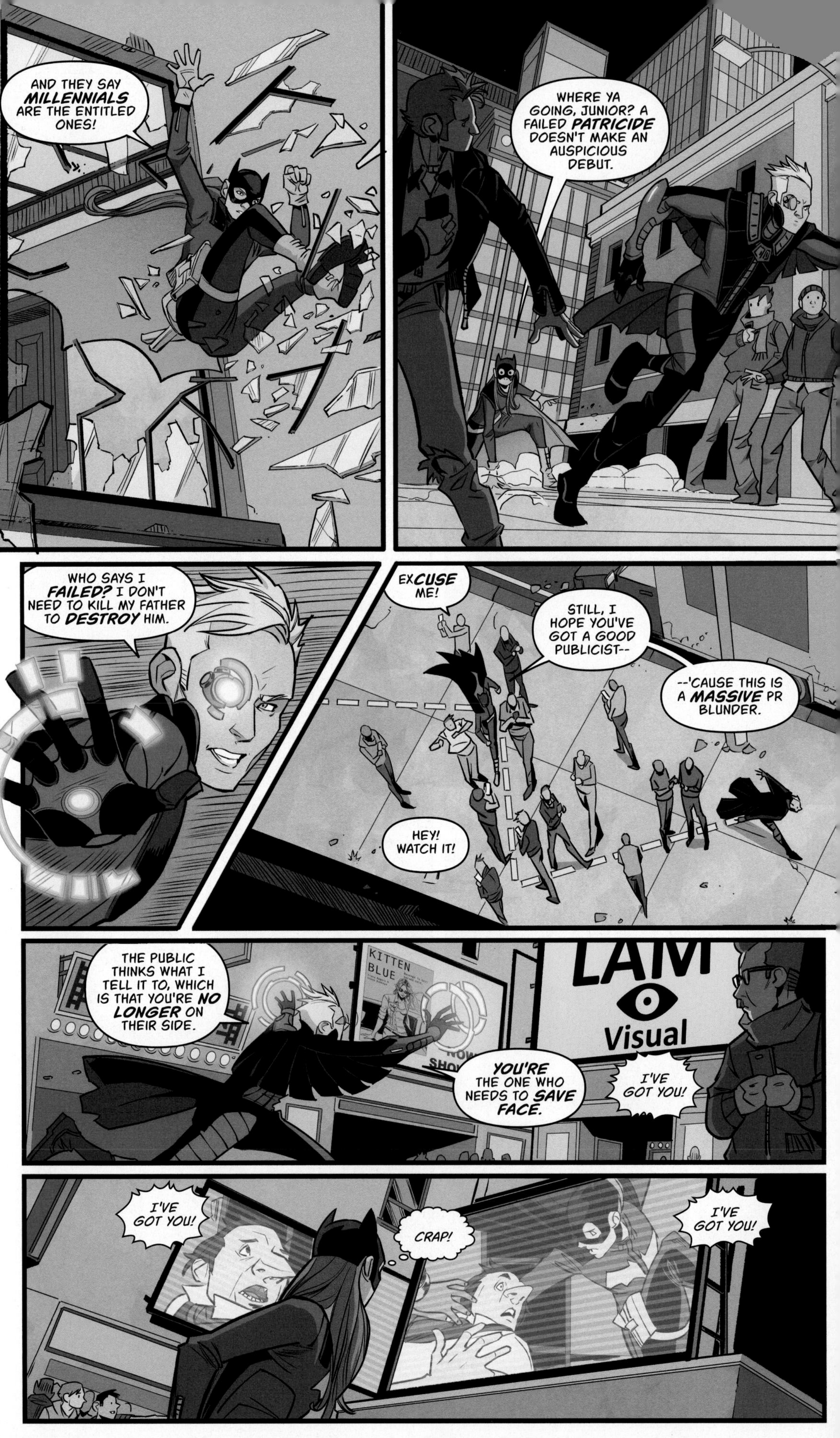
AND THEY SAY MILLENNIALS ARE THE ENTITLED ONES!
WHERE YA GOING, JUNIOR? A FAILED PATRICIDE DOESN'T MAKE AN AUSPICIOUS DEBUT.
WHO SAYS I FAILED? I DON'T NEED TO KILL MY FATHER TO DESTROY HIM.
EXCUSE ME!
STILL, I HOPE YOU'VE GOT A GOOD PUBLICIST--
--'CAUSE THIS IS A MASSIVE PR BLUNDER.
HEY! WATCH IT!
THE PUBLIC THINKS WHAT I TELL IT TO, WHICH IS THAT YOU'RE NO LONGER ON THEIR SIDE.
KITTEN BLUE
LAM
Visual
YOU'RE THE ONE WHO NEEDS TO SAVE FACE.
I'VE GOT YOU!
I'VE GOT YOU!
CRAP!
I'VE GOT YOU!

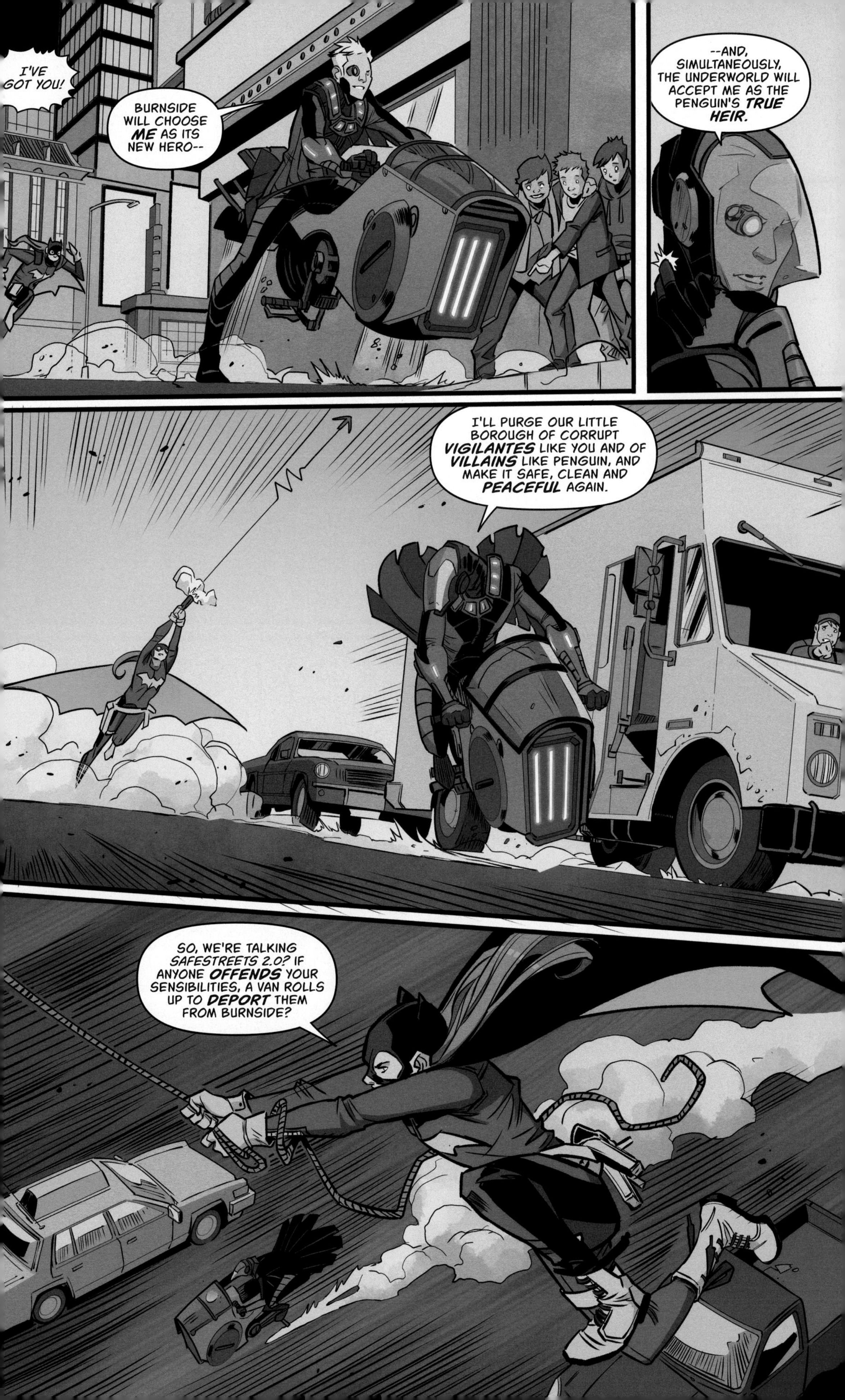
I'VE GOT YOU!
BURNSIDE WILL CHOOSE ME AS ITS NEW HERO--
--AND, SIMULTANEOUSLY, THE UNDERWORLD WILL ACCEPT ME AS THE PENGUIN'S TRUE HEIR.
I'LL PURGE OUR LITTLE BOROUGH OF CORRUPT VIGILANTES LIKE YOU AND OF VILLAINS LIKE PENGUIN, AND MAKE IT SAFE, CLEAN AND PEACEFUL AGAIN.
SO, WE'RE TALKING SAFESTREETS 2.0? IF ANYONE OFFENDS YOUR SENSIBILITIES, A VAN ROLLS UP TO DEPORT THEM FROM BURNSIDE?

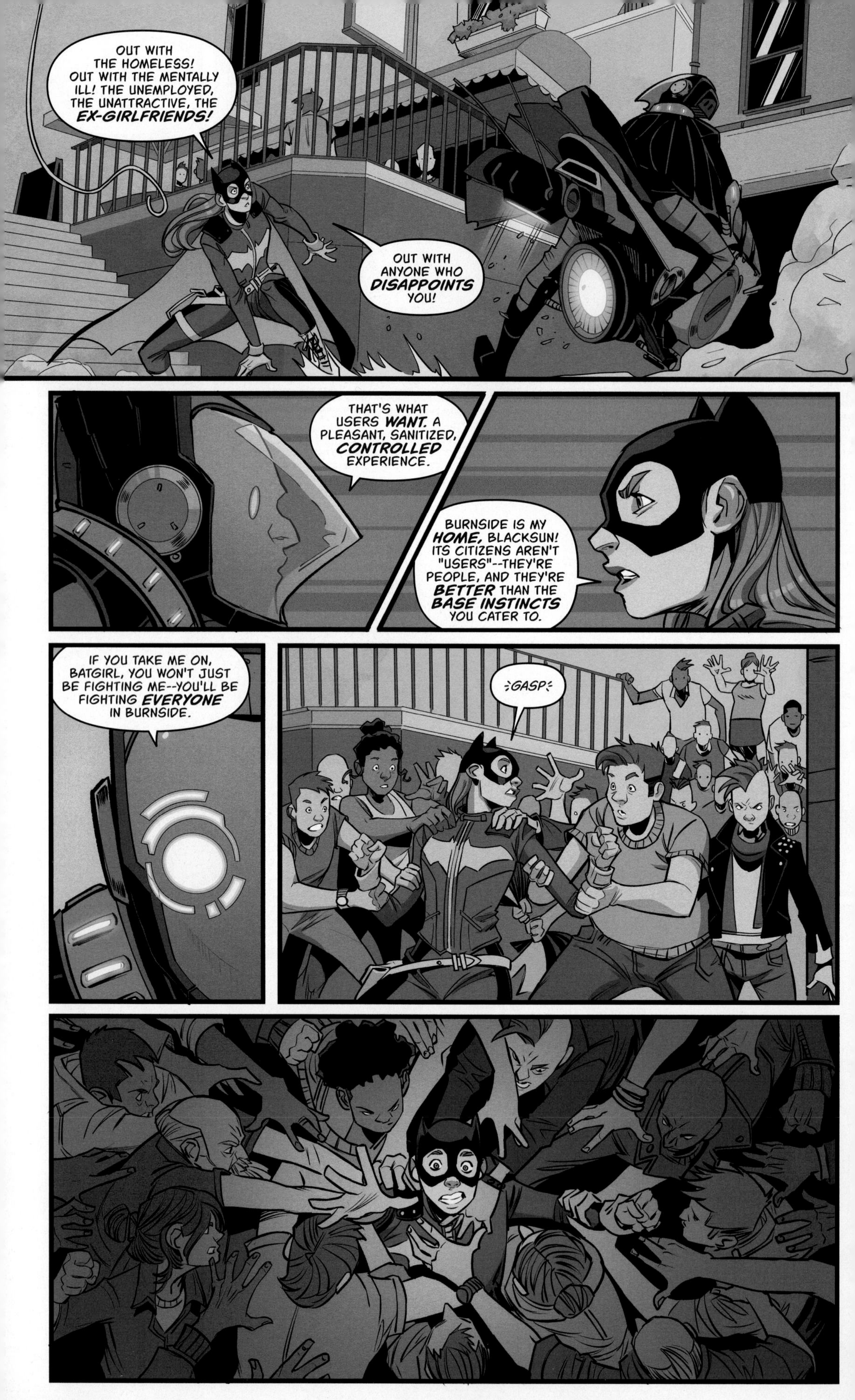
OUT WITH THE HOMELESS! OUT WITH THE MENTALLY ILL! THE UNEMPLOYED, THE UNATTRACTIVE, THE EX-GIRLFRIENDS!
OUT WITH ANYONE WHO DISAPPOINTS YOU!
THAT'S WHAT USERS WANT. A PLEASANT, SANITIZED, CONTROLLED EXPERIENCE.
BURNSIDE IS MY HOME, BLACKSUN! ITS CITIZENS AREN'T "USERS"--THEY'RE PEOPLE, AND THEY'RE BETTER THAN THE BASE INSTINCTS YOU CATER TO.
IF YOU TAKE ME ON, BATGIRL, YOU WON'T JUST BE FIGHTING ME--YOU'LL BE FIGHTING EVERYONE IN BURNSIDE.
GASP

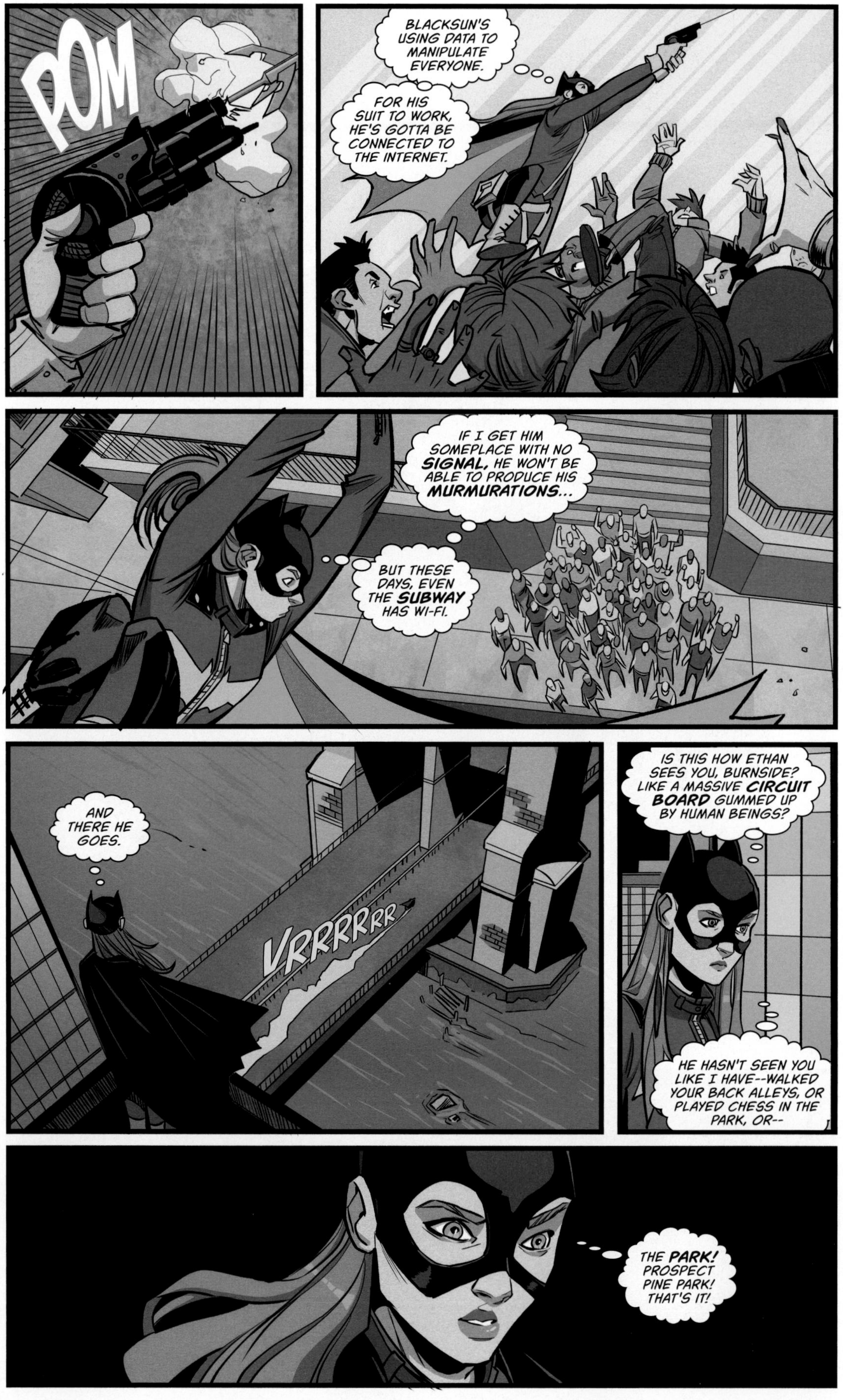
POM
BLACKSUN'S USING DATA TO MANIPULATE EVERYONE.
FOR HIS SUIT TO WORK, HE'S GOTTA BE CONNECTED TO THE INTERNET.
IF I GET HIM SOMEPLACE WITH NO SIGNAL, HE WON'T BE ABLE TO PRODUCE HIS MURMURATIONS...
BUT THESE DAYS, EVEN THE SUBWAY HAS WI-FI.
AND THERE HE GOES.
VRRRRRR
IS THIS HOW ETHAN SEES YOU, BURNSIDE? LIKE A MASSIVE CIRCUIT BOARD GUMMED UP BY HUMAN BEINGS?
HE HASN'T SEEN YOU LIKE I HAVE--WALKED YOUR BACK ALLEYS, OR PLAYED CHESS IN THE PARK, OR--
THE PARK! PROSPECT PINE PARK! THAT'S IT!

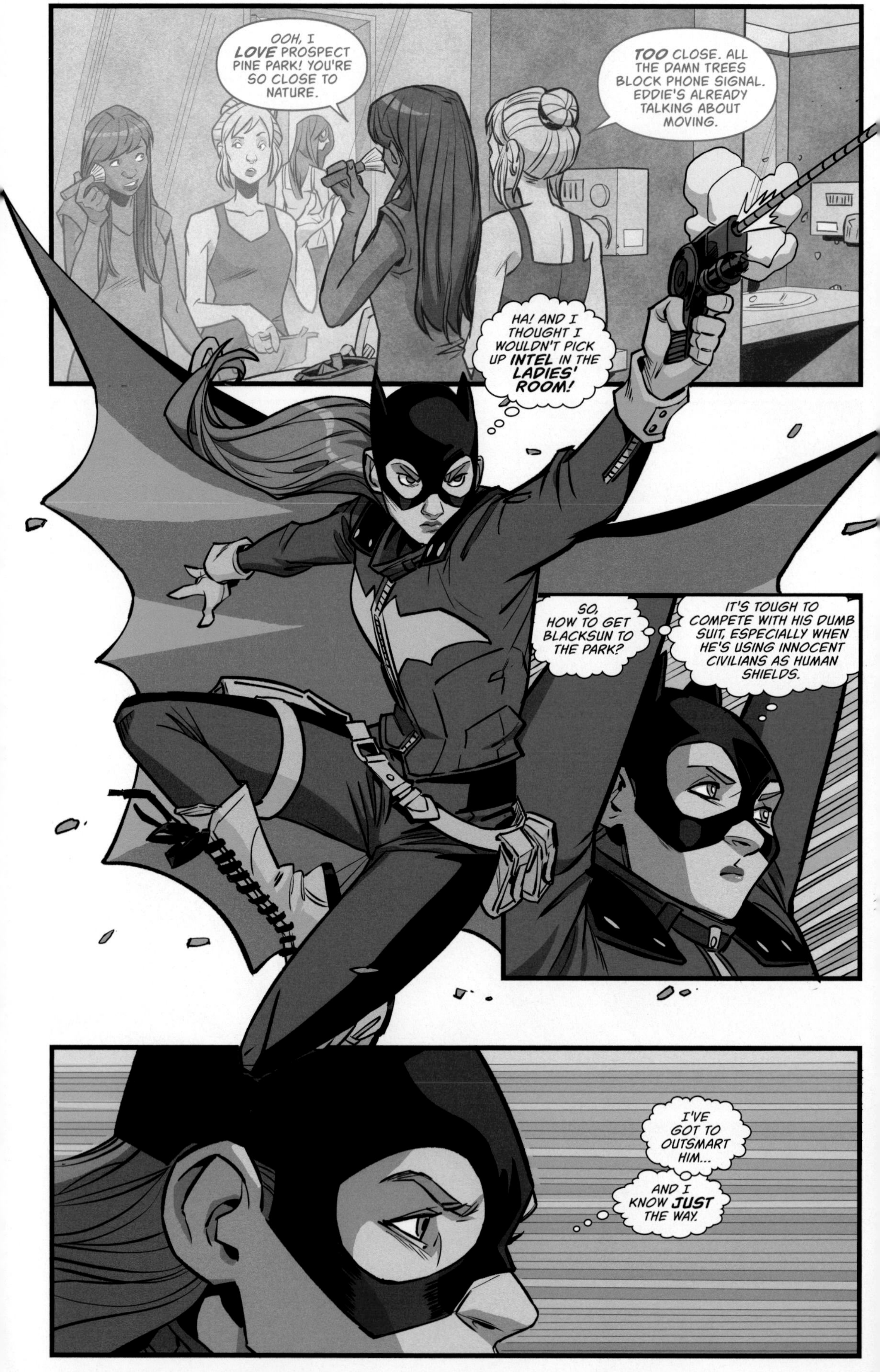

OOH, I LOVE PROSPECT PINE PARK! YOU'RE SO CLOSE TO NATURE.
TOO CLOSE. ALL THE DAMN TREES BLOCK PHONE SIGNAL. EDDIE'S ALREADY TALKING ABOUT MOVING.
HA! AND I THOUGHT I WOULDN'T PICK UP INTEL IN THE LADIES' ROOM!
SO, HOW TO GET BLACKSUN TO THE PARK?
IT'S TOUGH TO COMPETE WITH HIS DUMB SUIT, ESPECIALLY WHEN HE'S USING INNOCENT CIVILIANS AS HUMAN SHIELDS.
I'VE GOT TO OUTSMART HIM...
AND I KNOW JUST THE WAY.

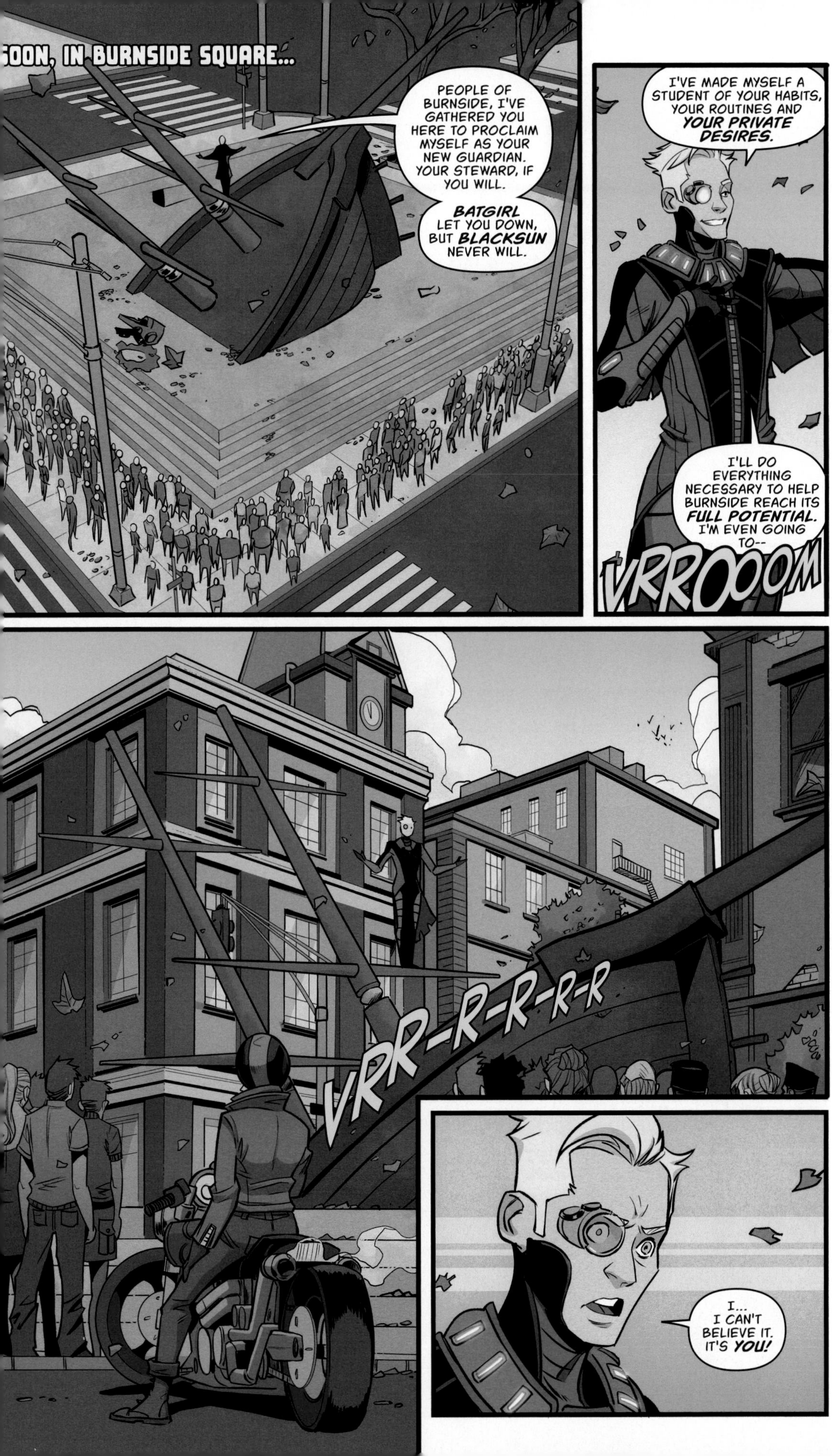

SOON, IN BURNSIDE SQUARE...
PEOPLE OF BURNSIDE, I'VE GATHERED YOU HERE TO PROCLAIM MYSELF AS YOUR NEW GUARDIAN. YOUR STEWARD, IF YOU WILL.
BATGIRL LET YOU DOWN, BUT BLACKSUN NEVER WILL.
I'VE MADE MYSELF A STUDENT OF YOUR HABITS, YOUR ROUTINES AND YOUR PRIVATE DESIRES.
I'LL DO EVERYTHING NECESSARY TO HELP BURNSIDE REACH ITS FULL POTENTIAL. I'M EVEN GOING TO--
VRROOOM
VRR-R-R-R-R
I... I CAN'T BELIEVE IT. IT'S YOU!

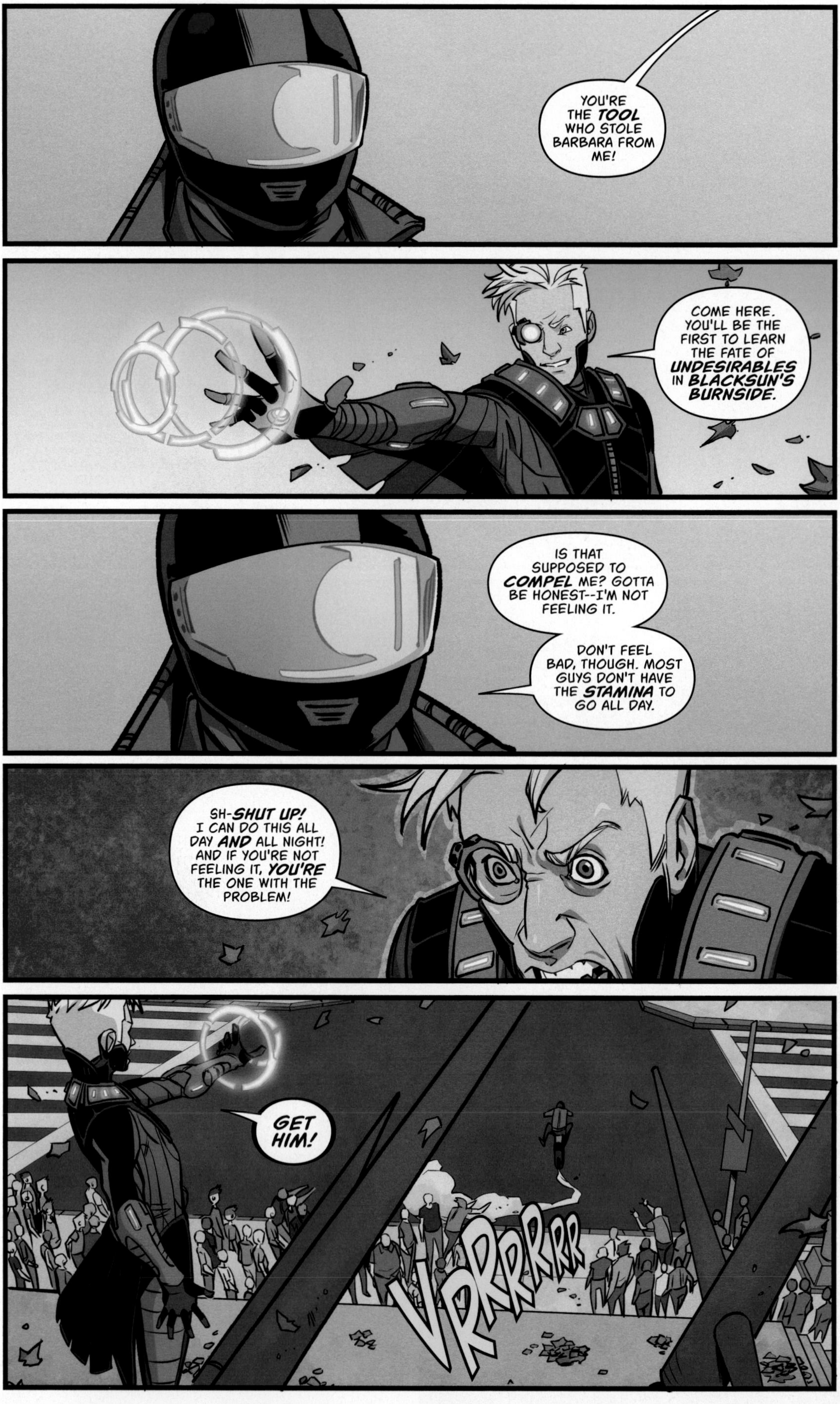
YOU'RE THE TOOL WHO STOLE BARBARA FROM ME!
COME HERE. YOU'LL BE THE FIRST TO LEARN THE FATE OF UNDESIRABLES IN BLACKSUN'S BURNSIDE.
IS THAT SUPPOSED TO COMPEL ME? GOTTA BE HONEST--I'M NOT FEELING IT.
DON'T FEEL BAD, THOUGH. MOST GUYS DON'T HAVE THE STAMINA TO GO ALL DAY.
SH-SHUT UP! I CAN DO THIS ALL DAY AND ALL NIGHT! AND IF YOU'RE NOT FEELING IT, YOU'RE THE ONE WITH THE PROBLEM!
GET HIM!
VRRRRRR

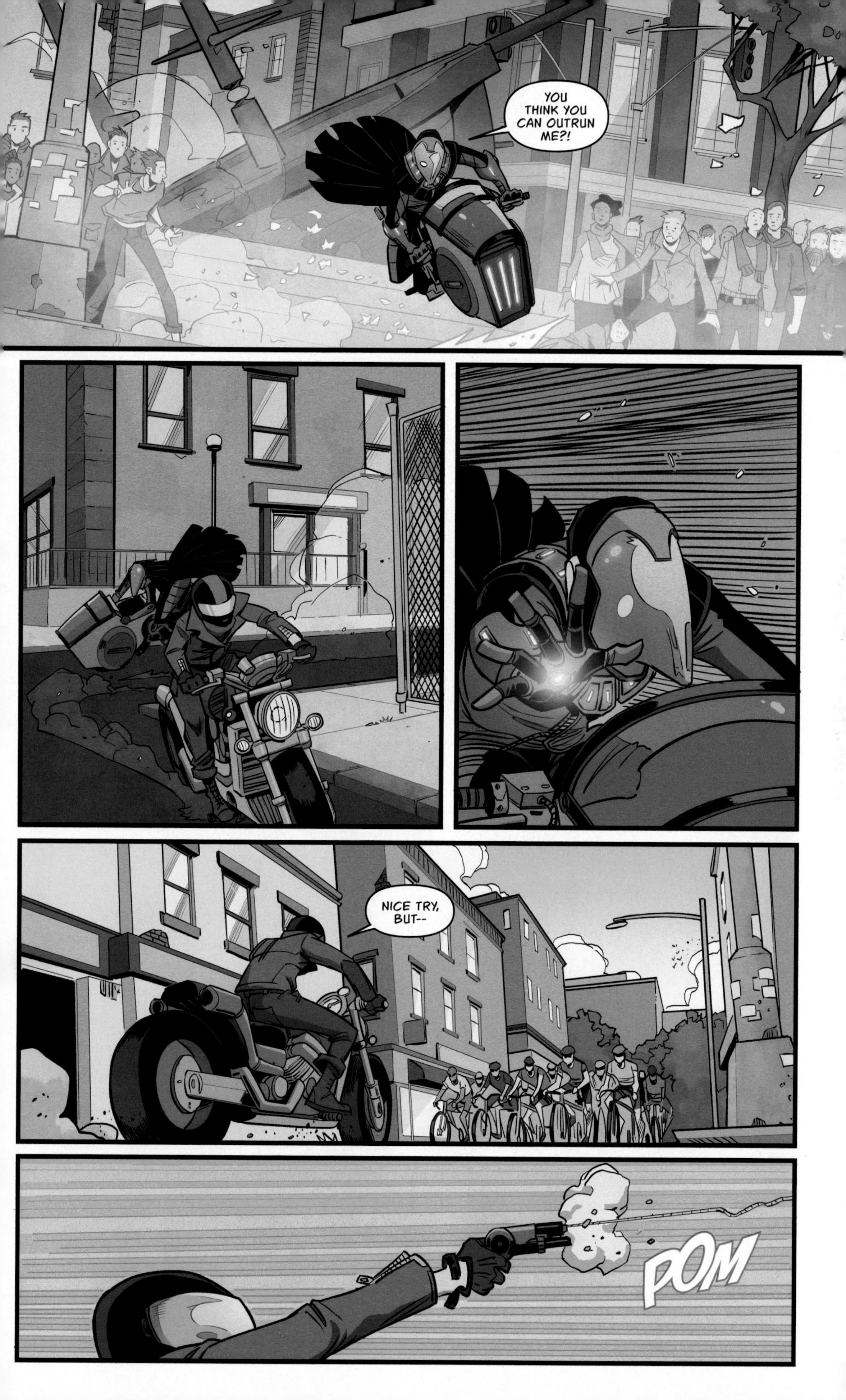
YOU THINK YOU CAN OUTRUN ME?!
NICE TRY, BUT--
POM

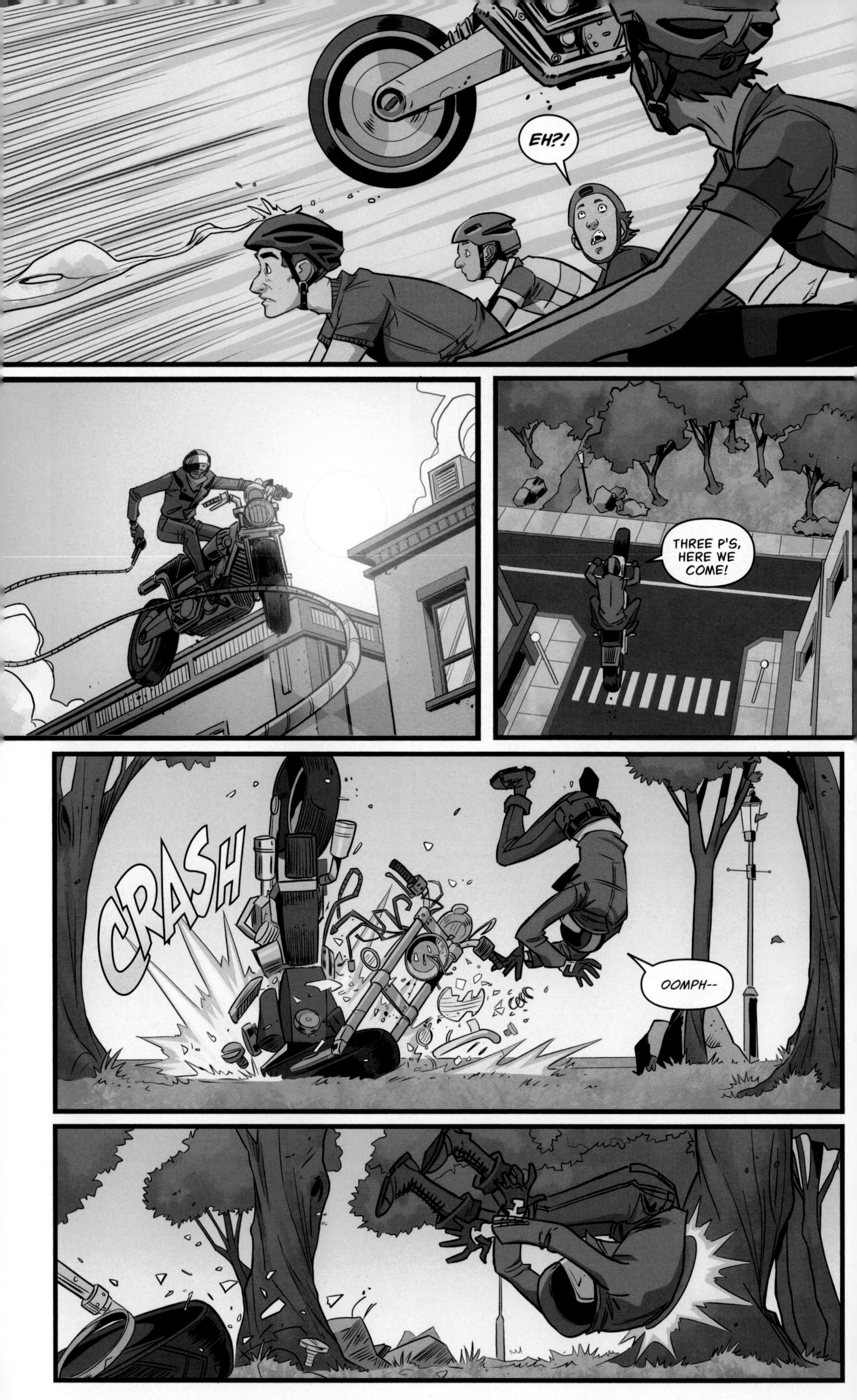
EH?!
THREE P'S, HERE WE COME!
CRASH
OOMPH--

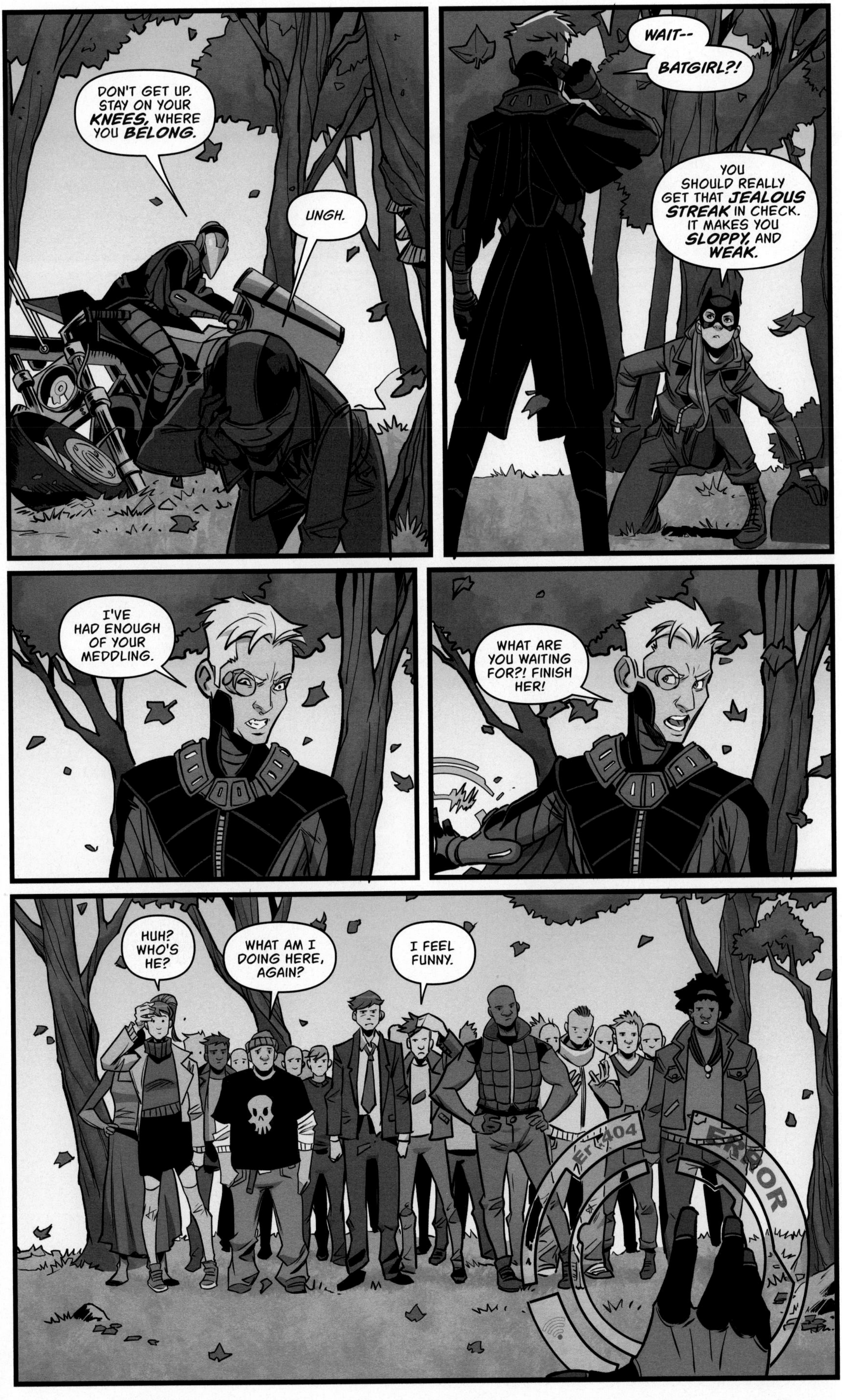
DON'T GET UP. STAY ON YOUR KNEES, WHERE YOU BELONG.
UNGH.
WAIT--
BATGIRL?!
YOU SHOULD REALLY GET THAT JEALOUS STREAK IN CHECK. IT MAKES YOU SLOPPY, AND WEAK.
I'VE HAD ENOUGH OF YOUR MEDDLING.
WHAT ARE YOU WAITING FOR?! FINISH HER!
HUH? WHO'S HE?
WHAT AM I DOING HERE, AGAIN?
I FEEL FUNNY.
Er 404
ERROR

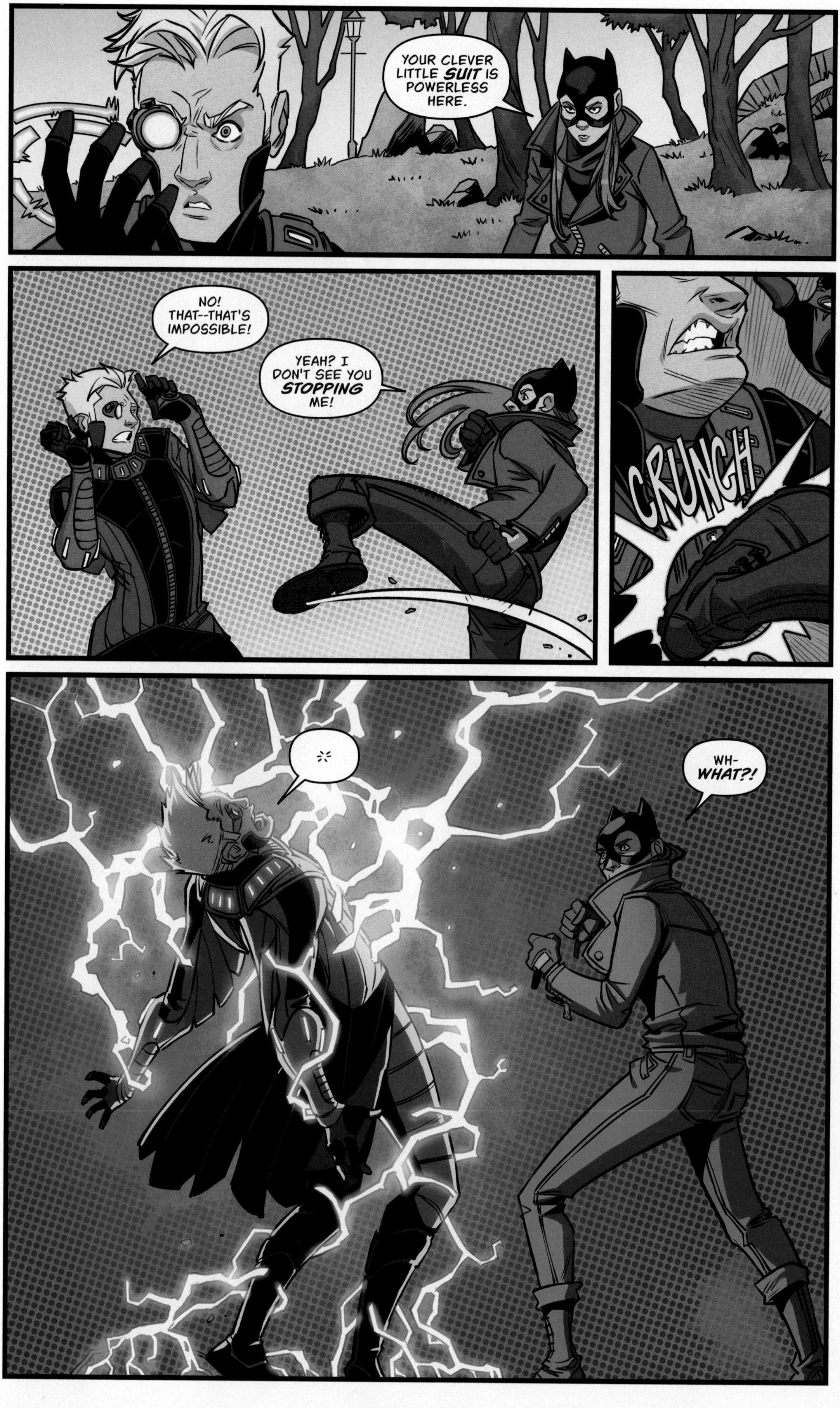
YOUR CLEVER LITTLE SUIT IS POWERLESS HERE.
NO! THAT--THAT'S IMPOSSIBLE!
YEAH? I DON'T SEE YOU STOPPING ME!
CRUNCH
:
WH-WHAT?!

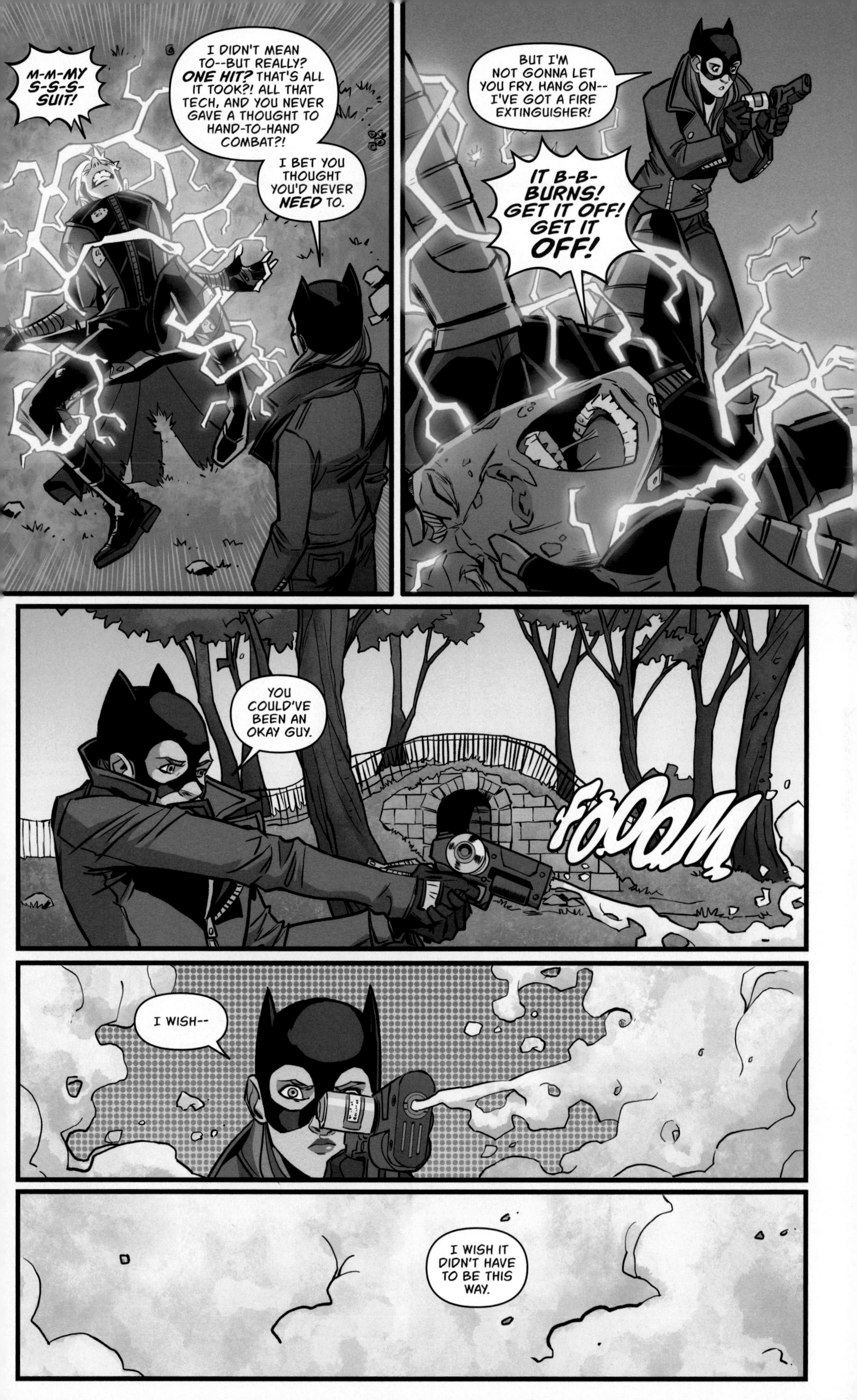
M-M-MY S-S-S-SUIT!
I DIDN'T MEAN TO--BUT REALLY? ONE HIT? THAT'S ALL IT TOOK?! ALL THAT TECH, AND YOU NEVER GAVE A THOUGHT TO HAND-TO-HAND COMBAT?!
I BET YOU THOUGHT YOU'D NEVER NEED TO.
BUT I'M NOT GONNA LET YOU FRY. HANG ON-- I'VE GOT A FIRE EXTINGUISHER!
IT B-B-BURNS! GET IT OFF! GET IT OFF!
YOU COULD'VE BEEN AN OKAY GUY.
FOOOM
I WISH--
I WISH IT DIDN'T HAVE TO BE THIS WAY.

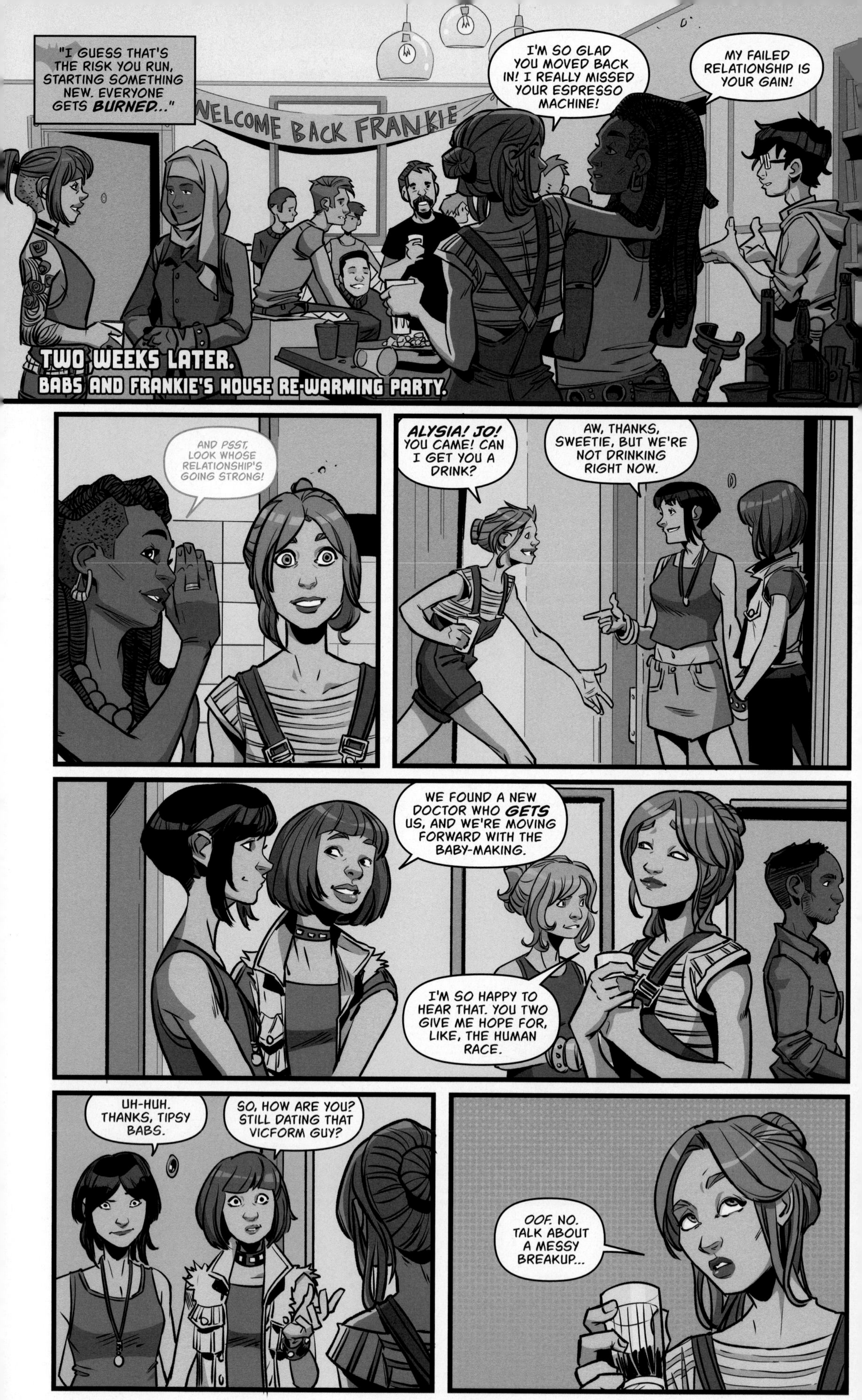
"I GUESS THAT'S THE RISK YOU RUN, STARTING SOMETHING NEW. EVERYONE GETS *BURNED...*"
WELCOME BACK FRANKIE
I'M SO GLAD YOU MOVED BACK IN! I REALLY MISSED YOUR ESPRESSO MACHINE!
MY FAILED RELATIONSHIP IS YOUR GAIN!
TWO WEEKS LATER.
BABS AND FRANKIE'S HOUSE RE-WARMING PARTY.
AND PSST, LOOK WHOSE RELATIONSHIP'S GOING STRONG!
ALYSIA! JO! YOU CAME! CAN I GET YOU A DRINK?
AW, THANKS, SWEETIE, BUT WE'RE NOT DRINKING RIGHT NOW.
WE FOUND A NEW DOCTOR WHO *GETS* US, AND WE'RE MOVING FORWARD WITH THE BABY-MAKING.
I'M SO HAPPY TO HEAR THAT. YOU TWO GIVE ME HOPE FOR, LIKE, THE HUMAN RACE.
UH-HUH. THANKS, TIPSY BABS.
SO, HOW ARE YOU? STILL DATING THAT VICFORM GUY?
OOF. NO. TALK ABOUT A MESSY BREAKUP...

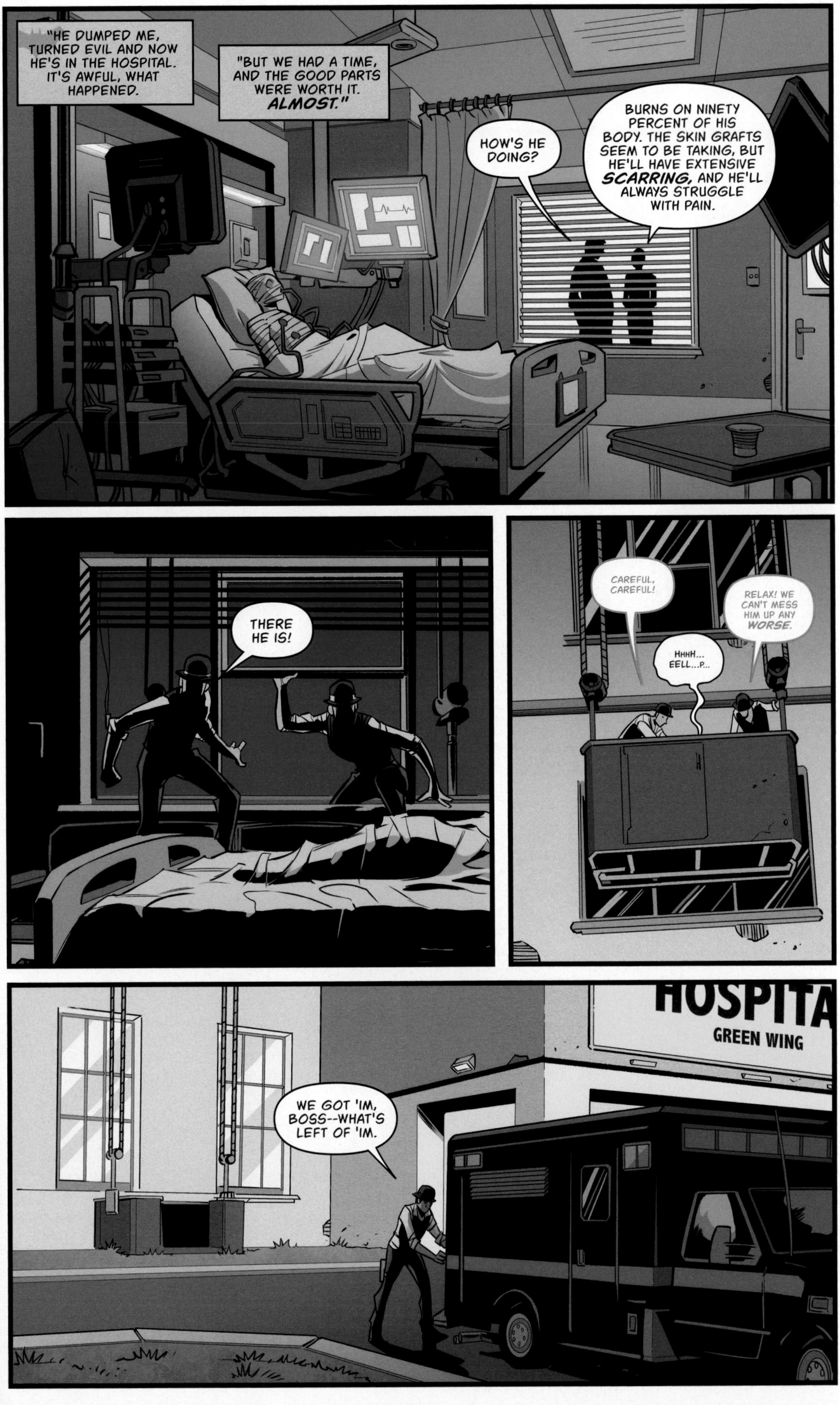
"HE DUMPED ME, TURNED EVIL AND NOW HE'S IN THE HOSPITAL. IT'S AWFUL, WHAT HAPPENED.
"BUT WE HAD A TIME, AND THE GOOD PARTS WERE WORTH IT. ALMOST."
HOW'S HE DOING?
BURNS ON NINETY PERCENT OF HIS BODY. THE SKIN GRAFTS SEEM TO BE TAKING, BUT HE'LL HAVE EXTENSIVE SCARRING, AND HE'LL ALWAYS STRUGGLE WITH PAIN.
THERE HE IS!
CAREFUL, CAREFUL!
HHHH... EELL...P...
RELAX! WE CAN'T MESS HIM UP ANY WORSE.
HOSPITA
GREEN WING
WE GOT 'IM, BOSS--WHAT'S LEFT OF 'IM.

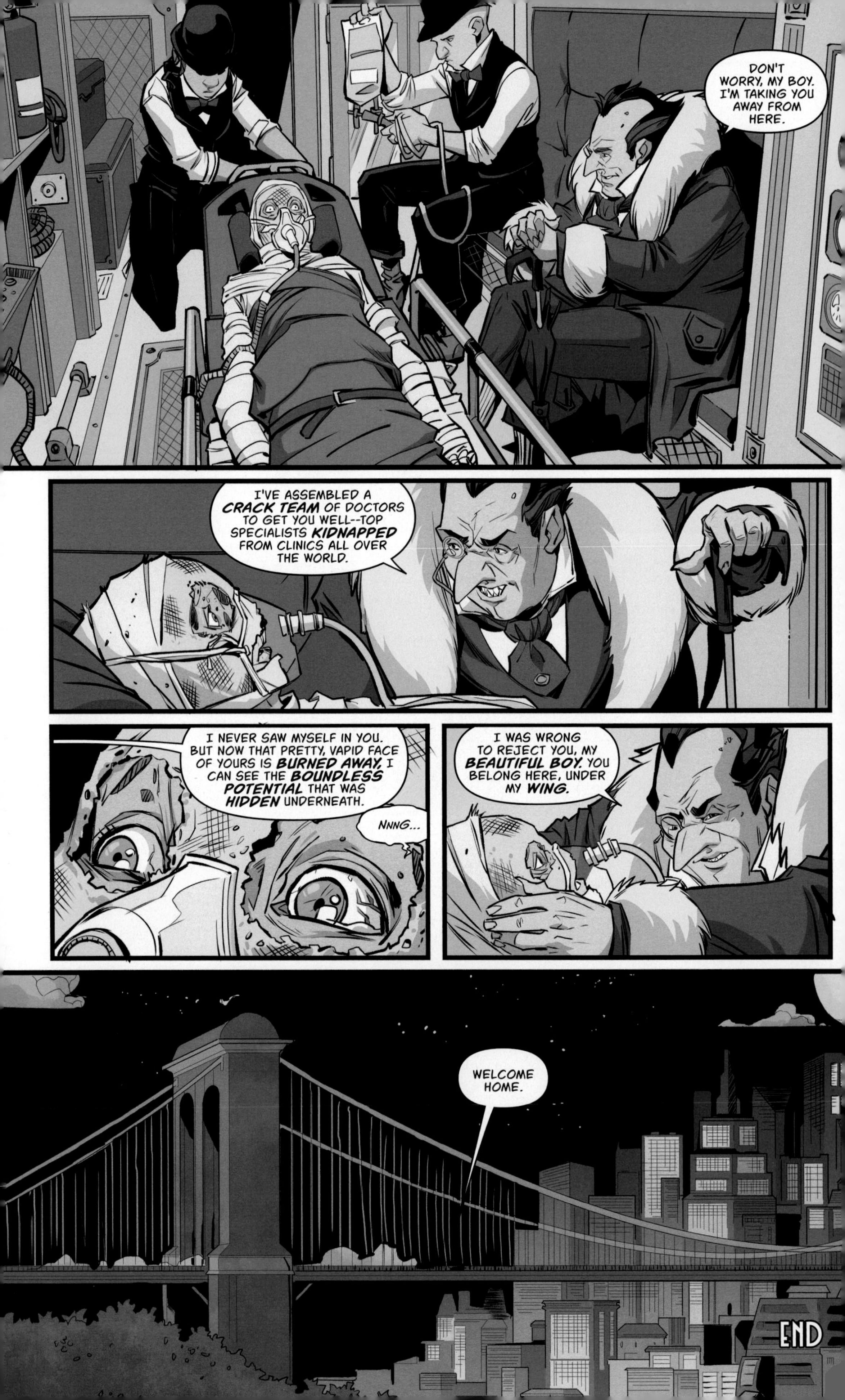
DON'T WORRY, MY BOY. I'M TAKING YOU AWAY FROM HERE.
I'VE ASSEMBLED A CRACK TEAM OF DOCTORS TO GET YOU WELL--TOP SPECIALISTS KIDNAPPED FROM CLINICS ALL OVER THE WORLD.
I NEVER SAW MYSELF IN YOU. BUT NOW THAT PRETTY, VAPID FACE OF YOURS IS BURNED AWAY, I CAN SEE THE BOUNDLESS POTENTIAL THAT WAS HIDDEN UNDERNEATH.
NNNG...
I WAS WRONG TO REJECT YOU, MY BEAUTIFUL BOY. YOU BELONG HERE, UNDER MY WING.
WELCOME HOME.
END

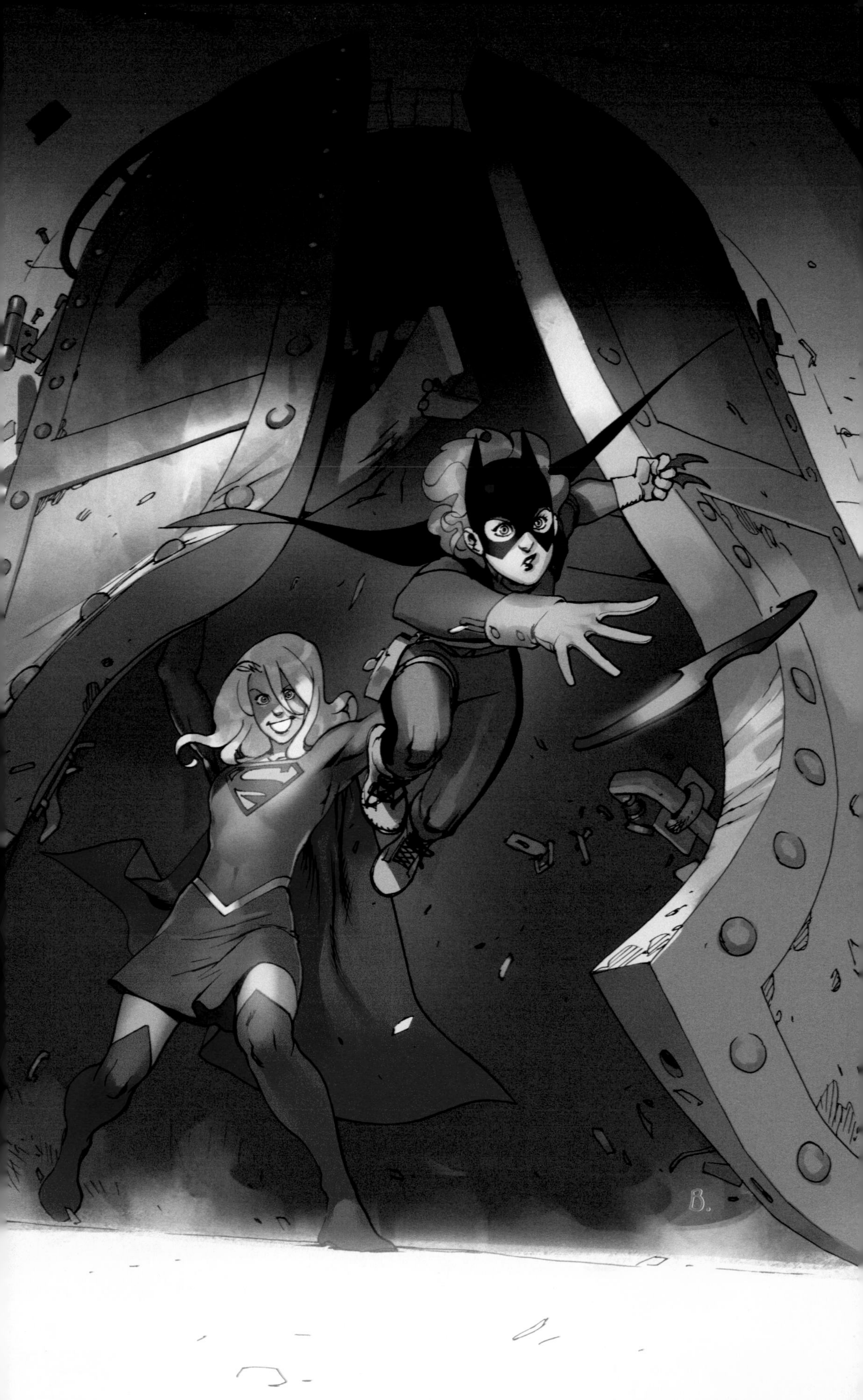

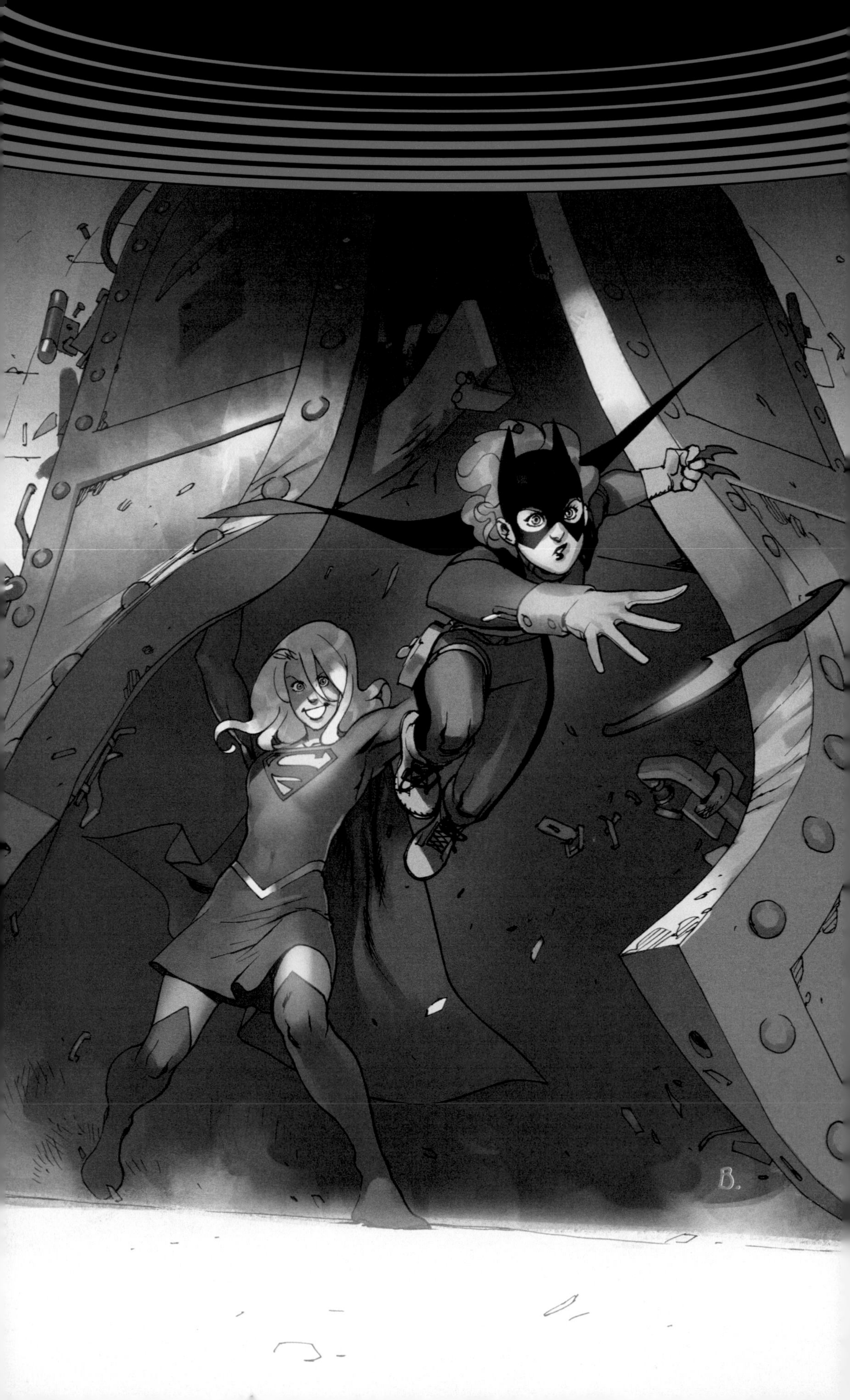

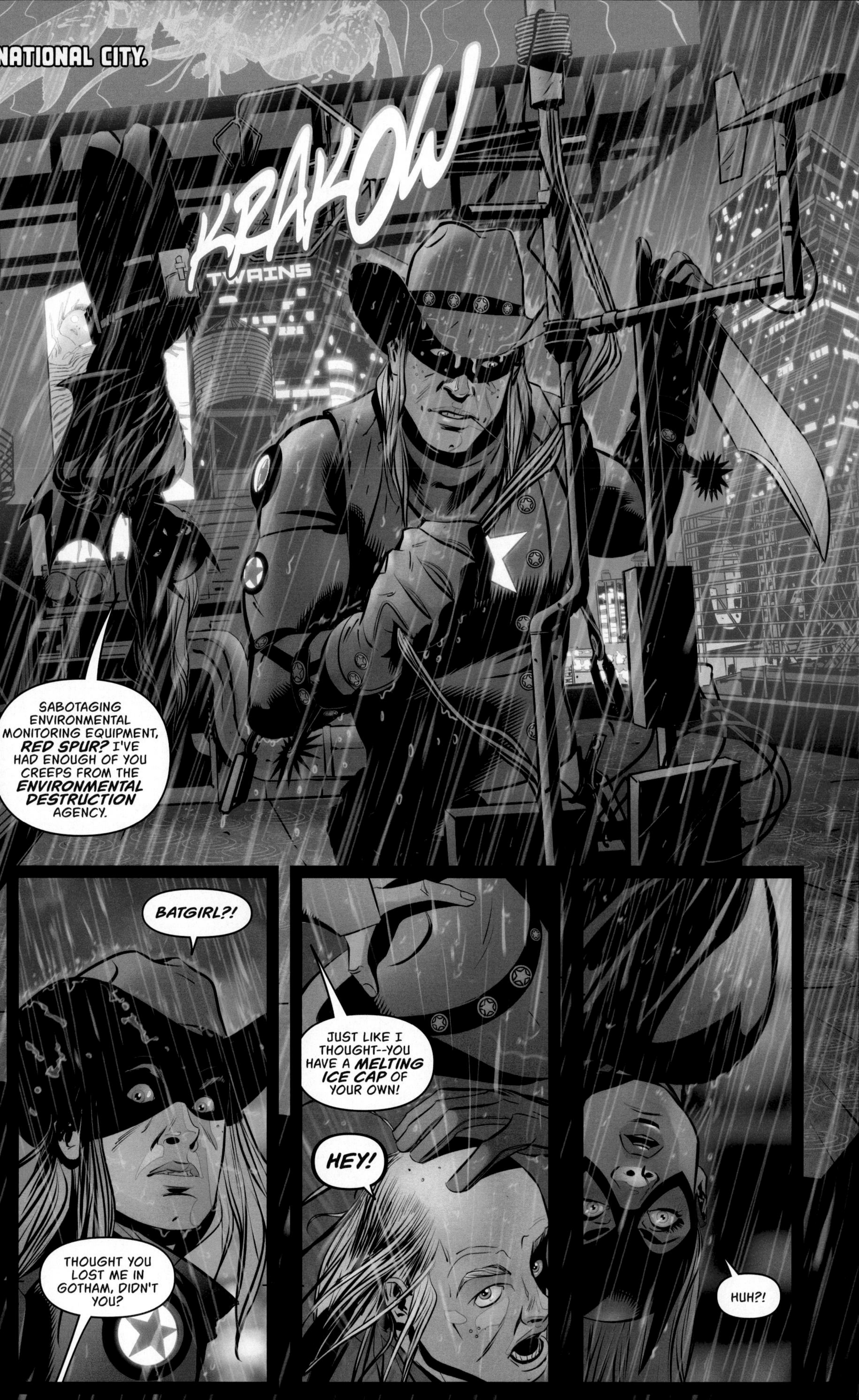

NATIONAL CITY.
KRAKOW
TWAINS
SABOTAGING ENVIRONMENTAL MONITORING EQUIPMENT, RED SPUR? I'VE HAD ENOUGH OF YOU CREEPS FROM THE ENVIRONMENTAL DESTRUCTION AGENCY.
BATGIRL?!
THOUGHT YOU LOST ME IN GOTHAM, DIDN'T YOU?
JUST LIKE I THOUGHT--YOU HAVE A MELTING ICE CAP OF YOUR OWN!
HEY!
HUH?!

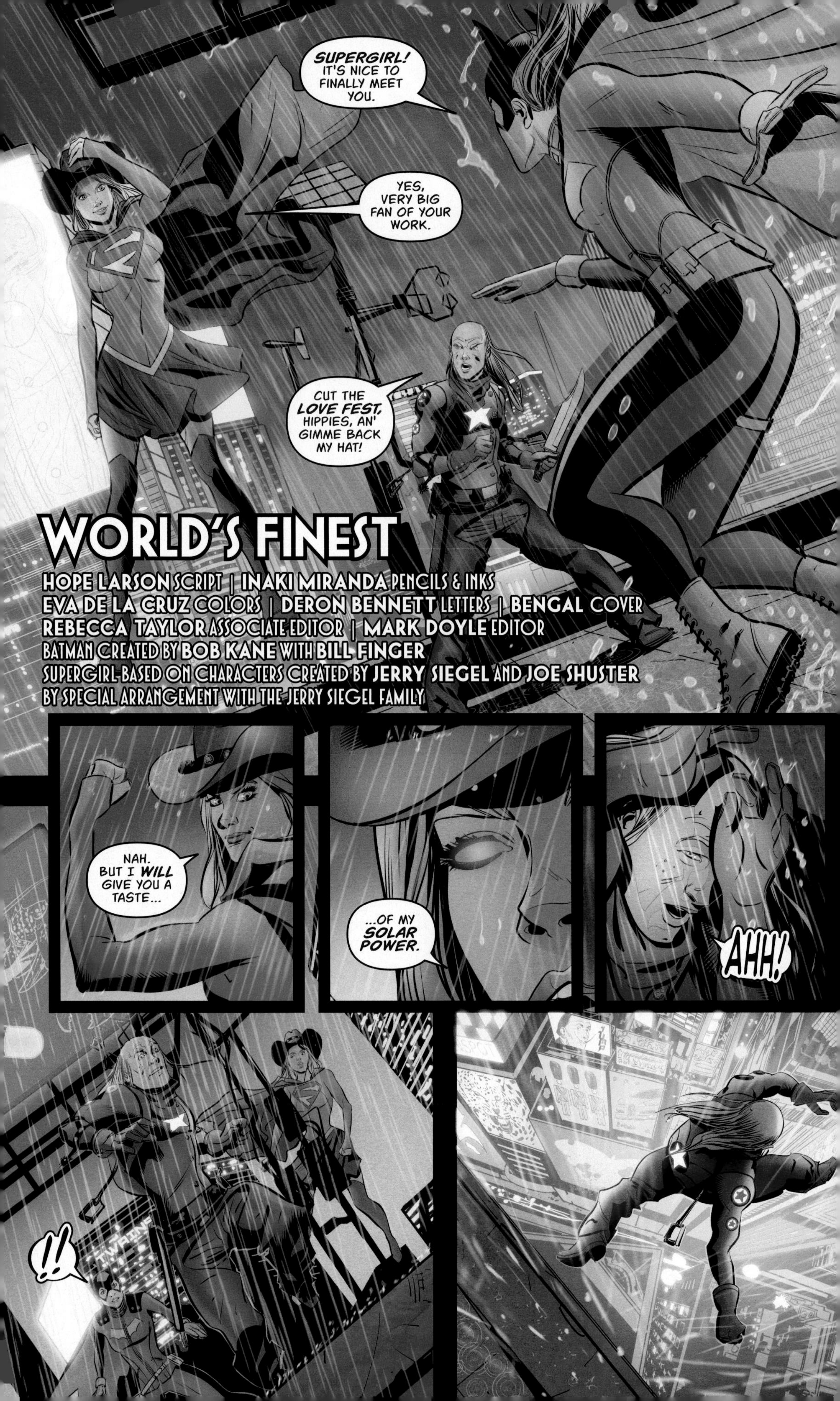
SUPERGIRL! IT'S NICE TO FINALLY MEET YOU.
YES, VERY BIG FAN OF YOUR WORK.
CUT THE LOVE FEST, HIPPIES, AN' GIMME BACK MY HAT!
WORLD'S FINEST
HOPE LARSON SCRIPT | INAKI MIRANDA PENCILS & INKS
EVA DE LA CRUZ COLORS | DERON BENNETT LETTERS | BENGAL COVER
REBECCA TAYLOR ASSOCIATE EDITOR | MARK DOYLE EDITOR
BATMAN CREATED BY BOB KANE WITH BILL FINGER
SUPERGIRL BASED ON CHARACTERS CREATED BY JERRY SIEGEL AND JOE SHUSTER
BY SPECIAL ARRANGEMENT WITH THE JERRY SIEGEL FAMILY
NAH. BUT I WILL GIVE YOU A TASTE...
...OF MY SOLAR POWER.
AHH!
!!

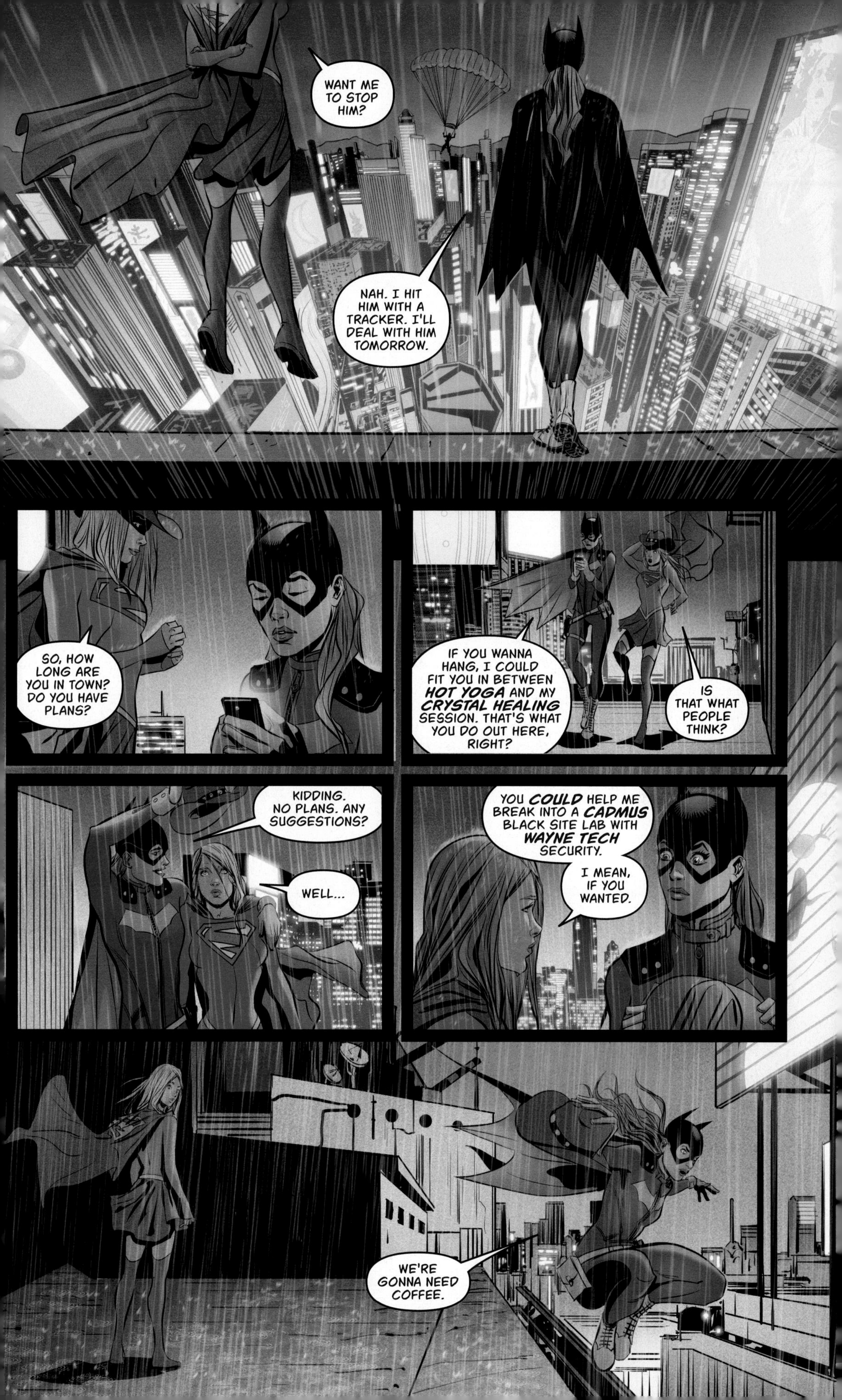
WANT ME TO STOP HIM?
NAH. I HIT HIM WITH A TRACKER. I'LL DEAL WITH HIM TOMORROW.
SO, HOW LONG ARE YOU IN TOWN? DO YOU HAVE PLANS?
IF YOU WANNA HANG, I COULD FIT YOU IN BETWEEN HOT YOGA AND MY CRYSTAL HEALING SESSION. THAT'S WHAT YOU DO OUT HERE, RIGHT?
IS THAT WHAT PEOPLE THINK?
KIDDING. NO PLANS. ANY SUGGESTIONS?
WELL...
YOU COULD HELP ME BREAK INTO A CADMUS BLACK SITE LAB WITH WAYNE TECH SECURITY.
I MEAN, IF YOU WANTED.
WE'RE GONNA NEED COFFEE.

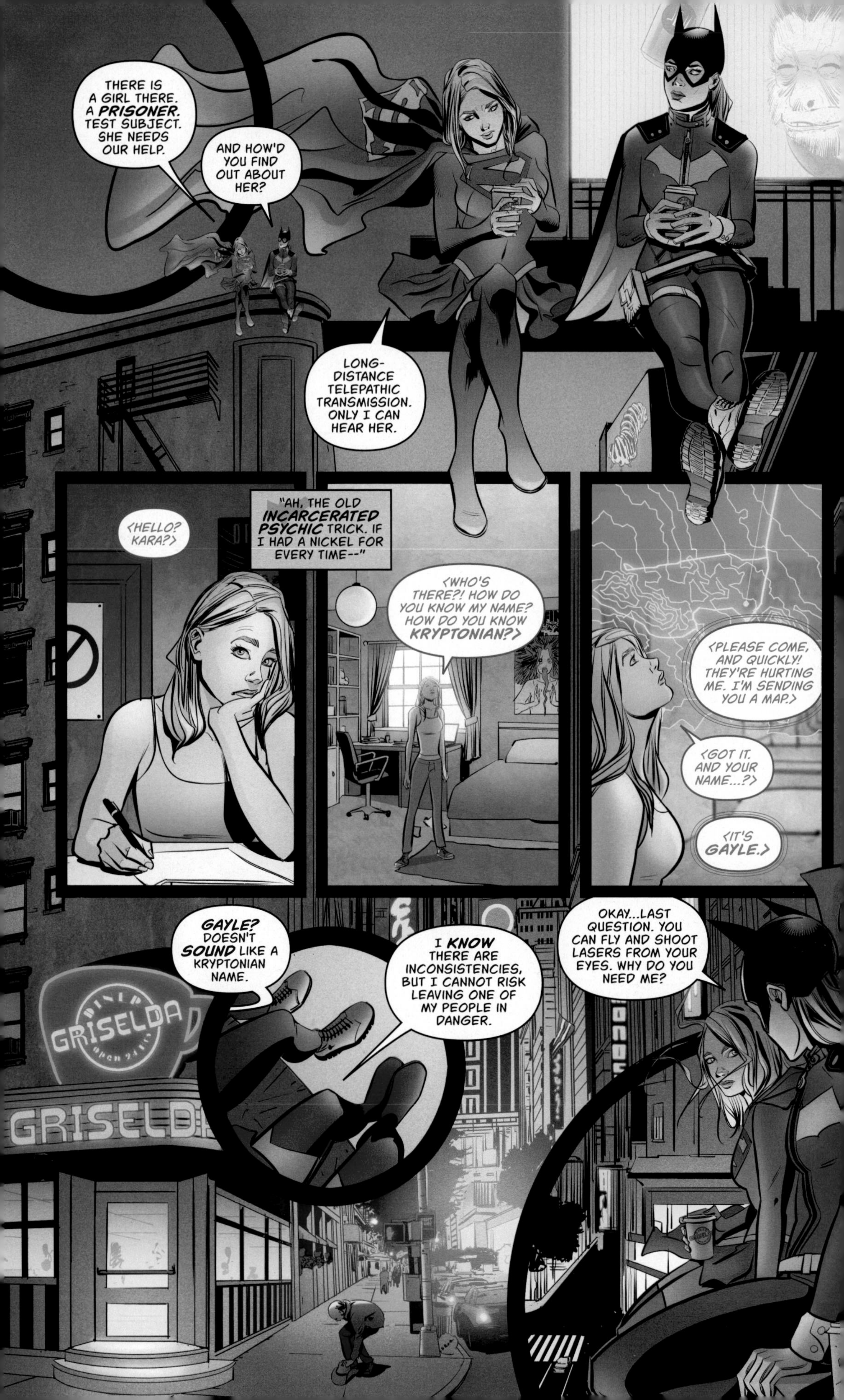
THERE IS A GIRL THERE. A PRISONER. TEST SUBJECT. SHE NEEDS OUR HELP.
AND HOW'D YOU FIND OUT ABOUT HER?
LONG-DISTANCE TELEPATHIC TRANSMISSION. ONLY I CAN HEAR HER.
<HELLO? KARA?>
"AH, THE OLD INCARCERATED PSYCHIC TRICK. IF I HAD A NICKEL FOR EVERY TIME--"
<WHO'S THERE?! HOW DO YOU KNOW MY NAME? HOW DO YOU KNOW KRYPTONIAN?>
<PLEASE COME, AND QUICKLY! THEY'RE HURTING ME. I'M SENDING YOU A MAP.>
<GOT IT. AND YOUR NAME...?>
<IT'S GAYLE.>
GAYLE? DOESN'T SOUND LIKE A KRYPTONIAN NAME.
I KNOW THERE ARE INCONSISTENCIES, BUT I CANNOT RISK LEAVING ONE OF MY PEOPLE IN DANGER.
OKAY...LAST QUESTION. YOU CAN FLY AND SHOOT LASERS FROM YOUR EYES. WHY DO YOU NEED ME?
GRISELDA
GRISELDA

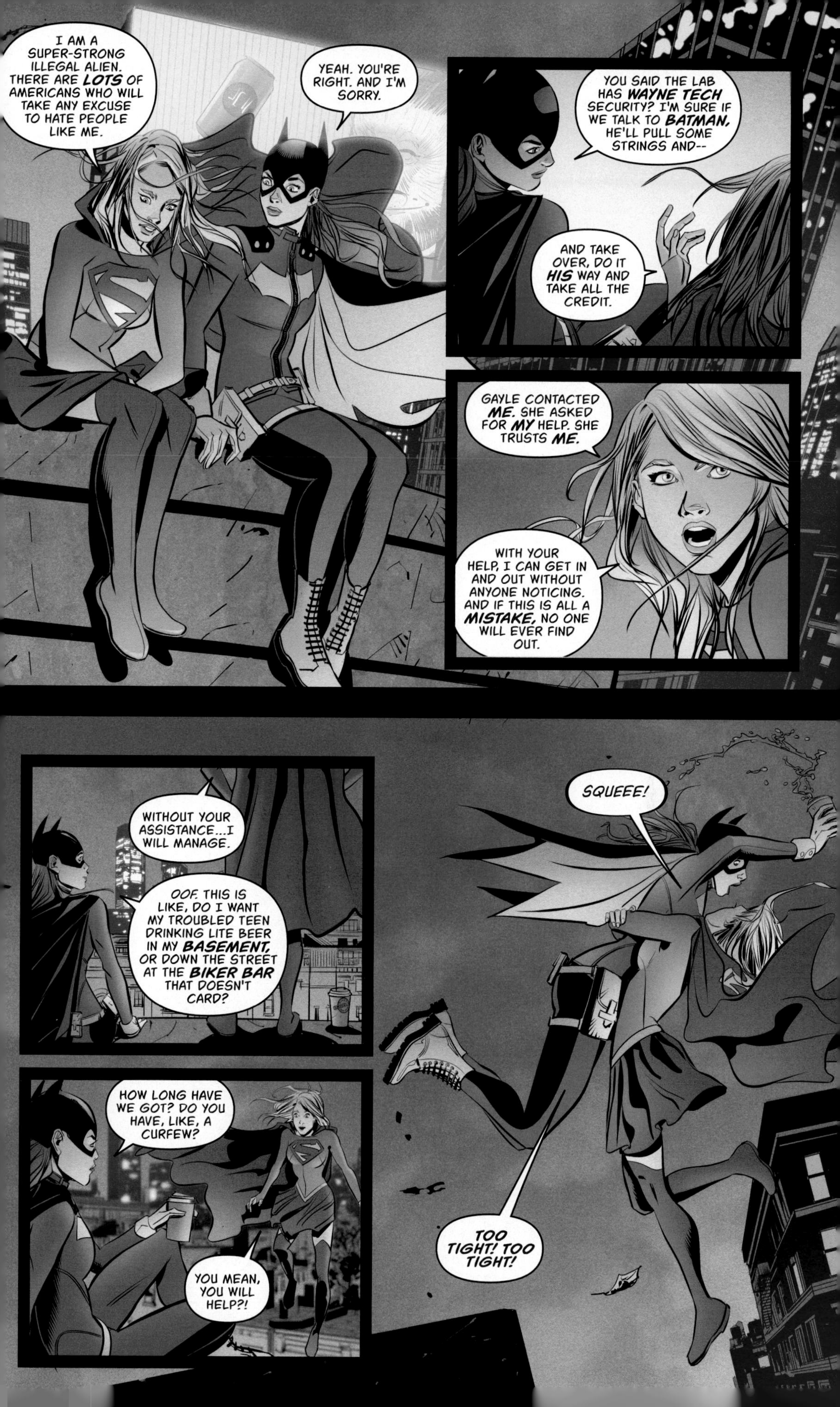
I AM A SUPER-STRONG ILLEGAL ALIEN. THERE ARE LOTS OF AMERICANS WHO WILL TAKE ANY EXCUSE TO HATE PEOPLE LIKE ME.
YEAH. YOU'RE RIGHT. AND I'M SORRY.
YOU SAID THE LAB HAS WAYNE TECH SECURITY? I'M SURE IF WE TALK TO BATMAN, HE'LL PULL SOME STRINGS AND--
AND TAKE OVER, DO IT HIS WAY AND TAKE ALL THE CREDIT.
GAYLE CONTACTED ME. SHE ASKED FOR MY HELP. SHE TRUSTS ME.
WITH YOUR HELP, I CAN GET IN AND OUT WITHOUT ANYONE NOTICING. AND IF THIS IS ALL A MISTAKE, NO ONE WILL EVER FIND OUT.
WITHOUT YOUR ASSISTANCE...I WILL MANAGE.
OOF. THIS IS LIKE, DO I WANT MY TROUBLED TEEN DRINKING LITE BEER IN MY BASEMENT, OR DOWN THE STREET AT THE BIKER BAR THAT DOESN'T CARD?
HOW LONG HAVE WE GOT? DO YOU HAVE, LIKE, A CURFEW?
YOU MEAN, YOU WILL HELP?!
SQUEEE!
TOO TIGHT! TOO TIGHT!

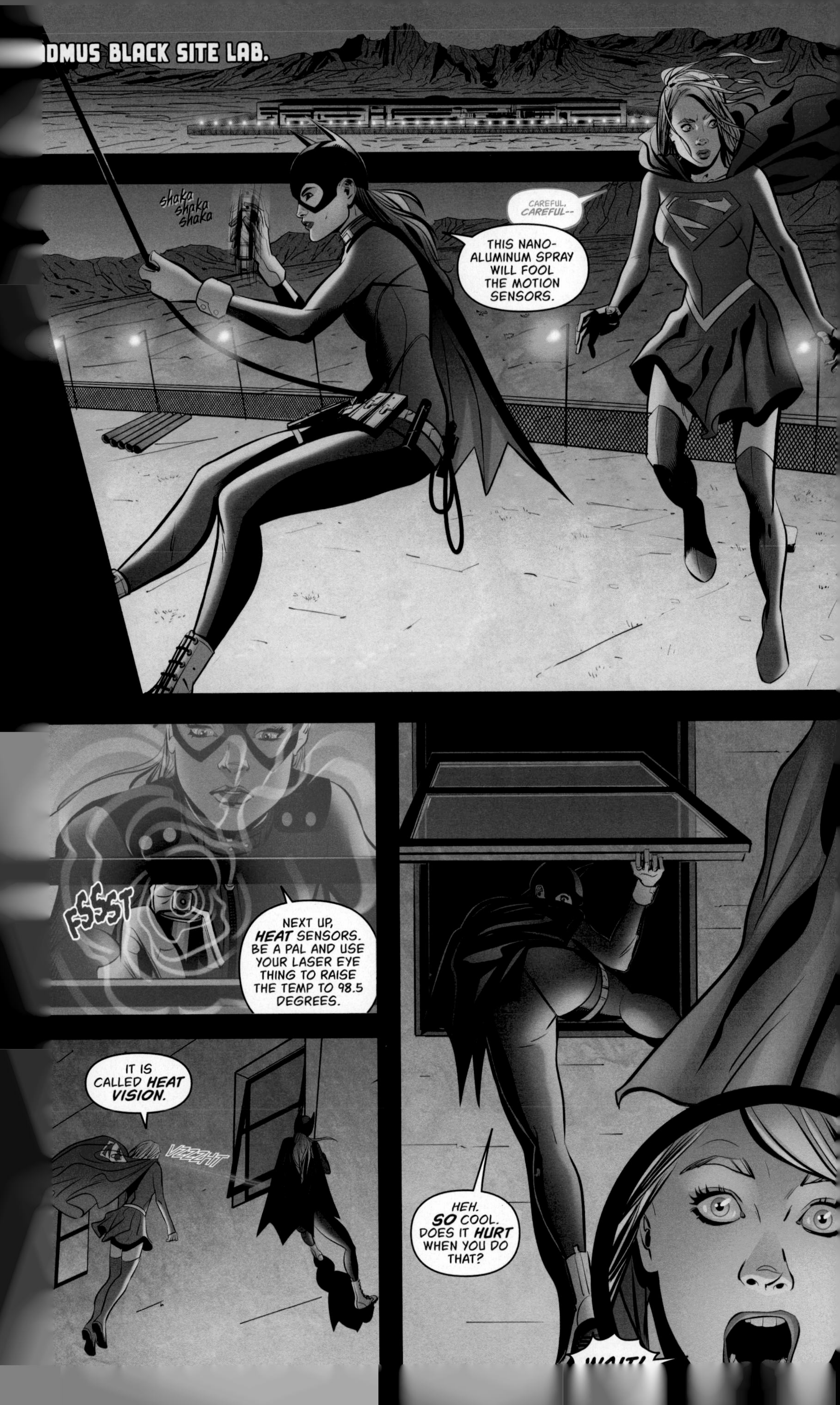
DMUS BLACK SITE LAB.
shaka shaka shaka
CAREFUL, CAREFUL--
THIS NANO-ALUMINUM SPRAY WILL FOOL THE MOTION SENSORS.
FSSST
NEXT UP, HEAT SENSORS. BE A PAL AND USE YOUR LASER EYE THING TO RAISE THE TEMP TO 98.5 DEGREES.
IT IS CALLED HEAT VISION.
VZZZHT
HEH. SO COOL. DOES IT HURT WHEN YOU DO THAT?

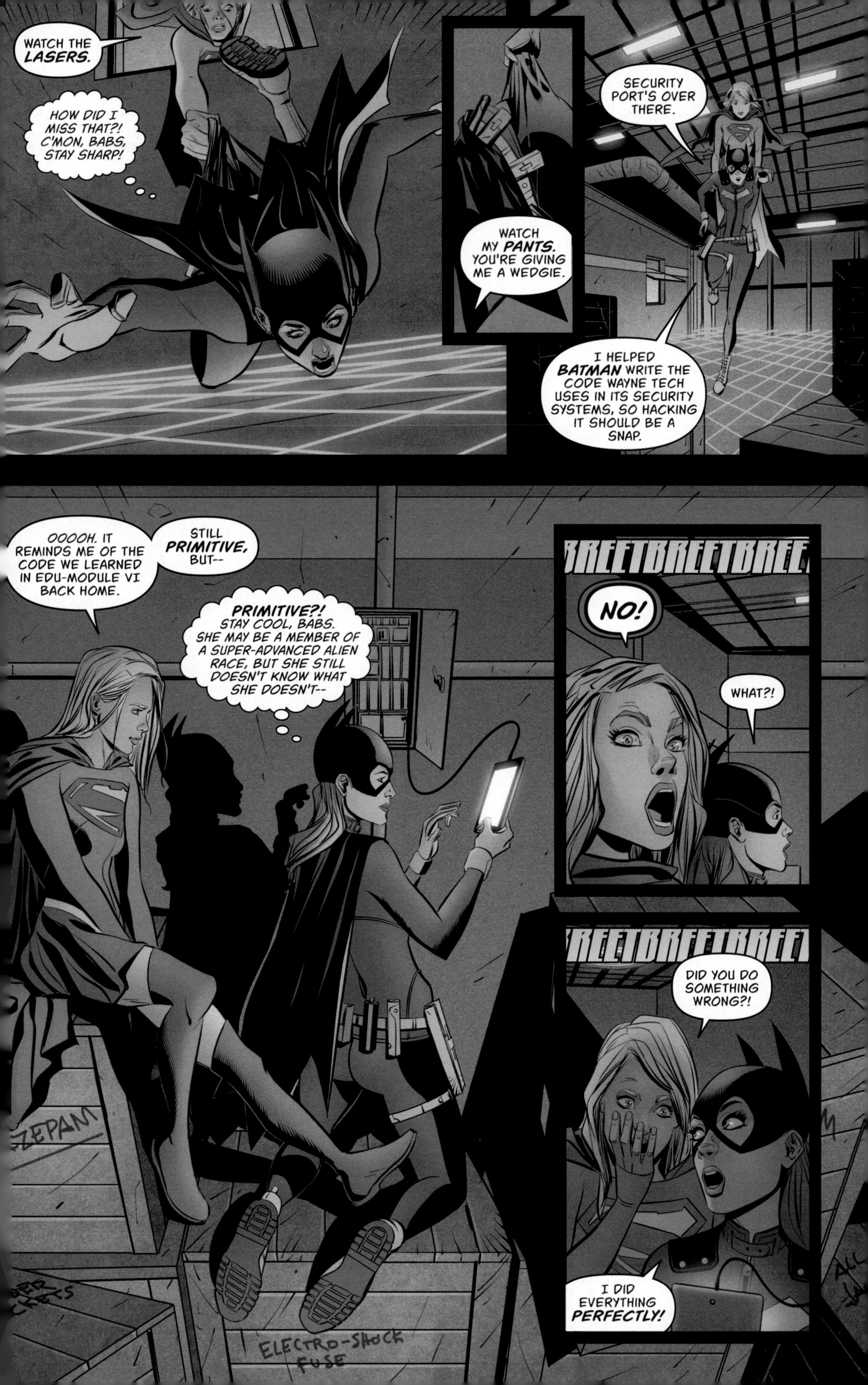
WATCH THE LASERS.
HOW DID I MISS THAT?! C'MON, BABS, STAY SHARP!
WATCH MY PANTS. YOU'RE GIVING ME A WEDGIE.
SECURITY PORT'S OVER THERE.
I HELPED BATMAN WRITE THE CODE WAYNE TECH USES IN ITS SECURITY SYSTEMS, SO HACKING IT SHOULD BE A SNAP.
OOOOH. IT REMINDS ME OF THE CODE WE LEARNED IN EDU-MODULE VI BACK HOME.
STILL PRIMITIVE, BUT--
PRIMITIVE?! STAY COOL, BABS. SHE MAY BE A MEMBER OF A SUPER-ADVANCED ALIEN RACE, BUT SHE STILL DOESN'T KNOW WHAT SHE DOESN'T--
ELECTRO-SHOCK FUSE
BREETBREETBREE
NO!
WHAT?!
BREETBREETBREE
DID YOU DO SOMETHING WRONG?!
I DID EVERYTHING PERFECTLY!

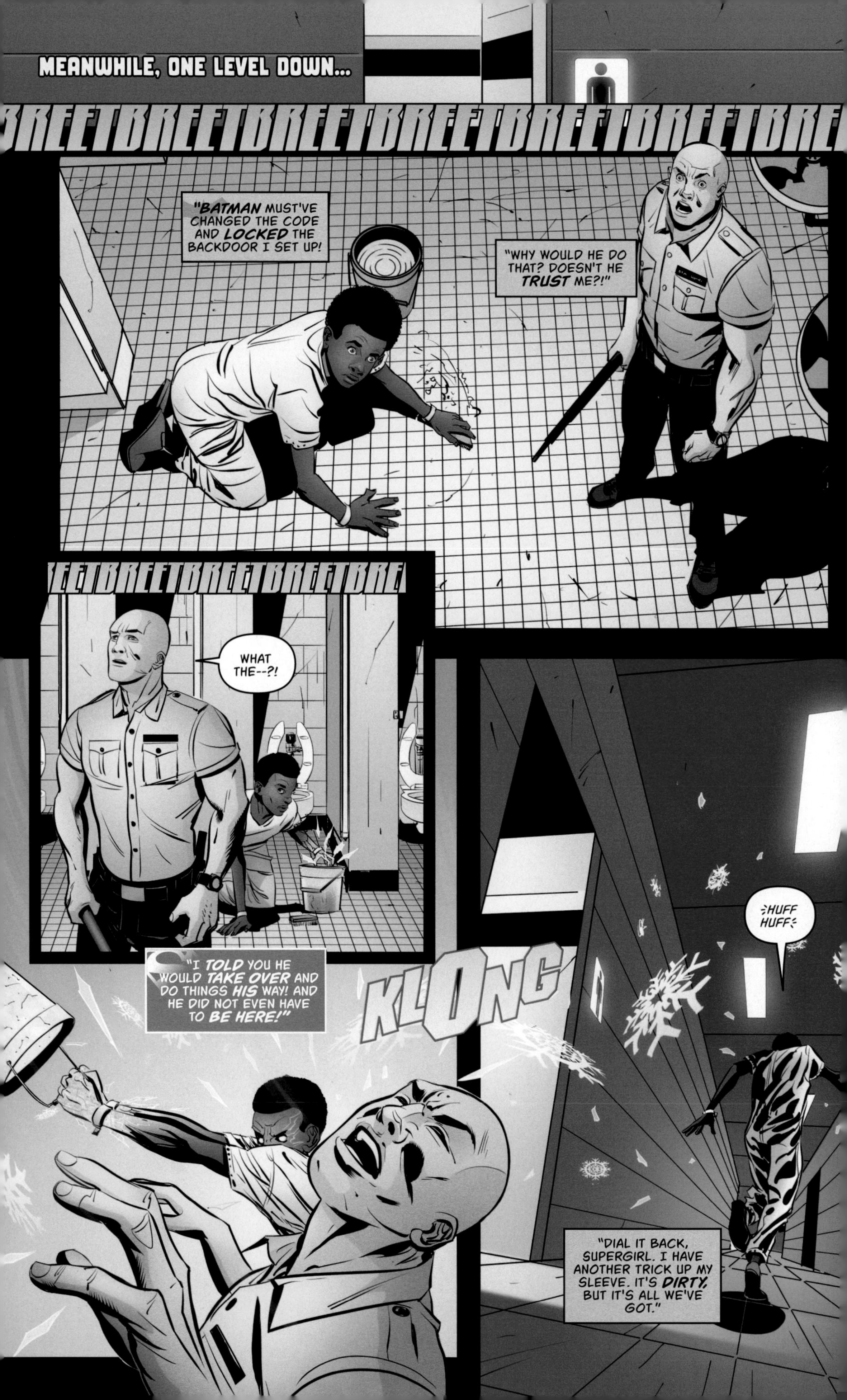
MEANWHILE, ONE LEVEL DOWN...
BREETBREETBREETBREETBREETBREETBRE
"BATMAN MUST'VE CHANGED THE CODE AND LOCKED THE BACKDOOR I SET UP!
"WHY WOULD HE DO THAT? DOESN'T HE TRUST ME?!"
EETBREETBREETBREETBRE
WHAT THE--?!
"I TOLD YOU HE WOULD TAKE OVER AND DO THINGS HIS WAY! AND HE DID NOT EVEN HAVE TO BE HERE!"
KLONG
HUFF HUFF
"DIAL IT BACK, SUPERGIRL. I HAVE ANOTHER TRICK UP MY SLEEVE. IT'S DIRTY, BUT IT'S ALL WE'VE GOT."

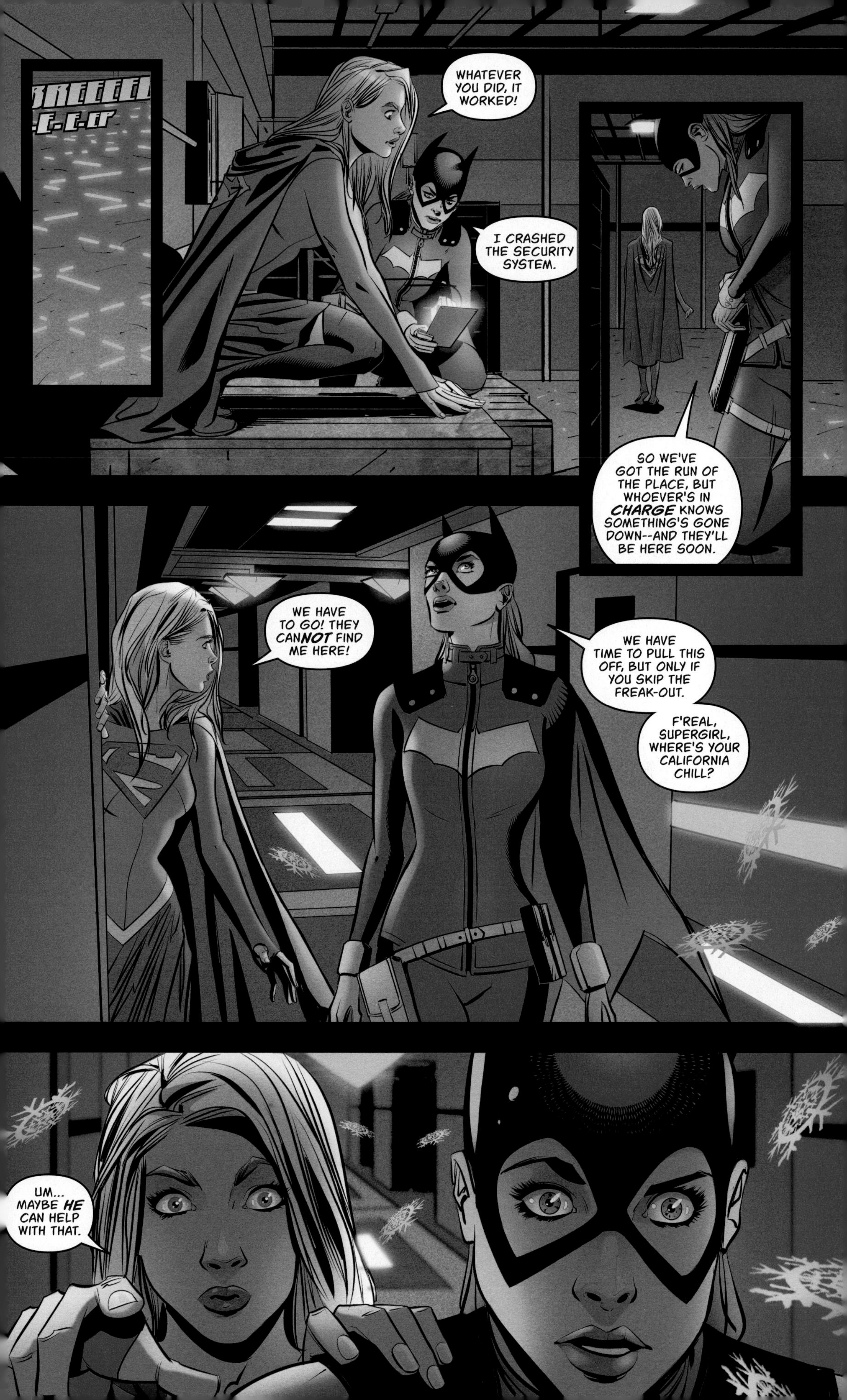
WHATEVER YOU DID, IT WORKED!
I CRASHED THE SECURITY SYSTEM.
SO WE'VE GOT THE RUN OF THE PLACE, BUT WHOEVER'S IN CHARGE KNOWS SOMETHING'S GONE DOWN--AND THEY'LL BE HERE SOON.
WE HAVE TO GO! THEY CANNOT FIND ME HERE!
WE HAVE TIME TO PULL THIS OFF, BUT ONLY IF YOU SKIP THE FREAK-OUT.
F'REAL, SUPERGIRL, WHERE'S YOUR CALIFORNIA CHILL?
UM... MAYBE HE CAN HELP WITH THAT.

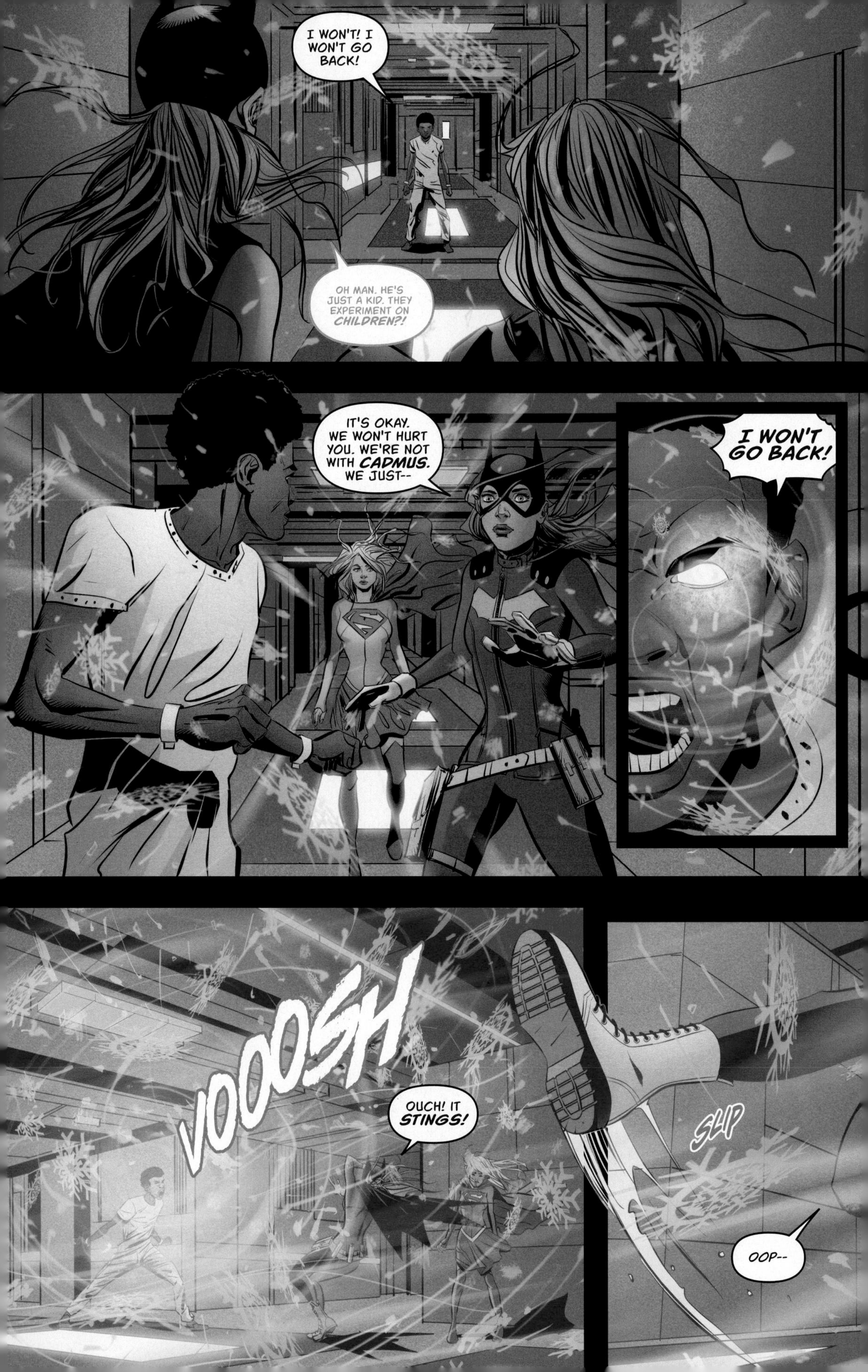
I WON'T! I WON'T GO BACK!
OH MAN. HE'S JUST A KID. THEY EXPERIMENT ON CHILDREN?!
IT'S OKAY. WE WON'T HURT YOU. WE'RE NOT WITH CADMUS. WE JUST--
I WON'T GO BACK!
VOOOSH
OUCH! IT STINGS!
SLIP
OOP--

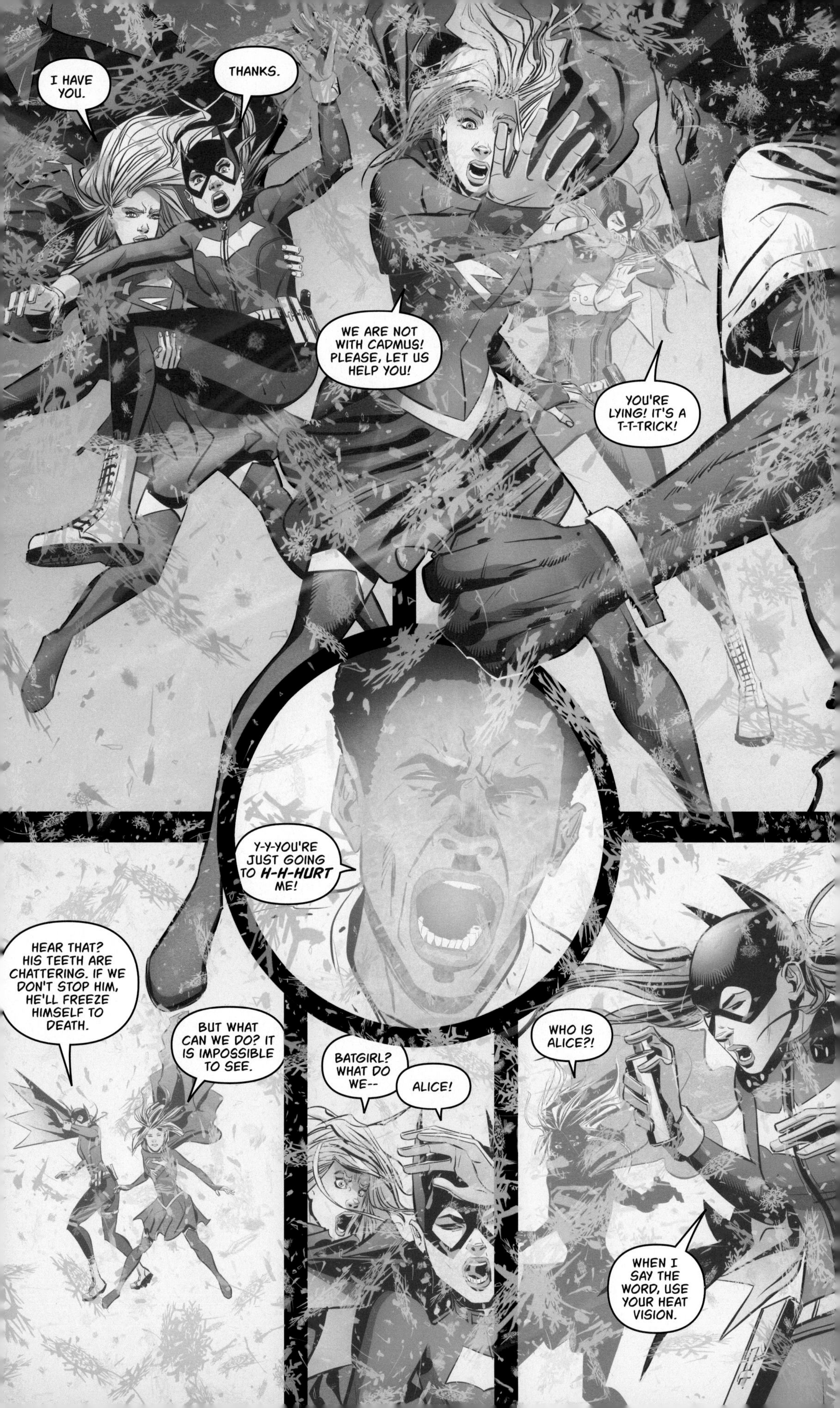

I HAVE YOU.
THANKS.
WE ARE NOT WITH CADMUS! PLEASE, LET US HELP YOU!
YOU'RE LYING! IT'S A T-T-TRICK!
Y-Y-YOU'RE JUST GOING TO **H-H-HURT** ME!
HEAR THAT? HIS TEETH ARE CHATTERING. IF WE DON'T STOP HIM, HE'LL FREEZE HIMSELF TO DEATH.
BUT WHAT CAN WE DO? IT IS IMPOSSIBLE TO SEE.
BATGIRL? WHAT DO WE--
ALICE!
WHO IS ALICE?!
WHEN I SAY THE WORD, USE YOUR HEAT VISION.

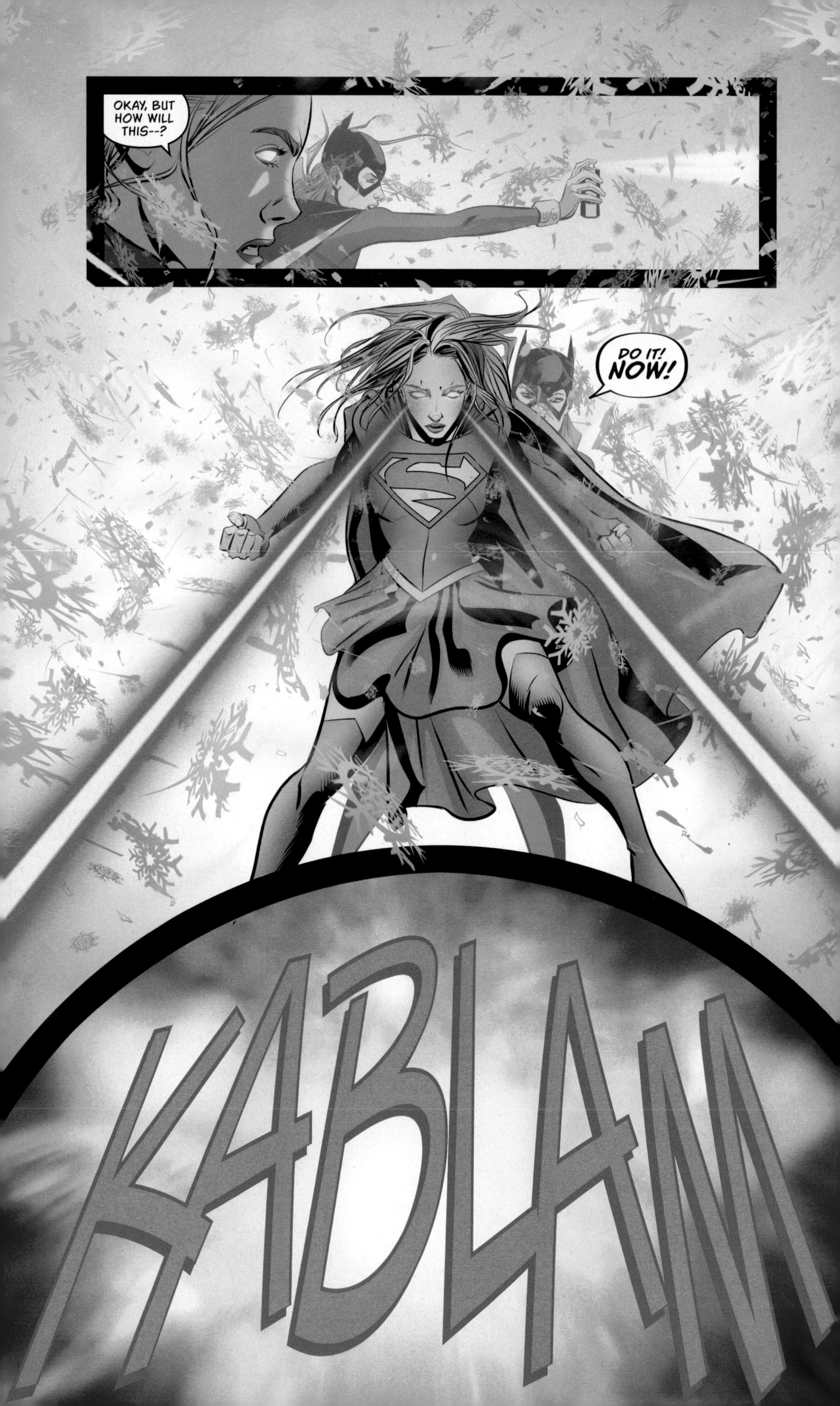
OKAY, BUT HOW WILL THIS--?
DO IT! NOW!
KABLAM

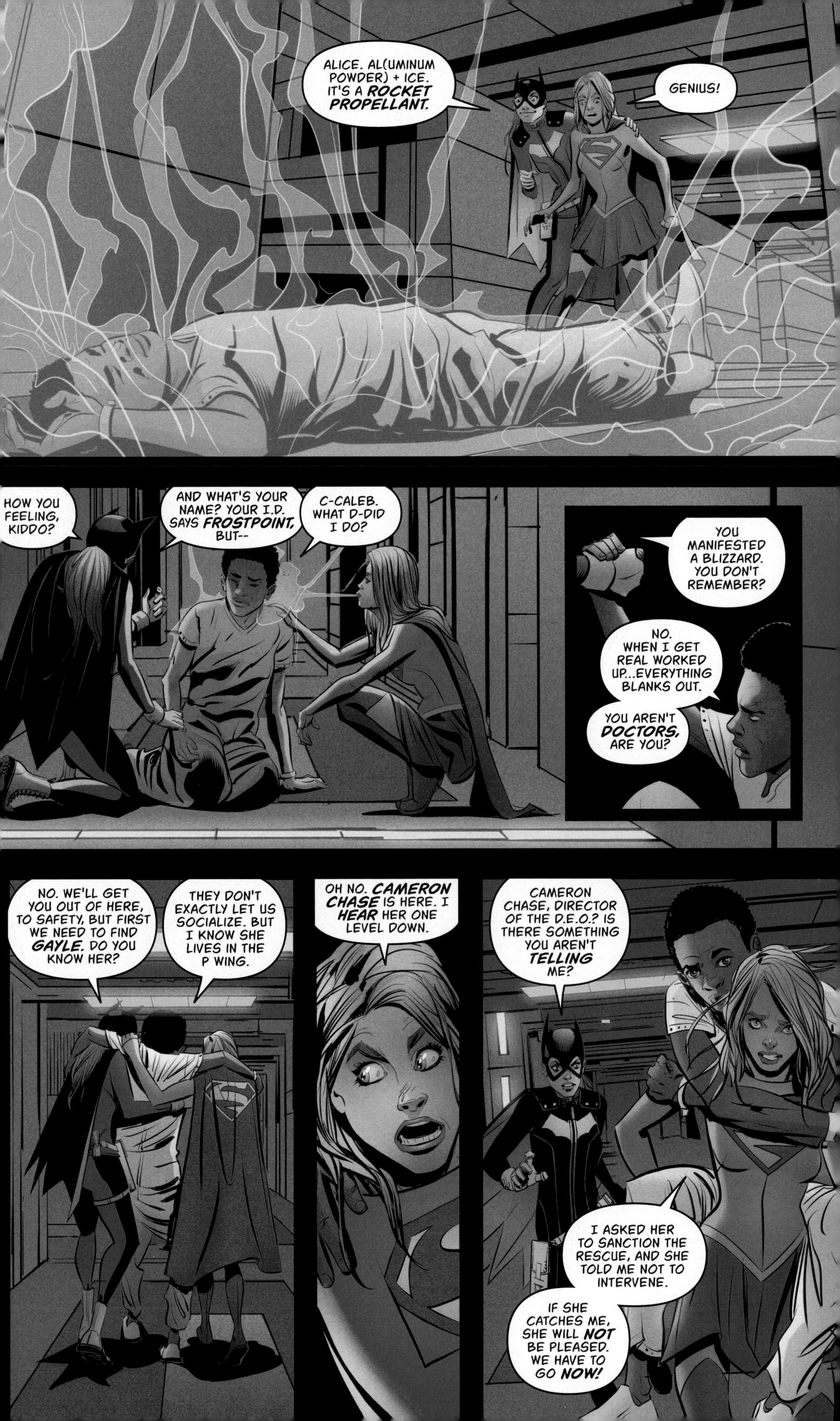
ALICE. AL(UMINUM POWDER) + ICE. IT'S A ROCKET PROPELLANT.
GENIUS!
HOW YOU FEELING, KIDDO?
AND WHAT'S YOUR NAME? YOUR I.D. SAYS FROSTPOINT, BUT--
C-CALEB. WHAT D-DID I DO?
YOU MANIFESTED A BLIZZARD. YOU DON'T REMEMBER?
NO. WHEN I GET REAL WORKED UP...EVERYTHING BLANKS OUT.
YOU AREN'T DOCTORS, ARE YOU?
NO. WE'LL GET YOU OUT OF HERE, TO SAFETY, BUT FIRST WE NEED TO FIND GAYLE. DO YOU KNOW HER?
THEY DON'T EXACTLY LET US SOCIALIZE. BUT I KNOW SHE LIVES IN THE P WING.
OH NO. CAMERON CHASE IS HERE. I HEAR HER ONE LEVEL DOWN.
CAMERON CHASE, DIRECTOR OF THE D.E.O.? IS THERE SOMETHING YOU AREN'T TELLING ME?
I ASKED HER TO SANCTION THE RESCUE, AND SHE TOLD ME NOT TO INTERVENE.
IF SHE CATCHES ME, SHE WILL NOT BE PLEASED. WE HAVE TO GO NOW!

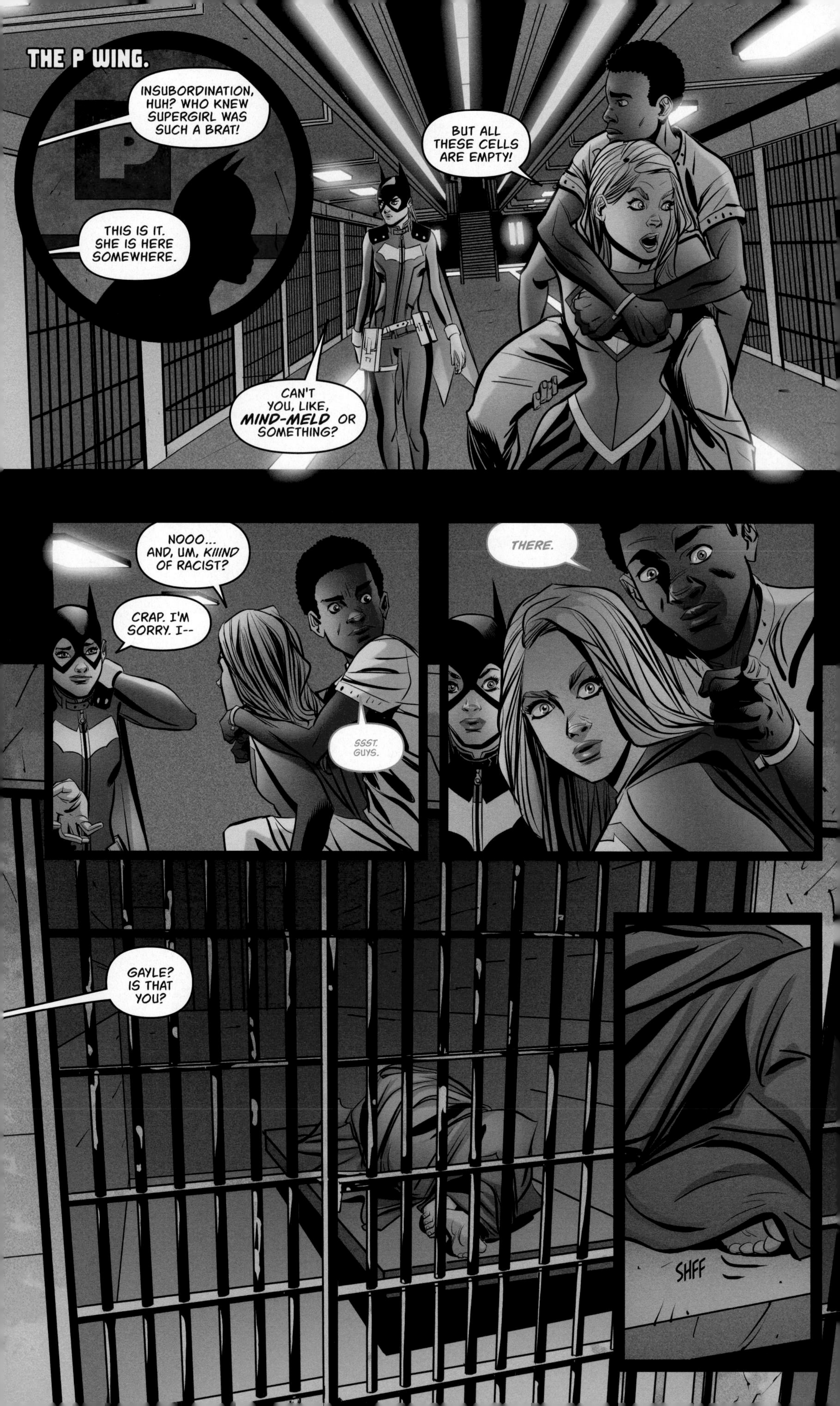
THE P WING.
INSUBORDINATION, HUH? WHO KNEW SUPERGIRL WAS SUCH A BRAT!
THIS IS IT. SHE IS HERE SOMEWHERE.
BUT ALL THESE CELLS ARE EMPTY!
CAN'T YOU, LIKE, MIND-MELD OR SOMETHING?
NOOO... AND, UM, KIIIND OF RACIST?
CRAP. I'M SORRY. I--
SSST. GUYS.
THERE.
GAYLE? IS THAT YOU?
SHFF

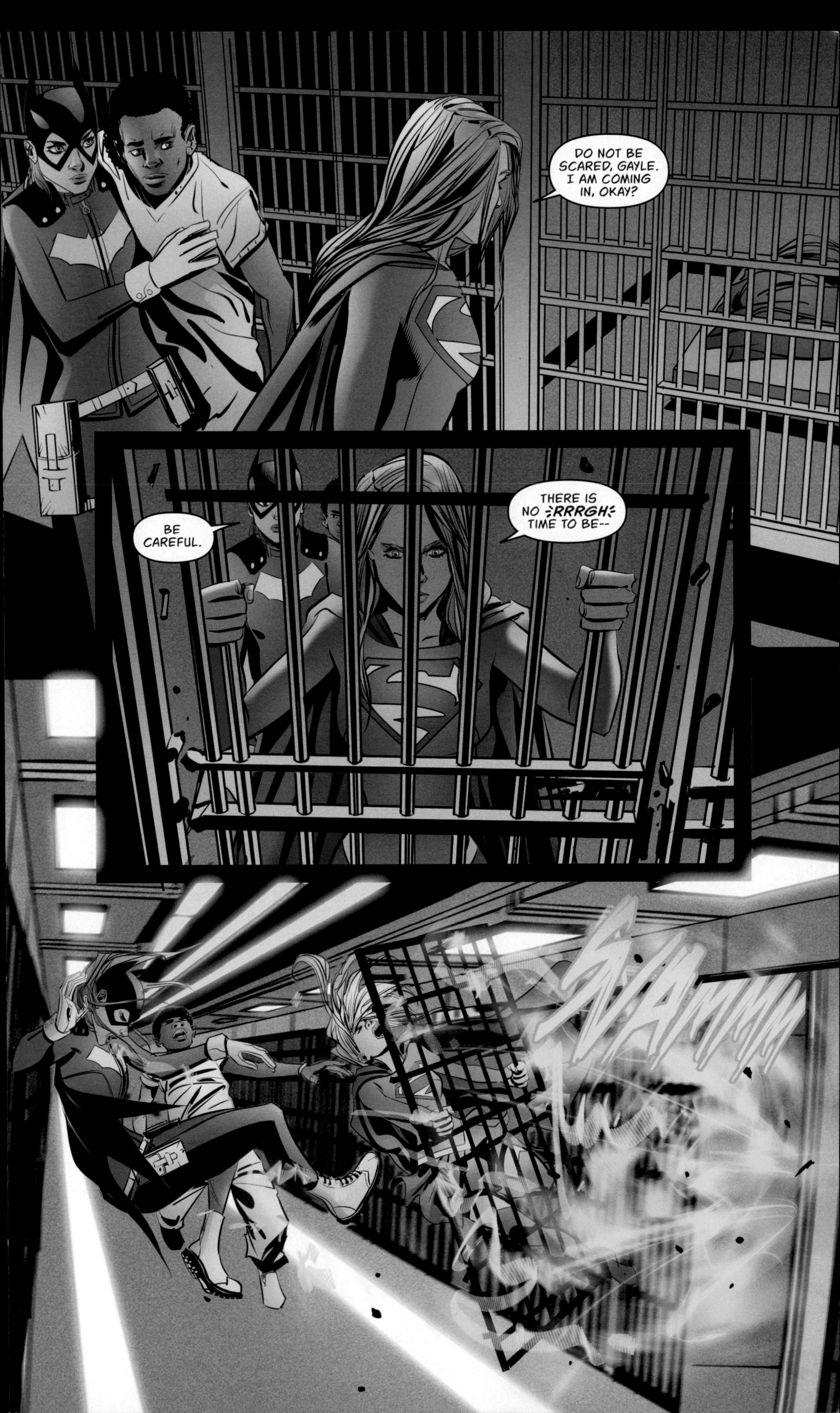
DO NOT BE SCARED, GAYLE. I AM COMING IN, OKAY?
BE CAREFUL.
THERE IS NO RRRGH TIME TO BE--

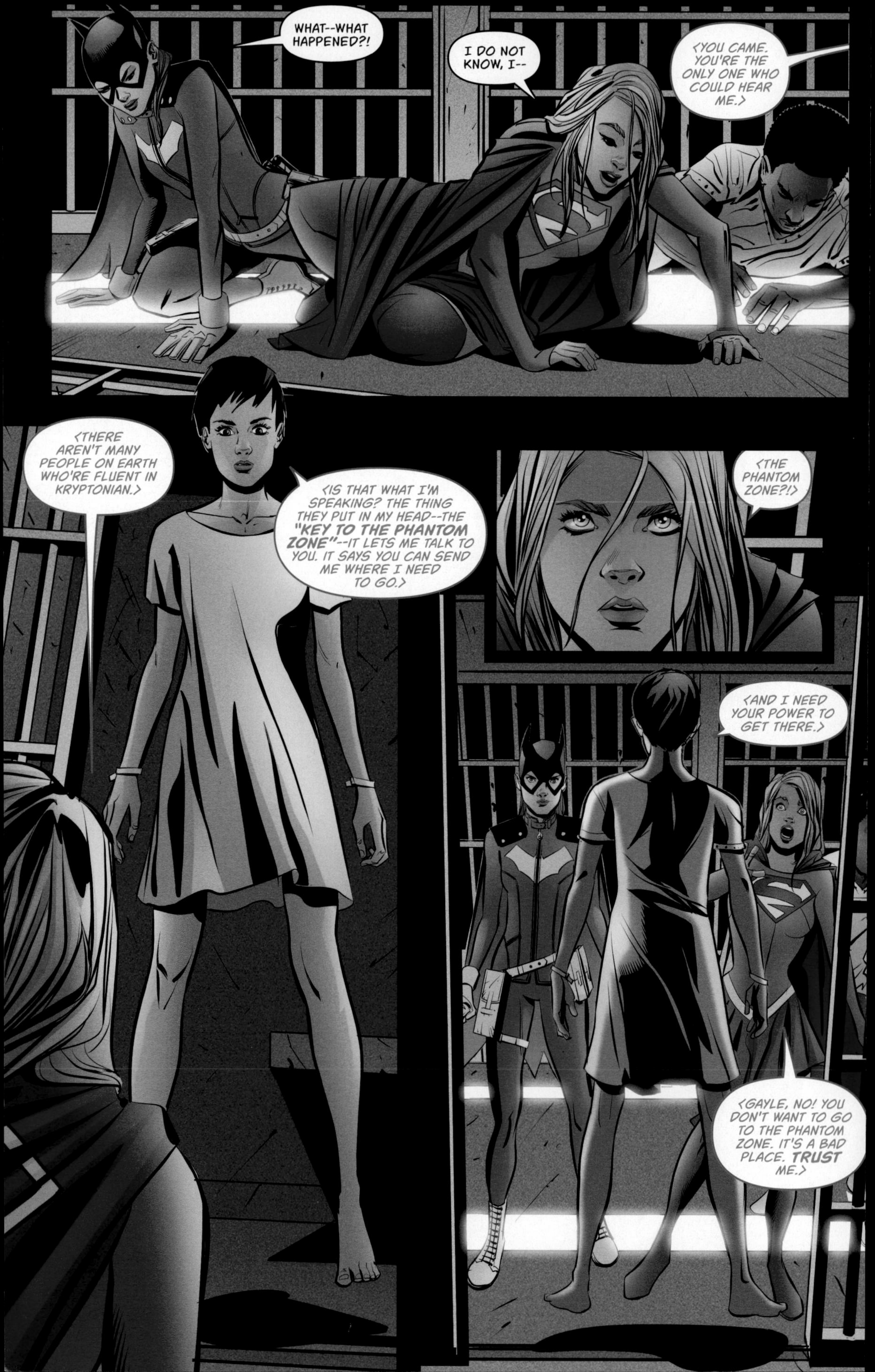
WHAT--WHAT HAPPENED?!
I DO NOT KNOW, I--
<YOU CAME. YOU'RE THE ONLY ONE WHO COULD HEAR ME.>
<THERE AREN'T MANY PEOPLE ON EARTH WHO'RE FLUENT IN KRYPTONIAN.>
<IS THAT WHAT I'M SPEAKING? THE THING THEY PUT IN MY HEAD--THE "KEY TO THE PHANTOM ZONE"--IT LETS ME TALK TO YOU. IT SAYS YOU CAN SEND ME WHERE I NEED TO GO.>
<THE PHANTOM ZONE?!>
<AND I NEED YOUR POWER TO GET THERE.>
<GAYLE, NO! YOU DON'T WANT TO GO TO THE PHANTOM ZONE. IT'S A BAD PLACE. TRUST ME.>

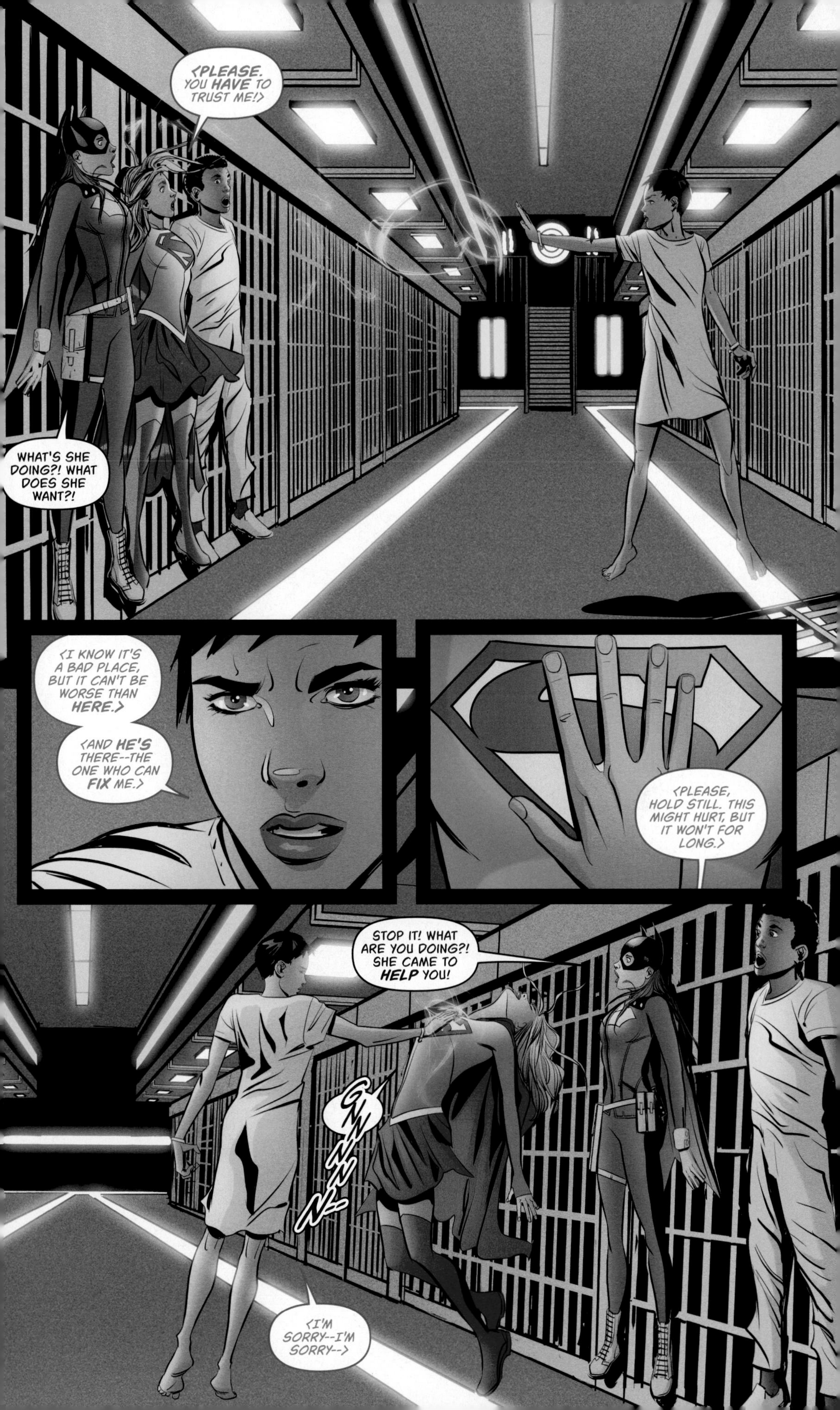
<PLEASE. YOU HAVE TO TRUST ME!>
WHAT'S SHE DOING?! WHAT DOES SHE WANT?!
<I KNOW IT'S A BAD PLACE, BUT IT CAN'T BE WORSE THAN HERE.>
<AND HE'S THERE--THE ONE WHO CAN FIX ME.>
<PLEASE, HOLD STILL. THIS MIGHT HURT, BUT IT WON'T FOR LONG.>
STOP IT! WHAT ARE YOU DOING?! SHE CAME TO HELP YOU!
GNNNNN-!
<I'M SORRY--I'M SORRY-->

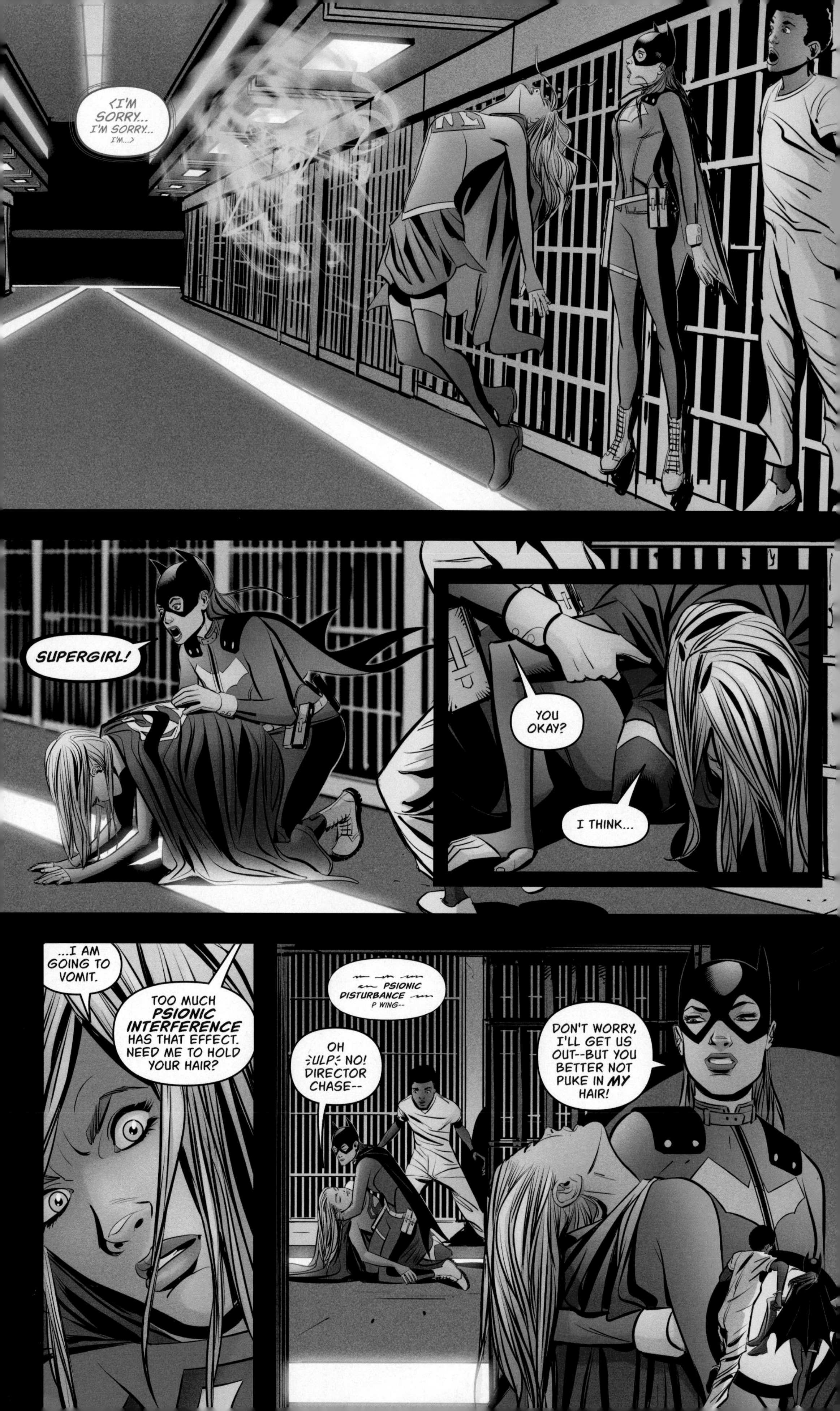

<I'M SORRY... I'M SORRY... I'M...>
SUPERGIRL!
YOU OKAY?
I THINK...
...I AM GOING TO VOMIT.
TOO MUCH PSIONIC INTERFERENCE HAS THAT EFFECT. NEED ME TO HOLD YOUR HAIR?
PSIONIC DISTURBANCE P WING--
OH -ULP- NO! DIRECTOR CHASE--
DON'T WORRY, I'LL GET US OUT--BUT YOU BETTER NOT PUKE IN MY HAIR!

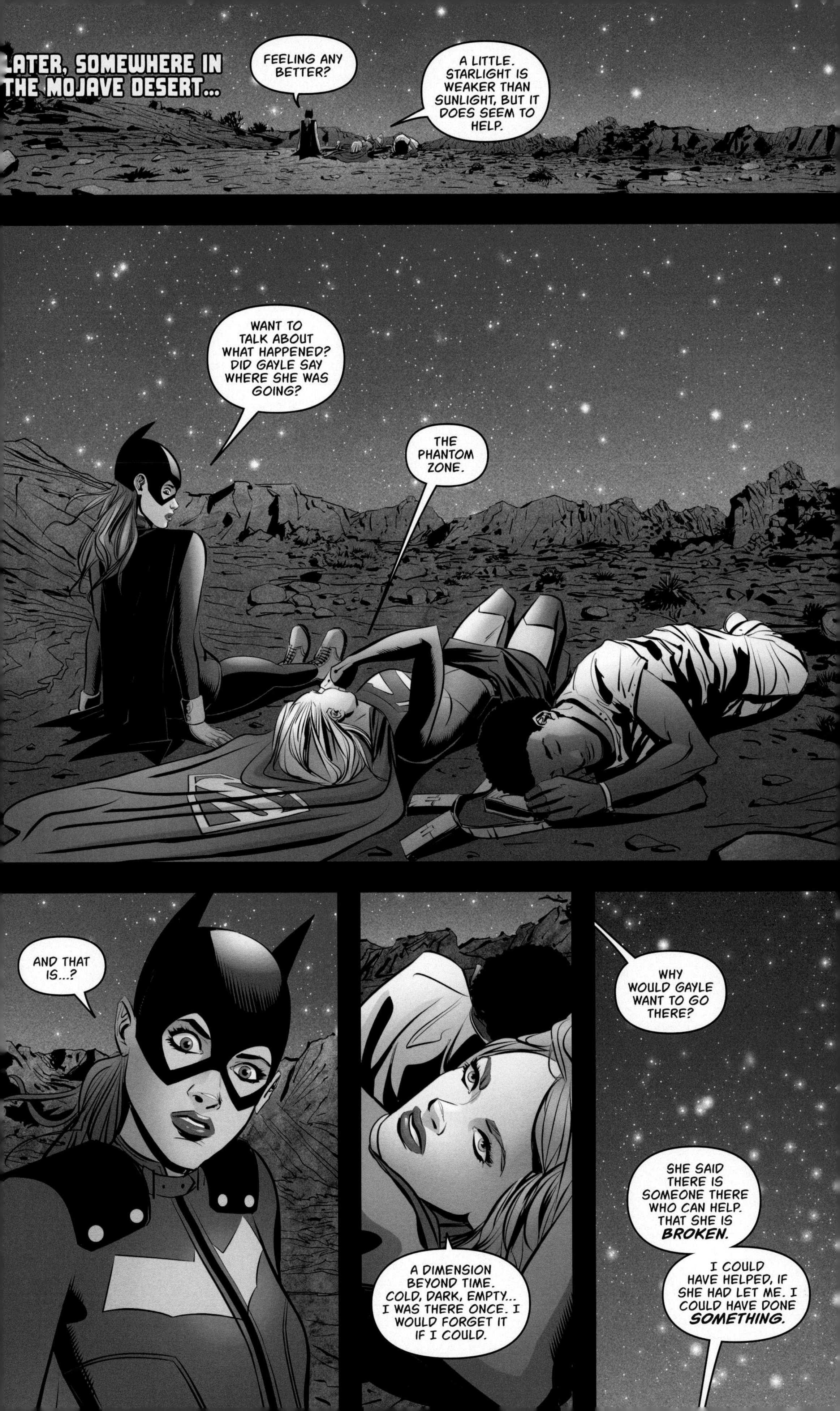
LATER, SOMEWHERE IN THE MOJAVE DESERT...
FEELING ANY BETTER?
A LITTLE. STARLIGHT IS WEAKER THAN SUNLIGHT, BUT IT DOES SEEM TO HELP.
WANT TO TALK ABOUT WHAT HAPPENED? DID GAYLE SAY WHERE SHE WAS GOING?
THE PHANTOM ZONE.
AND THAT IS...?
A DIMENSION BEYOND TIME. COLD, DARK, EMPTY... I WAS THERE ONCE. I WOULD FORGET IT IF I COULD.
WHY WOULD GAYLE WANT TO GO THERE?
SHE SAID THERE IS SOMEONE THERE WHO CAN HELP. THAT SHE IS BROKEN.
I COULD HAVE HELPED, IF SHE HAD LET ME. I COULD HAVE DONE SOMETHING.

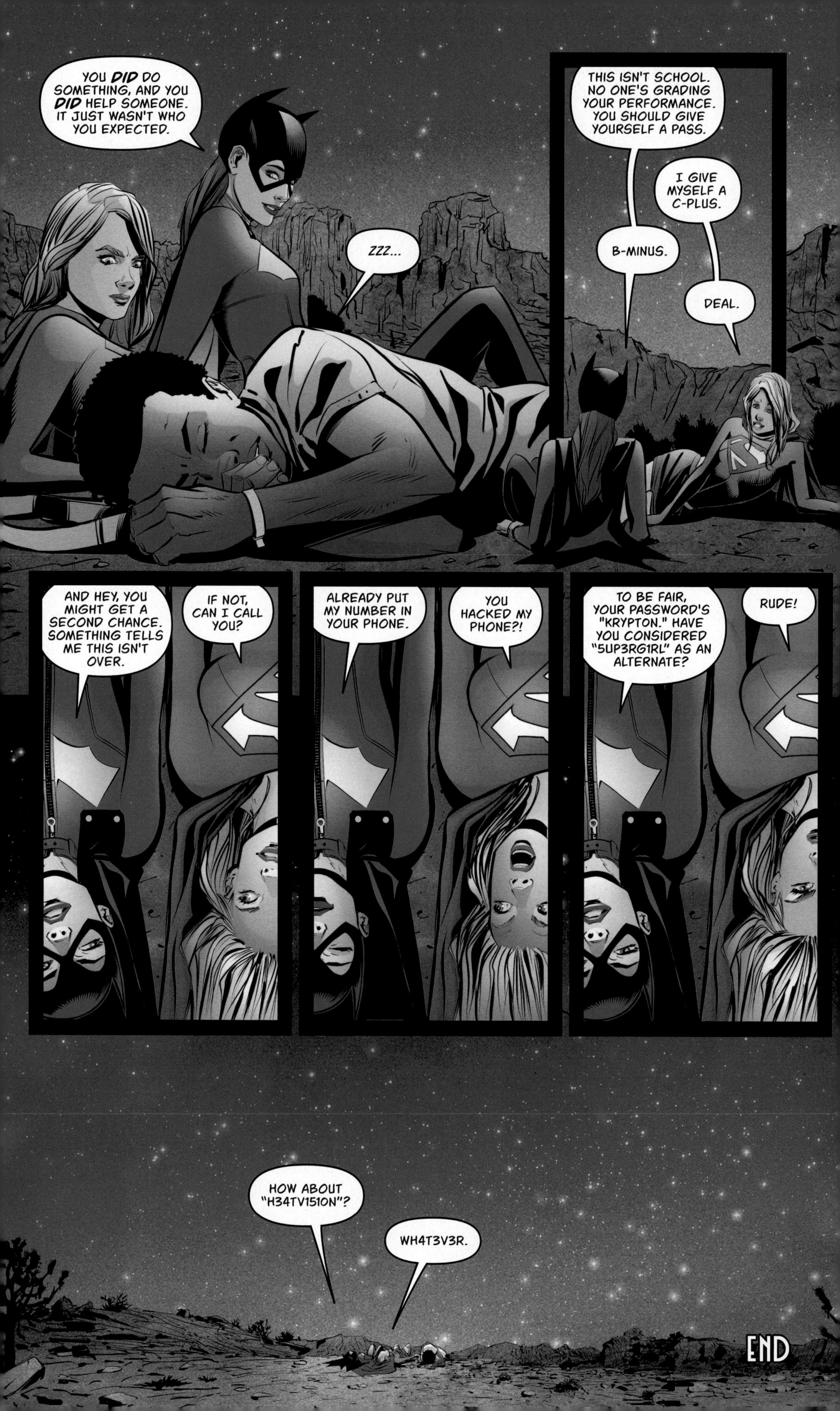
YOU DID DO SOMETHING, AND YOU DID HELP SOMEONE. IT JUST WASN'T WHO YOU EXPECTED.
ZZZ...
THIS ISN'T SCHOOL. NO ONE'S GRADING YOUR PERFORMANCE. YOU SHOULD GIVE YOURSELF A PASS.
I GIVE MYSELF A C-PLUS.
B-MINUS.
DEAL.
AND HEY, YOU MIGHT GET A SECOND CHANCE. SOMETHING TELLS ME THIS ISN'T OVER.
IF NOT, CAN I CALL YOU?
ALREADY PUT MY NUMBER IN YOUR PHONE.
YOU HACKED MY PHONE?!
TO BE FAIR, YOUR PASSWORD'S "KRYPTON." HAVE YOU CONSIDERED "5UP3RG1RL" AS AN ALTERNATE?
RUDE!
HOW ABOUT "H34TV1510N"?
WH4T3V3R.
END

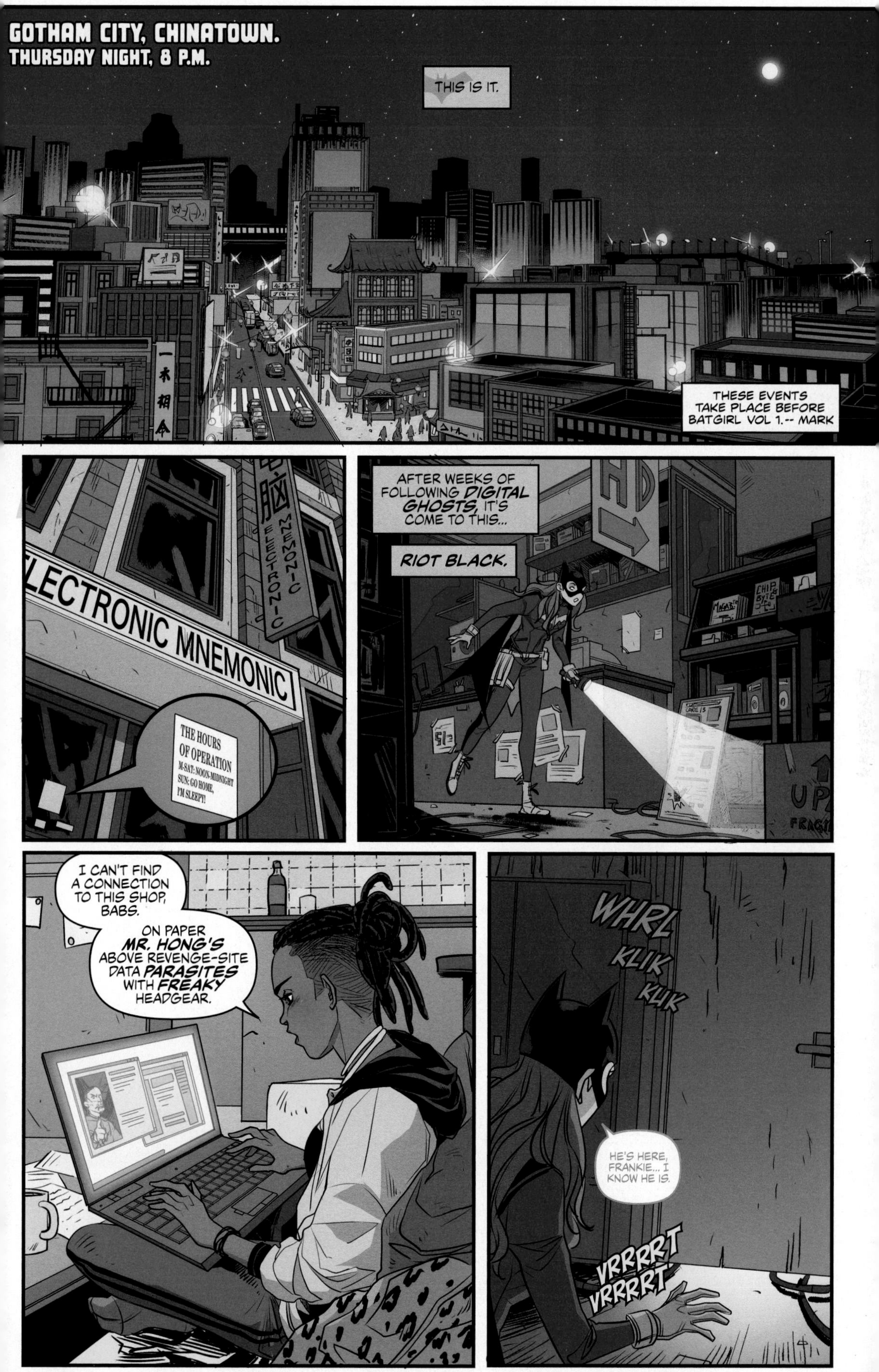
GOTHAM CITY, CHINATOWN.
THURSDAY NIGHT, 8 P.M.
THIS IS IT.
THESE EVENTS TAKE PLACE BEFORE BATGIRL VOL 1.-- MARK
ELECTRONIC MNEMONIC
ELECTRONIC MNEMONIC
THE HOURS OF OPERATION M-SAT: NOON-MIDNIGHT SUN: GO HOME, I'M SLEEPY!
AFTER WEEKS OF FOLLOWING DIGITAL GHOSTS, IT'S COME TO THIS...
RIOT BLACK.
I CAN'T FIND A CONNECTION TO THIS SHOP, BABS.
ON PAPER MR. HONG'S ABOVE REVENGE-SITE DATA PARASITES WITH FREAKY HEADGEAR.
WHRL
KLIK
KLIK
HE'S HERE, FRANKIE... I KNOW HE IS.
VRRRRT VRRRRT

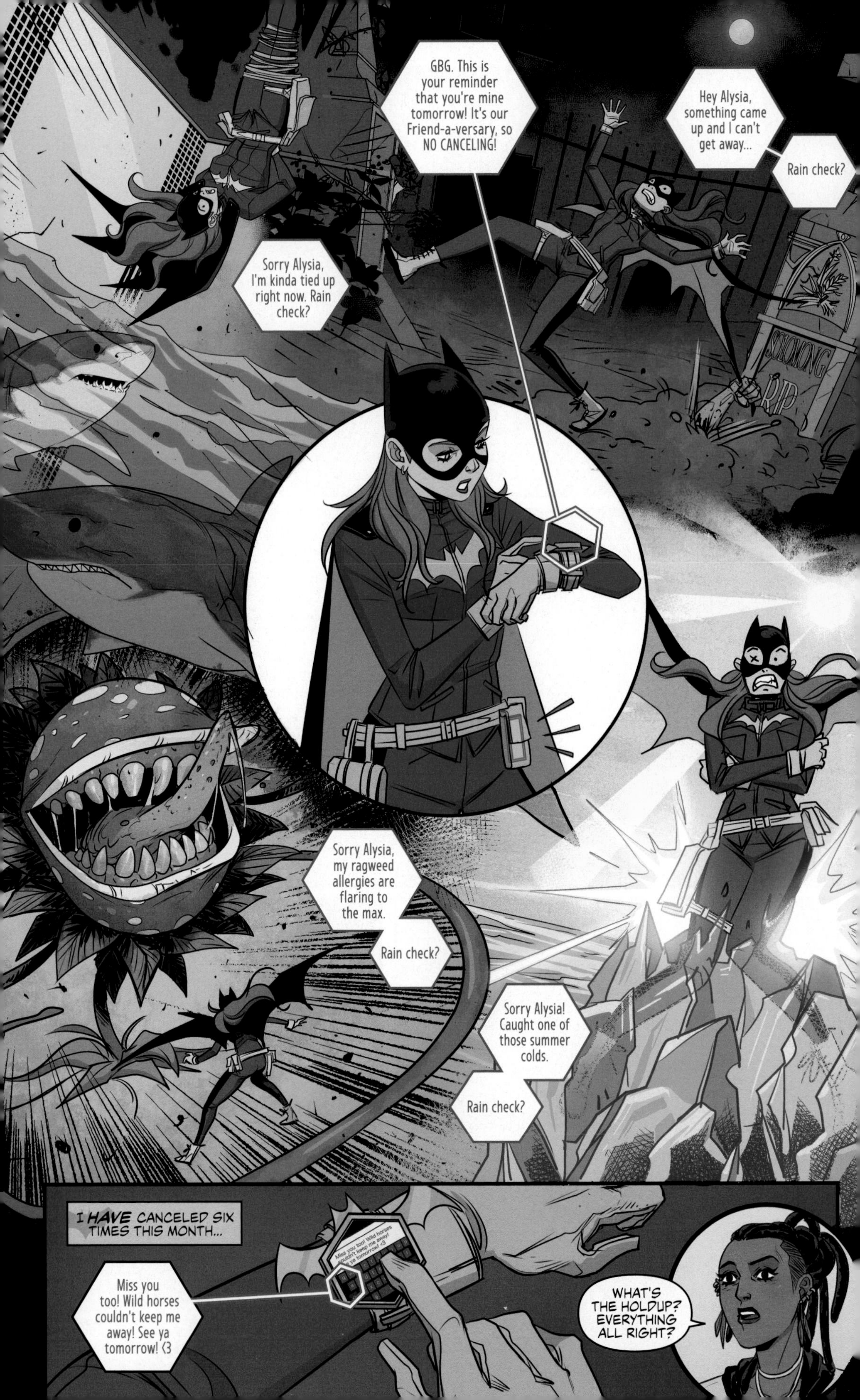
GBG. This is your reminder that you're mine tomorrow! It's our Friend-a-versary, so NO CANCELING!
Sorry Alysia, I'm kinda tied up right now. Rain check?
Hey Alysia, something came up and I can't get away...
Rain check?
SCHOMONG
RIP
Sorry Alysia, my ragweed allergies are flaring to the max.
Rain check?
Sorry Alysia! Caught one of those summer colds.
Rain check?
I HAVE CANCELED SIX TIMES THIS MONTH...
Miss you too! Wild horses couldn't keep me away! See ya tomorrow! <3
WHAT'S THE HOLDUP? EVERYTHING ALL RIGHT?

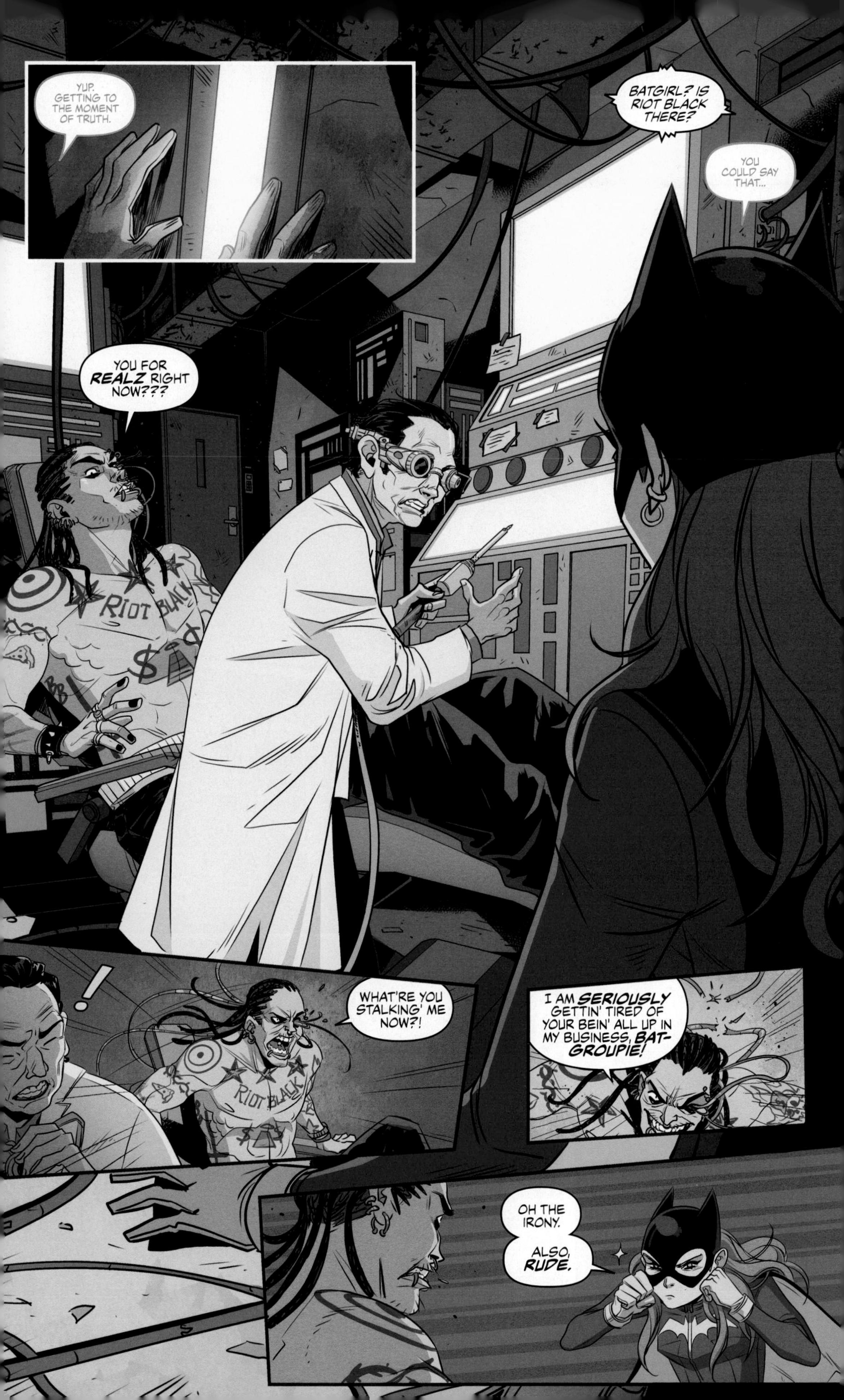
YUP. GETTING TO THE MOMENT OF TRUTH.
BATGIRL? IS RIOT BLACK THERE?
YOU COULD SAY THAT...
YOU FOR REALZ RIGHT NOW???
RIOT BLACK
WHAT'RE YOU STALKING' ME NOW?!
I AM SERIOUSLY GETTIN' TIRED OF YOUR BEIN' ALL UP IN MY BUSINESS, BAT-GROUPIE!
OH THE IRONY.
ALSO, RUDE.

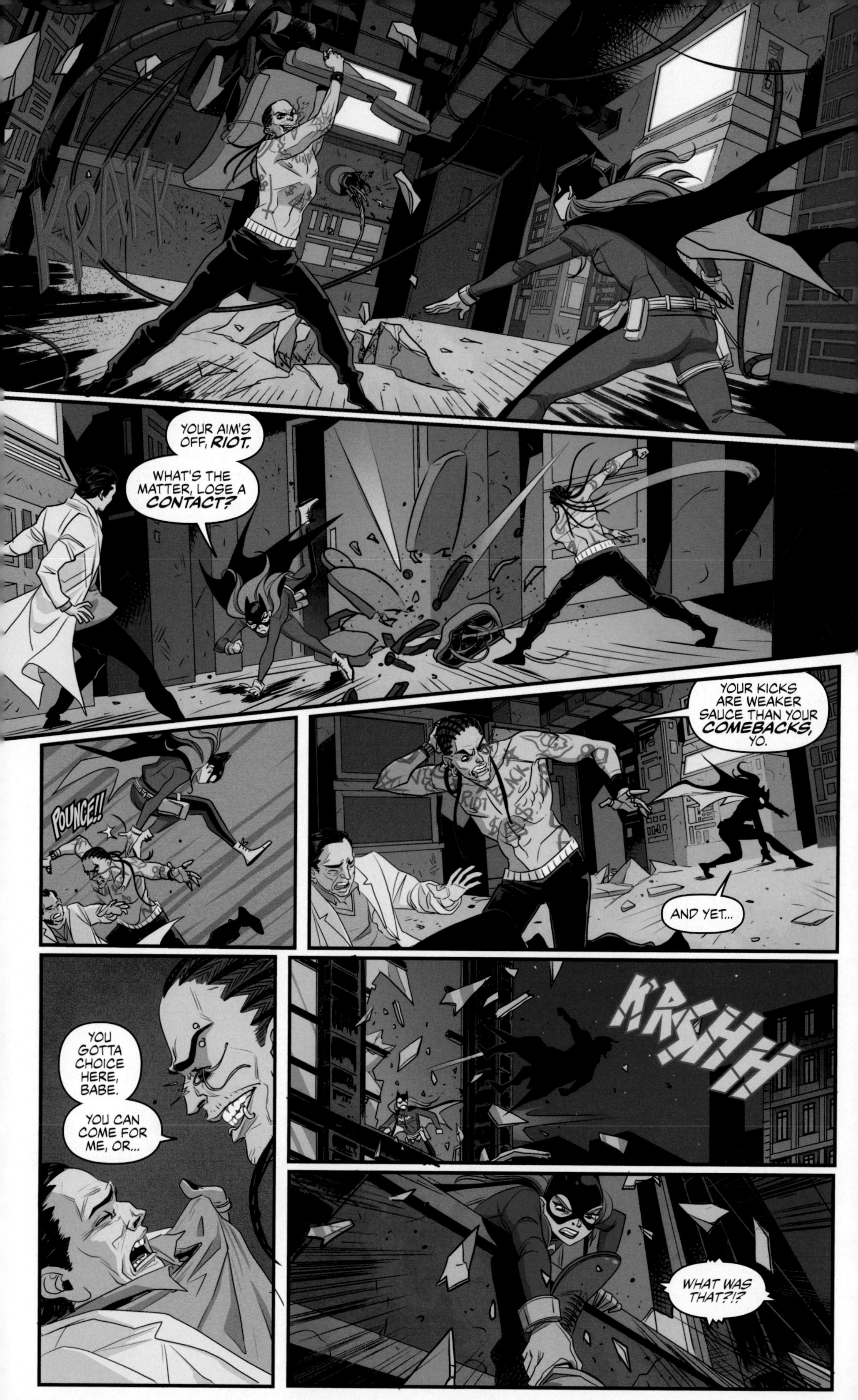
KRAKK
YOUR AIM'S OFF, RIOT.
WHAT'S THE MATTER, LOSE A CONTACT?
POUNCE!!
YOUR KICKS ARE WEAKER SAUCE THAN YOUR COMEBACKS, YO.
AND YET...
YOU GOTTA CHOICE HERE, BABE.
YOU CAN COME FOR ME, OR...
KRSHH
WHAT WAS THAT?!?

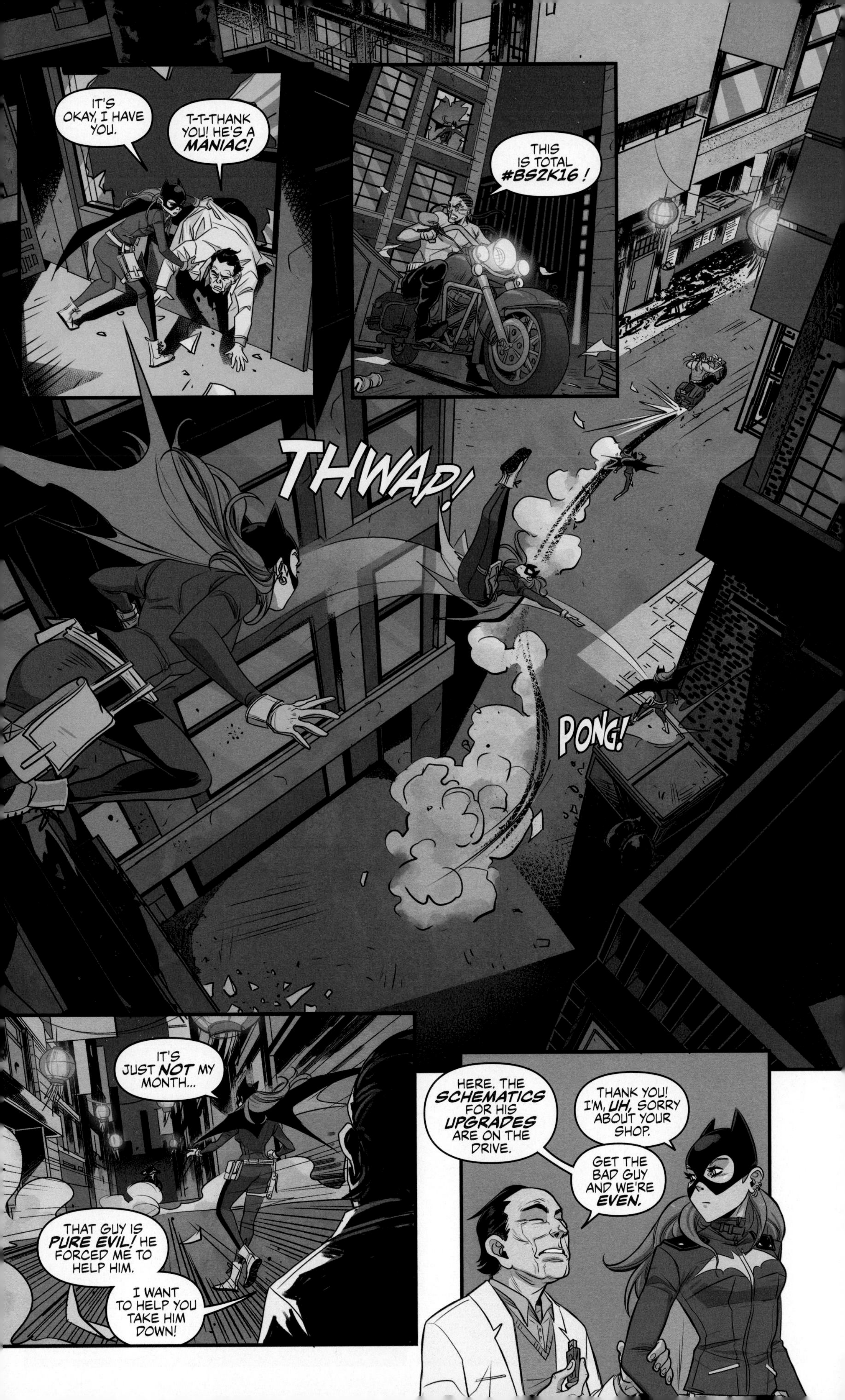
IT'S OKAY, I HAVE YOU.
T-T-THANK YOU! HE'S A MANIAC!
THIS IS TOTAL #BS2K16 !
THWAP!
PONG!
IT'S JUST NOT MY MONTH...
THAT GUY IS PURE EVIL! HE FORCED ME TO HELP HIM.
I WANT TO HELP YOU TAKE HIM DOWN!
HERE. THE SCHEMATICS FOR HIS UPGRADES ARE ON THE DRIVE.
THANK YOU! I'M, UH, SORRY ABOUT YOUR SHOP.
GET THE BAD GUY AND WE'RE EVEN.

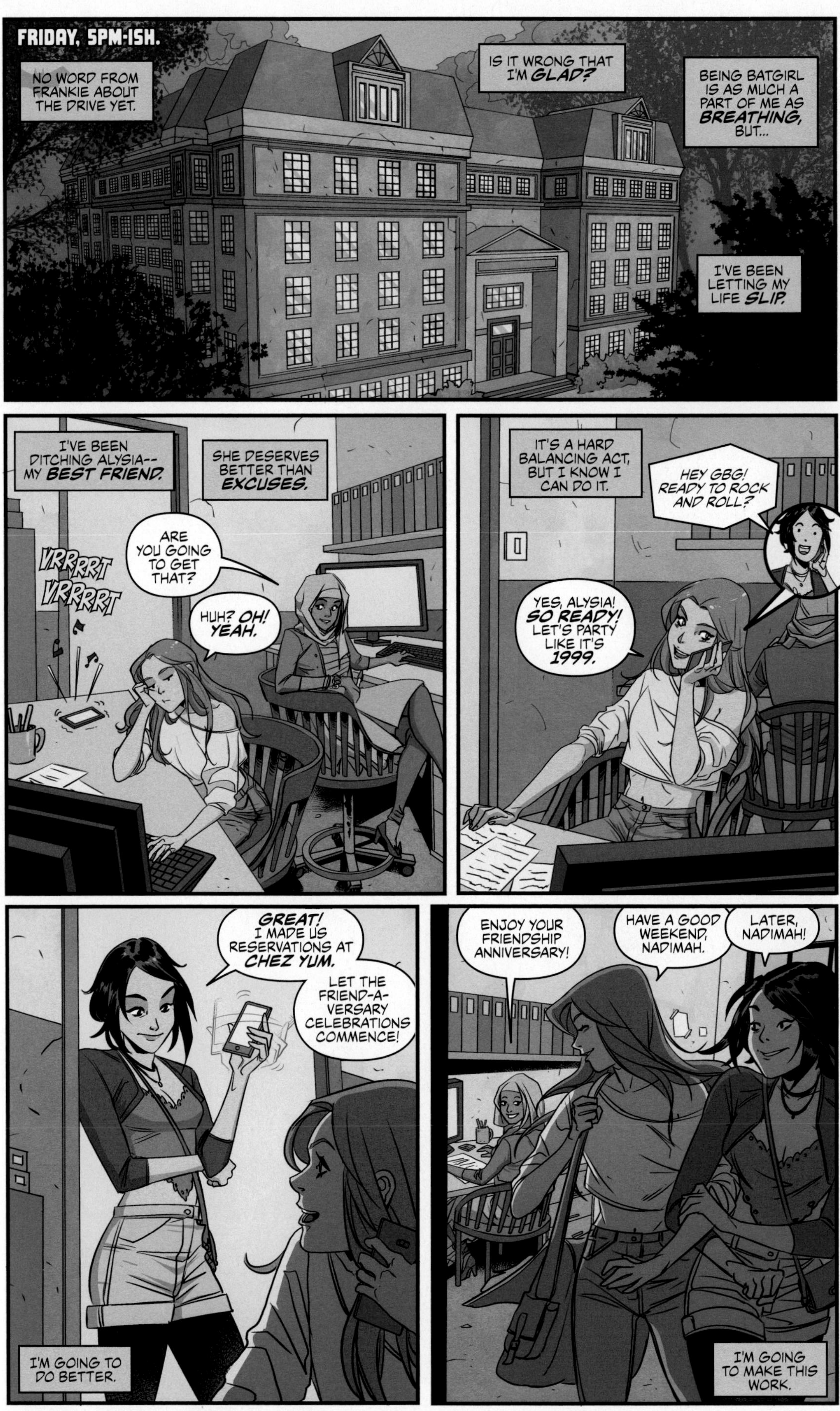
FRIDAY, 5PM-ISH.
NO WORD FROM FRANKIE ABOUT THE DRIVE YET.
IS IT WRONG THAT I'M GLAD?
BEING BATGIRL IS AS MUCH A PART OF ME AS BREATHING, BUT...
I'VE BEEN LETTING MY LIFE SLIP.
I'VE BEEN DITCHING ALYSIA-- MY BEST FRIEND.
SHE DESERVES BETTER THAN EXCUSES.
VRRRRT VRRRRT
ARE YOU GOING TO GET THAT?
HUH? OH! YEAH.
IT'S A HARD BALANCING ACT, BUT I KNOW I CAN DO IT.
HEY GBG! READY TO ROCK AND ROLL?
YES, ALYSIA! SO READY! LET'S PARTY LIKE IT'S 1999.
GREAT! I MADE US RESERVATIONS AT CHEZ YUM.
LET THE FRIEND-A-VERSARY CELEBRATIONS COMMENCE!
I'M GOING TO DO BETTER.
ENJOY YOUR FRIENDSHIP ANNIVERSARY!
HAVE A GOOD WEEKEND, NADIMAH.
LATER, NADIMAH!
I'M GOING TO MAKE THIS WORK.

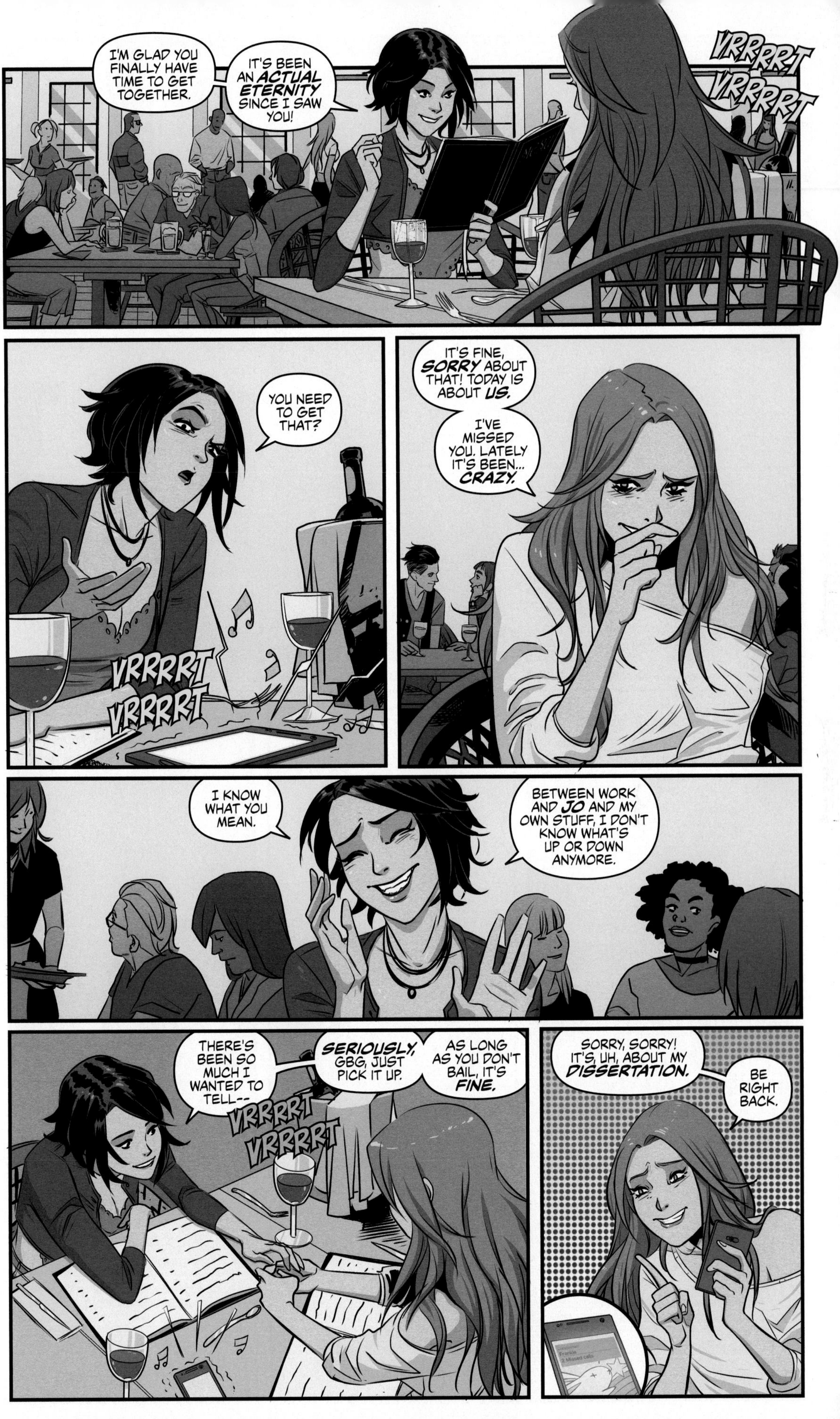
I'M GLAD YOU FINALLY HAVE TIME TO GET TOGETHER.
IT'S BEEN AN ACTUAL ETERNITY SINCE I SAW YOU!
VRRRRT VRRRRT
YOU NEED TO GET THAT?
VRRRRT VRRRRT
IT'S FINE, SORRY ABOUT THAT! TODAY IS ABOUT US.
I'VE MISSED YOU. LATELY IT'S BEEN... CRAZY.
I KNOW WHAT YOU MEAN.
BETWEEN WORK AND JO AND MY OWN STUFF, I DON'T KNOW WHAT'S UP OR DOWN ANYMORE.
THERE'S BEEN SO MUCH I WANTED TO TELL--
VRRRRT VRRRRT
SERIOUSLY, GBG, JUST PICK IT UP.
AS LONG AS YOU DON'T BAIL, IT'S FINE.
SORRY, SORRY! IT'S, UH, ABOUT MY DISSERTATION.
BE RIGHT BACK.
Frankie
2 Missed calls

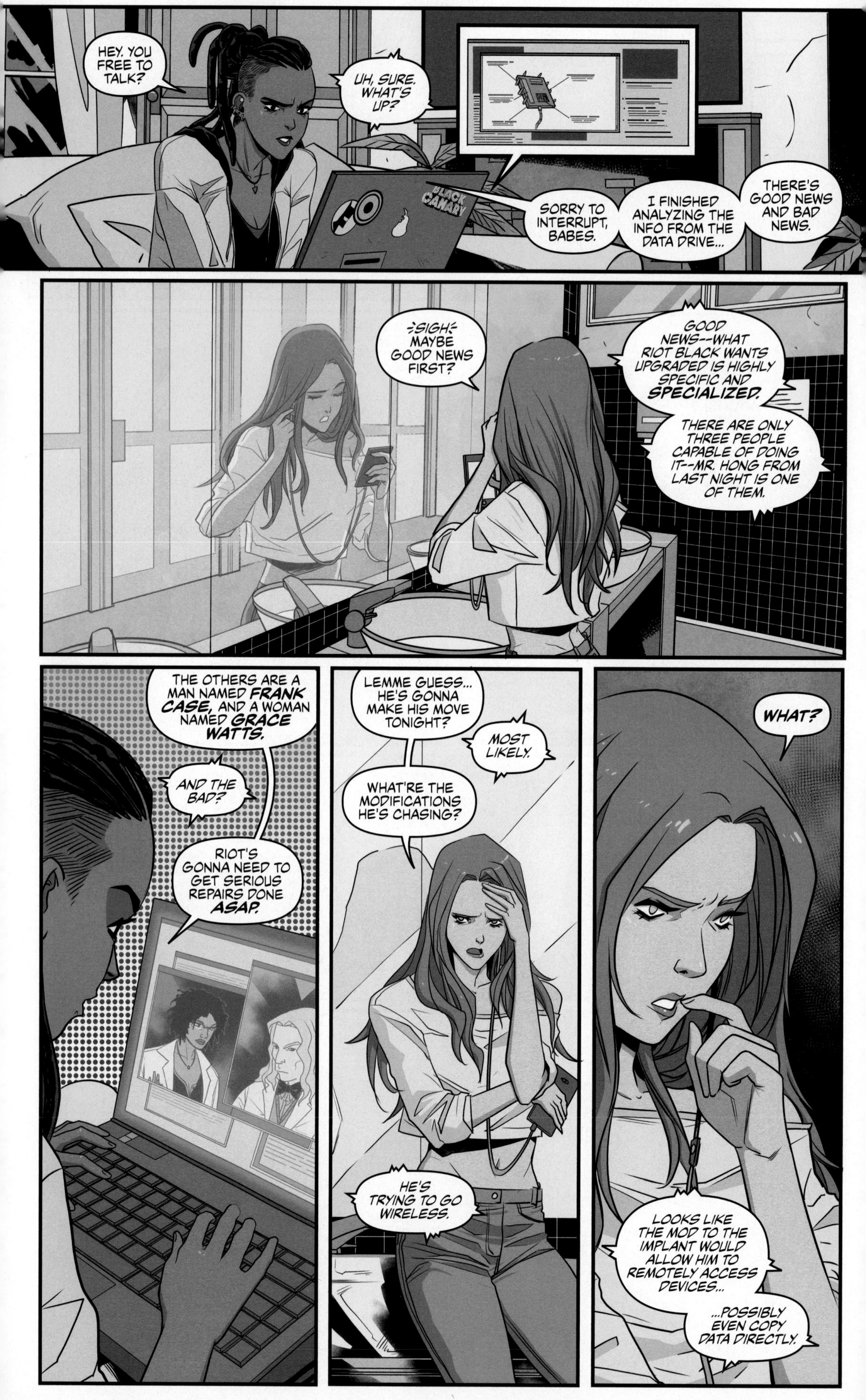
HEY. YOU FREE TO TALK?
UH, SURE. WHAT'S UP?
BLACK CANARY
SORRY TO INTERRUPT, BABES.
I FINISHED ANALYZING THE INFO FROM THE DATA DRIVE...
THERE'S GOOD NEWS AND BAD NEWS.
SIGH MAYBE GOOD NEWS FIRST?
GOOD NEWS--WHAT RIOT BLACK WANTS UPGRADED IS HIGHLY SPECIFIC AND SPECIALIZED.
THERE ARE ONLY THREE PEOPLE CAPABLE OF DOING IT--MR. HONG FROM LAST NIGHT IS ONE OF THEM.
THE OTHERS ARE A MAN NAMED FRANK CASE, AND A WOMAN NAMED GRACE WATTS.
AND THE BAD?
RIOT'S GONNA NEED TO GET SERIOUS REPAIRS DONE ASAP.
LEMME GUESS... HE'S GONNA MAKE HIS MOVE TONIGHT?
MOST LIKELY.
WHAT'RE THE MODIFICATIONS HE'S CHASING?
HE'S TRYING TO GO WIRELESS.
WHAT?
LOOKS LIKE THE MOD TO THE IMPLANT WOULD ALLOW HIM TO REMOTELY ACCESS DEVICES...
...POSSIBLY EVEN COPY DATA DIRECTLY.

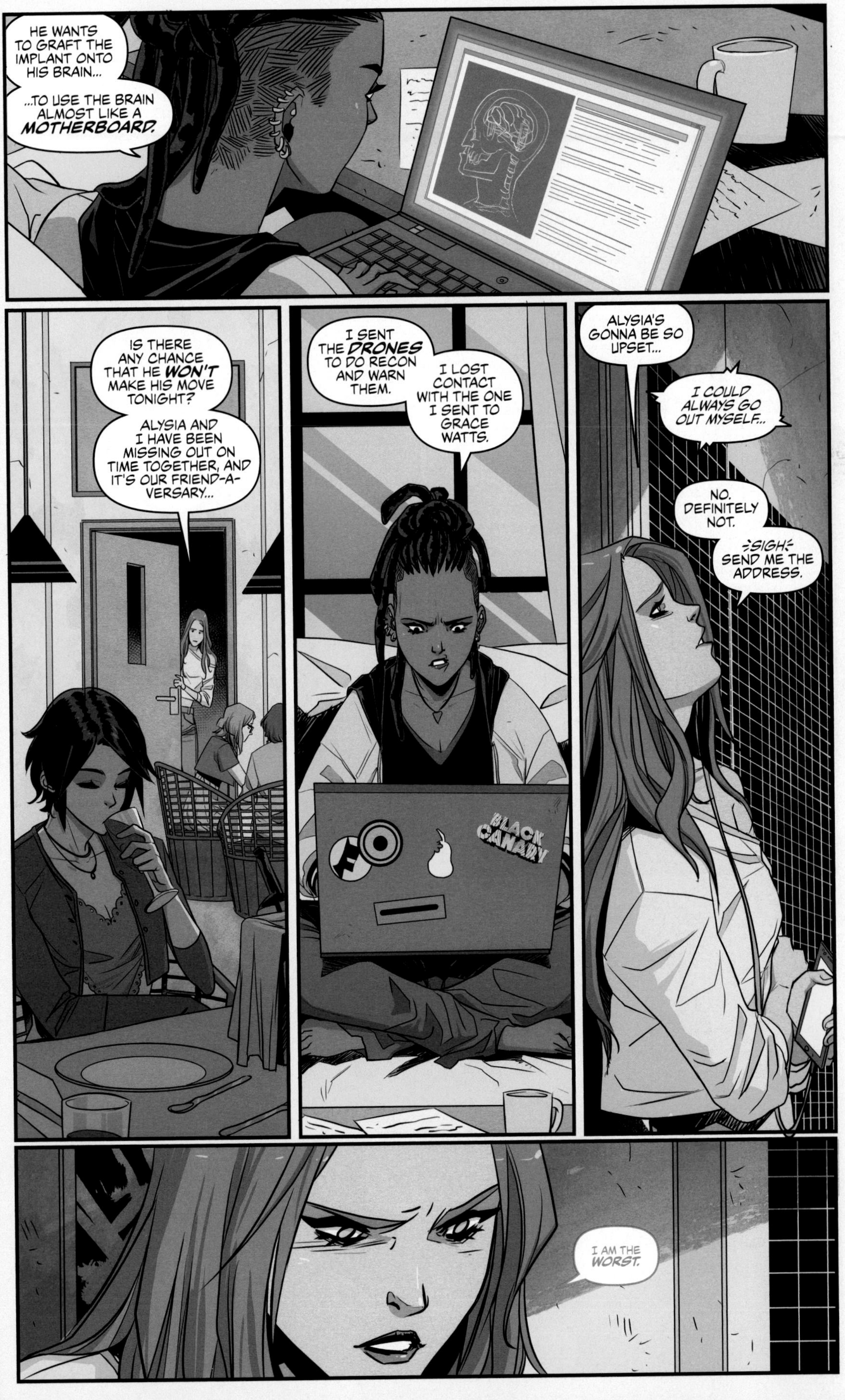
HE WANTS TO GRAFT THE IMPLANT ONTO HIS BRAIN...
...TO USE THE BRAIN ALMOST LIKE A MOTHERBOARD.
IS THERE ANY CHANCE THAT HE WON'T MAKE HIS MOVE TONIGHT?
ALYSIA AND I HAVE BEEN MISSING OUT ON TIME TOGETHER, AND IT'S OUR FRIEND-A-VERSARY...
I SENT THE DRONES TO DO RECON AND WARN THEM.
I LOST CONTACT WITH THE ONE I SENT TO GRACE WATTS.
BLACK CANARY
ALYSIA'S GONNA BE SO UPSET...
I COULD ALWAYS GO OUT MYSELF...
NO. DEFINITELY NOT.
SIGH
SEND ME THE ADDRESS.
I AM THE WORST.

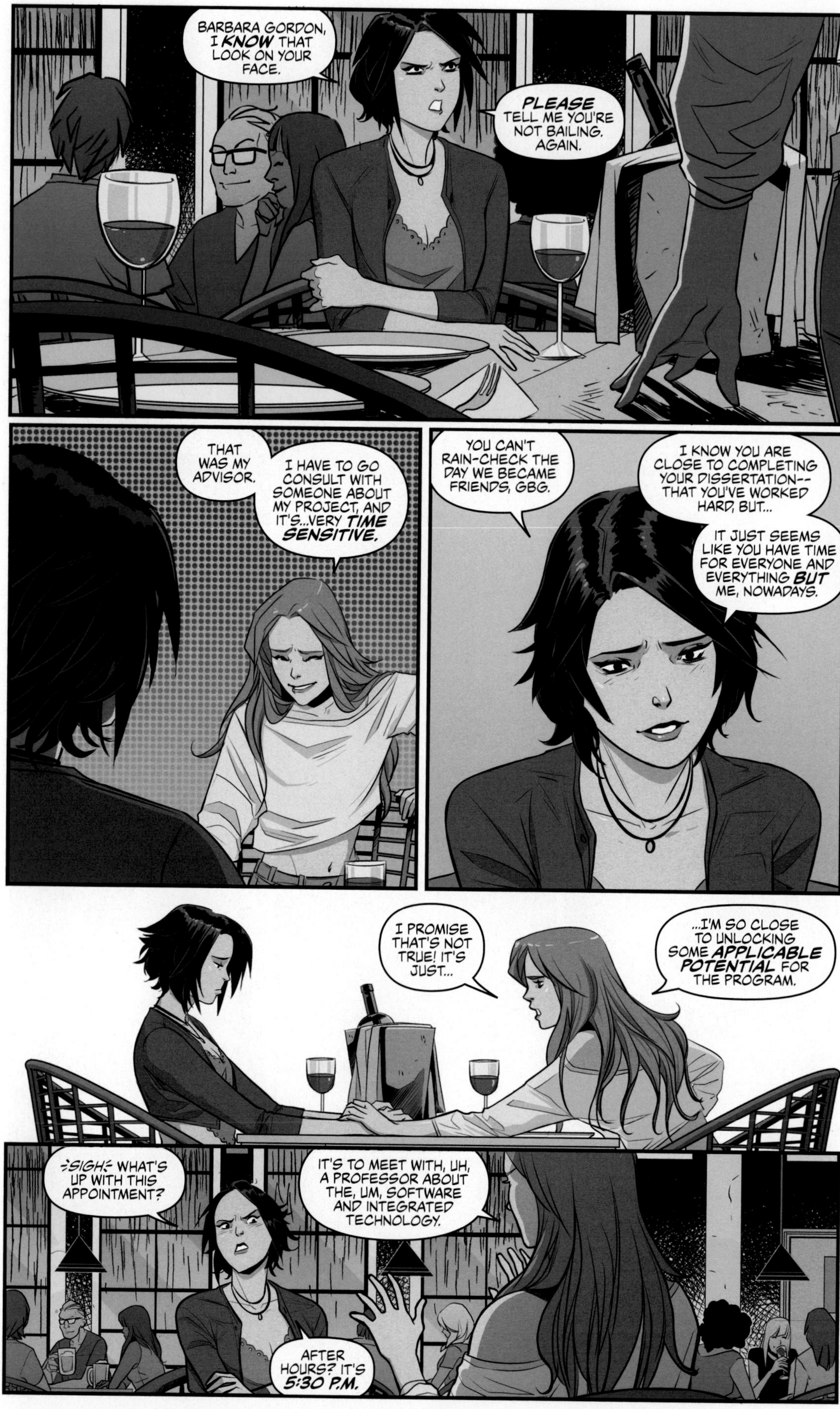
BARBARA GORDON, I KNOW THAT LOOK ON YOUR FACE.
PLEASE TELL ME YOU'RE NOT BAILING. AGAIN.
THAT WAS MY ADVISOR.
I HAVE TO GO CONSULT WITH SOMEONE ABOUT MY PROJECT, AND IT'S...VERY TIME SENSITIVE.
YOU CAN'T RAIN-CHECK THE DAY WE BECAME FRIENDS, GBG.
I KNOW YOU ARE CLOSE TO COMPLETING YOUR DISSERTATION-- THAT YOU'VE WORKED HARD, BUT...
IT JUST SEEMS LIKE YOU HAVE TIME FOR EVERYONE AND EVERYTHING BUT ME, NOWADAYS.
I PROMISE THAT'S NOT TRUE! IT'S JUST...
...I'M SO CLOSE TO UNLOCKING SOME APPLICABLE POTENTIAL FOR THE PROGRAM.
-SIGH- WHAT'S UP WITH THIS APPOINTMENT?
IT'S TO MEET WITH, UH, A PROFESSOR ABOUT THE, UM, SOFTWARE AND INTEGRATED TECHNOLOGY.
AFTER HOURS? IT'S 5:30 P.M.

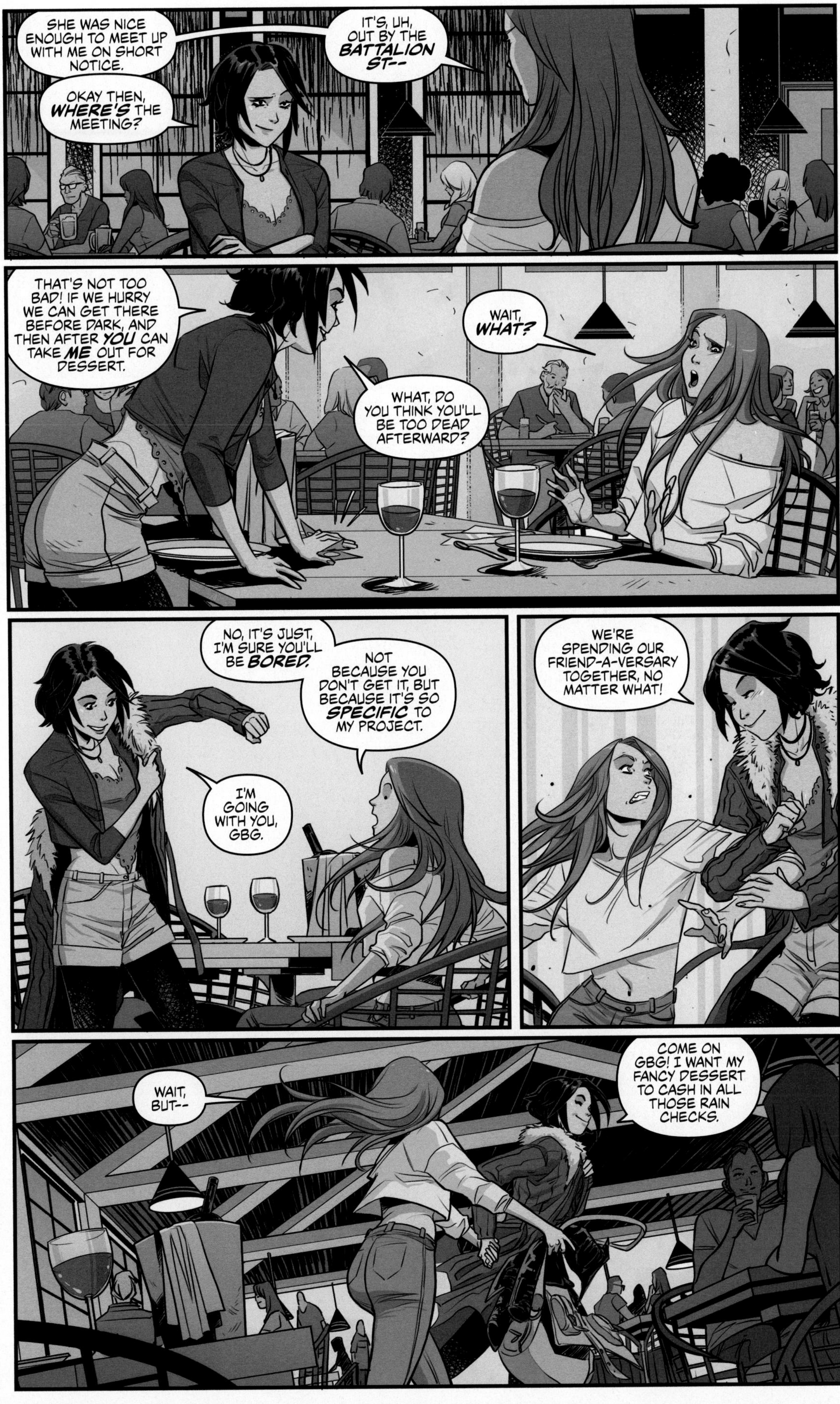

SHE WAS NICE ENOUGH TO MEET UP WITH ME ON SHORT NOTICE.
OKAY THEN, WHERE'S THE MEETING?
IT'S, UH, OUT BY THE BATTALION ST--
THAT'S NOT TOO BAD! IF WE HURRY WE CAN GET THERE BEFORE DARK, AND THEN AFTER YOU CAN TAKE ME OUT FOR DESSERT.
WAIT, WHAT?
WHAT, DO YOU THINK YOU'LL BE TOO DEAD AFTERWARD?
NO, IT'S JUST, I'M SURE YOU'LL BE BORED.
NOT BECAUSE YOU DON'T GET IT, BUT BECAUSE IT'S SO SPECIFIC TO MY PROJECT.
I'M GOING WITH YOU, GBG.
WE'RE SPENDING OUR FRIEND-A-VERSARY TOGETHER, NO MATTER WHAT!
WAIT, BUT--
COME ON GBG! I WANT MY FANCY DESSERT TO CASH IN ALL THOSE RAIN CHECKS.

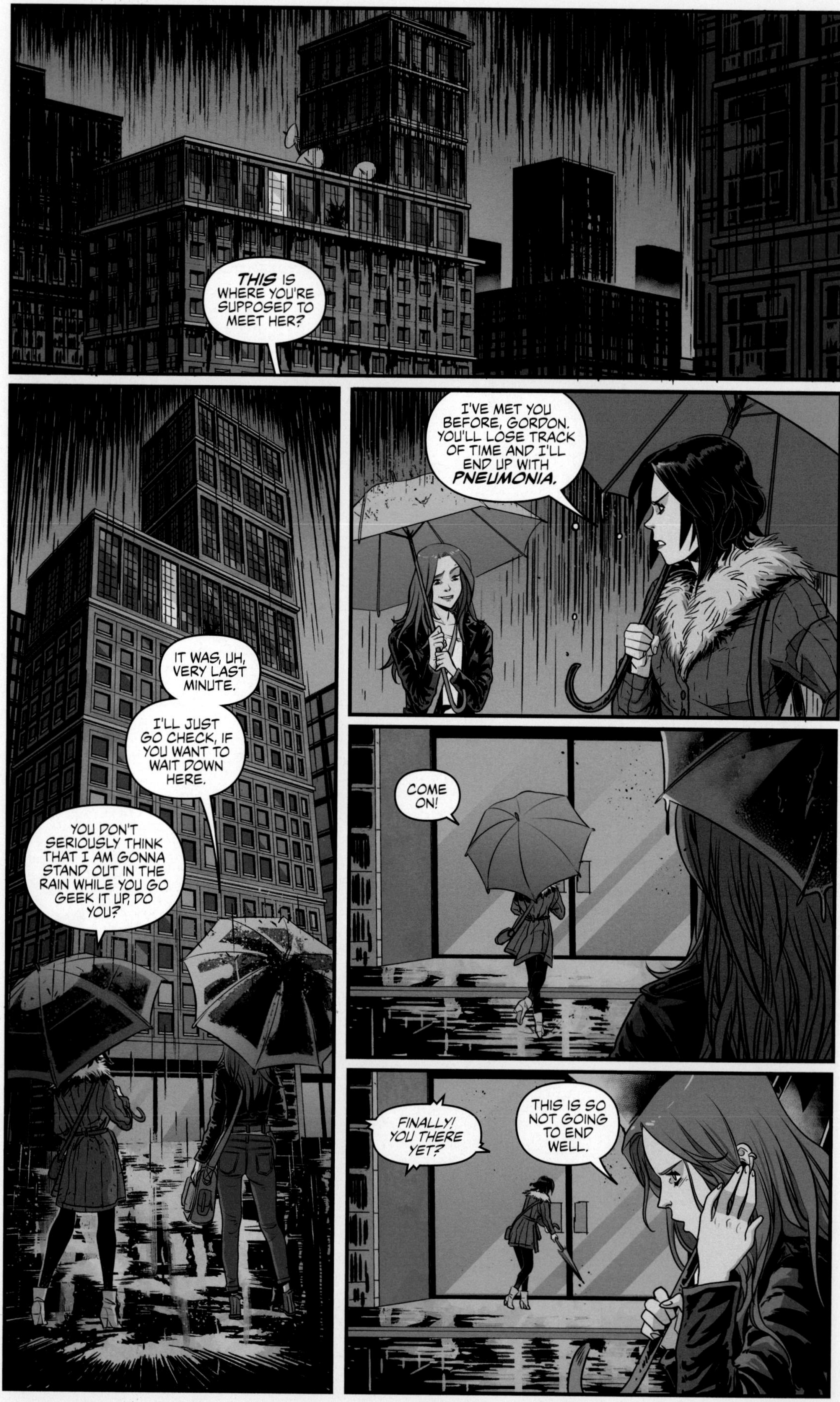
THIS IS WHERE YOU'RE SUPPOSED TO MEET HER?
IT WAS, UH, VERY LAST MINUTE.
I'LL JUST GO CHECK, IF YOU WANT TO WAIT DOWN HERE.
YOU DON'T SERIOUSLY THINK THAT I AM GONNA STAND OUT IN THE RAIN WHILE YOU GO GEEK IT UP, DO YOU?
I'VE MET YOU BEFORE, GORDON. YOU'LL LOSE TRACK OF TIME AND I'LL END UP WITH PNEUMONIA.
COME ON!
FINALLY! YOU THERE YET?
THIS IS SO NOT GOING TO END WELL.

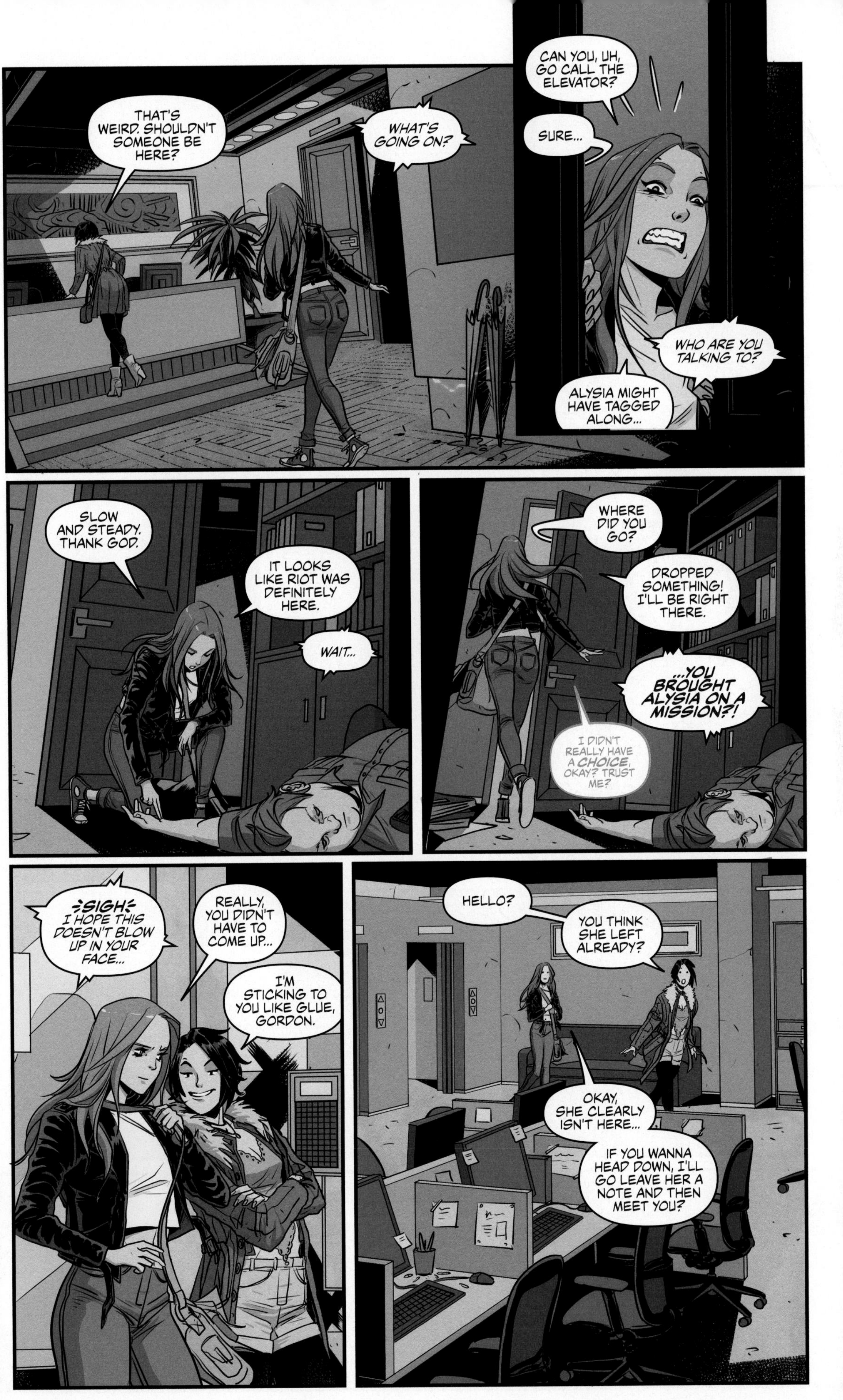
THAT'S WEIRD. SHOULDN'T SOMEONE BE HERE?
WHAT'S GOING ON?
CAN YOU, UH, GO CALL THE ELEVATOR?
SURE...
WHO ARE YOU TALKING TO?
ALYSIA MIGHT HAVE TAGGED ALONG...
SLOW AND STEADY. THANK GOD.
IT LOOKS LIKE RIOT WAS DEFINITELY HERE.
WAIT...
WHERE DID YOU GO?
DROPPED SOMETHING! I'LL BE RIGHT THERE.
...YOU BROUGHT ALYSIA ON A MISSION?!
I DIDN'T REALLY HAVE A CHOICE, OKAY? TRUST ME?
SIGH I HOPE THIS DOESN'T BLOW UP IN YOUR FACE...
REALLY, YOU DIDN'T HAVE TO COME UP...
I'M STICKING TO YOU LIKE GLUE, GORDON.
HELLO?
YOU THINK SHE LEFT ALREADY?
OKAY, SHE CLEARLY ISN'T HERE...
IF YOU WANNA HEAD DOWN, I'LL GO LEAVE HER A NOTE AND THEN MEET YOU?

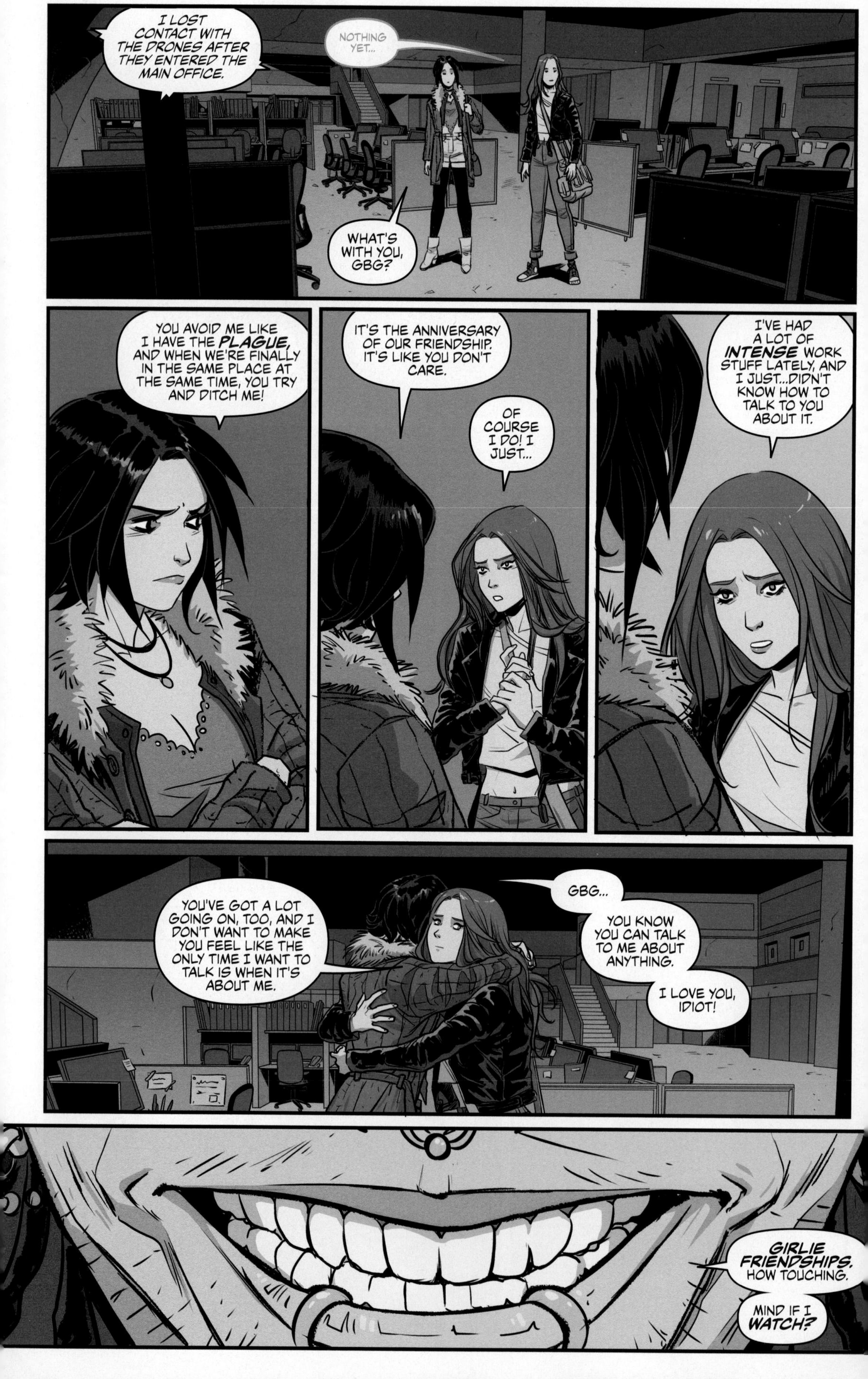
I LOST CONTACT WITH THE DRONES AFTER THEY ENTERED THE MAIN OFFICE.
NOTHING YET...
WHAT'S WITH YOU, GBG?
YOU AVOID ME LIKE I HAVE THE PLAGUE, AND WHEN WE'RE FINALLY IN THE SAME PLACE AT THE SAME TIME, YOU TRY AND DITCH ME!
IT'S THE ANNIVERSARY OF OUR FRIENDSHIP. IT'S LIKE YOU DON'T CARE.
OF COURSE I DO! I JUST...
I'VE HAD A LOT OF INTENSE WORK STUFF LATELY, AND I JUST...DIDN'T KNOW HOW TO TALK TO YOU ABOUT IT.
YOU'VE GOT A LOT GOING ON, TOO, AND I DON'T WANT TO MAKE YOU FEEL LIKE THE ONLY TIME I WANT TO TALK IS WHEN IT'S ABOUT ME.
GBG...
YOU KNOW YOU CAN TALK TO ME ABOUT ANYTHING.
I LOVE YOU, IDIOT!
GIRLIE FRIENDSHIPS. HOW TOUCHING.
MIND IF I WATCH?

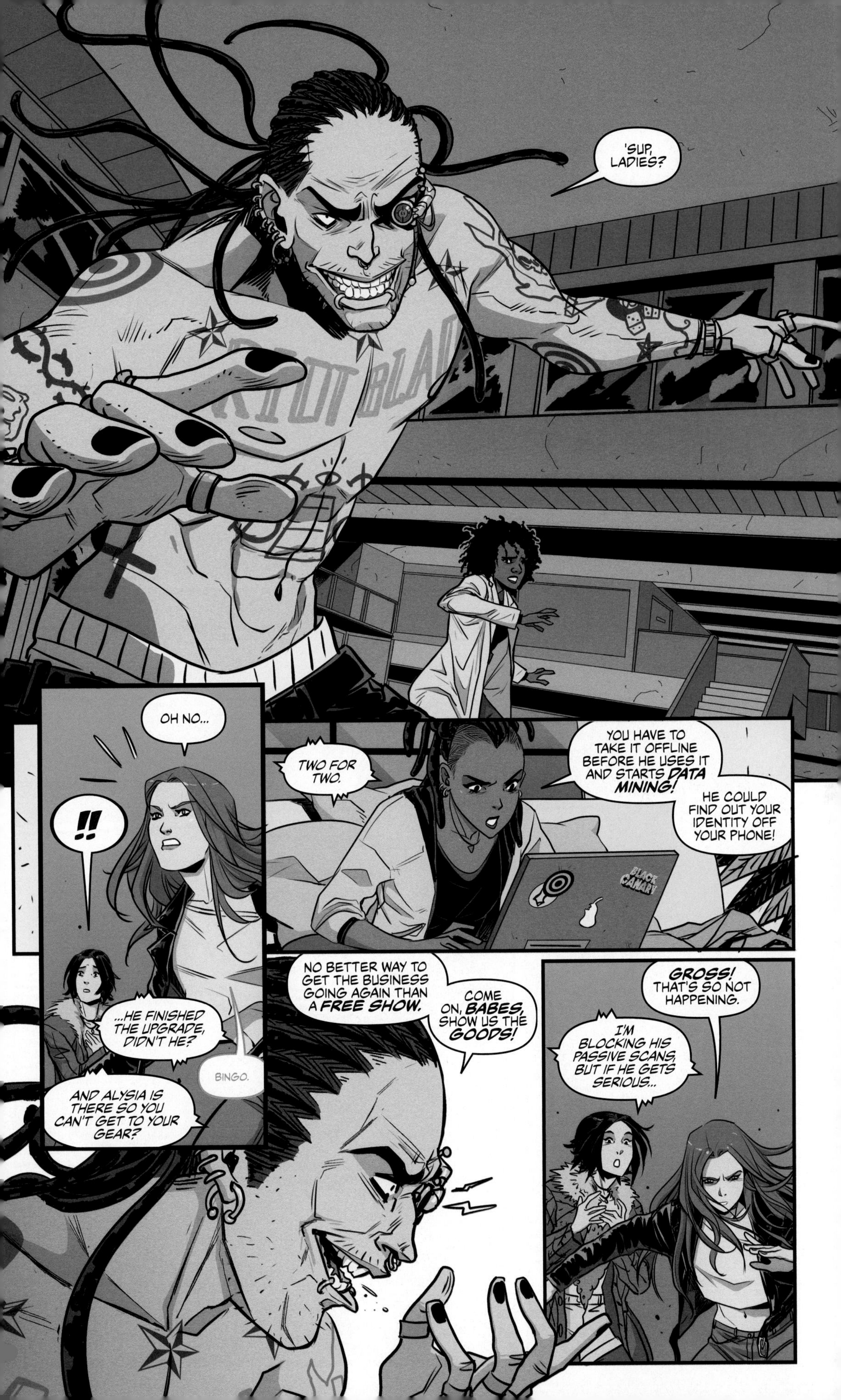

'SUP, LADIES?
OH NO...
!!
TWO FOR TWO.
YOU HAVE TO TAKE IT OFFLINE BEFORE HE USES IT AND STARTS DATA MINING!
HE COULD FIND OUT YOUR IDENTITY OFF YOUR PHONE!
...HE FINISHED THE UPGRADE, DIDN'T HE?
BINGO.
AND ALYSIA IS THERE SO YOU CAN'T GET TO YOUR GEAR?
NO BETTER WAY TO GET THE BUSINESS GOING AGAIN THAN A FREE SHOW.
COME ON, BABES, SHOW US THE GOODS!
GROSS! THAT'S SO NOT HAPPENING.
I'M BLOCKING HIS PASSIVE SCANS, BUT IF HE GETS SERIOUS...

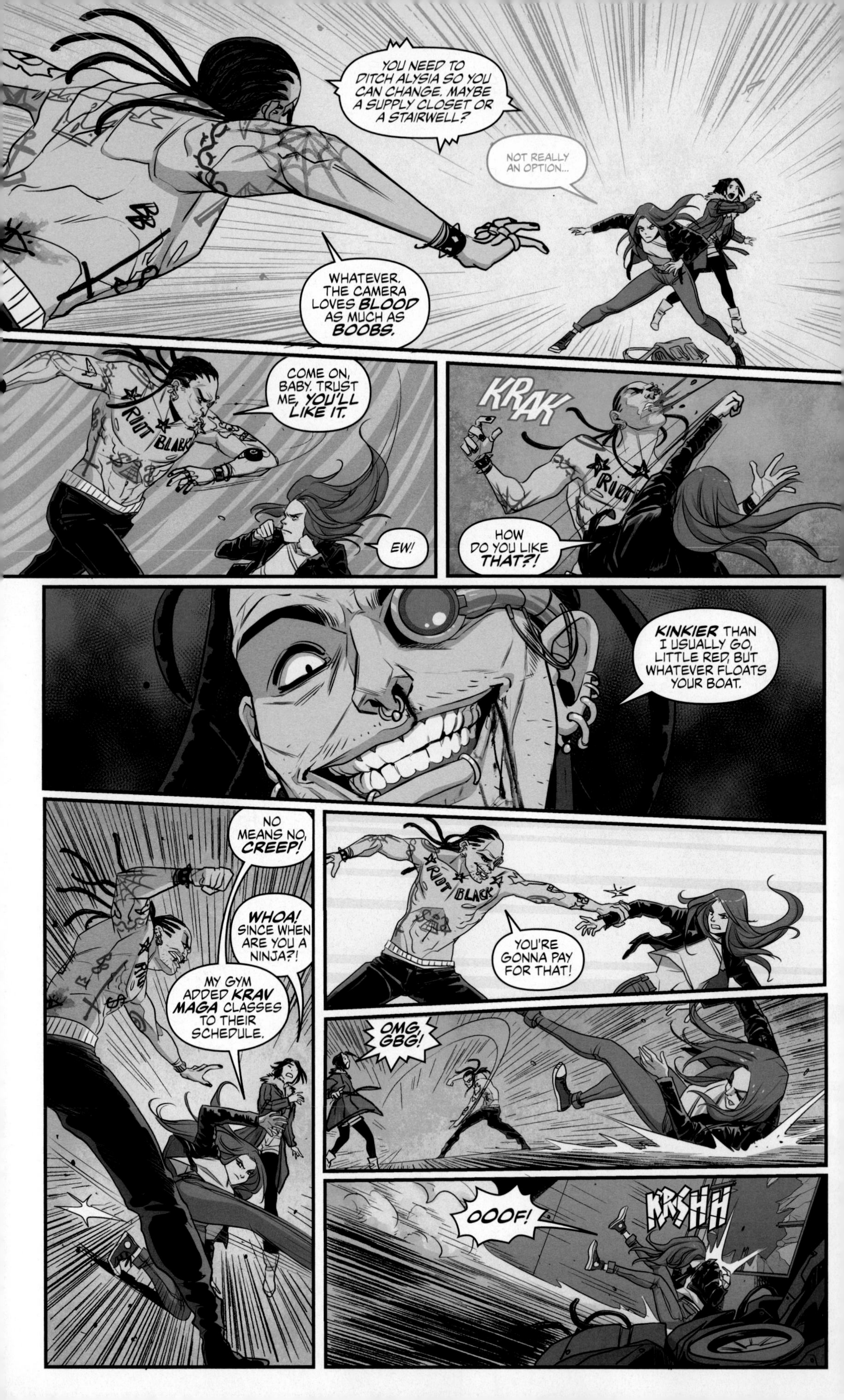
YOU NEED TO DITCH ALYSIA SO YOU CAN CHANGE. MAYBE A SUPPLY CLOSET OR A STAIRWELL?
NOT REALLY AN OPTION...
WHATEVER. THE CAMERA LOVES BLOOD AS MUCH AS BOOBS.
COME ON, BABY. TRUST ME, YOU'LL LIKE IT.
EW!
KRAK
HOW DO YOU LIKE THAT?!
KINKIER THAN I USUALLY GO, LITTLE RED, BUT WHATEVER FLOATS YOUR BOAT.
NO MEANS NO, CREEP!
WHOA! SINCE WHEN ARE YOU A NINJA?!
MY GYM ADDED KRAV MAGA CLASSES TO THEIR SCHEDULE.
YOU'RE GONNA PAY FOR THAT!
OMG, GBG!
OOOF!
KRSHH

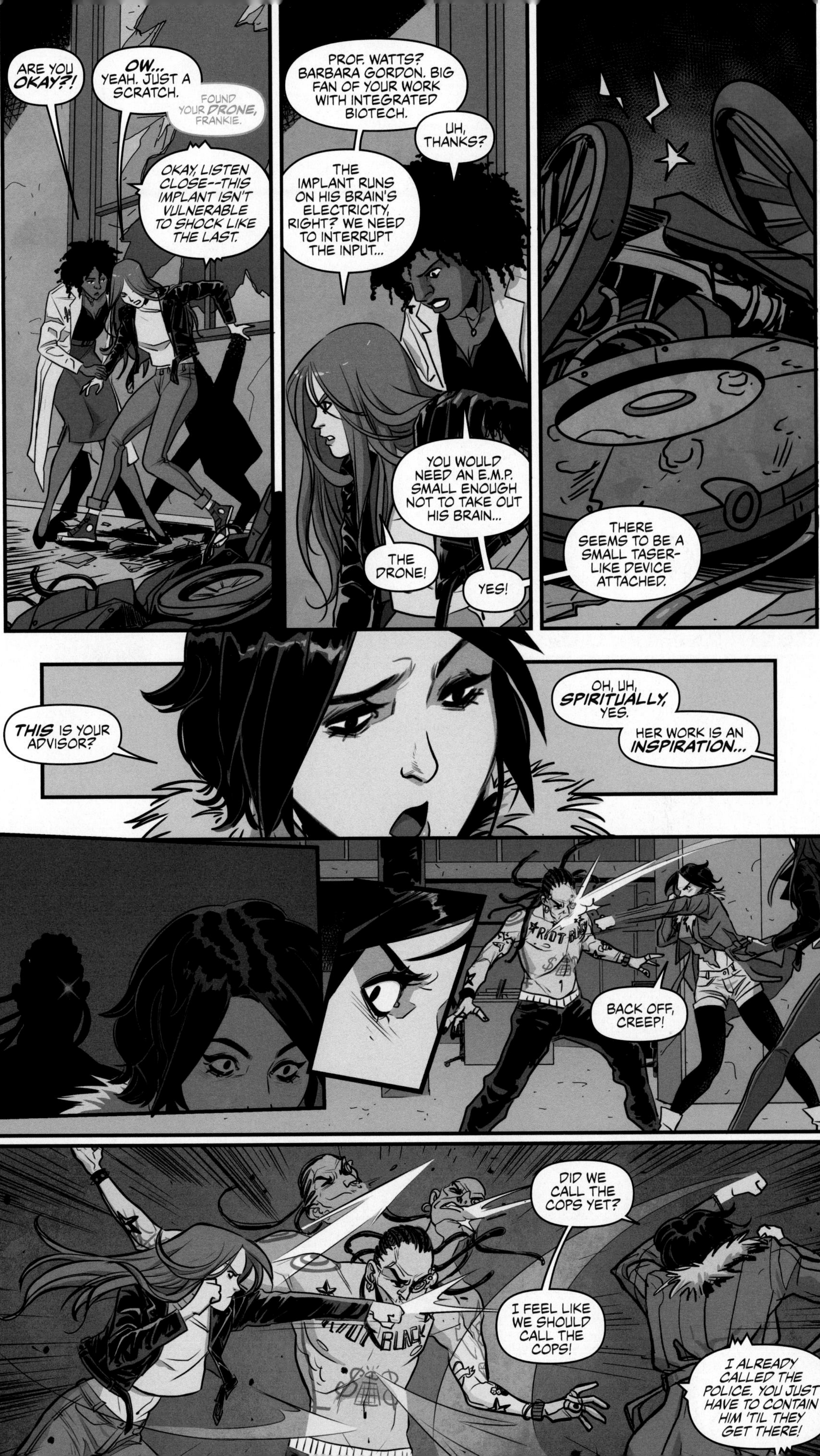
ARE YOU OKAY?!
OW... YEAH. JUST A SCRATCH.
FOUND YOUR DRONE, FRANKIE.
OKAY, LISTEN CLOSE--THIS IMPLANT ISN'T VULNERABLE TO SHOCK LIKE THE LAST.
PROF. WATTS? BARBARA GORDON. BIG FAN OF YOUR WORK WITH INTEGRATED BIOTECH.
UH, THANKS?
THE IMPLANT RUNS ON HIS BRAIN'S ELECTRICITY, RIGHT? WE NEED TO INTERRUPT THE INPUT...
YOU WOULD NEED AN E.M.P. SMALL ENOUGH NOT TO TAKE OUT HIS BRAIN...
THE DRONE!
YES!
THERE SEEMS TO BE A SMALL TASER-LIKE DEVICE ATTACHED.
THIS IS YOUR ADVISOR?
OH, UH, SPIRITUALLY, YES.
HER WORK IS AN INSPIRATION...
BACK OFF, CREEP!
DID WE CALL THE COPS YET?
I FEEL LIKE WE SHOULD CALL THE COPS!
I ALREADY CALLED THE POLICE. YOU JUST HAVE TO CONTAIN HIM 'TIL THEY GET THERE!

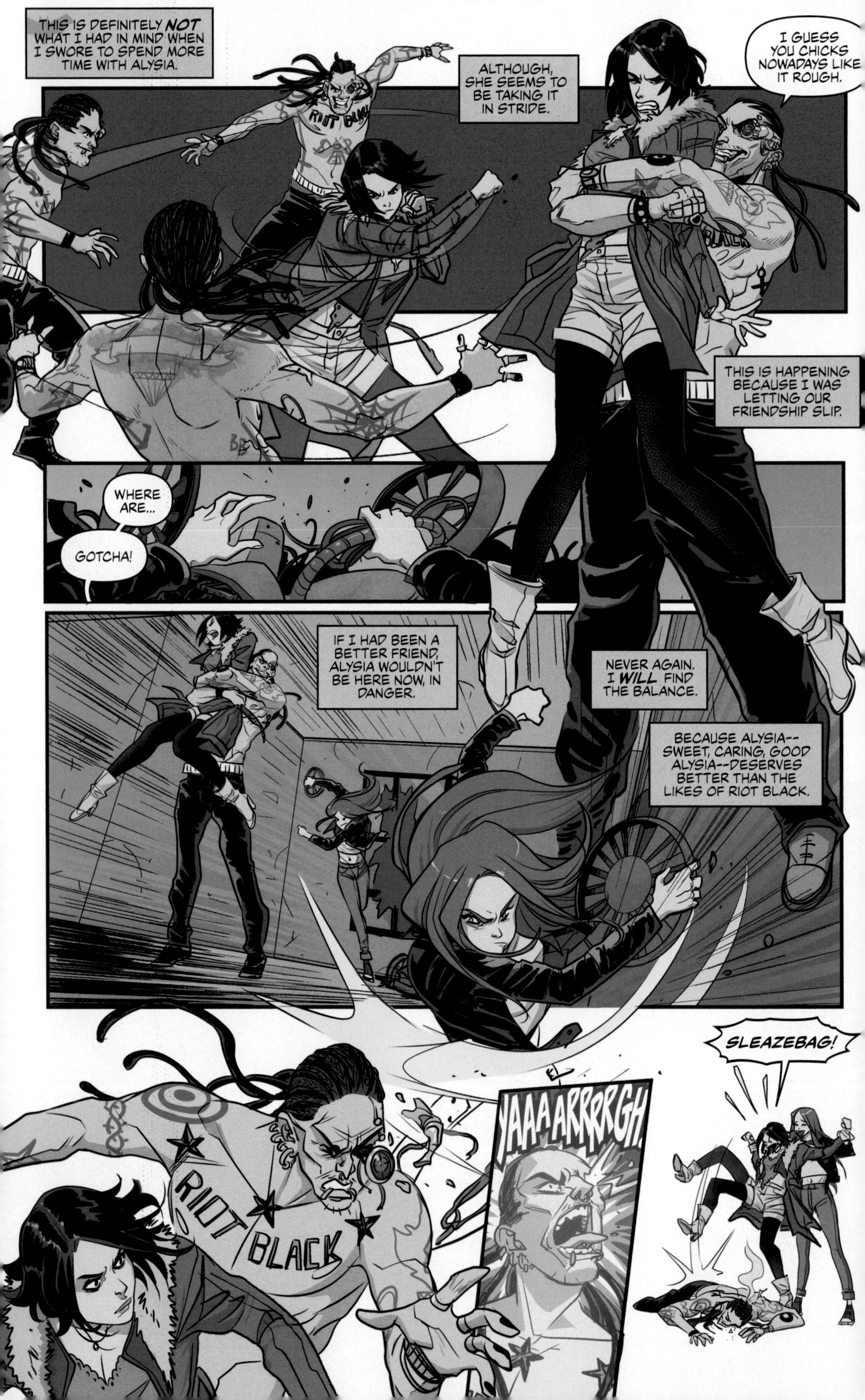
THIS IS DEFINITELY NOT WHAT I HAD IN MIND WHEN I SWORE TO SPEND MORE TIME WITH ALYSIA.
ALTHOUGH, SHE SEEMS TO BE TAKING IT IN STRIDE.
RIOT BLACK
I GUESS YOU CHICKS NOWADAYS LIKE IT ROUGH.
THIS IS HAPPENING BECAUSE I WAS LETTING OUR FRIENDSHIP SLIP.
WHERE ARE...
GOTCHA!
IF I HAD BEEN A BETTER FRIEND, ALYSIA WOULDN'T BE HERE NOW, IN DANGER.
NEVER AGAIN. I WILL FIND THE BALANCE.
BECAUSE ALYSIA--SWEET, CARING, GOOD ALYSIA--DESERVES BETTER THAN THE LIKES OF RIOT BLACK.
RIOT BLACK
YAAAARRRRGH!
SLEAZEBAG!

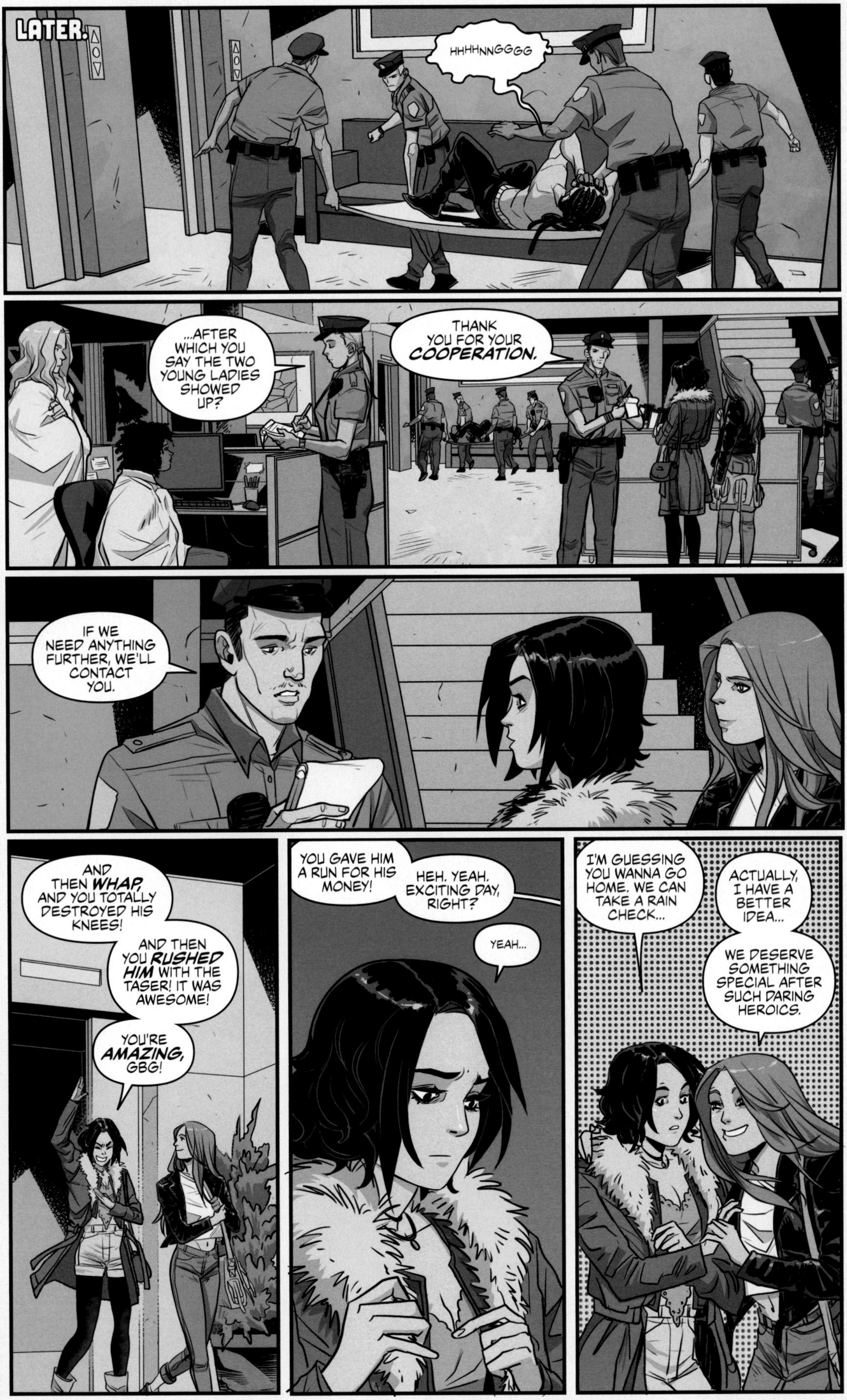
LATER.
HHHHNNGGGG
...AFTER WHICH YOU SAY THE TWO YOUNG LADIES SHOWED UP?
THANK YOU FOR YOUR COOPERATION.
IF WE NEED ANYTHING FURTHER, WE'LL CONTACT YOU.
AND THEN WHAP, AND YOU TOTALLY DESTROYED HIS KNEES!
AND THEN YOU RUSHED HIM WITH THE TASER! IT WAS AWESOME!
YOU'RE AMAZING, GBG!
YOU GAVE HIM A RUN FOR HIS MONEY!
HEH. YEAH. EXCITING DAY, RIGHT?
YEAH...
I'M GUESSING YOU WANNA GO HOME. WE CAN TAKE A RAIN CHECK...
ACTUALLY, I HAVE A BETTER IDEA...
WE DESERVE SOMETHING SPECIAL AFTER SUCH DARING HEROICS.

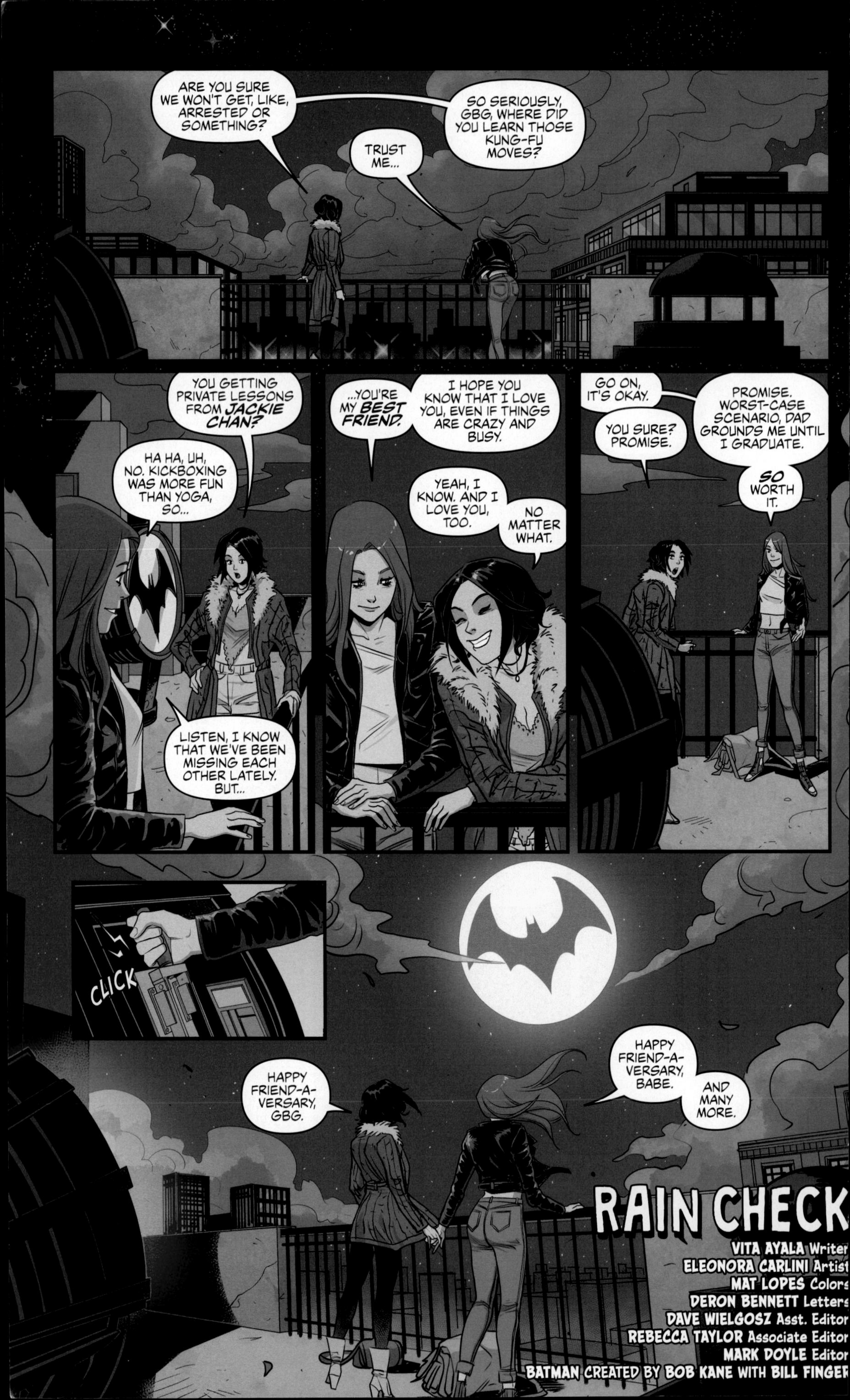

ARE YOU SURE WE WON'T GET, LIKE, ARRESTED OR SOMETHING?
TRUST ME...
SO SERIOUSLY, GBG, WHERE DID YOU LEARN THOSE KUNG-FU MOVES?
YOU GETTING PRIVATE LESSONS FROM JACKIE CHAN?
HA HA, UH, NO. KICKBOXING WAS MORE FUN THAN YOGA, SO...
LISTEN, I KNOW THAT WE'VE BEEN MISSING EACH OTHER LATELY. BUT...
...YOU'RE MY BEST FRIEND.
I HOPE YOU KNOW THAT I LOVE YOU, EVEN IF THINGS ARE CRAZY AND BUSY.
YEAH, I KNOW. AND I LOVE YOU, TOO.
NO MATTER WHAT.
GO ON, IT'S OKAY.
YOU SURE? PROMISE.
PROMISE. WORST-CASE SCENARIO, DAD GROUNDS ME UNTIL I GRADUATE.
SO WORTH IT.
CLICK
HAPPY FRIEND-A-VERSARY, GBG.
HAPPY FRIEND-A-VERSARY, BABE.
AND MANY MORE.
RAIN CHECK
VITA AYALA Writer
ELEONORA CARLINI Artist
MAT LOPES Colors
DERON BENNETT Letters
DAVE WIELGOSZ Asst. Editor
REBECCA TAYLOR Associate Editor
MARK DOYLE Editor
BATMAN CREATED BY BOB KANE WITH BILL FINGER

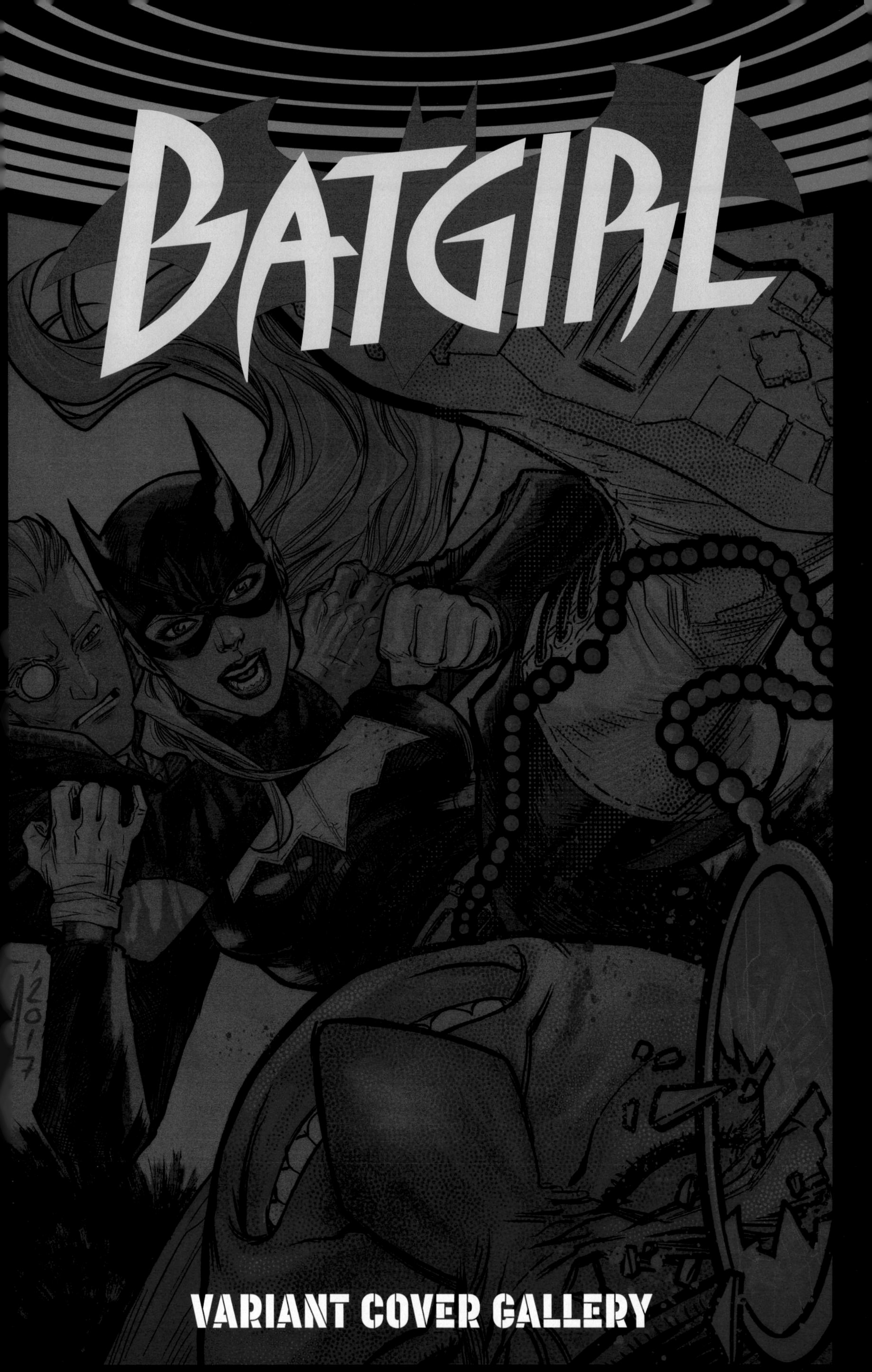
BATGIRL
VARIANT COVER GALLERY

BATGIRL #7 variant by FRANCIS MANAPUL

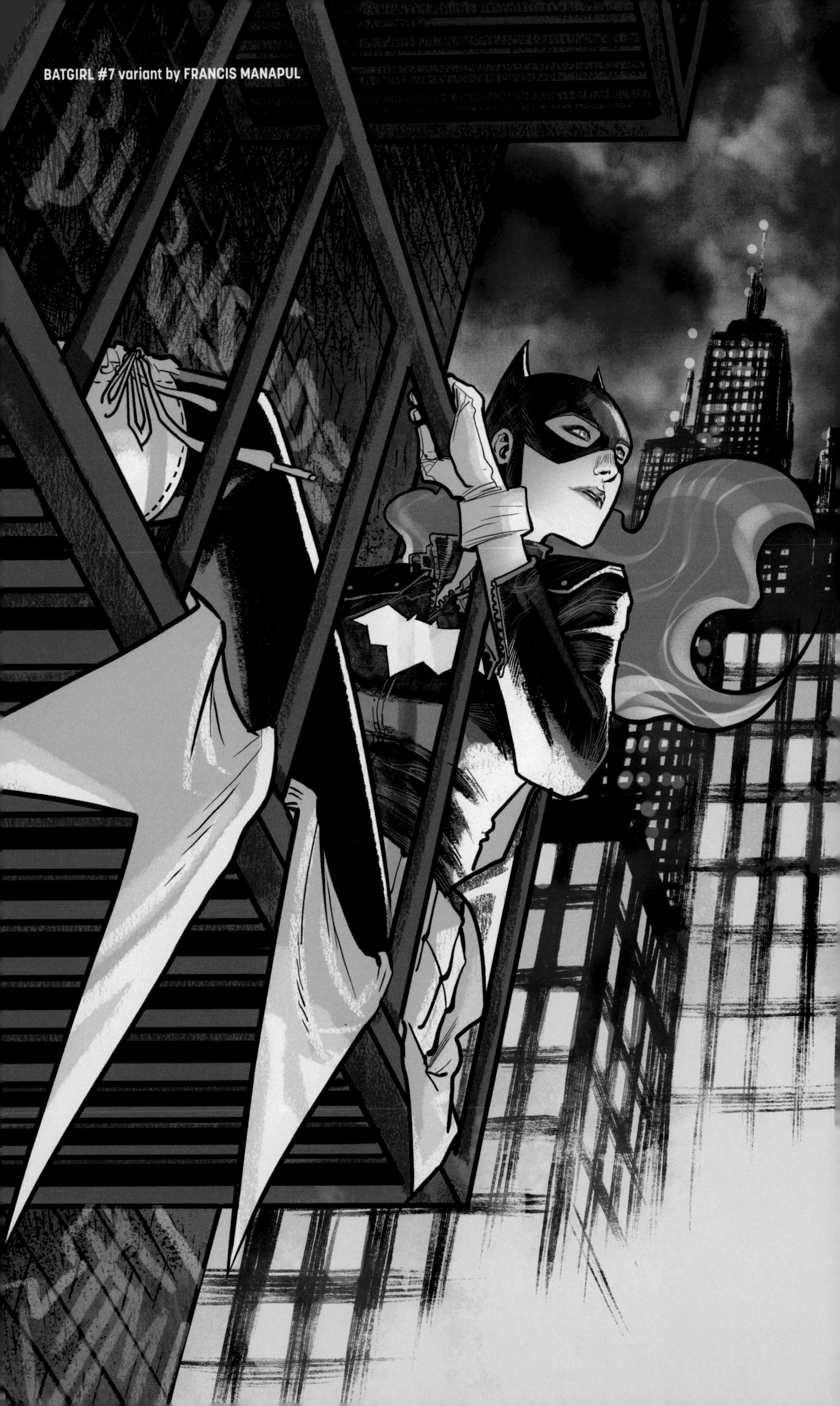

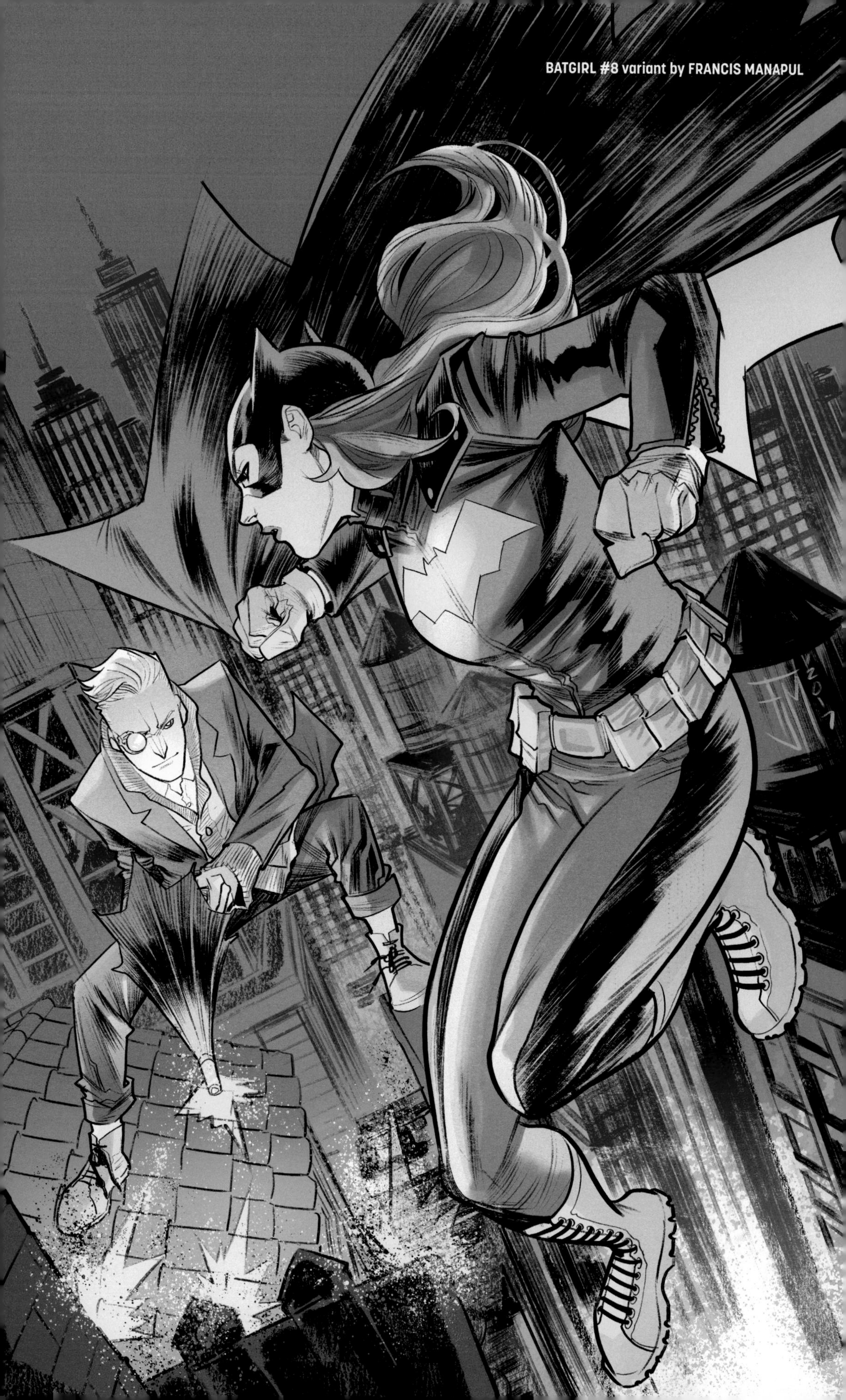

BATGIRL #8 variant by FRANCIS MANAPUL

BATGIRL #9 variant by FRANCIS MANAPUL

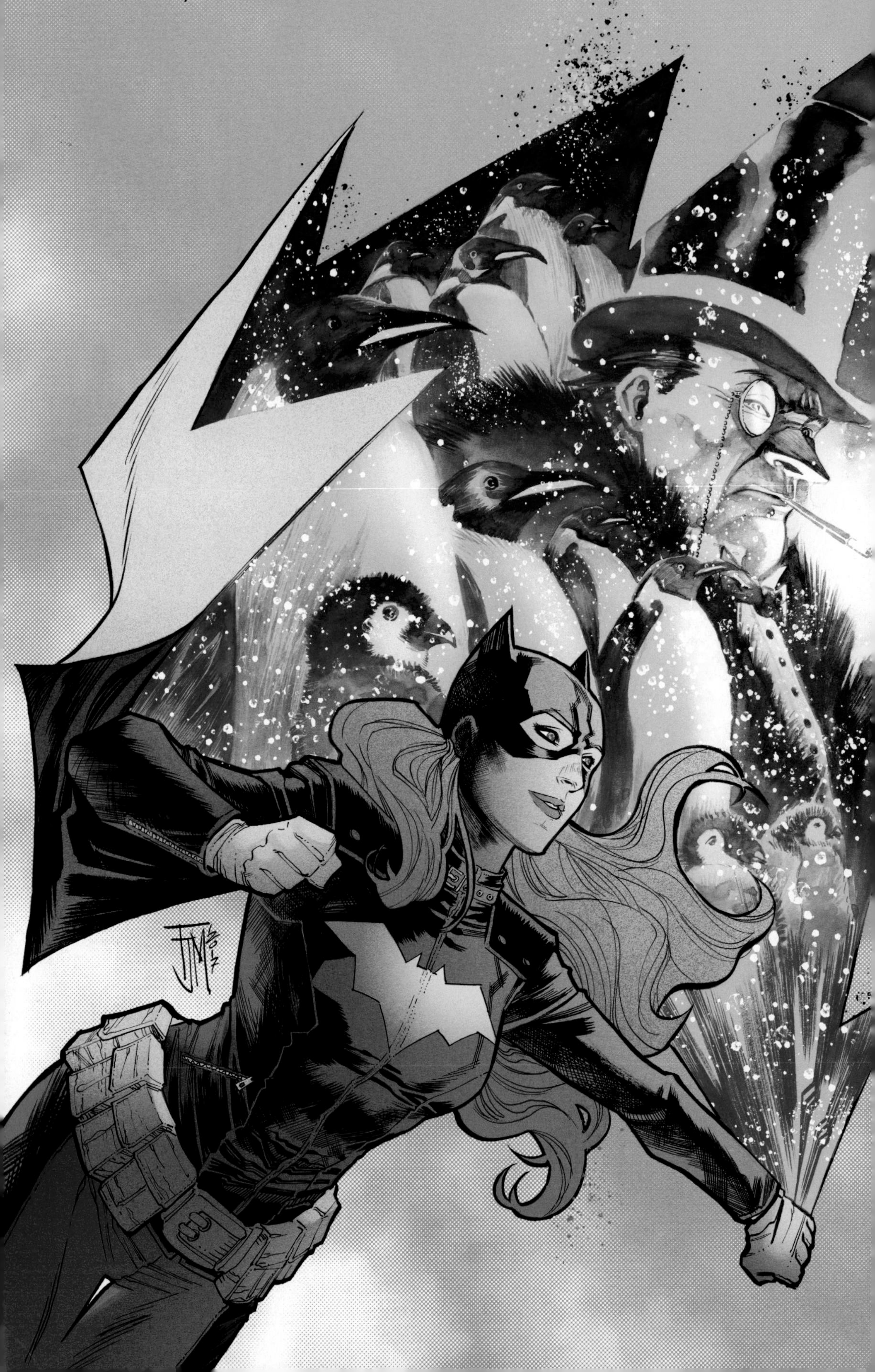

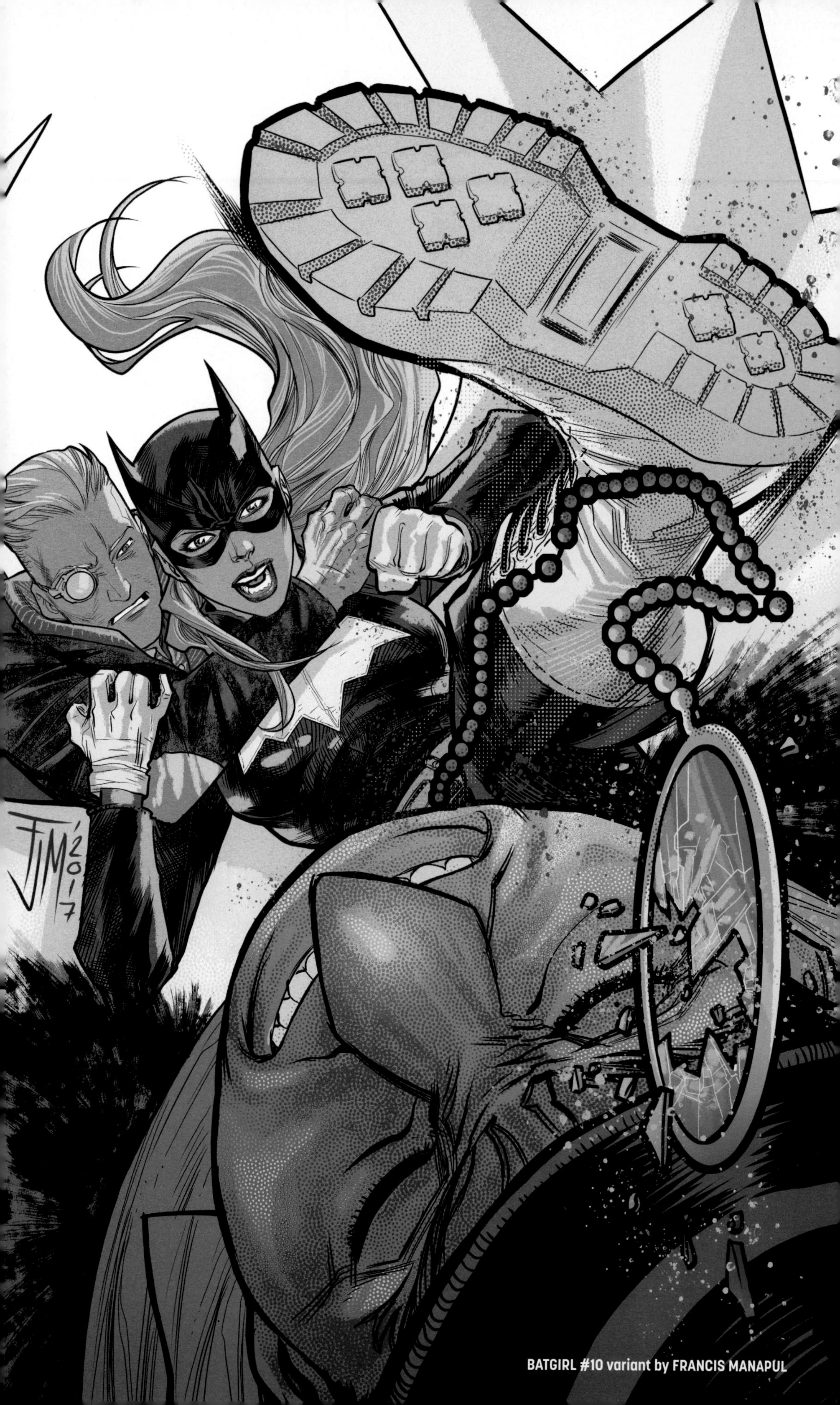
FJM 2017
BATGIRL #10 variant by FRANCIS MANAPUL

BATGIRL #11 variant by FRANCIS MANAPUL

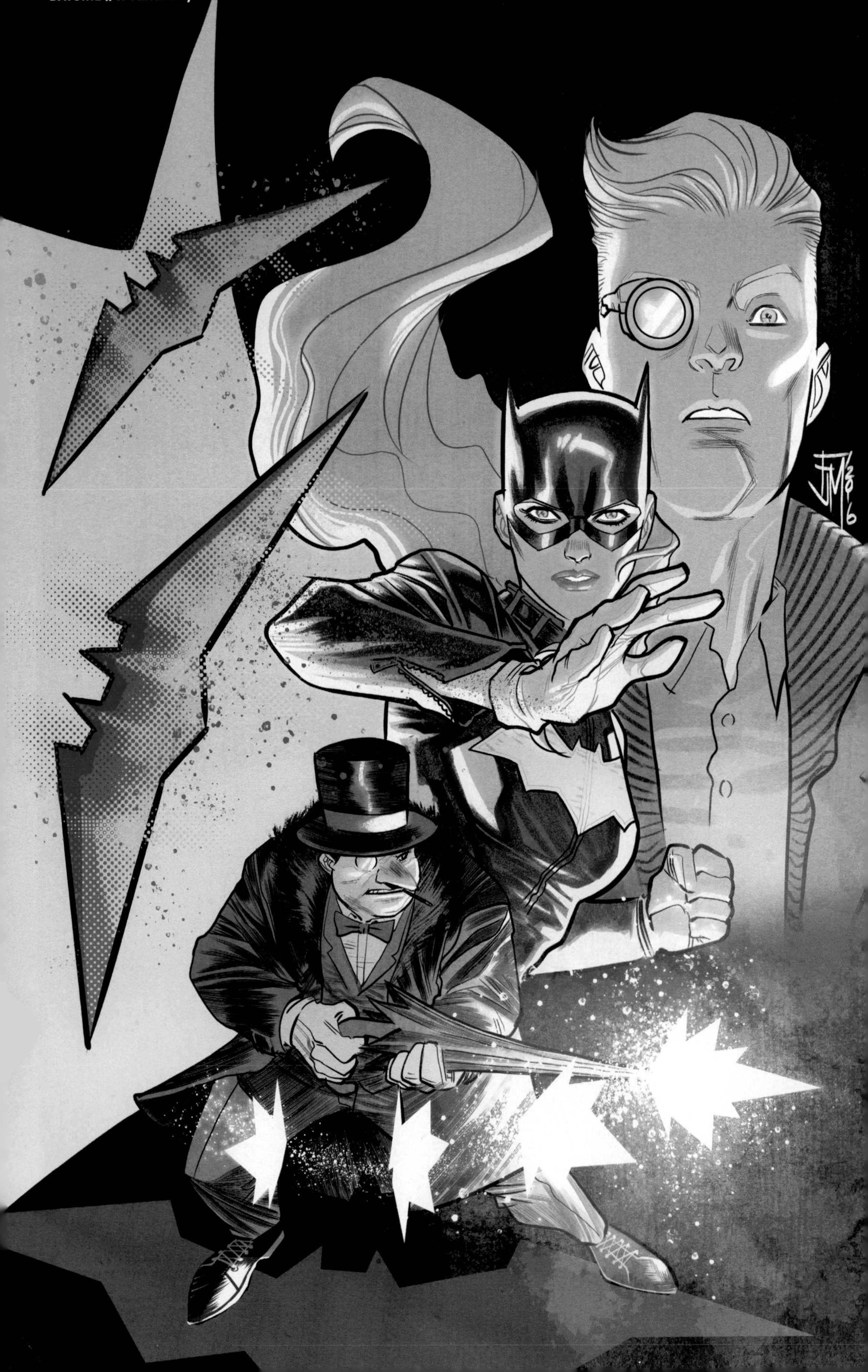

CHARACTER STUDIES
by CHRIS WILDGOOSE

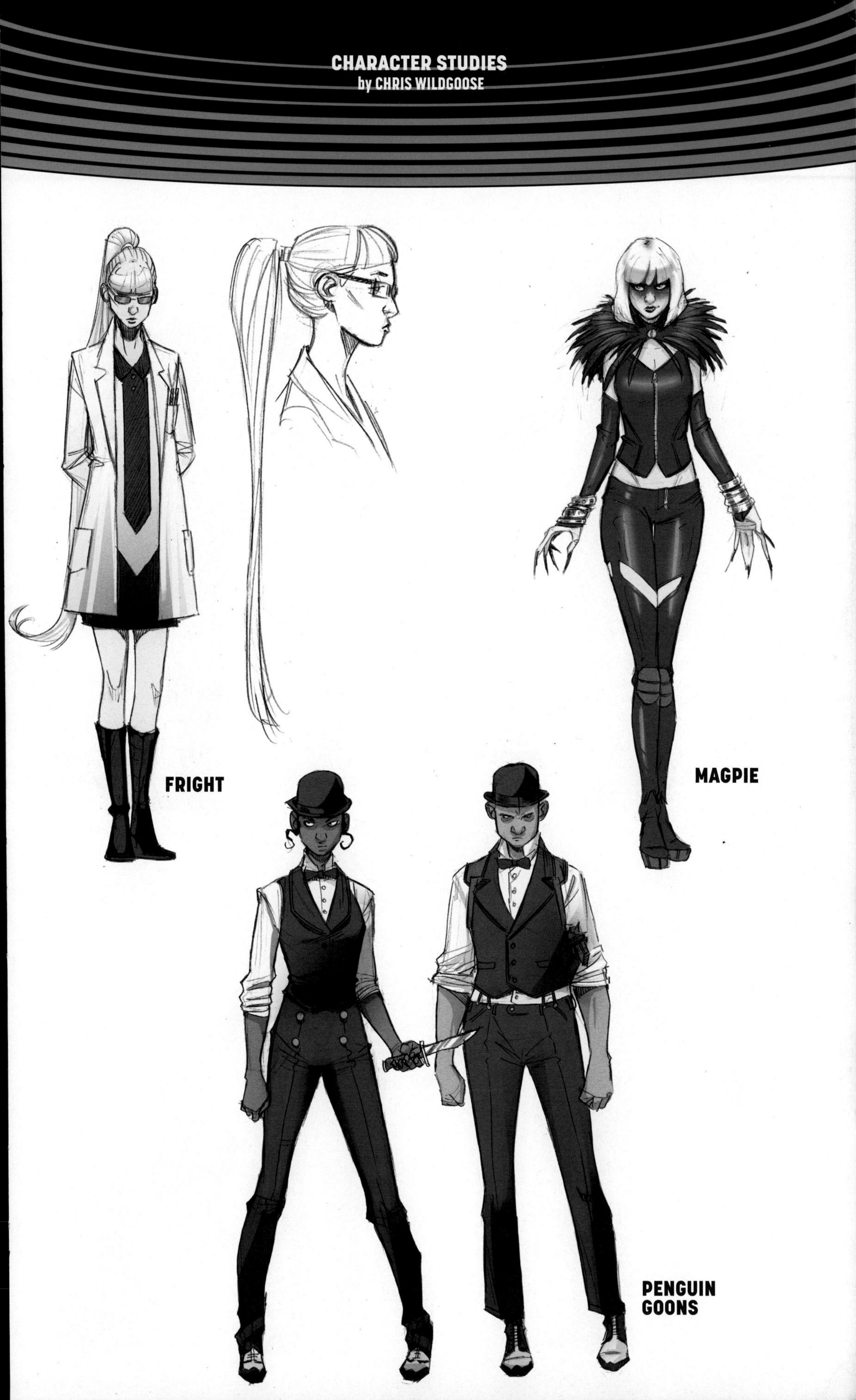
FRIGHT
MAGPIE
PENGUIN
GOONS

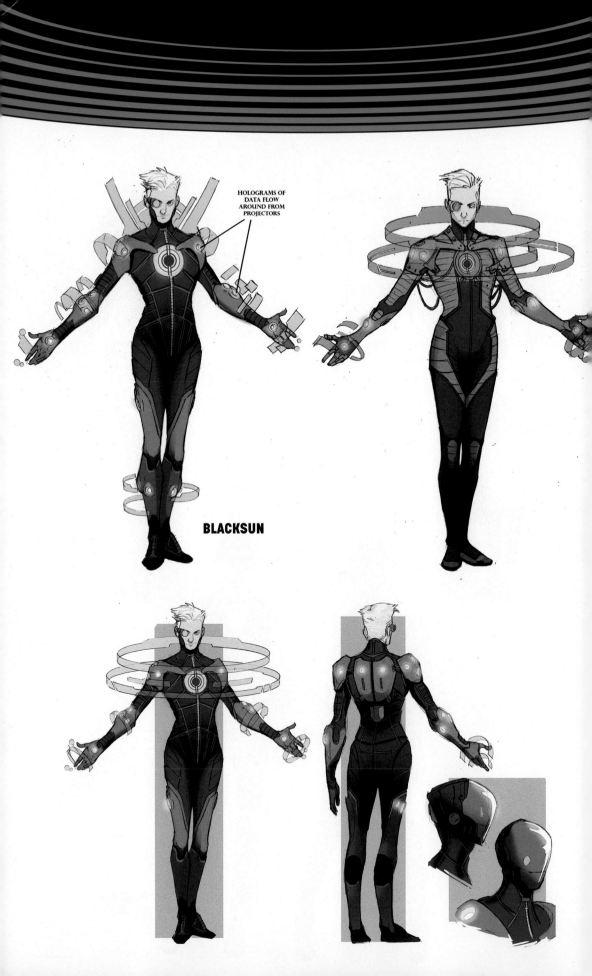

HOLOGRAMS OF
DATA FLOW
AROUND FROM
PROJECTORS

BLACKSUN

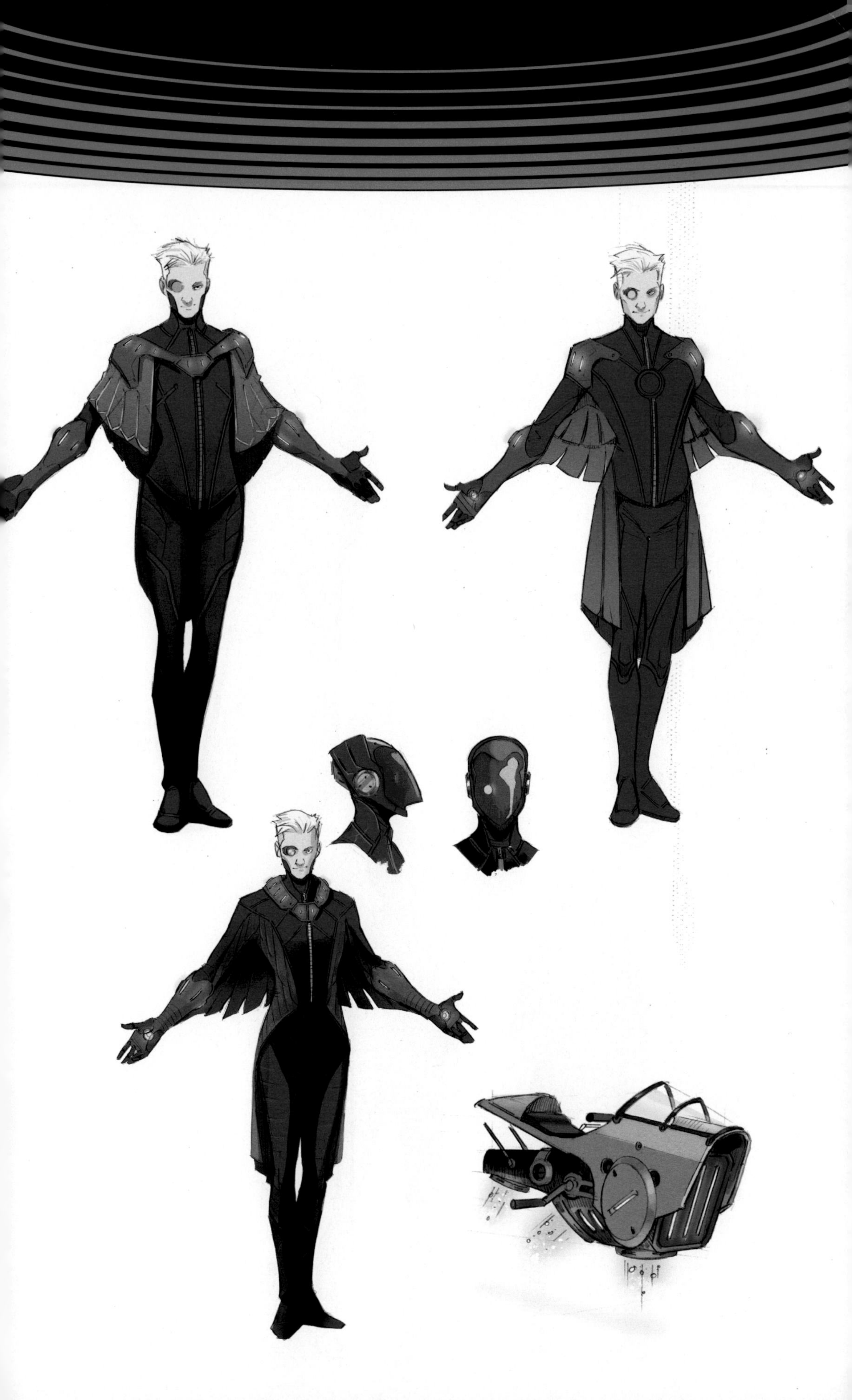

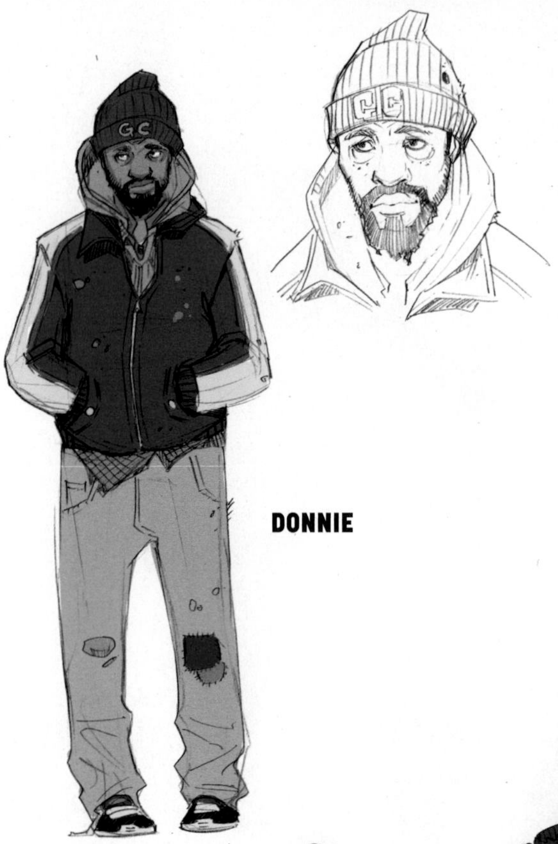
GC
GC

DONNIE

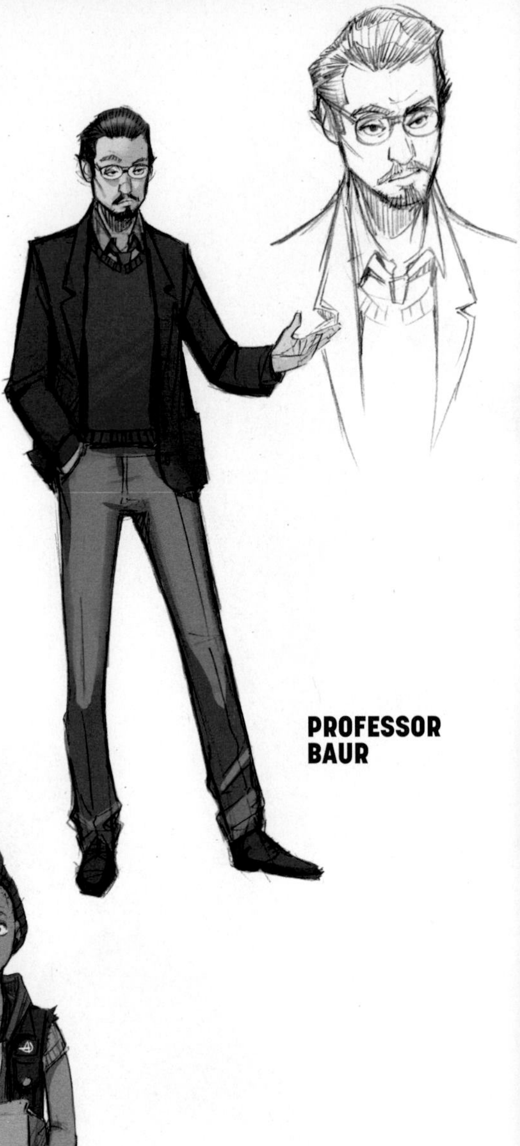

PROFESSOR BAUR

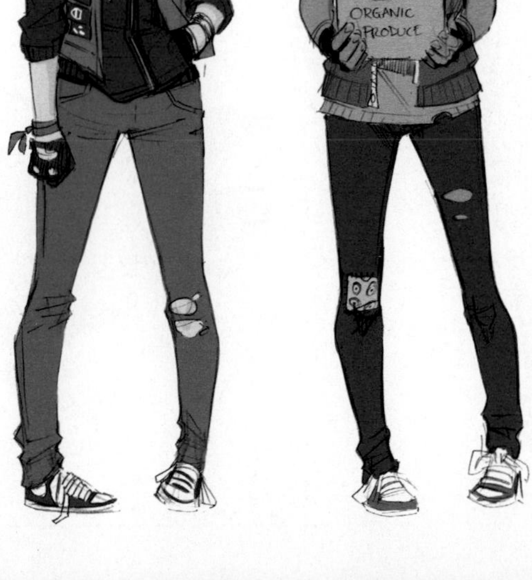
ORGANIC PRODUCE

MIRA & CRYSTAL

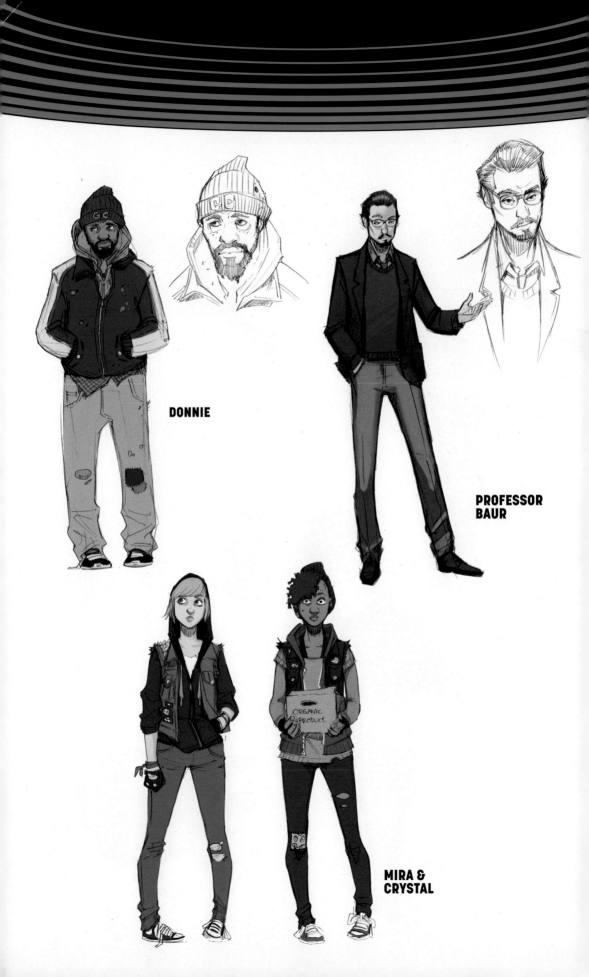

COVER SKETCHES FOR BATGIRL #7-11
by CHRIS WILDGOOSE

ISSUE #7

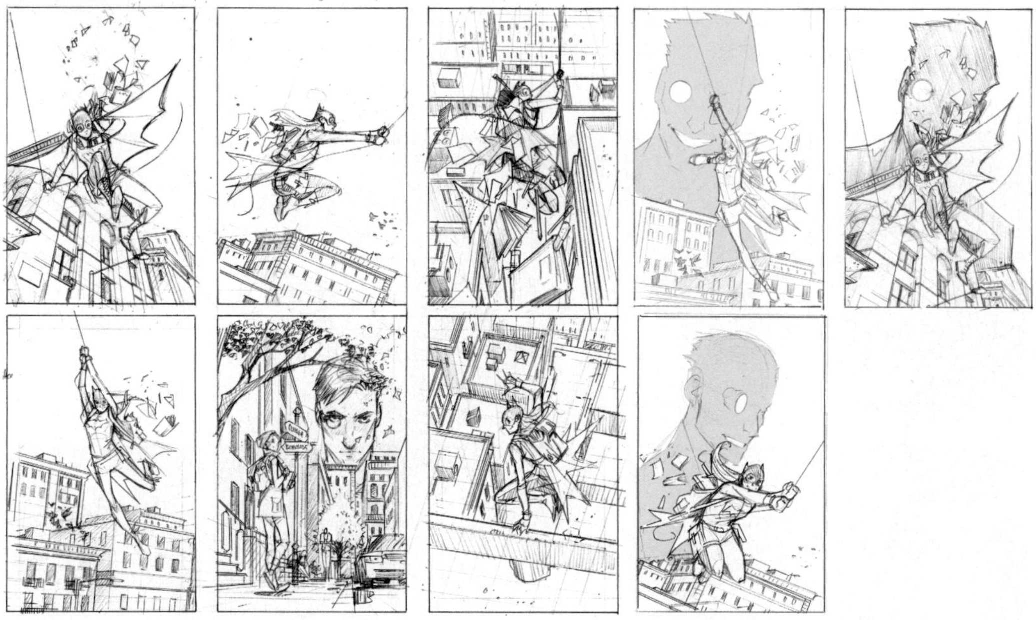

ISSUE #8

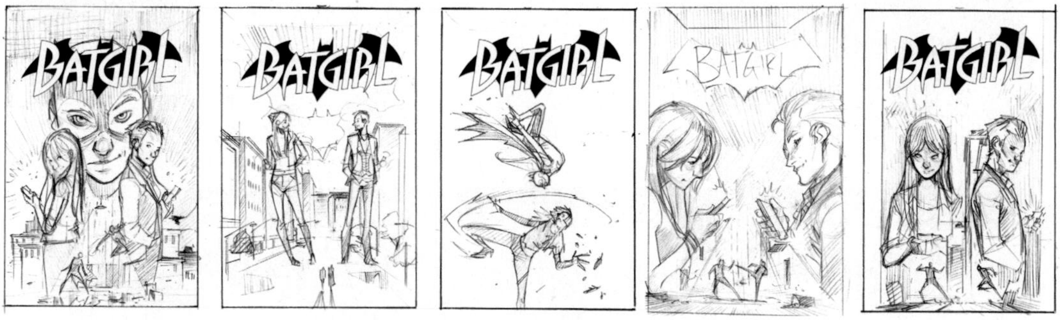
BATGIRL

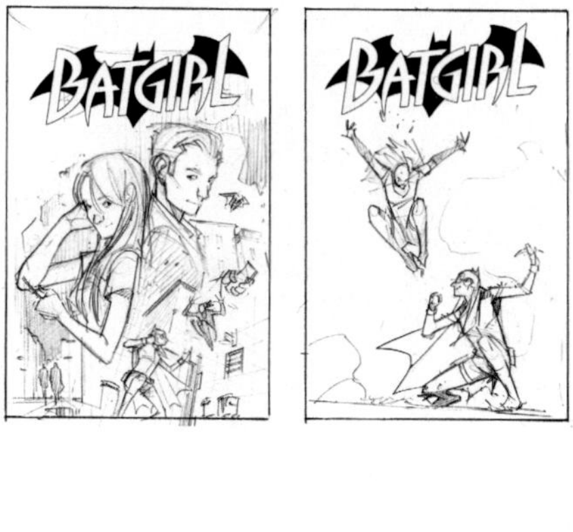
BATGIRL

ISSUE #9

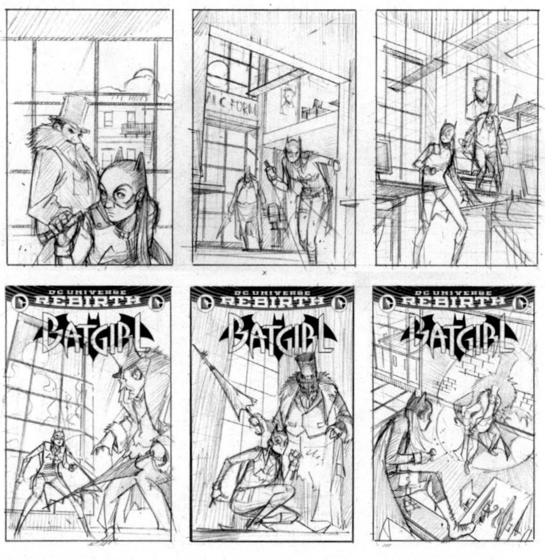
DC UNIVERSE
REBIRTH
BATGIRL

ISSUE #10

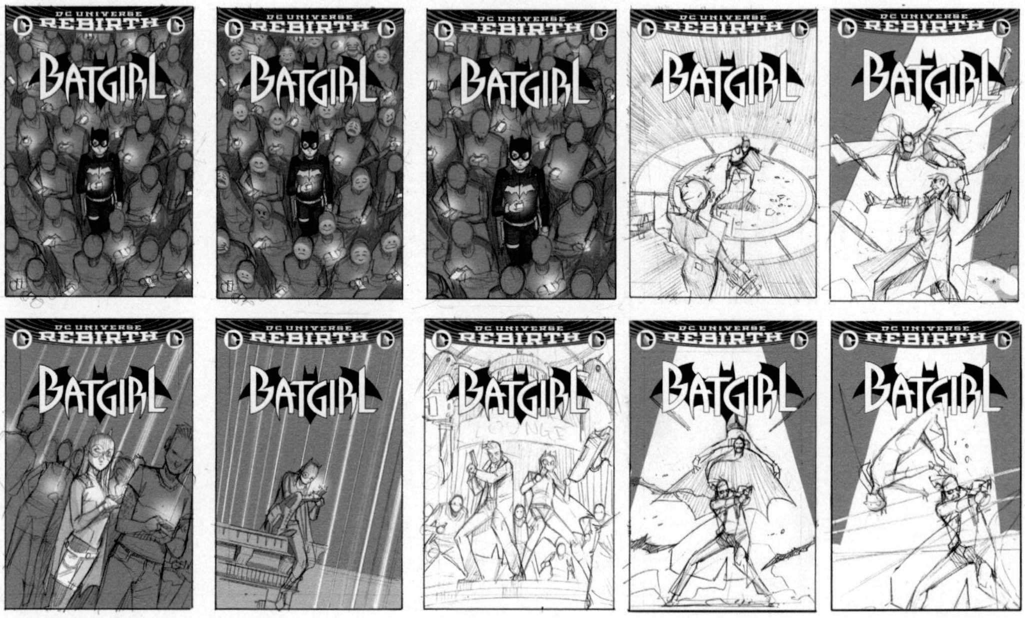
DC UNIVERSE
REBIRTH
BATGIRL
LOUNGE

ISSUE #11

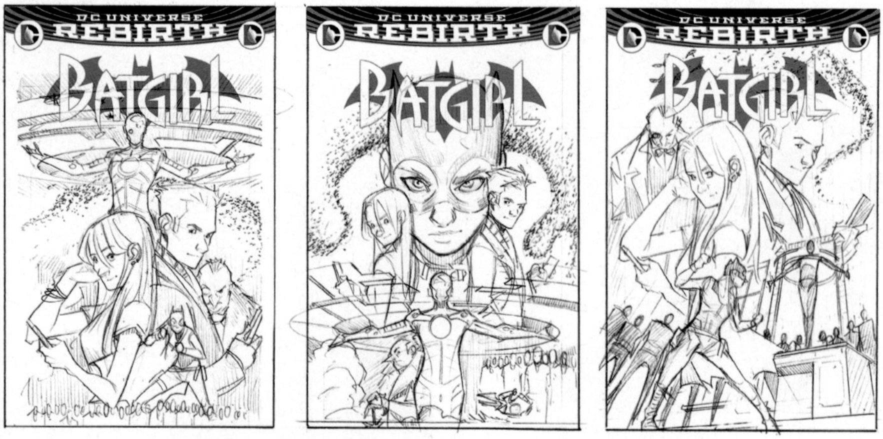
DC UNIVERSE
REBIRTH
BATGIRL